Patternmaking with Stretch Knit Fabrics

Patternmaking with Stretch Knit Fabrics

Julie Cole

Fairchild Books
An imprint of Bloomsbury Publishing Inc

BLOOMSBURY
NEW YORK · LONDON · OXFORD · NEW DELHI · SYDNEY

I dedicate this book to the women in my family who all share my love of fashion.

Carol Clark
Hannah Cole
Eva Becos-Cole
Judith Cole

Fairchild Books
An imprint of Bloomsbury Publishing Inc

1385 Broadway	50 Bedford Square
New York	London
NY 10018	WC1B 3DP
USA	UK

www.bloomsbury.com

FAIRCHILD BOOKS, BLOOMSBURY and the Diana logo
are trademarks of Bloomsbury Publishing Plc

First published 2016

© Bloomsbury Publishing Inc, 2016

Library of Congress Cataloging-in-Publication Data
Cole, Julie, author.
Patternmaking with stretch knit fabrics / Julie Cole.
pages cm
ISBN 978-1-5013-0504-7 (paperback)
1. Dressmaking--Pattern design. 2. Knit goods--Design. 3. Stretch woven fabrics. I. Title.
TT520.C66 2016
646.4'072--dc23
2015028067

ISBN:	HB:	978-1-5013-0504-7
	ePDF:	978-1-5013-0505-4

Typeset by Lachina
Illustrations: Graphic World Inc.
Photography: Jean Qualman Dent
Printed and bound in Canada

EXTENDED CONTENTS

PREFACE

Many designers include stretch knit garments in their collections. American designer Ralph Lauren's signature polo shirt is one example. Designers such as Norma Kamali produce complete collections in stretch knits. Other well-known designers such as Isabel Marant, Stella McCartney, and Alexander Wang, to name just a few, include a selection of garments in stretch knits as part of their collections. Adidas and Nike are well-known businesses whose focus is activewear constructed from stretch knit fabrics. For this reason, learning to design and work with stretch knit fabrics should not be ignored in fashion schools.

In my own experience as a designer, stretch knit garments were always part of creating each new season's collection. Customers loved wearing knits because they were so functional and practical. The fact that knits stretched and felt so comfortable was the drawing card. In design school, I had not learned about stretch knits. For this reason, I adapted the slopers for woven fabric into slopers for stretch knits for use when designing. This was not a smooth process. Consequently, when the opportunity came my way to teach in fashion design programs, and the focus was a stretch knit design course, I developed my own unique sloper system.

It is very important to understand that stretch knit fabrics do not all stretch to the same degree. For this reason, knit fabrics are divided into stretch categories: *minimal stretch*, *moderate stretch*, *very stretchy*, and *super stretchy*. The slopers are developed in the same stretch categories

that knits are divided into. The stretch categories are not sizes. For example, a T-shirt cut and stitched in each stretch category and fitted on the form will look the same; only the amount of stretch differs.

How to Use this Textbook

To draft the slopers for stretch knits, you must begin by drafting the hip and top foundations. The foundations are partial patterns that are the base for forming the slopers for each garment group. Once the foundations are drafted in each stretch category (minimal stretch, moderate stretch, very stretchy, and super stretchy), you can jump to the relevant chapter (tops; dresses; skirts; pants; jackets, cardigans, and sweater-jackets; lingerie; and swimwear) and begin developing the slopers and patterns for the relevant style.

The slopers are developed to have a fitted silhouette. This is the starting point for each pattern. However, because the fabric stretches, you are not restricted to designing tightly fitted garments. Stretch knit garments can also be loose-fit and oversized.

This textbook is an intermediate-level book. Consequently, this work assumes some basic knowledge of pattern drafting. Not all pattern-drafting dimensions for knits are the same dimensions that are used for drafting patterns for garments constructed from woven fabric. For this reason, this textbook outlines some basic pattern drafting techniques that designers must understand specifically for knits. The styles illustrated in the textbook are not trends but basic styles. This is intentional because the patternmaking techniques are flexible in use. By inter-mixing knowledge, creativity, and current fashion trends, you can develop your own creative pattern designs.

Note that Keith Richardson's textbook, *Designing and Patternmaking for Stretch Fabrics*, categorizes knits to include one-way stretch, two-way stretch, and four-way stretch. In this textbook, this system is streamlined to include two-way stretch and four-way stretch categories only.

It is my joy to share my experience of working with stretch knit fabrics and empower you as fashion design students by imparting my knowledge.

Instructive Features

The following features are included in *Patternmaking with Stretch Knit Fabrics*. The goal of each section is to provide foundational material to support you in what you need to know and do when patternmaking for stretch knit fabrics.

- **Tables and Charts**
  The tables and charts throughout the textbook set out in a clear methodical way important material that you need to know. The "Knit Fabric Chart," "Fabric Evaluation Worksheet," "The Knit Family of Slopers Transform into Garments," "Grading Measurement Chart," and "Stretchable Stitches Chart" are some examples of the resources available.

- **Stitching Tip**
  The "Stitching Tip" boxes aim to bring together the relationship between pattern drafting and stitching. They explain how a particular pattern, when cut and stitched, forms a specific part of the garment.

- **Pattern Tip**
  The "Pattern Tips" are designed to give you additional pattern drafting knowledge. They may explain how a simple pattern modification can change the design. Or they may demonstrate how a particular pattern drafting technique from another chapter can also be utilized in the chapter at hand.

- **Important**
  The "Important" boxes emphasize significant aspects of pattern drafting relating to a chapter. They may call attention to the importance of choosing the appropriate fabric weight or type for a certain style. Or they may give advice on what slopers to use to draft the patterns for a particular style.

- **Stitching Order**
  The Stitching Orders teach you, as beginning designers, the process of how to stitch a particular garment. Seam ripping knits needs care because the knit can hole easily. Knowing what to stitch first, second, and third can prevent this from happening and simplifies the stitching process.

End-of-Chapter Features

- **Knit It Together**
  This section is a checklist summary. It draws together the major central subject matter taught in each chapter.

- **Stop: What Do I Do If . . .**
  The goal of this section is to answer critical questions about a pattern drafting problem. I cannot provide instructions on how to draft every possible pattern in this textbook because of page limits. In the "Stop: What Do I Do If . . ." section, you are encouraged to use the pattern drafting techniques in a flexible way. This may require you to engage several chapters to resolve a pattern drafting question. When you follow this methodology, your patternmaking skills will advance.

- **Self-Critique**
  The Self-critique section asks a series of questions to test your knowledge about what has been taught in each chapter. It aims to highlight the concepts that you have learned and understood. It also aims to reveal what you do not understand and need to follow up and learn.

Supplementary Resources

- **Instructor's Guide and Test Bank**

  The instructor's guide is an additional resource and tool for instructors to use in a classroom setting. It is designed to be used in conjunction with this textbook, *Patternmaking for Stretch Knits*. The resources provide additional skill building for students. A test bank is also available for instructors.

Patternmaking with Stretch Knit Fabrics STUD!O

Fairchild Books has a long history of excellence in textbook publishing for fashion education. Our new online STUDIOS are specially developed to complement this book with rich media ancillaries that students can adapt to their visual learning styles. *Patternmaking with Stretch Knit Fabrics STUDIO* features online self-quizzes with scored results and personalized study tips and flashcards with terms/definitions to help students master concepts and improve grades; plus downloadable files of half-size top and hip foundations and slopers to practice pattern drafting. The foundations can be used to draft the slopers, and the slopers can be used to develop the patterns outlined throughout the text.

STUDIO access cards are offered free with new book purchases and also sold separately through Bloomsbury Fashion Central (www.BloomsburyFashionCentral.com).

Acknowledgments

First, I would like to thank Cheryl Turnauer, from Harper College, who presented me with the opportunity of developing and teaching a course in stretch knits in the fashion design program. I am also grateful to Bloomsbury for the opportunity to author this textbook and to put into print my classroom knowledge. In particular, I'd like to thank Amanda Breccia, Amy Butler, and Edie Weinberg for their wonderful support and guidance in the development of this textbook.

Second, I want to express my gratitude to my husband, Graham Cole, an author in his own right, who has helped, encouraged, and stood by my side throughout the writing process. Even though his discipline is not fashion design, his advice, wisdom, and comments were always insightful. I also want to thank my family and friends who have walked this journey with me. In particular, I am grateful to Julie Babarik for her contribution. She tirelessly read each chapter and made very helpful edits and comments.

I also want to thank my students at Harper College who participated in the Advanced Diversified Apparel Design courses, as they all played an integral part in the development of the sloper system for stretch knits. Other students who I taught in the Advanced Knits: Lingerie and Swimwear design course were also integral to the development of Chapters 11 and 12. In particular, I want to thank Genevieve Jauquet Perez for her helpful contribution and thorough testing of the sloper system.

I am also very grateful to Jean Dent for her expertise and tireless patience shooting the photographs for this book. I appreciate the professionalism she evidenced. Additionally, I want to thank Amanda Maxwell for giving her time as a model for the photographs.

I also want to express my gratitude to the University of Alabama fashion department for their kindness in allowing the use of a fashion classroom for the photography.

I also thank Graphic World Inc for their expertise and careful attention given to creating the illustrations.

Finally, I'd like to thank the reviewers for their expertise and constructive suggestions: Dr. Theresa C. Alexander, University of the Incarnate Word; Cindy Bainbridge, Art Institute of Colorado; Kelly Cobb, University of Delaware; Patricia Crockett, Art Institute of Portland; Lori Gann-Smith, Brenau University; Adriana Gorea, University of Delaware; Susan Kaye Owens, Purdue University; Mary McCarthy, IADT Orlando; Pamela Powell, College of DuPage; Paula Robinson, University of Alabama; Mary Simpson, Baylor University; J. Sissons, Nottingham Trent University; Catherine Stephenson, Art Institute of Portland; and Kathie L. Taylor, Art Institute of San Diego.

1

Getting the Knack of Knits

Why bother with knits? Working with knits is a joy because you're creating clothing with stretchability, elasticity, and flexibility. Victoria Beckham says, "There is nothing better than seeing a woman in clothes she loves to wear. Her comfort is what you see first."[1]

It was Coco Chanel who liberated women by introducing inexpensive cotton knits into her collection of women's wear. (At this stage, jersey was used only for men's undergarments.) She was known as "Jersey Girl" because she used her imagination and resourcefulness by incorporating jersey into her collection of garments.[2]

To get the knack of knits, you first must understand knit fabric principles. Designing for knits is an entirely different process than designing for woven fabric because knit fabric stretches. Among the most important features of a knit fabric are the direction the knit stretches and the capacity of stretch each knit has. This chapter explains these important features and explores how they affect the design.

This chapter aims to set you on the path to getting the knack of knits.

Fabrics fall into two categories: knit or woven. Knit fabric and woven fabric are structured differently, so let's distinguish between the two.

What Is a Knit?

Knit fabric is a stretchable material constructed on huge knitting machines and formed by a series of horizontal interlocking loops (see Figure 1.1). The sizes of the needles and yarns used determine whether the knit will be fine or chunky. Knit fabrics come in a variety of fibers and vary in type, structure, texture, and weight. Some knits are knitted with a smooth surface. Other surfaces are textured and may be knotty, nubby, loopy, brushed, embossed, or textured. How the loops are arranged determines what type of knit you are using. Using a **pick glass** to magnify the fabric surface will help you see the loop formation of the knit you are working on.

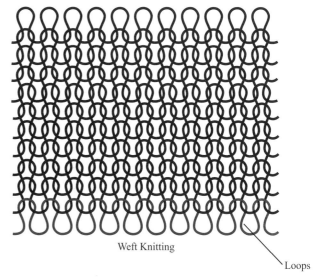

Weft Knitting

Loops

Figure 1.1 Knit fabric

Knits can be knitted from *natural fibers* derived from animals and plants (e.g., wool, cotton, linen, and silk), *regenerated fibers* manufactured from natural

1 Hal Rubenstein, "Designer Profile: Donna Karan," *InStyle*, November 2013, 149–150.
2 Justine Picardie, "The Secret Life of Coco Chanel," *Harpers Bazaar*, June 2011, 159. http://www.harpersbazaar.com/fashion/fashion-articles/coco-chanel-secret-life; Sarah Brown, "Jersey Girl Relaxed Chic with a Dash of Liberation, Bottled," *Vogue*, November 2011, 210.

materials such as wood pulp (e.g., bamboo, rayon, viscose, and modal), or *synthetics fibers* formed by chemical compounds (e.g., polyester, acrylic, spandex, and nylon). Knits can be a blend of two or more fibers to combine the best qualities of each fiber (cotton/polyester, for example). The weight of knit fabrics can vary from light and drapey to heavy and structured.

Woven fabric is formed when lengthwise *warp* and horizontal *weft* yarns interlace over and under each other. Woven fabric has "give" on the bias grain; however, this does not make it a stretchable fabric.

Why Knit Fabrics Stretch

The loop formation enables a knit fabric to stretch. The loops expand in the width or in the length when the fabric is stretched (see Figures 1.2a and b). The stretch of knit fabrics can vary from just a little stretch to a large amount of stretch.

How Working with Knits Differs from Working with Wovens

The stretch factor in knits creates many differences when working with knits in contrast to working with woven fabrics. Following are a few major differences you will encounter:

- Pattern drafting is simpler because darts and fitting lines to create shape are generally not necessary; the fabric stretches to fit the body. (There are a few exceptions—for example, a jacket, top, or dress made in a knit with minimal stretch.) Nevertheless, stretch knits *can* have style lines as a design element. For this reason, slopers are required specifically for drafting patterns for garments constructed in stretch knit fabrics.

- Bust darts may be necessary in some styles. For example, a dress with an empire waist will benefit from having darts to shape the bustline above the empire

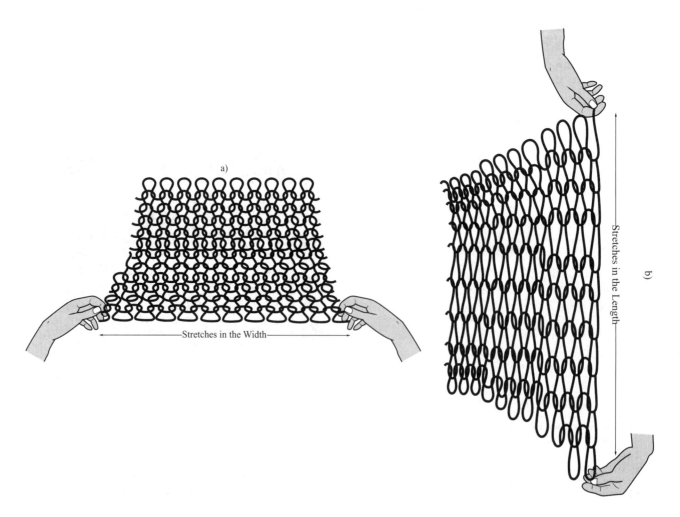

a)

Stretches in the Width

Stretches in the Length

b)

Figures 1.2a and b The loops expand when a knit is stretched; **a)** Crosswise stretch; **b)** Lengthwise stretch

line. Bust darts may also be needed when creating a custom-fit garment for a person with a full bust.

- Knits are quicker and easier to sew because construction techniques are simpler. Zippers are most often not required because the fabric stretches to fit over the body. In contrast, most dresses constructed from woven fabric require a zipper closure. Skirts and pants in knits are pull-on garments with an elasticized waist; therefore, a zipper opening is not required.
- Garments in woven fabric take more time to fit. Knits are easier and less time-consuming to fit because the fabric stretches to conform to the body shape.
- When garments in woven fabrics are constructed, they require frequent pressing. Knits require little or no pressing.

Structure of Knits

Knits are produced in various ways, so there is no "standard" knit. For example, some knits (such as jersey) have two distinctive sides to the fabric, and in other knits (such as double knit), both sides of the fabric look the same. Some knits are knitted with a smooth surface. Other surfaces are textured and may be knotty, nubby, loopy, or brushed.

How the loops are arranged determines what type of knit you are using. Knit fabrics are knitted using two basic structures: weft knitting and warp knitting. Each type is structured differently.

A **weft knit** is knitted with one continuous yarn that forms rows of *horizontal* loops across the width of the fabric (refer to Figure 1.1). As each new row is knitted, new loops link through the previous row of stitches. Weft knits are more elastic in the width than warp knits. Weft knits include interlock, rib knit, fleece, knitted terry, velour, and sweater knits.

Four basic stitches can be used to manufacture weft knits:[3]

- *Flat jersey stitches* are also known as plain stitches. The jersey stitch has vertical lines on the correct side of the fabric called **ribs** (or **wales**). The underside has loops called **courses** that run across the width of the fabric. (Look ahead to Chapter 4 and Figures 4.2a and b on p. 41 to see the loops.) The jersey stitch produces a jersey knit; when the stitch is varied, it produces terry and velour.

- *Purl stitches* produce knits that look the same on both sides of the fabric. This stitch is often used to produce bulky sweaters.
- *Rib stitches* produce columns of wales on both sides of the fabric. The rib stitch produces "ribbing," which has excellent elasticity. Ribbing is used for neck bands.
- *Interlock stitches* are a variation of rib stitches. The knit looks the same on both sides of the fabric. These fabrics are usually heavier in weight. A double knit is knitted with interlock stitches.

Weft knits can be single or double knits:

- A **single knit** is knitted with a *single* set of needles. Single knits include jersey, activewear knits, velour, and French terry. Single knits are light to medium weight. The most popular single knit is a jersey knit (which has two distinctive sides).
- A **double knit** is knitted with double needles that knit in unison; therefore, the fabric is double the thickness of a single knit. This makes a double knit a two-faced fabric, meaning that both sides of the fabric look the same and have vertical ribs (just like the correct side of jersey). Double knits include wool double knit, Ponte, and interlock.

A **warp knit** is constructed with yarn loops formed in a lengthwise *warp* direction (see Figure 1.3). As one needle moves in a zigzag direction, the loops interlock together. Warp knits are more elastic in the lengthwise

Figure 1.3 Warp Knit

3   Unit III Topic A: Fibers and Fabrics, "Knit Fabrics," accessed November 2, 2014, http://www.uen.org/cte/family/clothing-2 /downloads/textiles/knit.pdf, 87.

direction. Warp knits include tricot (including swimwear fabric), Raschel knits (characterized by its lacy construction), mesh, and Powernet.

Table 1.1 catalogs a number of popular knits and how to recognize the structure of each. The table also catalogs the styles that would suit each type of knit.

TABLE 1.1 Knit fabric chart

Type of Knit	Appearance	Weight	Direction of Stretch	Suitable Styles
Jersey (Weft knit)	Two distinctive sides.	Light to medium weight	Two-way and four-way stretch	Tops, dresses, skirt, pants, cardigans, camisoles, and hoodies
The most popular knit for all types of clothing	*Correct side*—vertical ribs create a smooth surface	One hundred percent cotton does not drape well. Silk and rayon jerseys have a beautiful drape.		Use four-way stretch for bodysuit and panties.
	Underside—horizontal loops called courses (refer to Figure 1.2)			
Double knit (Weft knit) • Ponte • Interlock • Wool jersey double knit • Boiled wool	Both sides of the fabric look the same; both sides have vertical ribs.	Medium to heavy weight	Generally two-way stretch	Skirts, pants, dresses, and jackets Styles often need seamlines for fitting purposes if the knit has minimal stretch.
Sweater knits (Weft knit)	Can be loosely knitted and looks like a hand knit	Bulkier and thicker knits	Two-way stretch	Skirts, sweaters, cardigans, and dresses
Ribbing (Weft knit) Series of plain and purl stitches knitted in more prominent ribs	Both sides of the fabric look the same; both sides have vertical ribs.	Varying weights	Two-way stretch One hundred percent cotton ribbing does not have good recovery after stretching. Garments will stretch out of shape over time. If a cotton/polyester blend is used or Lycra is added, ribbing will have better stretch and recovery.	Tank tops and collars Bands for neckline, armhole, wrist, ankle, and hems
Activewear knits Require moisture-wicking properties to function well during vigorous activity	Many activewear knits are jersey.	Medium weight	Four-way stretch knits with Lycra	Workout gear for yoga and exercise Tops, dresses, pants, and leggings
French terry (Weft knit)	*Correct side*—smooth knitted surface *Underside*—loopy texture	Medium weight		Infant onesies, vests, hoodies, bath robes, loungewear, sweatshirts, and sweatpants
Stretch terry (Weft knit)	*Correct side*—cut loops *Underside*—smooth knitted surface	Medium to heavy weight	Two-way stretch	Bath robe
Velour (Weft knit) (Napped fabric)	*Correct side*—soft plush pile *Underside*—smooth knitted surface	Medium weight	Two-way stretch	Tracksuits, vests, hoodies, sweatpants, loungewear, and bathrobes
Sweatshirt fleece (Weft knit)	*Correct side*—smooth knitted surface *Underside*—soft brushed pile	Medium weight	Two-way stretch	Tracksuits, vests, hoodies, and sweatpants
Fleece (Weft knit)	Brushed on both sides	Medium to heavy weight	Two-way minimal stretch	Vests, hoodies, jackets; makes a super-warm jacket lining

Type of Knit	Appearance	Weight	Direction of Stretch	Suitable Styles
Mesh (Warp knit) Large hole mesh	Open-holes; both sides look the same.	Medium weight	Two-way stretch	Fun tops, tunics, hoodies
Athletic mesh		Medium weight	Two-way stretch	Basketball uniform; hoodie lining
Mini mesh		Light weight; sheer	Two-way and four-way stretch	Tops, swimsuit lining (must be four-way stretch)
Powernet		Heavy weight	Two-way stretch	Undergarments
Stretch lace (Warp knit)	Opaque textured lace with sheer mesh	Light to medium weight		Tops, dresses, camisoles, chemises, teddies, bras, and panties Stretch lace trims for lingerie
Tricot (Warp knit)	*Correct side*—dull surface; vertical ribs, like jersey (refer to Figure 1.1) *Underside*—shiny surface; horizontal zigzag loop formation (refer to Figure 1.2)	Medium weight	Two-way stretch	Camisoles and chemises (Tricot will not feel as luxurious as a silk knit.) Excellent lining for undertops and dresses
Swimwear fabric (Warp knit) Part of the tricot family	Shiny or matte surface	Heavy weight	Four-way stretch	Swimsuits, bikinis, leggings, cycling shorts, skating and dance costumes, leotards, catsuits, and unitards
Raschel knit (Warp knit)	Delicate open-worked design	Fine mesh to thicker weights	Two-way stretch in *length* (not width), so care must be taken when cutting because of the direction of stretch	Tops, dresses, skirts, and cardigans

Why Knits?

In design school, students mainly focus on designing and pattern drafting for woven fabric. Of course, this skill is important, but when you look around on a given day, most people are wearing at least one stretch knit garment. It is advantageous for designers to include a selection of stretch knit garments in their collections because the fabric is so functional, comfortable, and versatile to wear year-round and for any occasion. In addition, many knits in plain and print patterns are available at more reasonable prices.

With knowledge and skill of working with knits, beginning designers can expand their opportunities for future employment in the fashion industry.

Advantages of Wearing Knits

There are many benefits to wearing stretch knit garments:

- *Elasticity*—The fabric stretches and moves with the body and feels comfortable.

- *Fit flexibility*—The fabric adjusts to the wearer's shape and size.
- *Wearability*—Knits mix and match easily; a single item can yield several different looks.
- *Easy care*—Knits require little or no ironing, which is perfect for busy people on the go.
- *Wrinkle-resistance*—Knits require less pressing and care.
- *Travel essential*—Knits can be rolled up and tucked into luggage.
- *Affordability*—Knits are cheaper to produce and require minimal yardage and stitching time.
- *Fabric weight*—Many knit garments are a lighter weight than garments in woven fabrics.
- *Fit choices*—Knits are available in body-hugging or loose-fit styles.
- *Shape retention*—Knits stretch and then recover and bounce back to the original shape.
- *Quick dry*—After laundering, the fabric dries quickly.

- *Fabric selection*—Knits are produced in a variety of fibers, weights, and textures.
- *Drapability*—Because of their elasticity, knits drape better than wovens.

Designing for Knits

The following sections address several important features of the fabric, such as spandex versus Lycra, direction of stretch, stretch capacity, and fabric selection. Designers need to be aware of these aspects because they influence the design, the slopers used, pattern drafting, and cut and fit of garments.

Spandex versus Lycra

Spandex is a generic fiber name. **Lycra**® is the trademark name for spandex made by DuPont. This synthetic elastic fiber is known for its extraordinary ability to stretch many times its original length and then bounce back to its initial size. (In garment labels, *Lycra, spandex*, and *elastane* are interchangeable terms.) When a percentage of spandex is added to a knit, the fabric has more stretch, provides more comfort and freedom of movement, improves the fit (and prevents bagging), and offers wrinkle-free and moisture-wicking properties and odor control. Garments with spandex will never go out of shape because the fabric always returns to its original shape or size after stretching.

The amount of spandex a garment requires to function well differs. For example, 15 percent spandex permits a figure-hugging shape and adds shape retention to swimsuits when wet. A tightly fitted T-shirt requires only 3 to 7 percent spandex.

IMPORTANT 1.1: WOVEN/ STRETCH FABRIC DISTINGUISHED

A woven/stretch fabric stretches only (minimally) when a small percentage (3 to 5 percent) of spandex/Lycra is added. However, this does *not* make it a stretch knit fabric! A woven/stretch fabric cannot be substituted for a knit fabric. The garment will not perform well, and the fit will be compromised. Even though both fabrics have spandex, a woven fabric is not knitted with the loop formation that enables the fabric to stretch (refer to Figure 1.2a).

Direction of Stretch

By definition, knits stretch. However, they do not all stretch in the same direction and to the same degree. Knits can be *two-way stretch* or *four-way stretch*. Designers must determine the direction the knit stretches before deciding on the style because the direction of stretch influences what garment to choose for a particular knit.

In this text, two-way stretch and four-way stretch are defined as follows.

Two-way Stretch

A **two-way stretch** knit stretches *across* the width of the fabric (refer to Figure 1.2a). Two-way stretch knits can be used for everyday garments and for some athletic activities. For example, for some sports (think basketball uniforms) and for general everyday activities, tops, skirts, and pants in a two-way stretch knit allow adequate stretch and comfort. Two-way stretch knits may or may not have spandex in the mix. A two-way stretch knit *without* spandex has **mechanical stretch** and stretches from the loop formation only (refer to Figure 1.2a).

Four-way Stretch

Four-way stretch knits stretch *across* the width of the fabric and *up* and *down* in the length (refer to Figures 1.2a and b). Four-way stretch *always* has spandex/Lycra added in the warp direction for supplementary stretch. These fabrics are often heavier and have more body and greater stretch than two-way stretch fabrics. Knits for swimming, dancing, cycling, skating, or skiing *must* be constructed of a four-way stretch knit to allow for vigorous activity and excellent performance. Four-way stretch knits typically have a higher component of spandex.

The following section explains how knits do not stretch to the same degree or in a uniform manner.

Stretch Capacity

The **stretch capacity** refers to the amount of stretch in the knit. Knits do not stretch the same amount; they stretch to different degrees. A suitable fabric with the "appropriate" amount of stretch *must* be chosen for the design; otherwise, it will not fit or function correctly. To know the stretchiness of a knit, you use a stretch gauge (see Figure 1.4).

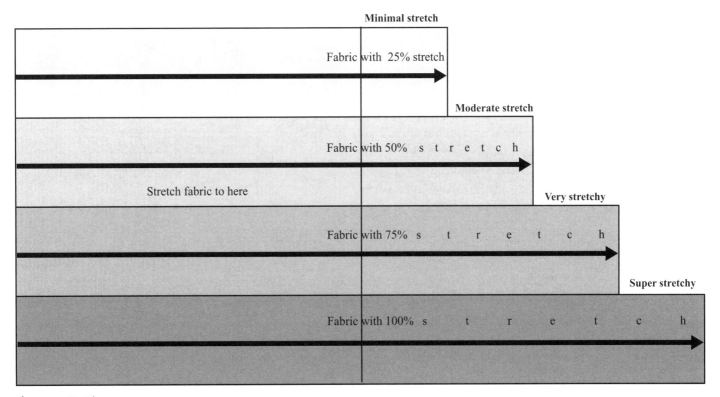

Figure 1.4 Stretch gauge

Stretch Categories

Stretch categories divide knits into groupings according to the amount of stretch the knit has. The stretch categories are as follows:

- **Minimal stretch knits** have the least amount of stretch (as little as ½" more than the original length). They are referred to as stable knits and stretch only in the width. Some minimal stretch knits are double knit, interlock, sweatshirt fleece, fleece, Raschel knits, sweater knits, and tricot.
- **Moderate stretch knits** stretch 50 percent more than the original length. Moderate stretch knits can be made into fitted styles. Many jersey knits are moderate stretch.
- **Very stretchy knits** stretch 75 percent more than the original length. These knits are often classified as activewear knits because they are four-way stretch with spandex for maximum movement.
- **Super stretchy knits** stretch 100 percent or more than the original length. These four-way stretch knits are called performance knits (except for a rib knit, which is two-way stretch). These knits have 15 to 50 percent spandex in the mix for maximum movement.[4] Swimwear fabric is a super stretchy knit.

To understand the concept of stretch categories further, look at Figure 1.5. At first glance, the T-shirts look as if they are in different sizes. However, they are *not*! These garments are all made in the same style, in *one* size, and they all fit the same body. They are in increments because they have been constructed from knits in each stretch category. All these T-shirts stretch to the same size as the arrows point out. What differs is the amount of stretch each T-shirt has. In sum, the style is the same, the fit is the same, but the amount of stretch in each top is different.

To know the stretch category of a particular knit, you need to complete a stretch test.

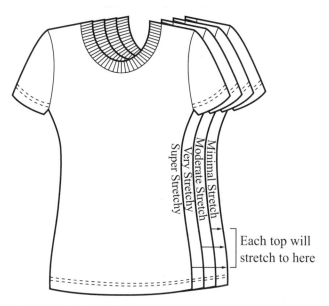

Figure 1.5 T-shirt stretch comparison

---

4   Claire Shaeffer, *Fabric Sewing Guide* (Iola, WI: Krause Publications, 1994), 77.

How to Do a Stretch Test

Prepare a fabric swatch by following these steps (see Figure 1.6):

1. Cut a fabric swatch 4" × 4" "on grain." (Refer to "Cutting the Fabric 'On Grain'" in Chapter 4 for further information.)
2. Fold the fabric piece in half on the crossgrain. (For four-way stretch, fold the fabric on the crossgrain and lengthwise grain.)
3. Hold the edge firmly to the left side of the stretch gauge, and stretch the fabric to the right as far as it will go.
4. Document the stretch category.

Stretch and Recovery

The most important characteristic in knits is the **stretch and recovery**. Good stretch and recovery means that after the fabric is stretched and released, it should bounce back to its original shape. After conducting a stretch test, be wary of using a knit that does not return to its original shape. Fabrics that do not have good recovery do not fit properly. Loose knits constructed with fewer *courses* and *wales* per inch tend to stretch and sag and not have good recovery.[5]

---

5   Unit III Topic A: Fibers and Fabrics, "Knit Fabrics," 87.

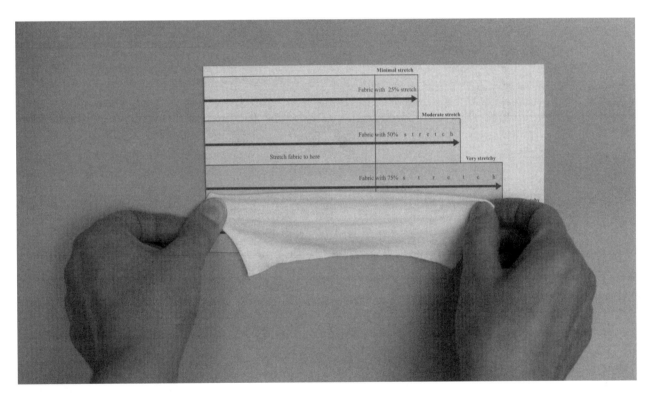

Figure 1.6 The stretch test

Napped Fabric

The way knits are knitted creates a slight shading difference. For this reason, knits are **napped fabrics**. This means that when the pattern pieces are placed on the fabric, they must face in *one* direction for a "nap layout." To observe the shading, drape the fabric around the form so that the lengthwise edges butt together on the center front. Then look down the fabric (from the top of the form) to see the shading difference (see Figure 1.7). In some knits, the shading difference is obvious. In other knits, it is more subtle. Chapter 4 describes how to lay out the patterns following a nap layout.

Fabric Selection

A good-quality fabric is the key to making clothes that fit well and last. Donna Karan's advice in Important 1.2 says that the *fabric* is the key to all decisions that need to be made about the design, pattern drafting, and stitching. These decisions involve determining the fabric weight and drape, the direction of stretch, and the stretchiness. Karan's advice is to listen to the fabric talk so that you choose the correct knit fabric for the design.

The importance of the fabric can be summed up this way:

- The fabric is the designer's medium.
- The characteristics of the fabric influence what style the fabric would suit.
- The weight of the fabric directs what design will suit a certain fabric.
- The fiber content of the fabric influences the amount of stretch and the fit of the garment.
- The amount of stretch in the fabric influences the chosen design.
- The design must suit the fabric.

Here are some tips to follow when selecting the appropriate fabric for a particular design:

- *Fabric weight*—The most practical way to determine a fabric's weight is to take the fabric in your hand and sense what you feel. Then define the fabric weight: light, medium, or heavy. Tops are generally made from lighter-weight knits. Pants, skirts, and jackets are commonly made from weightier knits. However, this does not discount the possibility of using a lightweight sheer knit to make a fabulous skirt and adding a lining.

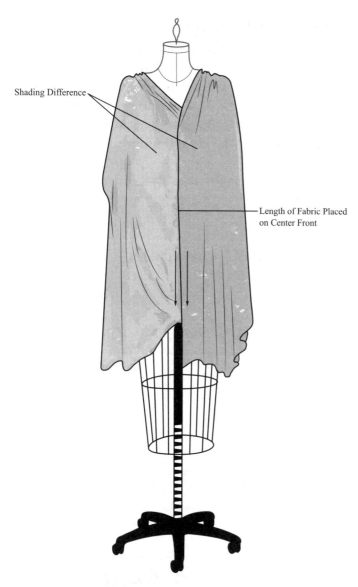

Shading Difference

Length of Fabric Placed on Center Front

Figure 1.7 Fabric shading in knits

IMPORTANT 1.2: FABRIC TALKS

Whether you choose a woven or a knit fabric, Donna Karan advises, "It's all about the fabric . . . it's as if the fabric talks to me. As I start playing with it, it begins to dictate how it wants to fall and move against the body. That's when everything just comes alive and all my creative juices start to flow."[6]

---

6 Rubenstein, "Designer Profile: Donna Karan," 149–150.

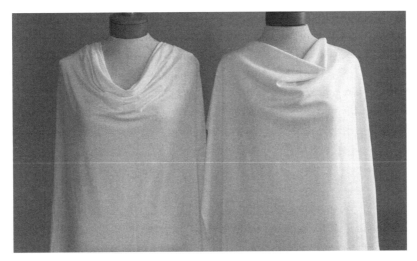

Figure 1.8a Fabric with excellent drape   **Figure 1.8b** Fabric that does not drape well

- *Directions of stretch*—Determine if the knit you are working with has two-way or four-way stretch because this fact influences the design. For example, a top, dress, or skirt requires only two-way stretch to function well on the body. In contrast, a swimsuit or bike shorts for cycling *must* be made in a knit that has four-way stretch.
- *Stretch capacity*—The stretch capacity directs what style is suitable for a particular fabric. For example, after doing a stretch test, if you discover the knit you are working with is four-way stretch (and the fabric weight is correct), then you know it is suitable for swimwear or cycling shorts or a pair of leggings. Note that a top, dress, or skirt *can* also be constructed from any four-way stretch knit. (The lengthwise stretch is inactive in these styles.) In addition, you can design a four-way stretch knit into loose-fitting styles when you use the suitable fabric weight.

IMPORTANT 1.3: FABRIC DRAPE

Discern how the fabric drapes. To get a true picture, place the fabric on the form with the lengthwise grain aligned on the center front. Then pin the fabric to the shoulders of the form. Fabric that is fluid drapes into rounded folds, as illustrated in Figure 1.8a. In Figure 1.8b, the angular fold that flops to the side indicates that the fabric does not drape well.

Choosing Garment Fabric

The "correct" fabric type *must* be chosen for a particular style because it affects the fit, function, wearability, and ultimately the salability of the garment.

It is important that the design and chosen fabric are in sync. For example, if you were planning to make active-wear pants from a certain fabric, the fabric must be of medium weight, have enough stretch for vigorous exercise, and wick moisture. The fiber content and the fabric's characteristics are important for these reasons:

- *Movement*—When you are working out or playing sports, movement *must* come with ease. (Spandex aids in comfort and ease.)
- *Quick-dry finish*—This characteristic is essential for swimwear. (Nylon and spandex dry quickly.)
- *Moisture-wicking properties*—Moisture-wicking fabrics pull moisture away from the skin and then release it for evaporation so you feel comfortable during vigorous activity.[7] (Many new synthetics offer moisture-wicking properties.)
- *Comfort*—Lightweight organic, Pima, and combed cotton are soft fibers that prevent chafing of delicate skin and are ideal for sleepwear and infants' clothing.
- *Warmth*—Wool, cashmere, mohair, and acrylic knits feel cozy on wintery days.
- *Coolness*—Cotton and linen knits facilitate coolness in hot, humid weather.

---

7   "Wicking Fabric Demystified," *Healthy Wage Blog*, July 9, 2010, http://healthywage.wordpress.com/2010/07/09/wicking-fabric-demystified/.

- *Fabric cost*—A deluxe silk knit is expensive, whereas cottons, rayon, and synthetics are more cost-effective. The cost of the fabric influences the final cost of the garment.
- *Fabric care*—Synthetics and regenerated fibers are easy to care for. The care of the fabric influences the customer's preferences.

Choosing Muslin

The muslin you choose to test-fit a garment can be a cheaper knit fabric or the actual garment fabric. It is important that the muslin you use is the same weight and stretches as much as the final fabric stretches. Polyester interlock is an inexpensive lightweight two-way stretch knit that makes excellent muslin. To test-fit a swimsuit, always use the final fabric for muslin to ensure a perfect fit.

IMPORTANT 1.4: FITTING KNITS: HOW TO TELL IF YOU'RE PULLING THE FABRIC TOO TIGHTLY WHEN FITTING A GARMENT

When you're fitting knits, be guided by the fabric. Some garments are designed to have a tight fit (swimsuits and bike shorts with spandex), whereas other garments (T-shirts and pajamas made in 100 percent cotton) are not designed to fit tightly. The fiber content impacts the fit. Some fabrics can be pulled in to fit tightly, but others cannot.

Choosing Lining

It is not imperative that knits have a lining. The choice of whether a garment needs a lining may be purely practical. Using a lining may be the fastest and most economical way to stitch the garment. An evening dress is one example in which a lining would create a clean finish (with no topstitching) and adds a high-quality finish to the inside of the garment.

Various linings are available in two-way and four-way stretch. Tricot is one two-way stretch knit that makes an excellent lining for a skirt, dress, or pants. A nylon/spandex sheer mesh has a four-way stretch that makes an excellent swimsuit lining. Even a polyester woven/stretch lining can be used to line skirts, dresses, and jackets that have two-way minimal stretch.

Fabric Evaluation

The Fabric Evaluation Worksheet in Table 1.2 is a tool that you can use to test your fabric and document your results. Testing the fabric before drafting the patterns or cutting and stitching the garment helps prevent any fabric disasters.

Follow these instructions to test the fabric:

1. Cut *two* identical 4" × 4" fabric swatches "on grain."
2. Launder *one* swatch following the care instructions for the fiber content; do *not* launder the other swatch. After laundering the first swatch, compare the swatch size to the other swatch and calculate any shrinkage over 36" for the length and width. For example, if the laundered fabric has shrunk $\frac{1}{8}$" in the width, then over 36", the shrinkage would be $1\frac{1}{8}$" (36" ÷ 4 = 9"; next, 9 × $\frac{1}{8}$" = $1\frac{1}{8}$"). This amount of shrinkage would affect the fit of the garment after it is laundered.
3. Test the stretch capacity using the stretch gauge shown previously in Figure 1.4. (Refer to the "Stretch Categories" section.)
4. Test the stretch and recovery. After stretching the fabric, let it relax. Notice whether the knit bounces back to its original shape. If it does bounce back to exactly the 4" square, it has excellent recovery.
5. After testing, place the correct sides of both swatches facing up, with rib-lines placed in the vertical direction. Then attach both swatches to the Fabric Evaluation Worksheet and fill in the worksheet.

TABLE 1.2 Fabric Evaluation Worksheet

	Fabric Weight (Circle)	Stretch Recovery (Circle)	Shrinkage after Laundering (Circle)
Type of Knit _____ **Fiber Content** _____ **Care Instructions** _____ **What is distinctive about my fabric?** _____ _____ **Change to fabric surface after laundering? Yes/No** (Add Comments) _____ _____ **Suitable Styles** _____ _____	Light weight Medium weight Heavy weight	Poor Fair Good Excellent	Calculate over 36" width Calculate over 36" length

	Type of Stretch (Circle)	Stretch Capacity (Circle) **Width**	Stretch Capacity (Circle) **Length**
Attach both fabric swatches here; place washed swatch on top of unwashed swatch. Cut fabric swatch 4" × 4"	Mechanical Stretch Two-way Stretch Four-way Stretch	Minimal Stretch Moderately Stretchy Very Stretchy Super Stretchy	Minimal Stretch Moderately Stretchy Very Stretchy Super Stretchy

Knit It Together

This checklist summarizes what you have learned about knit fabrics in this chapter.

- ✓ Knit fabric stretches because it is knitted with loops.
- ✓ Woven fabric with a percentage of Lycra does not make it a knit fabric.
- ✓ Designers need to be aware of the type of knit they are using, fiber content, stretch capacity, and care instructions because these characteristics direct the end use of the fabric.
- ✓ Knit fabric can be two-way stretch or four-way stretch.
- ✓ Knit fabrics stretch to different amounts.
- ✓ To determine the stretch capacity of a knit, complete a stretch test using the stretch gauge featured in Figure 1.4.

Stop: What Do I Do If . . .

. . . I can't recognize the difference between a woven and knit fabric structure?

Obtain a pick glass from your instructor to help you distinguish each one. Place the fabric under the glass, and it will magnify the surface. Then you'll see the loop formation of a knit and the warp and weft yarns of a woven fabric.

. . . I purchased fabric without checking if it had the correct amount of stretch for my design? The design worked well. So why use the stretch gauge in the future?

Next time, not checking the stretch may lead to a disaster because the fabric may not have the correct stretch percentage when you construct your design. Carry your stretch gauge with you whenever you look for a knit fabric so you can be sure the fabric has adequate stretch for the design.

Self-Critique

1. Why does knit fabric stretch?
2. How does the stretch factor impact on patternmaking for knits? (Refer to the "How Working with Knits Differs from Working with Wovens" section).
3. Is a woven fabric with Lycra a knit?
4. What is the difference between a two-way stretch and four-way stretch knit?
5. Donna Karan's advice is to "Listen to the fabric talk." How do you do this? (Refer to the "Fabric Selection" section.)
6. If you were marketing a knit garment, how would you endorse the fabric's qualities?
7. How do you recognize a jersey knit? (Refer to Table 1.1.)
8. Evaluate the fabric.
   - Purchase ⅛ yard of a selection of knit fabrics (jersey single knit, double knit, interlock, ribbing, sweater knit, swimwear fabric, activewear knit, sheer mini mesh or other sheer knit, fleece, stretch terry, or French terry).
   - Cut 4" × 4" swatches. Evaluate each fabric type and fill in the relevant information on the Fabric Evaluation Worksheet in Table 1.2.

Key Terms	Single Knit
Courses	Spandex
Double Knit	Stretch and Recovery
Four-way Stretch	Stretch Capacity
Knit Fabric	Stretch Categories
Lycra	Super Stretchy Knits
Mechanical Stretch	Two-way Stretch
Minimal Stretch Knits	Very Stretchy Knits
Moderate Stretch Knits	Wales
Napped Fabric	Warp Knit
Pick Glass	Weft Knit
Ribs	Woven Fabric

2

The Knit Family of Slopers

This chapter explains the sloper system and how to use it. As the chapter unfolds, you will discover how the "knit family" has birthed a variety of slopers from the hip and top foundations. From the slopers, you can create a vast collection of garments for everyday wear, business wear, sportswear, and activewear. When you have excellent slopers, fitting and testing are the preliminary stages essential for designing and producing stretch knit garments with perfect fit.

Sloper System Explained

The **sloper system** is a method of creating slopers for drafting patterns for garments constructed from stretch knit fabrics. As previously discussed in Chapter 1, in the "How Working with Knits Differs from Working with Wovens" section, slopers for woven fabrics (incorporating dart and ease) cannot be used to draft the patterns for stretch knit fabrics. Stretch knit garments require unique slopers that do not have darts or ease incorporated into the slopers. The fabric's stretch replaces the darts and ease.

The method requires you to draft hip and top foundations. A foundation is the base, source, or the groundwork of something. These foundations form the base of the slopers for skirts, pants, panties, swimsuits, and tops. From the slopers, you can draft any pattern for a stretch knit garment, as you will see in Tables 2.1 and 2.2.

Hip and Top Foundations

The hip and top foundations are not complete patterns in themselves, nor are they slopers. The hip and top Foundations are partial patterns (see Figure 2.1). The **hip foundation** represents the lower part of the body from the waist to the hip. The **top foundation** represents

the upper part of the body from the waist up to the shoulders. The hip and top foundations are drafted from the form or body measurements. No ease is added to the patterns because the stretch factor in knits *is* the ease. For this reason, the foundations look taut when they are cut, stitched, and fitted on the form (see Figure 5.10 on p. 74 and Figure 5.30 on p. 84).

The stretchiness of knits varies. For this reason, the foundations are prepared for use in two-way and four-way stretch and in the stretch categories (*minimal stretch, moderate stretch, very stretchy,* and *super stretchy*) to match the stretch categories shown previously in Figure 1.4 on p. 7.

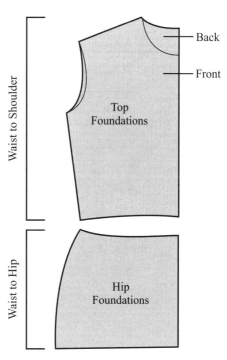

Figure 2.1 Hip and top foundations

Hip and Top Foundations Transform into Slopers

This is a unique system because all the slopers are developed from the two-way stretch and four-way stretch hip and top foundations, as shown in Table 2.1. The unifying theme in this text is how the sloper system uses the foundations to create all the slopers—skirt, pant, panty, swimwear, and top. The red outline in Table 2.1 demonstrates how the slopers are developed from the foundations. When cut, stitched, and fitted on the form, the slopers will also have a taut fit. (Refer to Figures 6.12a and b on p. 106 to see the top sloper stitched in muslin.) The relevant chapters describe how to make each specific sloper.

The advantage of using the sloper system is that once the foundations are completed, you can jump to the relevant chapter and commence developing the slopers for the garment of your choice.

Slopers Transform into Garments

The slopers can be used to draft the patterns for any garment made in a stretch knit fabric. In Table 2.1, each family of slopers is identified in garment form (top, skirt, pants, panty, and swimwear). Below each sloper in Table 2.2 is a list of the garments that can be created from that sloper. Table 2.2 also shows how you would use the

TABLE 2.1 Hip and top foundations transform into slopers

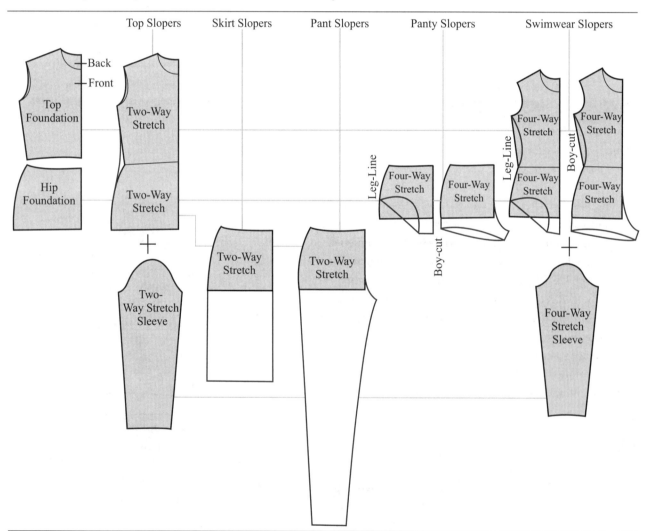

top slopers to draft the patterns for a dress, cardigan, or camisole. To create leggings, you would choose the pant slopers to draft the pattern. To create a jumpsuit, you would combine the two-way stretch top foundations and pant slopers to draft the patterns.

How to Use the Sloper System

Just as the foundations are drafted in stretch categories (*minimal stretch, moderate stretch, very stretchy,* and *super stretchy*) so are the slopers. There is a 2" difference between each sloper because each knit has less stretch. The *moderate stretch* top sloper in Table 2.3 is cut larger than the *super stretchy* top sloper because a

moderate stretch knit has less stretch. When the knit has less stretch, the garment must be made bigger to fit the same size body.

Before drafting the patterns for a particular garment, designers need to determine the stretchiness of the knit they are working with (using the stretch gauge shown in Figure 1.4 on p. 7). They also need to have in mind how the garment will fit.

Fit Flexibility: Adding Extra Room into Garments

Just because the fabric stretches, a garment does not have to be taut and tightly fitted on the body. The garment can also have a loose fit. In such garments, **fit flexibility**

TABLE 2.2 The knit family of slopers transform into garments

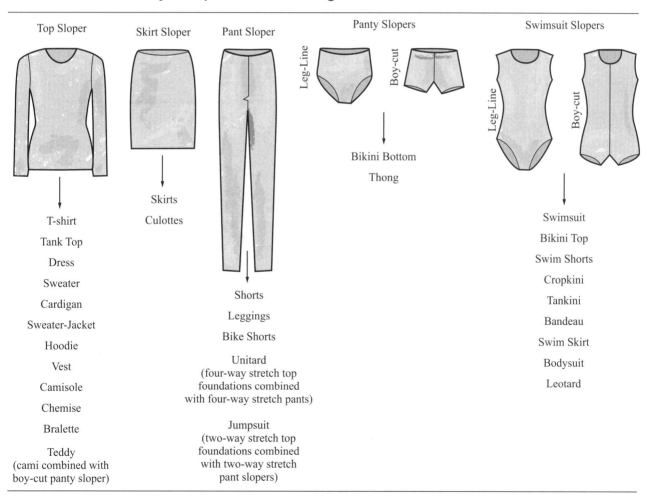

Top Sloper	Skirt Sloper	Pant Sloper	Panty Slopers		Swimsuit Slopers
			Leg-Line	Boy-cut	Leg-Line / Boy-cut

Skirts
Culottes

T-shirt
Tank Top
Dress
Sweater
Cardigan
Sweater-Jacket
Hoodie
Vest
Camisole
Chemise
Bralette
Teddy
(cami combined with boy-cut panty sloper)

Bikini Bottom
Thong

Shorts
Leggings
Bike Shorts
Unitard
(four-way stretch top foundations combined with four-way stretch pants)
Jumpsuit
(two-way stretch top foundations combined with two-way stretch pant slopers)

Swimsuit
Bikini Top
Swim Shorts
Cropkini
Tankini
Bandeau
Swim Skirt
Bodysuit
Leotard

comes into play, as demonstrated in Table 2.3. Even though the slopers are drafted into stretch categories to match the stretch categories of knits, designers have options when choosing which slopers to use to draft the patterns for a particular garment.

How to Choose Slopers

You can choose the sloper to meet different needs using the following two methods:

- **Method 1: Choose the sloper in the *same* stretch category as the stretch capacity of your knit for a fitted look.**
  In this method you choose the "stretch capacity of sloper" to draft the patterns for your garment that matches the knit stretch capacity. For example, by

following this method, you would choose the *very stretchy* top sloper to draft the patterns for a top constructed from a *very stretchy knit* for a *fitted* look.

- **Method 2: Choose *another* stretch category of sloper for a roomier fit to allow ease.**
  In this method you choose the sloper according to the "fit of garment." Table 2.3 lists the fit categories: slim-fit, semi slim-fit, semi loose-fit, and loose-fit. The arrows point from left to right toward another stretch category of sloper to indicate the other slopers you can choose to draft the patterns for a more generous fit. For instance, by following this method, you could choose the *minimal stretch* slopers to draft the pattern for a *very stretchy* knit to create a loose-fitting garment with a more generous fit. (The side seam can also be changed to create a relaxed fit as shown.) Additionally, if you desire an oversized top, you can grade the

TABLE 2.3 Fit flexibility: adding extra room into the garment

minimal stretch slopers larger for additional room. (You learn how to do this in Chapter 8 in the section "Slopers for Jackets, Cardigans, and Sweater-Jackets.") Even though these slopers are designed for sweaters, cardigans, and sweater-jackets, they can be used to create any style of top.

Knit It Together

This checklist summarizes what you have learned about the knit family of slopers in this chapter.

- ✓ The hip and top foundations are partial patterns drafted to the form measurements.
- ✓ All slopers are developed from the hip and top foundations.
- ✓ Any stretch knit garment can be developed from the knit family of slopers.
- ✓ There is flexibility when choosing which sloper to use to draft the patterns.

Stop: What Do I Do If . . .

. . . I can't see a bathrobe listed in Table 2.2? I'd like to draft the pattern, but I don't know what slopers to use.

Not every garment is listed in Table 2.2. In fact, one of the exercises in the "Self-Critique" section is to add other garments to the list. The patterns for a bathrobe would be drafted from the cardigan and sweater slopers created in Chapter 8. These slopers are created from the top slopers. Now you know where to list the bathrobe.

. . . I want to add extra room into a skirt or pant and create a loose-fit? Does the same fit flexibility concept in Table 2.3 still apply?

Yes, you can use the fit flexibility concept for any garment.

Self-Critique

1. The sloper system is a method of creating slopers for stretch knit fabrics. Two partial patterns are required to draft all the slopers for stretch knits. What are they?

2. What two foundations are used to form the top slopers? How do they join into one sloper? (Refer to Table 2.1. Also look forward to Figure 6.4 on p. 98.)

3. What is the advantage of using this sloper system described in the section "Hip and Top Foundations Transform into Slopers?"

4. Why are the slopers created in stretch categories (minimal stretch, moderate stretch, very stretchy, and super stretchy)?

5. The chapter addresses fit flexibility. The relevant section indicates that the slopers can be chosen in two different ways. Explain how the slopers can be chosen. (Refer to Table 2.3.)

6. Explain the difference between two-way and four-way stretch.

7. In the following table, check the box to indicate the direction of stretch required for each garment to function at its best. (Refer to Table 2.1.)

Garment	Two-way Stretch	Four-way Stretch
Tank top		
Cardigan		
Dress		
Bodysuit		
Sweater-jacket		
Jumpsuit with waist casing		
Swim skirt		
Bike shorts		
Skirt		
Leggings		
Pajama shorts		
Palazzo pants		

8. List any other garments that can be added to Table 2.2.

Key Terms	Sloper System
Fit Flexibility	Top Foundation
Hip Foundation	

3
Pattern Drafting for Knits

This chapter outlines important principles and key definitions for use when drafting slopers and patterns for stretch knit garments. To draft patterns successfully, you must employ the correct drafting tools. This chapter explains what those tools are and how to use them.

The chapter also explains how to communicate and organize aspects of the patterns such as seam and hem allowances, pattern markings, grainlines, and pattern labeling. Correct pattern drafting is vital to creating an easy process when you begin laying out, cutting, and stitching a garment.

The main supplies—other than the fabric required for knits—are interfacing and elastic. The chapter explains each one and where to use them on garments.

Pattern Drafting Tools

Working with the right tools makes the pattern drafting process easier. The essential patternmaking tools are illustrated in Figure 3.1. Figures 3.2 and 3.3 illustrates where to use each tool when drafting patterns.

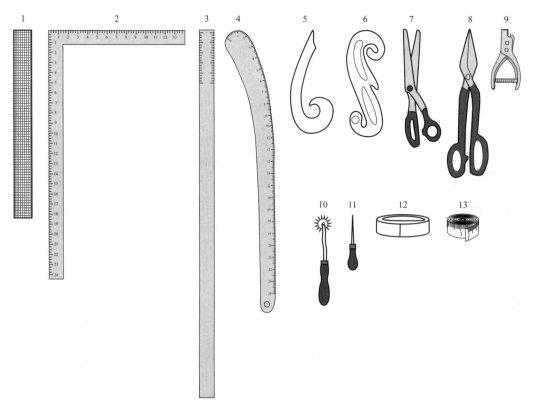

Figure 3.1 Patternmaking tools. **1)** 18" graph ruler, **2)** L-square metal ruler, **3)** Straight metal ruler, **4)** Hip curve, **5)** French curve, **6)** Sleigh curve, **7)** Paper scissors, **8)** Pattern shears, **9)** Notcher, **10)** Needle-point tracing wheel, **11)** Awl,**12)** Masking tape, **13)** Tape measure

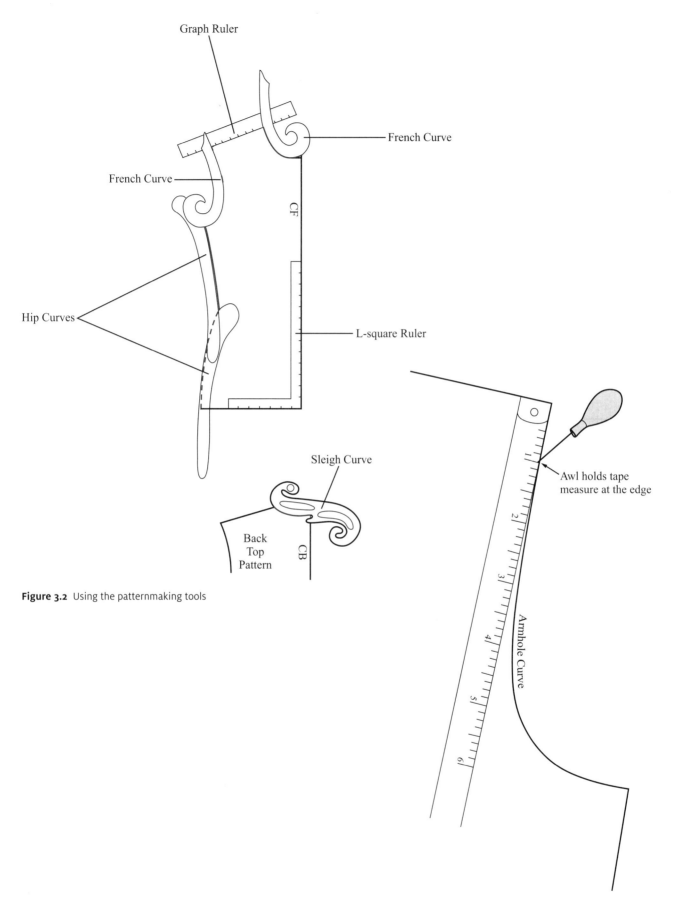

Graph Ruler

French Curve

French Curve

CF

Hip Curves

L-square Ruler

Sleigh Curve

Back
Top
Pattern

CB

Figure 3.2 Using the patternmaking tools

Armhole Curve

Awl holds tape
measure at the edge

Figure 3.3 Walking the tape measure

Patternmaking Symbols

Familiarizing yourself with the symbols in Table 3.1 is especially important because they are used throughout the text for drafting patterns for knits.

Key Definitions and Pattern Drafting Principles

Many of the pattern drafting principles in this text for drafting slopers and patterns follow standard definitions

TABLE 3.1 Patternmaking symbols

Patternmaking Symbols	
Center Front CF Center Back CB	Measurement Indicator
Intersecting Lines	Matchpoint
Guide Mark/Guideline	Notches
Squared-off Angle (90% Angle/Right	Directional Grainline
Squared Line (Vertical or Horizontal)	Cut on Fold Grainline
Cross-mark	Trace Pattern
Slash/Spread	Stitch Line
Slash/Separate	Finished Pattern Outline
Align Patterns	Buttonhole and Button Placement

and principles. A number of definitions are applicable only to stretch knits.

Key Definitions

Dress/pant form—A replica of a part of a woman's body with no head or arms; sometimes it has legs. Designers and dressmakers use a form for draping fabric, testing patterns, and fitting garments during construction. In this text, no set size of form is required. You can use the form of your choice because the slopers are drafted to the form measurements. In Chapter 5, the form is taped in preparation for pattern drafting.

Flat patternmaking—The method used to draft slopers and patterns. The patterns are drafted directly on pattern paper to a set of measurements using the patternmaking tools illustrated in Figure 3.1.

Sloper—A basic pattern shaped to the natural neckline, shoulders, armholes, bust, waist, and hip of the form. Slopers (or *blocks* may be the preferred term) are not made to a particular design, nor do they have style lines or seam allowance. Slopers are made in *oak-tag*, a heavyweight paper. Oak-tag patterns can be traced and retraced and will hold up to constant use.

Positive and negative ease—Slopers for woven fabric have **positive ease**. The slopers are cut larger than the body measurements with ease incorporated for comfort and movement. Knit slopers have no ease because the stretch factor in knits provides the ease and flexibility for movement and comfort. A garment can also be designed with positive ease; this is "wearing ease," with a few extra inches to allow room for comfortable, nonrestricted movement. (Chapter 8 outlines how to draft top slopers with wearing ease.) Garments can also have "design ease," which is ease added for the design to follow a certain silhouette.

In some cases, knit patterns may require **negative ease**. This means that the patterns are cut smaller than the actual body measurements.

Pattern grading—The process of scaling patterns to a mathematical formula to increase or decrease the pattern dimensions. In this text, slopers are graded into stretch categories rather than graded into sizes.

Muslin—A prototype of the actual garment (or section of a garment). Muslin is also the fabric used to test-fit a garment. For stretch knits, the muslin *must* be a knit fabric that has the same stretch capacity as the garment fabric.

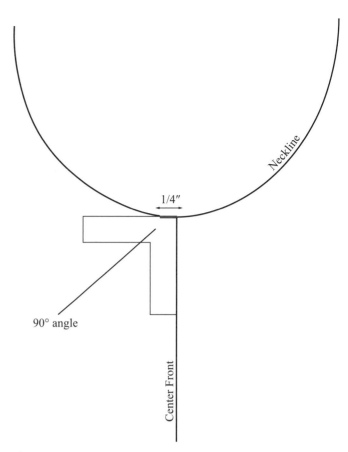

Figure 3.4 Pattern drafting using a squared line

Pattern Drafting Principles

Working pattern—The pattern where the lines are plotted following the sketch of the garment. The pattern pieces are then traced from the working patterns, separated, and finalized. (Figure 6.44a on p. 131 shows a working pattern. Figure 6.44b on p. 132 shows the patterns that have been traced from the working pattern.)

Pattern plotting—The process of planning and drawing the pattern outline or silhouette (neckline, armhole, and hem length) and arranging the placement of seams on the working pattern.

Intersecting lines—Vertical and horizontal lines drawn on pattern paper that meet at a 90° right angle (see Figure 3.15).

Right angle—An angle of 90°. It is the corner of a square or the intersection of two perpendicular straight lines (see Figure 3.4).

Squared line—A line drawn perpendicular to another line. There must be an existing line to draw a squared line. In Figure 3.4, a ¼" squared line is drawn on the center front neckline of the front pattern. When a pattern piece is "cut on fold" and opened out flat, the neckline will continue into a smooth curved line because a squared line was used.

Squared-off angle—A 90° angle drawn with two connecting ¼" lines. (Draw using a graph ruler or L-square.) Figure 3.5 indicates where to draw squared-off angles on a bodice pattern. Drawing squared-off angles ensures smooth blending armhole, waistline, and underarm curves when the pattern seams are aligned.

Parallel lines—Lines that are drawn an equal distance from each other.

Crossmark—Two short ¼" intersecting lines to mark and locate various parts of the pattern (such as the apex in Figure 5.31 on p. 85).

Trueing seams—The process of establishing correct seam lengths and smoothing, straightening, blending, and establishing correct angles.

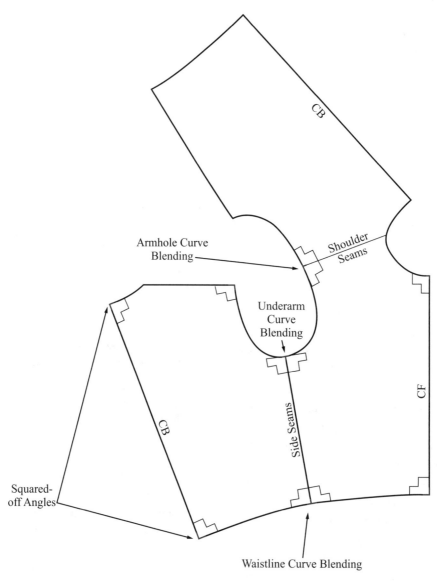

Figure 3.5 Pattern drafting using squared-off angles

Blending—The process of drawing a smooth continuous line to round any angular lines. Blending is essential in pattern drafting where two pattern seams, when placed together, form an angle, as shown in Figures 3.6a and b.

Equalizing—The process of drawing a new line to eliminate irregularities in line lengths. Figure 3.7 illustrates how to equalize two uneven line lengths.

Pattern manipulation—The process of changing the pattern design by using the slash/spread and slash/separate techniques.

Slash/spread technique—The process of changing the pattern design by cutting a line to a pivot point and spreading the pattern to add fullness to create volume and flare (see Figure 6.33b on p. 124).

Slash/separate technique—The process of changing the pattern design by cutting through a line to separate the patterns to add fullness to use for gathering, tucks, or pleats (see Figure 6.39b on p. 127).

Directional seamline—A seamline that follows exactly the shape of the seam.[1] A directional seamline ensures

---

1 Fashionbook, "Terminology Common to Drafting & Draping," accessed September 12, 2014, http://fashionbook.forza6.com/catalogo/term_116.html.

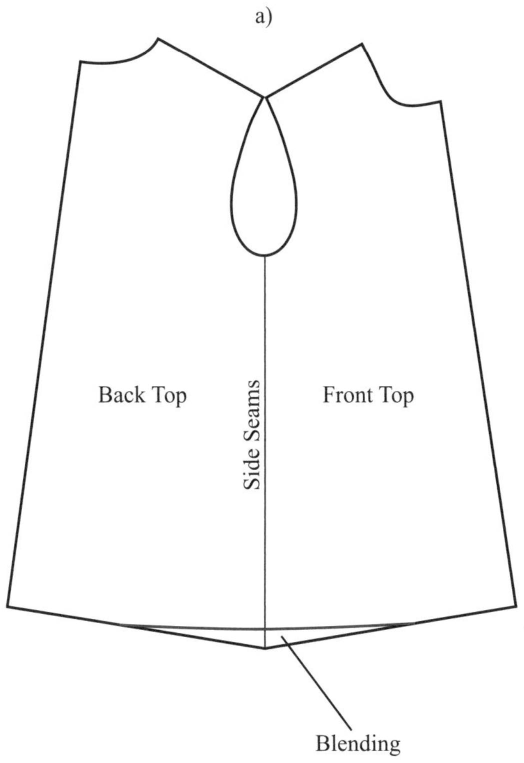

a)

Back Top   Side Seams   Front Top

Blending

Figure 3.6a Blending the hemline

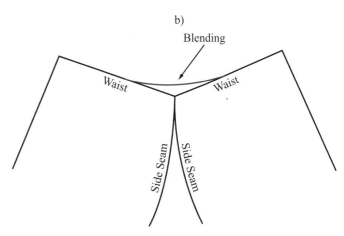

b)

Blending

Waist   Waist

Side Seam   Side Seam

Figure 3.6b Blending the waistline

that the section being stitched is the correct length and will not look puckered (if too short) or bulky (if excess length has not been removed); see Figures 3.8a and b.

Directional grainline—A grainline that indicates how a pattern is to be placed on the fabric and cut. In this text, a "T" is the base of the grainline and an arrow is the tip. (Look ahead to Figures 3.12 and 3.13.)

Seam allowance—The area between the seamline and the cut edge of the pattern. Seam allowance widths vary depending on the type of knit and the seam technique being stitched. (Look ahead to Figures 3.12 and 3.13.)

Final patterns—Patterns that have been trued with seam and hem allowance added, notches and grainlines indicated, and patterns labeled (see Figure 3.12).

Stabilizers for Knits

A **stabilizer** is a product that is used in clothing construction to add structure to garments. *Interfacing* is one type of stabilizer that is used to support garment parts such as the collar, placket, and cuffs. *Stabilizing tape* is another stabilizer that is used to prevent garment edges and seams from stretching. *Elastic* is also a stabilizer that is used to control the elasticity of openings, such as the waistline of pants and skirts, necklines, or openings of a swimsuit.

Interfacing

Interfacing can be two-way stretch, four-way stretch, or nonstretch. Each interfacing has a different use.

- **Two-way stretch interfacing** is ideal for use on two-way stretch knits because it stretches in the same direction.

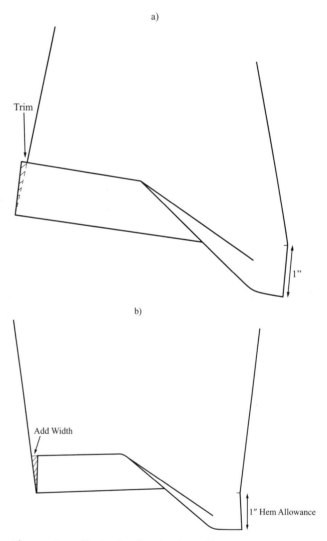

Figure 3.7 Equalizing uneven shoulder lengths

Figure 3.8a and b Cutting directional seamlines

- **Four-way stretch interfacing** stretches up and down the length and across the width in the same way a four-way stretch knit stretches, as shown in Figures 1.2a and b on p. 2. One popular type is Sofknit. It is referred to as an "all bias" interfacing because it stretches in every direction.
- *Nonstretch interfacing* does not stretch. A nonstretch interfacing can be an appropriate interfacing to use when the stretch of the knit needs to be removed from a section of the garment (such as the collar).
- *Stabilizing tape* prevents garment edges and seams from stretching. It can be purchased on a roll (Seams Great, fusible bias tape, or knit stay tape), or a narrow ⅜" to ½" strip can be cut from interfacing. (Refer to Figure 6.51d on p. 137 to see stabilizing being used on the neckline of a top.)

Elastic

Elastic is categorized by its construction. **Woven elastic** is constructed by weaving. **Knitted elastic** is knitted as knit fabric is. **Braided elastic** is identified by horizontal narrow ribs. Various types of elastic are shown in Table 3.2.

Some seams and garment openings need to be elasticized, as indicated in Figure 3.9. The type of elastic you use is directed by the *type* of garment, *placement* of the elastic, and the *construction* method employed to stitch the elastic in place. For example, the leg openings of a swimsuit require elastic that will endure saltwater and chlorine. The elastic to keep the edge of a dress stabilized requires lightweight clear elastic. Elastic for waistbands of skirts and pants requires firm nonroll 1" or wider elastic to ensure the garment stays firmly on the waistline.

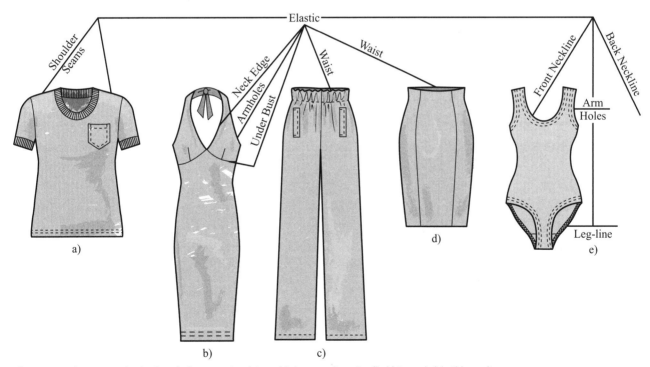

Figure 3.9 Where to apply elastic to knit garments: **a)** tops, **b)** dresses, **c)** pants, **d)** skirts, and **e)** bathing suits

TABLE 3.2 Types of elastic

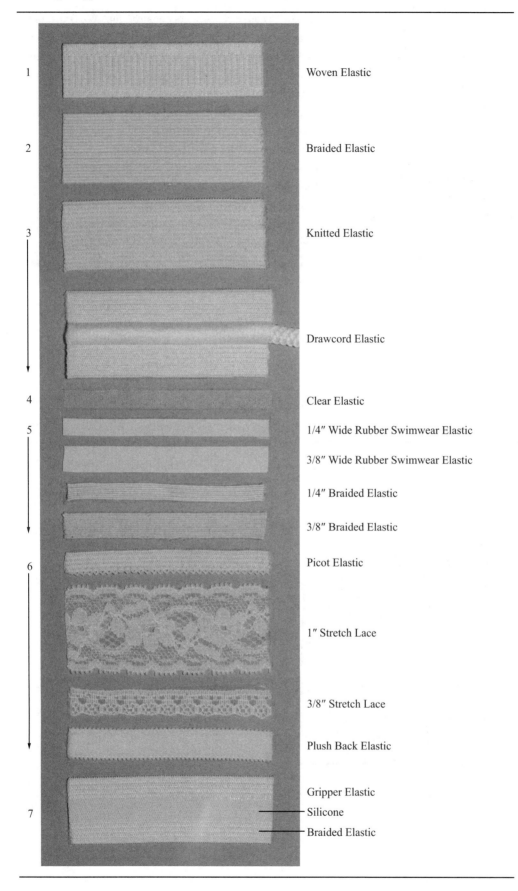

1 — Woven Elastic

2 — Braided Elastic

3 — Knitted Elastic

Drawcord Elastic

4 — Clear Elastic

5 — 1/4″ Wide Rubber Swimwear Elastic

3/8″ Wide Rubber Swimwear Elastic

1/4″ Braided Elastic

3/8″ Braided Elastic

6 — Picot Elastic

1″ Stretch Lace

3/8″ Stretch Lace

Plush Back Elastic

Gripper Elastic

Silicone

7 — Braided Elastic

TABLE 3.3 Elastic chart

Type of Elastic	Width Required	Where to Use
1. Woven Elastic		
Nonroll elastic. Can be topstitched.	¾"–1½"	Waistbands of skirts and pants
Can be inserted into a casing.	Varying widths	Elasticized bands for wrist and hems
	¾"–1"	Strapless garments
2. Braided Elastic		
Lightweight, soft, pliable elastic. It is the softest of all three types and narrows when stretched.	1" or wider for waistbands	Serge elastic to waistbands because braided elastic rolls within a casing.
	¼" wide	Use for swimwear.
	⅛" wide	Use for baby wear.
3. Knitted Elastic		
Soft yet stable elastic and *does not* roll. It has a *smooth* surface and therefore looks *flat* after application.	¾"–1½"	Waistline of skirts and pants
	¾"–1"	Strapless garments
Drawcord elastic is knitted elastic with a cord encompassed within it.		
4. Clear Elastic		
Made from 100 percent polyurethane.	¼" and ⅜" widths	Stitch not stretched to stabilize shoulder seams
Is lightweight, bulk free, and has the ability to stretch up to three times its original length.		Stitch stretched to seams to help the garment fit snugly on the body
5. Swimwear Elastic		
Available in two types: rubber and braided	¼" and ⅜" widths	Use the ¼" width to elasticize openings of a swimsuit to prevent stretching.
		Use ⅜" width to elasticize waistline of bikini bottom and edge of bikini top.
6. Lingerie Elastic		
Must feel soft against the skin. Picot elastic is the most popular type.		
Picot Elastic	¼" and ⅜" widths	Elasticized opening of panties and camisoles
Stretch Lace	Use ¾"–1" widths for waist opening and straps. Use ¼" and ⅜" widths for leg openings	Elasticized openings of panties and camisoles and shoulder straps
Plush Back Elastic	Use ½" – 1"	Shoulder straps and under the bust of built-in bra
7. Gripper Elastic		
This elastic has a ⅜" strip of silicone in the center of the elastic that grips the body firmly to hold the garment in place.	1" wide	Stitch to top edge of bandeau or strapless top/dress.
		Stitch to hem of bike shorts.

IMPORTANT 3.1: CHOOSING ELASTIC

It is important to choose the elastic before you draft your pattern because the width of elastic directs the amount that you must add to the pattern for stitching and turning the elastic edge. Table 3.3 helps you choose the appropriate elastic for your garment.

The length to which the elastic is cut is critical to the success of the garment. When you apply elastic, you must cut the elastic shorter than the seam length of the garment opening (see chapters for specific garments). Doing so ensures that the elastic lies flat after it is stitched in place (shoulder elastic is the exception).

The Patterns

If you want to produce a quality garment, your pattern must be first-rate because it directly influences how the garment will fit and hang on the body. Part of the pattern-making process is trueing the seams to make sure that all the seamlines fit together precisely. When two patterns have uneven seam lengths, you can easily stretch the shorter seam to fit the longer seam when stitching the pieces together. However, when you do this, the garment will look skewed (see Figure 3.10a). A garment will hang correctly when the seams are perfectly aligned (see Figure 3.10b).

Symmetrical and Asymmetrical Patterns

Garments can be symmetrical or asymmetrical. In a symmetrical garment, both sides of the garment look the same (see Figure 3.11a). In an asymmetrical garment, both sides of the garment look different (see Figure 3.11b). Whether the garment is symmetrical or asymmetrical influences how the patterns are drafted and labeled. Note that the asymmetrical striped tank dress must be constructed from a knit with four-way stretch because the stripes are placed on the lengthwise and crossgrain of the fabric. (Refer to Figure 4.7 on p. 45 to see the fabric layout.)

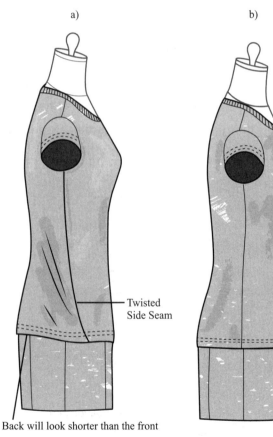

a)   b)

Twisted Side Seam

Back will look shorter than the front

Figure 3.10a Skewed T-shirt

Figure 3.10b T-shirt perfectly aligned

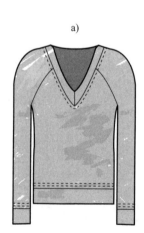

a)

Figure 3.11a Symmetrical V-neck sweater with raglan sleeves

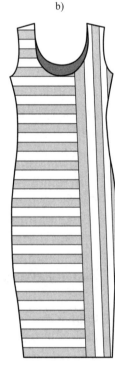

b)

Figure 3.11b Asymmetrical striped tank dress

Symmetrical

Symmetrical patterns can be drafted as half pattern pieces because both sides of the garment are the same. The fabric pieces can be cut from folded fabric. The neckband pattern is included, but the wrist and hem bands are not. These bands are drafted in a similar way to the neckband. Figure 3.12 shows the symmetrical patterns for the V-neck sweater.

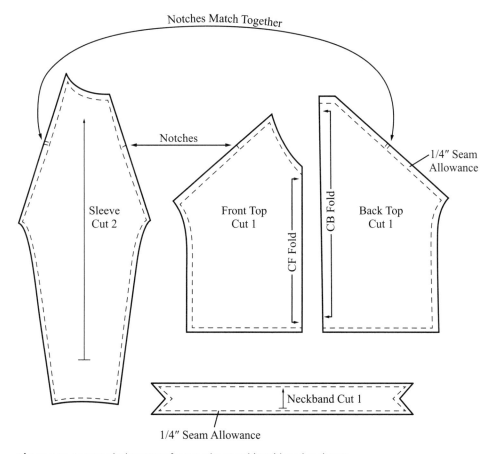

Figure 3.12 Symmetrical patterns for V-neck sweatshirt with raglan sleeves

Asymmetrical

Asymmetrical patterns are drafted as full pattern pieces for both sides of the garment. The patterns are labeled right side up (R.S.U.), so they are placed on the fabric correctly (according to the design). Figure 3.13 shows the asymmetrical patterns for the striped tank dress in Figure 3.11b.

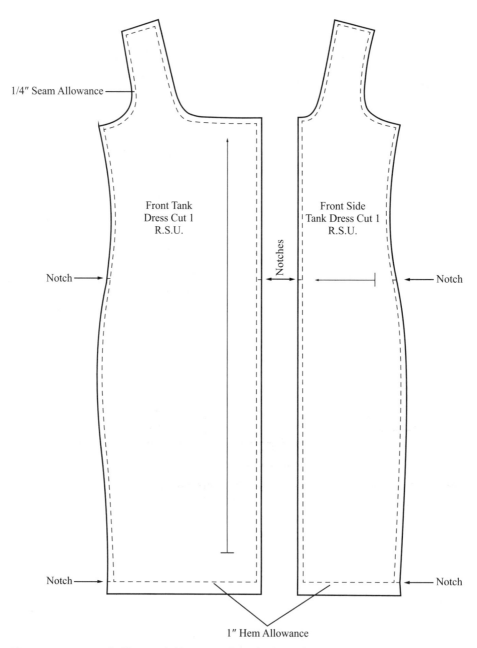

1/4″ Seam Allowance

Front Tank
Dress Cut 1
R.S.U.

Front Side
Tank Dress Cut 1
R.S.U.

Notches

Notch

Notch

Notch

Notch

1″ Hem Allowance

Figure 3.13 Asymmetrical front and side patterns for striped tank dress

Seam and Hem Allowances

After the patterns are drafted and finalized, seam and hem allowances are added beyond the pattern outline, as shown in Figures 3.12 and 3.13. The original outline then becomes the stitching line. The width of seam allowance added will vary. Some knits are fine and smooth, whereas others are thick and textured, and this affects the width required. Always stitch a sample seam in the fabric you plan to use to determine the exact width of seam allowance.

Seam Allowance

Keep in mind the following tips about seam allowances:

- On fabrics with stable neat edges, add ¼" seam allowances.
- If you plan to add a neckline, wrist, or hem band, add ¼" seam allowances.
- Stitch stable knits with ½" open seams.
- Knit fabrics that curl need a wider seam allowance. Use ⅜" to ½".
- Loosely knitted fabrics that unravel may need ½" to 1" seam allowances to make the stitching process more manageable. The final seam can then be serged back to ¼".

Hem Allowance

Keep in mind the following tips about hem allowances:

- Before adding the hem allowance, make sure the pattern has a smooth, even hemline (see Figure 3.6a).
- An average width of hem allowance for tops, skirts, dresses, and pants is 1" (see Figure 3.13).
- Make sure the hem allowance has directional seamlines. If you do not address this issue, after you turn back and stitch the hem allowance, it will look puckered (if too short) or bulky (if excess width has not been removed); see Figure 3.8.

Grainlines

Knits need a nap layout, so you need to draw **directional grainlines** on every pattern piece. A directional grainline indicates that the pattern must be placed on the fabric facing in one direction. If the pattern is to be "cut on fold," this is indicated by drawing the grainline with arrows pointing toward the center front/back of the pattern (see the patterns in Figure 3.12).

Notches

Notches indicate the pieces that need to be matched together in the stitching process. On the **working pattern**, notches are marked as short lines squared to the seamline. Minimal notches are used in knits (see Figure 3.13). After the patterns are finalized, a notcher punches small U-shaped cuts to indicate the notches. When the fabric is cut, the notches are small scissor "snips" cut in the fabric.

Matchpoints

Matchpoints indicate where two points are placed together for stitching purposes (see Figure 6.27a on p. 119 to see the matchpoints for the boatneck). In Figure 6.28 on p. 120, the boatneck is stitched by aligning the matchpoints together. Matchpoints are also used to indicate the placement of pockets. To indicate matchpoints, push the awl through the pattern to make hole marks. If the garment is symmetrical and has two pockets, you don't need to differentiate between the right and left side (see Figure 3.14a). If a design has one pocket, mark the matchpoints on one side of the pattern (see Figure 3.14b). Then document *left side only* (L.S.O.).

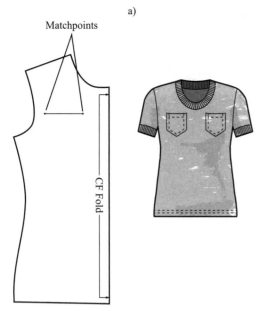

a)

Matchpoints

CF Fold

Figure 3.14a Matchpoints indicate two pockets

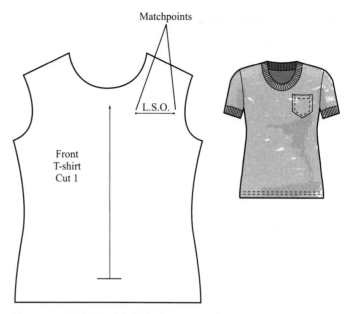

Matchpoints

L.S.O.

Front
T-shirt
Cut 1

Figure 3.14b Matchpoints indicate one pocket

Pattern Labeling

Labeling patterns communicates the name of every pattern piece and the number of fabric piece to be cut (Cut 1, Cut 2, and so on), as shown in Figures 3.12 and 3.13. In production, the pattern pieces also need to be numbered (1, 2, 3, and so on) so that the cutter knows how many pieces need to be cut.

Label the following:

- Indicate the *name* of the pattern piece.
- Indicate the *number* of patterns to cut.
- Indicate whether *interfacing* is to be cut.
- Label the *center front* (C.F.) and *center back* (C.B.).
- Label *right side up* (R.S.U.) on the patterns if the design is asymmetrical. The patterns in Figure 3.13 are labeled accordingly to cut the asymmetrical striped dress in Figure 3.11b.

PATTERN TIP 3.1: THE PATTERNMAKING PROCESS

Well-made patterns produce beautifully fitted garments that sell!

- Use light-colored, lightweight drafting paper that can be folded. This type of paper is translucent, and pattern pieces can be traced from the working pattern.
- Trace the appropriate slopers onto pattern drafting paper.
- Draft the working pattern.
- Plot the silhouette and design lines.
- Mark notches and matchpoints.
- Draw grainlines on the patterns during the pattern drafting process.
- Trace each pattern piece from the working pattern; do not cut the working pattern.
- Manipulate the pattern if necessary,
- To finalize the patterns, add seam and hem allowances and grainlines. Then label the patterns.

Grading System Explained

Pattern grading is the process of changing the pattern dimensions up or down while maintaining the shape, balance, and scale of the original pattern. The **master pattern** is the first pattern to be drafted; it is used to make all the grading moves. The master patterns (in minimal stretch) will be graded into each stretch category to match the stretch categories (moderate stretch, very stretchy, and super stretchy) that knit fabrics are categorized into. The more stretch a knit has, the smaller the pattern needs to be cut. In this text, you use a 2" grade. The 2" difference is *not* for sizing but rather to allow for the change in stretch capacity. The more stretch a knit has, the smaller the pattern needs to be cut.

You can do the grading system here on a table using a ruler, pencil, and grading plan. Once you know the grading techniques, you can grade any pattern by following the same grading technique outlined in this chapter.

The Grading Grid

To grade, you need a **grading grid**, which consists of drawing intersecting (vertical and horizontal) lines (see Figure 3.15). The vertical line is labeled D. A set of measurements identified by a letter/number code are also marked on the horizontal line, as indicated in Figure 3.16. The grading grid allows you to move the pattern in a **positive direction** to *increase* the pattern (for a knit with less stretch) or in a **negative direction** to *decrease* the pattern (for a knit with more stretch).

In each chapter, the text clearly sets out the measurements that are required when grading takes place and provides clear illustrations of each grading move. (Refer to the "Grading Measurement Chart" in Table 3.4.)

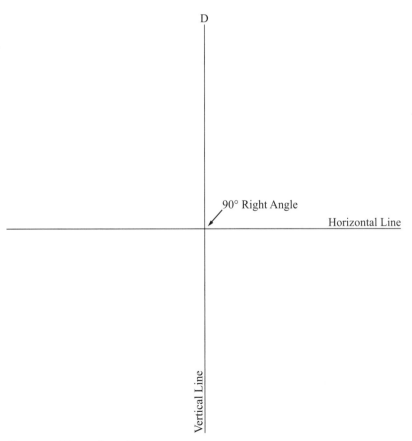

Figure 3.15 The grading grid

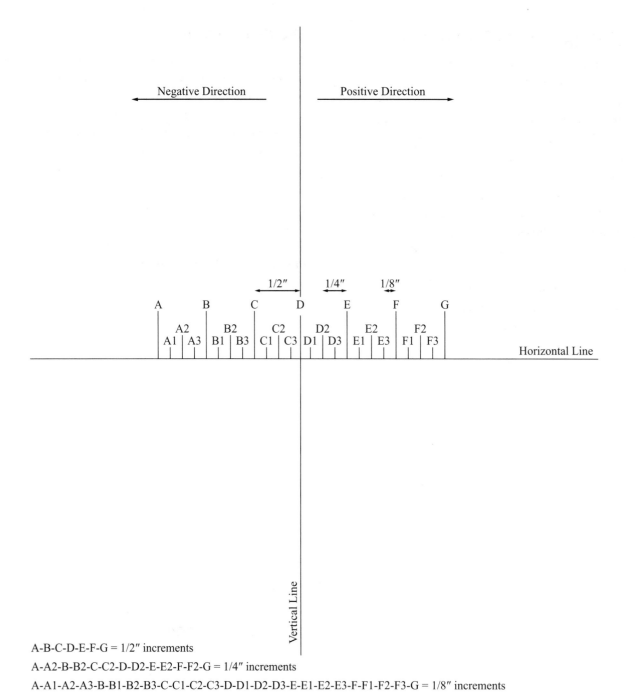

A-B-C-D-E-F-G = 1/2″ increments

A-A2-B-B2-C-C2-D-D2-E-E2-F-F2-G = 1/4″ increments

A-A1-A2-A3-B-B1-B2-B3-C-C1-C2-C3-D-D1-D2-D3-E-E1-E2-E3-F-F1-F2-F3-G = 1/8″ increments

Figure 3.16 Grading measurements marked on the grading grid

TABLE 3.4 Grading measurement chart

	Grading in a Positive Direction			
Total Body Increase	**Quarter Body Increase**	**Shoulder Increase**	**Sleeve Cap Increase**	**Bicep Increase**
2"	½" (E)	¼" (D2)	$^1/_8$" (D1)	¼" (D2)
3"	¾" (E2)	$^3/_8$"(D3)	"	$^3/_8$" (D3)
4"	1" (F)	½" (E)	¼" (D2)	½" (E)
5"	1¼" (F2)	$^5/_8$" (E1)	3/16"	$^5/_8$" (E1)
6"	1½" (G)	¾" (E2)	$^3/_8$" (D3)	¾" (E2)
	Grading in a Negative Direction			
Total Body Decrease	**Quarter Body Decrease**	**Shoulder Decrease**	**Sleeve Cap Decrease**	**Bicep Decrease**
2"	½" (C)	¼" (C2)	1/16"	¼" (C2)
3"	¾" (B2)	$^3/_8$"(C1)	$^1/_8$" (C3)	$^3/_8$" (C3)
4"	1" (B)	½" (C)	¼" (C2)	½" (C)
5"	1¼" (A2)	$^5/_8$" (E1)	$^3/_{16}$"	$^5/_8$" (E1)
6"	1½" (G)	¾" (B2)	$^3/_8$" (C1)	¾" (B2)

The Horizontal Balance Line

A **horizontal balance line** (called HBL) guides and balances the grading. It is drawn on the pattern used for grading and squared to the center front/back. The placement of HBL varies depending on what you are grading.

The grading method is exactly the same wherever you place HBL. In Figure 3.17a, HBL is the hipline of the hip foundation. In Figure 3.17b, HBL is squared at the center front of the bodice (top foundation) and drawn across the underarm. (When grading is done in sizes, the placement of HBL may differ from this example.)

b)

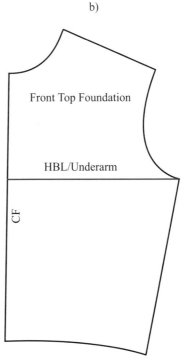

a)

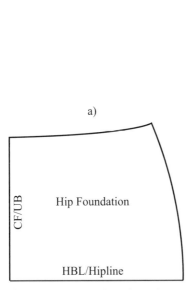

Figure 3.17a Hipline is horizontal balance line

Figure 3.17b Underarm is horizontal balance line

How to Grade

1. Make sure the patterns used for grading are made in oak-tag and cut with smooth edges (not uneven rough edges). Pattern paper is too flimsy to use for grading because you run the risk of drawing inaccurate lines when tracing soft paper.
2. On the master pattern, mark an (X) on HBL at the center front/back.
3. Align sloper (X) on (D) and on the horizontal line, and then trace the sloper. The sloper outline is simply there to show the comparison between the outline and the grading. If the grading is not done correctly, the error is easily noticeable.

4. Use the master pattern to make every grading move at 90° to the vertical line in a positive or negative direction. Place the (X) on the appropriate letter/number code with HBL aligned on the horizontal line. Then trace the appropriate pattern section. (Refer to Figures 3.18 and 3.19.) When all the patterns have been graded and outlined (from largest to smallest) on the grading grid, you have a **graded nest** of patterns. (Refer to Figure 5.36 on p. 90.) (Many commercial patterns are sold like this.)
5. Each pattern is then traced from the graded nest.

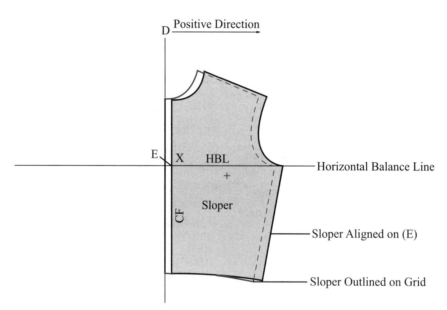

Figure 3.18 Grading in a positive direction to make the pattern larger

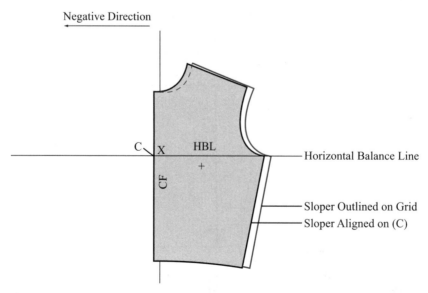

Figure 3.19 Grading in a negative direction to make the pattern smaller

Knit It Together

This checklist summarizes what you have learned about pattern drafting for knit fabrics in this chapter.

✓ Working with the correct patternmaking tools makes the pattern drafting process easier.

✓ Quality patternmaking involves trueing the seams, blending angled lines, and equalizing uneven line lengths to create smooth transitioning lines.

✓ Interfacing, stabilizing tape, and elastic are all stabilizers used in knit clothing.

✓ Patterns *must* have grainlines drawn, notches and matchpoints marked, and labels to communicate how to cut each fabric piece.

Stop: What Do I Do If . . .

. . . I didn't true my patterns? Does it really matter?

Trueing the patterns is essential because it establishes correct angles and seam lengths, smoothes angular lines, and equalizes uneven line lengths.

. . . I use the grading method explained in this chapter to grade my own pattern design into another stretch category?

You can use the same pattern grading techniques to grade any pattern design into another stretch category. Grade your patterns in a positive direction to enlarge the dimensions for a knit with less stretch.

Self-Critique

1. Why is it important to have a working pattern?
2. Explain why the two T-shirts in Figures 3.10a and b look different.
3. Why is it necessary to draw grainlines and label every pattern piece? What type of grainline is required for knits?
4. Elastic is a very important component of producing successful knit garments. Can any elastic be used for any garment?
5. What type of elastic is required for each of the garments in Figure 3.9? (Refer to Tables 3.2 and 3.3.)
6. At what stage of product development does the designer need to decide on the type and width of elastic to use for a particular garment?
7. Do you need to use a specific interfacing for knits? If so, why?
8. To ensure the elastic sits flat after it is stitched in place, what length must it be cut?

_____ cut longer than the seam length.

_____ cut shorter than the seam length

_____ cut the same length as the seam length.

Key Terms		
Asymmetrical Patterns	Horizontal Balance Line	Positive Direction
Braided Elastic	Knitted Elastic	Positive Ease
Directional Grainlines	Master Pattern	Stabilizer
Four-way Stretch Interfacing	Matchpoints	Symmetrical Patterns
Graded Nest	Negative Direction	Two-way Stretch Interfacing
Grading Grid	Negative Ease	Working Pattern
	Pattern Grading	Woven Elastic

4 Laying Out, Cutting, and Stitching Knits

Correct layout and cutting are important skills to learn because cutting knit fabric "on grain" impacts how the garment hangs on the body. Whether the fabric is plain, nubby, or patterned or has a repeat print, stripes, or checks influences how you cut the fabric. Excellent pattern preparation communicates how to lay out each pattern and cut the fabric. The design and the fabric must be in sync.

Layout and Cutting Tools

An L-square ruler and a tape measure are required tools you need for laying out and cutting knits. The remaining tools you need are as follows (see also Figure 4.1):

1. *Fabric shears*—Use 8" to 10" *sharp* shears.
2. *Rotary cutter*—Use a rotary cutter with a 1¾" (or 45 mm) blade to cut straight lines, long strips, and geometric shapes. Smaller blades (1", or 25 mm) cut smoothly around tight curves.
3. *Pattern weights*—Use these small, heavy objects to hold patterns on the fabric. You can purchase weights specifically for this purpose or use your own pattern weights from around your home (e.g., a door stop or can of soup).
4. *Pins*—Use pins to fasten *soft paper* patterns to the fabric. They are also used to connect seams together or to secure a pocket to a T-shirt prior to stitching and used for fitting purposes.
   - Use *ballpoint* or *super fine pins* because they will not snag knits.
   - Use *flat flower pins* to pin loosely knitted fabrics because the 2" length and flower head will not slip through open sections of the knit.

5. *Fabric markers*—Use these markers to outline oak-tag patterns onto the fabric and to transfer *internal* markings such as a pocket or button placement onto the fabric. Use a color that is visible on the fabric.
   - *Chaco markers* trace *fine* lines that brush away easily.
   - *Tailor's chalk* does not leave permanent marks and can be brushed off easily. However, the marking lines are not as fine.
   - *Water and air-erasable fabric marking pens* have a fine-point tip that draws fine lines that vanish in 24 to 72 hours.

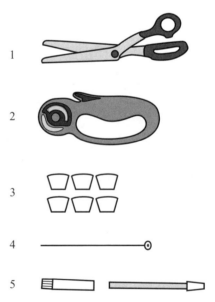

Figure 4.1 Layout and cutting tools

Fabric Preparation

Before layout, marking, and cutting, examine the fabric carefully (see Figures 4.2a and b). Be sure to do the following:

- *Determine whether your knit has a right and wrong side.* Jersey and tricot have distinct right and wrong sides. Some knits look the same on both sides. Choose which side will be the "correct" side and chalk-mark an X on the *wrong* side of the cut fabric pieces.
- *Determine if there are any snags or other flaws in the fabric.* Mark any flaws with a small piece of masking tape so you can cut around them.
- *Determine if the knit runs.* Some knits run from the end last knitted. Gently stretch the fabric in both directions to see whether the knit runs like nylon hose runs. If the knit runs, then place the hemline of the pattern toward that end.[1]
- *Determine if your knit has a striped, check, motif, or repeat pattern that must be matched.* For fabrics with these characteristics, planning the layout takes more time because the stripe/print must be matched on the seam joins.

---

1 Keith Richardson, *Designing and Patternmaking for Stretch Fabrics* (New York: Fairchild Books, 2008), 19.

Preshrinking Knits

All knits shrink to some degree (especially cotton knits), so it is advisable to preshrink the fabric yardage prior to cutting the fabric.

1. Do not use detergent.
2. Using cold water, begin washing the fabric on the rinse cycle.
3. Tumble dry or air-dry flat.

To preshrink "dry clean only" knits, do the following:

1. Hold an iron above the fabric surface and give it a shot of steam over the entire yardage.
2. Do not move the fabric until dry.

Pressing Knits

Knits require little pressing during a garment's construction; however, sometimes pressing is required.

- Press from the *wrong side* of the fabric, or press from the correct side using a press cloth to protect the fabric because the iron can leave shine marks.
- Use a press-lift-press motion when pressing to avoid stretching the fabric out of shape.
- If any seams have stretched in the stitching process, steam-pressing will help to bring the seams back into shape.

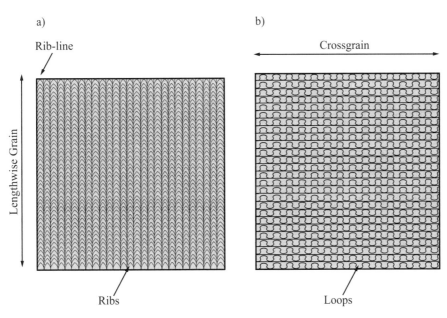

a) Rib-line Lengthwise Grain Ribs

b) Crossgrain Loops

Figures 4.2 Jersey knit. **a)** Correct side, **b)** wrong side

Cutting the Fabric on Grain

Figure 4.3

Cut the fabric yardage on grain before the pattern pieces are placed on the fabric. The fabric piece must be cut on grain and squared at a 90° angle on each corner of the fabric.

To cut the fabric on grain, follow these steps:

1. Lay the fabric flat on the table.
2. Cut the length of the fabric (on both sides) along a predominant **rib-line**. A rib-line is a column of little "v" stitches. Remember to cut off the selvages. (Draw a line with a ruler or cut using your eye judgment.) For knits that do not have a rib-line to follow (such as a Raschel knit, mesh, or stretch lace), cut off the selvage with sharp shears to straighten the edge.
3. To cut on the crossgrain, turn the fabric to the *wrong* side and cut across the fabric following a row of *loops*. Or draw a chalkline across the crosswise grain with an L-square ruler.

4. After completing the preceding steps, if the fabric is *not* squared at a 90° angle, stretch the fabric diagonally across the bias to bring it into alignment.

Knits Need a Nap Layout

Napped fabrics have an obvious shading difference and reflect the light differently. French terry, velour, stretch velvet, and fleece all have a raised pile and are napped fabrics. When stroked in one direction, the surface feels smooth; when stroked in the opposite direction, the surface feels rough. Knits show a slight shade difference when looking up and down the length of fabric. For this reason, knits require a nap pattern layout to keep the color uniform (see Figure 1.7 on p. 10). In a **nap layout**, the top of every pattern piece is placed toward the same end of the fabric and in the same direction. The directional grainlines on the patterns indicate a nap layout.

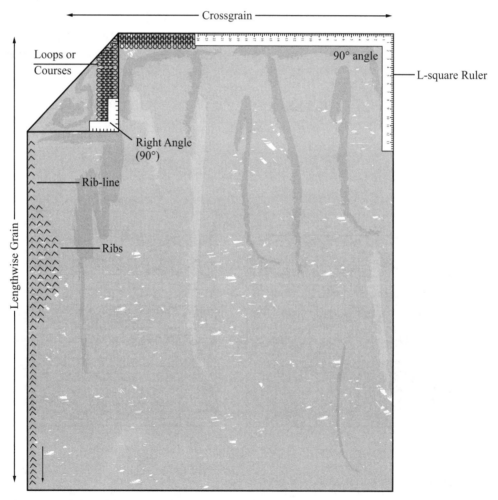

Figure 4.3 Fabric yardage cut on grain

PATTERN TIP 4.1: ZERO-WASTE PATTERN CUTTING TECHNIQUE

People working in the fashion industry are becoming more aware of how our resources are wasted when 15% of fabric is laying in waste on the factory floor after a garment is manufactured. This is not good for the environment, nor is it economical. One way to consciously think about fabric waste is to use the "zero-waste design technique."[2] It is an integrated design process that involves drafting zero-waste patterns to fit the entire fabric space to minimize wastage. It means keeping an open mind about the final design because the pattern shapes may change during the process. When you're working with knits, the zero-waste pattern-cutting technique has an extra challenge. The patterns need to be placed on the fabric in one direction because of the shading difference. This issue was pointed out in the "Knits Need a Nap Layout" section. (Refer to the "Stop: What Do I Do If . . ." section on page 65 to find out if you can lay out the patterns in both directions.)

Placing the Patterns on Grain

The purpose of this section is to demonstrate how to cut single lengthwise folded fabric; double lengthwise fold; single spread of fabric; and circular/tubular knits and patterned, check, striped, and askew fabrics. Each pattern piece must be placed on the fabric on grain. Not placing the patterns on grain can cause fitting problems. The garment will also look out of shape. The zero-waste design technique is not used in this section. Many of the fabric layouts are for cutting muslin fabric for fitting the slopers. You cannot use the zero-waste cutting technique to do this. Nevertheless, do be mindful of how you lay out the patterns on the fabric and decide how you can use the fabric waste.

Here are some tips about placing patterns:

- Press the fabric if it is wrinkled or creased.
- Generally, place patterns on the *wrong side* of the fabric. However, to see the rib-line (or to match a striped or checked fabric), lay out the pattern pieces on the correct side.

- Place the patterns on the fabric with the direction of stretch going around the body.
- Place the pattern grainline parallel to the straightened fabric edge or the folded edge.
- Arrange the patterns on folded fabric or a single spread of fabric if necessary.

Single Lengthwise Folded Fabric

Figures 4.4 and 4.5

In a single lengthwise fold, one garment piece can be placed on or near the fold, and the other pattern piece is placed next to it. This layout is perfect for cutting a pair of pants or a cardigan.

1. Fold the fabric on a rib-line. Pin along the foldline to keep the ribs on the fold. When both lengthwise edges have been straightened (as advised in the previous section) and placed together, the lengthwise fold will automatically be on grain. (If you find it difficult to find the rib-line to fold the fabric, lay out the patterns on a single layer of fabric.)
2. Lay the patterns on the fabric with the grainlines placed in the fabric's lengthwise direction. Use a tape measure to make sure that the grainlines are parallel to the foldline.

Double Lengthwise Folded Fabric

Figure 4.6

The double lengthwise fold is the perfect layout when both the front and back patterns need to be placed on the fold of the fabric.

1. Fold each lengthwise edge toward the middle of the fabric.
2. Measure both ends of the fabric so they are an equal distance from the foldline to the fabric edge.
3. Place the center front and back patterns on the fabric foldlines and pin in place.

---

2   "The EcoChic Design Award Zero-Waste Design Technique," accessed September 3, 2015, http://www.ecochicdesignaward.com/wp-content /blogs.dir/3/files/2013/07/LEARN_Zero-waste_ENG.pdf.

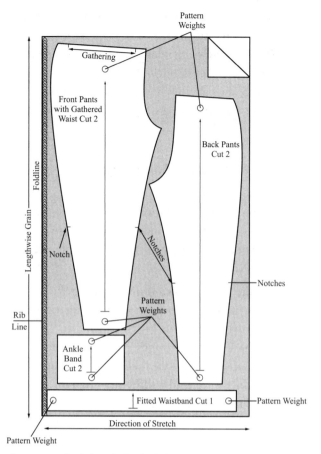

Figure 4.4 Single lengthwise folded fabric: pattern layout for pant patterns drafted in Figures 10.45a–c on pp. 370–371

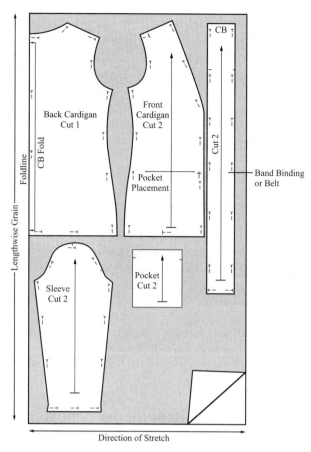

Figure 4.5 Single lengthwise folded fabric: pattern layout for V-neck cardigan patterns drafted in Figures 8.16a–b on pp. 224–225

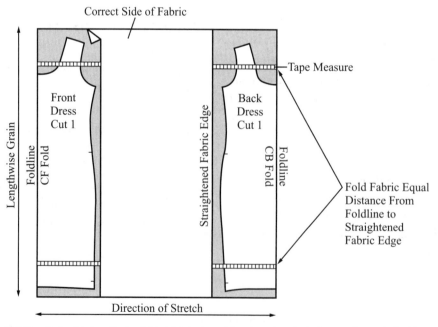

Figure 4.6 Double lengthwise folded fabric: layout for sleeveless tank dress patterns drafted in Figures 7.7a and b on p. 171

Single Spread of Fabric

Figure 4.7

When the style is asymmetrical, arrange the patterns on a single layer of fabric. Also use this layout for cutting striped or checked fabric or fabric with a repeat print that must be matched on the seams.

1. Place the patterns right side up (R.S.U.) on the correct side of the fabric.
2. Align pattern grainlines parallel to the straightened fabric edge.
3. For striped fabric, match the stripes on the side seams in the pattern layout as shown.

Circular or Tube Knits

Circular or tube knits have two foldlines with permanent creases. Never place a pattern piece on a creaseline because the creaseline is usually permanent.

1. Cut along one creaseline and open the fabric into a single layer.
2. Prewash the fabric and press the creaseline flat.
3. Avoid placing any pattern pieces on the creaseline because it may show on the garment.

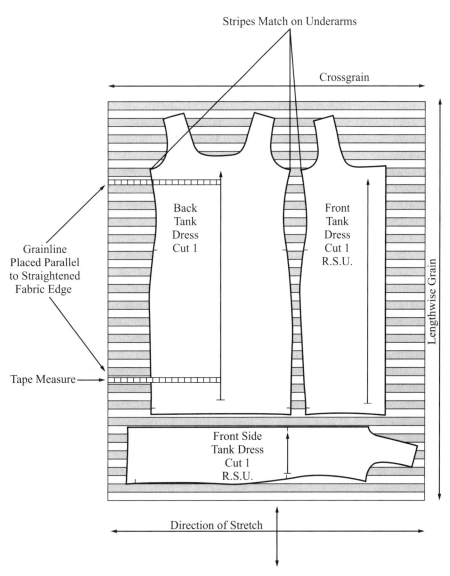

Figure 4.7 Single spread of fabric: pattern layout for asymmetrical striped tank dress shown in Figure 3.11b on p. 30

Using Various Layouts: Repeat Pattern, Check, and Striped Fabrics

For a repeat pattern and striped or check fabrics, you must place the pattern pieces on the fabric so they correspond perfectly and match up on the seamlines. This way, you ensure that the fabric design is uninterrupted around the garment.

Repeat Pattern

Figure 4.8
When you use fabric with a repeat pattern, extra yardage is required. Measure the length of the repeat from the top of the motif to the same spot in the motif below. Add this amount to each yard of fabric required. Lay out the patterns on a single spread.

1. Place the center front pattern on the center of a motif.
2. **Drop-match** the front pattern piece if the repeat pattern cannot be matched when the pattern pieces are placed side by side. To drop-match, place the front pattern piece lower than the back pattern for the purposes of matching the fabric print.

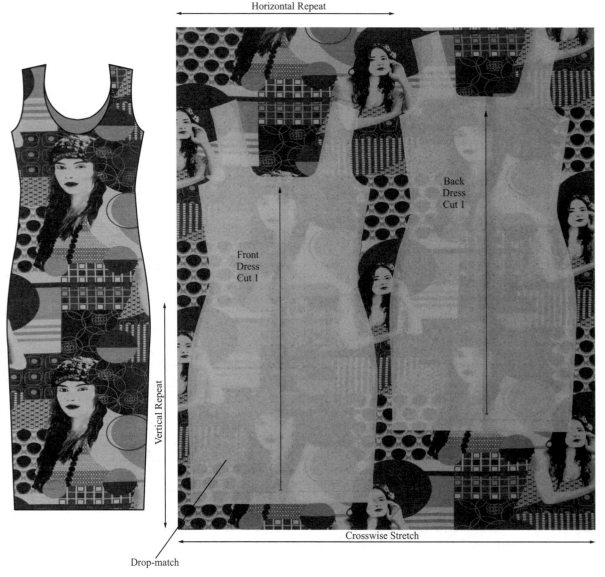

Figure 4.8 Pattern layout for a repeat fabric pattern

Check Fabric

Figure 4.9

1. Carefully position the patterns on a single layer of fabric so the *seamlines* (on front and back underarm/side seams) perfectly line up *horizontally*.

Also line up the checks *vertically* on the shoulder seam.

2. Place the *hemline* on the edge of a prominent check (not in the middle of a check).

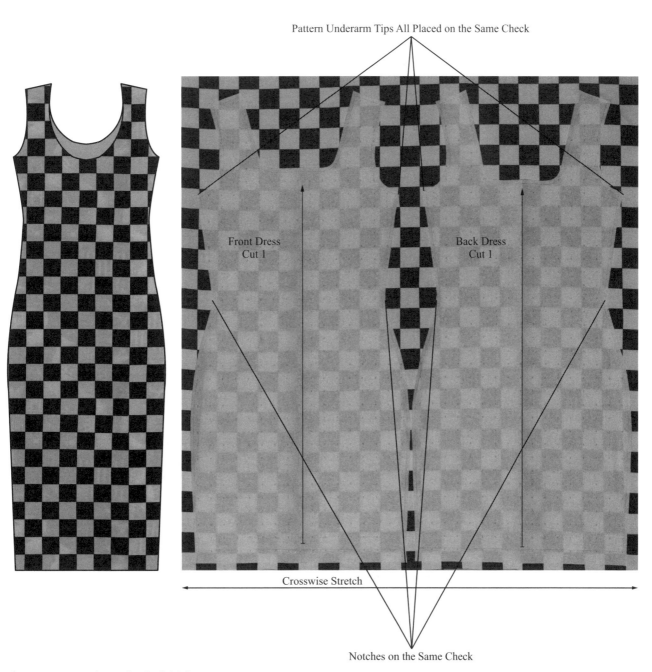

Pattern Underarm Tips All Placed on the Same Check

Front Dress
Cut 1

Back Dress
Cut 1

Crosswise Stretch

Notches on the Same Check

Figure 4.9 Pattern layout for check fabric

Striped Fabric

For striped fabric, the fabric layout can be for a single *spread* or *folded* fabric. In Figure 4.7, the dress patterns for the striped asymmetrical dress are placed on a single spread of fabric. For just under a yard of fabric, you can cut the short-sleeve striped T-shirt from double lengthwise folded fabric, as shown in Figure 4.10.

1. Place the garment patterns on the center front and back of the folded fabric with the underarm tips on the same stripe so that they match together along the side seams.

2. Place the tip of the sleeve underarm patterns on the same stripe as the front/back underarms, as shown in Figure 4.10. (In this figure, the sleeves are cut as single pieces because it is more economical in this layout.)

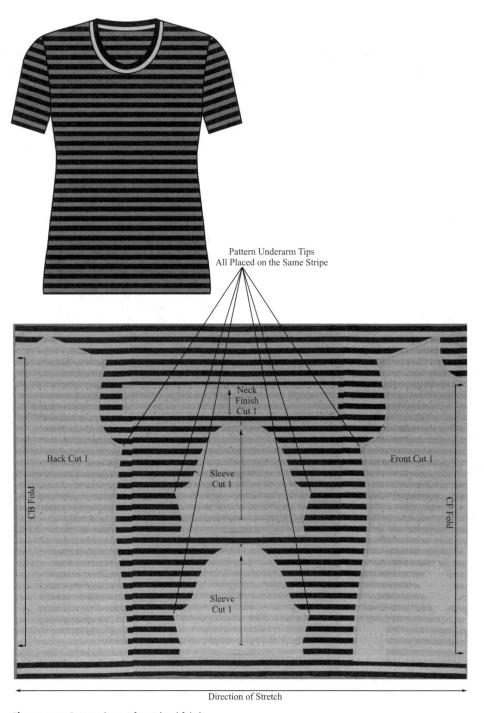

Figure 4.10 Pattern layout for striped fabric

Askew Knit

Figure 4.11

Knit yardage that is distorted and "off grain" is an askew knit.

1. *Do not* follow the selvage or lengthwise fabric edge to determine the lengthwise grain.
2. Cut the fabric edges on grain or fold the fabric along a rib-line, as shown.
3. Lay out and cut the fabric pieces.

Marking and Cutting Knits

1. Secure the patterns on the fabric with pattern weights (see Figure 4.4).
2. Carefully pin the patterns to the fabric (see Figure 4.5).
3. Do not pin oak-tag patterns to the fabric; instead, trace around them with a fabric marker in a noticeable color. When you're finished, carefully lift the patterns off the fabric.
4. Transfer pattern markings to loosely knitted sweater knits or open work knits with small pieces of masking tape, thread mark, or a safety pin.
5. Transfer matchpoints by placing a pin through the pattern holes. Do not push an awl into knits to mark matchpoints because a small hole grows into a *large* hole. Mark matchpoints with a *small* (x) on one side or both sides of the fabric for pockets (see Figure 4.12).
6. Cut *inside* the marking line.
7. Using sharp shears or a rotary cutter to cut the fabric pieces, cut long direct strokes on straight edges and shorter strokes around curved edges. Do not cut off any pattern paper!
8. *Never* move the fabric when cutting.
9. Snip short ⅛" notches (and no longer).

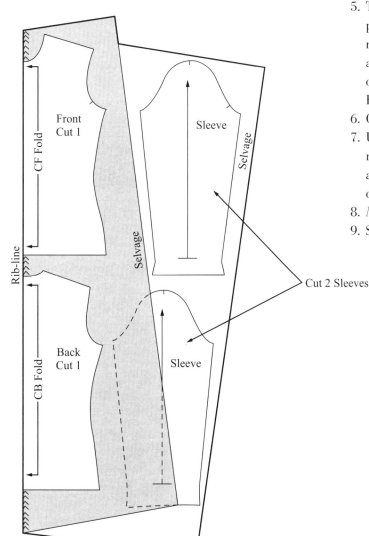

Figure 4.11 Pattern layout for askew fabric

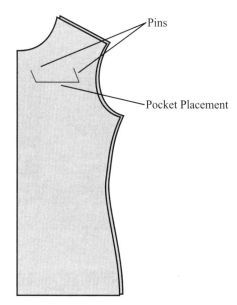

Figure 4.12 Marking matchpoints for pockets

Laying Out Patterns for Garments

The following sections illustrate how to lay out the patterns for various garments. Some pattern layouts have already been discussed, so the pattern layouts for these garments (tops, pants, and cardigans) are referenced. The garment patterns are either laid out on *single spread of fabric, lengthwise folded fabric,* or on *double lengthwise folded* fabric.

Top

To lay out and cut a top from double lengthwise folded fabric, see Figure 4.10. You can use this layout for striped or plain fabrics. A top can also be cut from a single spread of fabric if the pattern pieces need to be matched in the layout.

Dress

To lay out and cut a dress from double folded fabric, refer to Figure 4.6. To lay out and cut a dress from a single spread of fabric see Figures 4.7, 4.8, and 4.9.

Cardigan

To lay out and cut a cardigan, refer to the pattern layout in Figure 4.5.

Skirt

In Figure 4.13, the front/back patterns are placed on the fold of the fabric. A skirt can also be cut from a single spread of fabric.

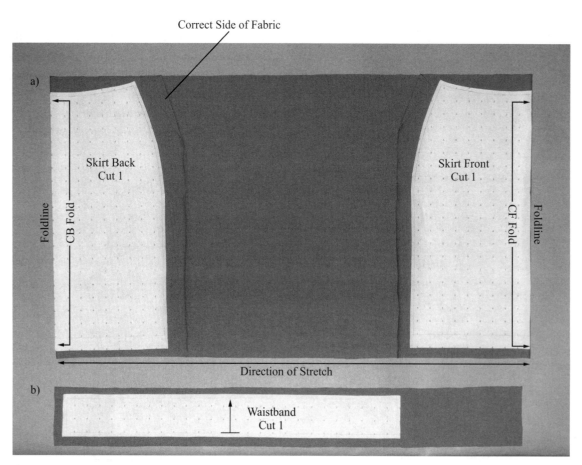

Figure 4.13 Pattern layout for a skirt

Pants

For pants, refer to Figure 4.4 and interlock the patterns as shown if the fabric is not wide enough to place the front and back patterns side by side. Pant patterns can also be cut from a single spread of fabric.

Leggings/Unitard

Cutting leggings is straightforward because you need only a one-piece pattern, as shown in Figure 4.14.

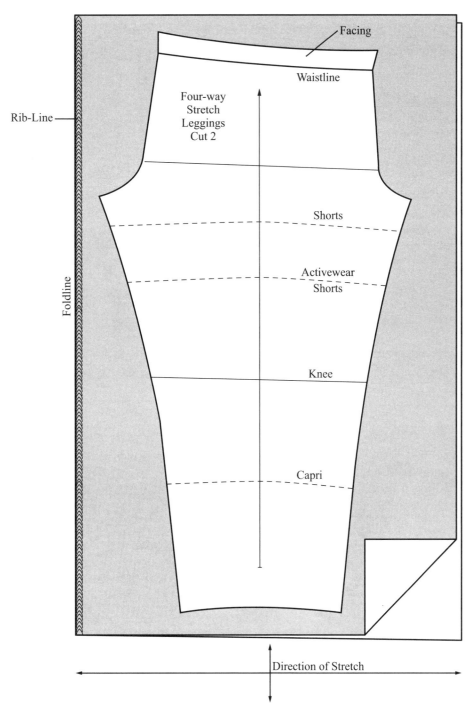

Figure 4.14 Pattern layout for leggings or unitard

Camisole

In Figure 4.15, the camisole patterns are placed on double lengthwise folded fabric. The remaining fabric has enough scope for placing the strap and neckline binding patterns on the crosswise, lengthwise, or bias grain.

Leg-line Panty and Bikini Bottom

To lay out leg-line panty or bikini bottom patterns, follow the layout in Figure 4.16.

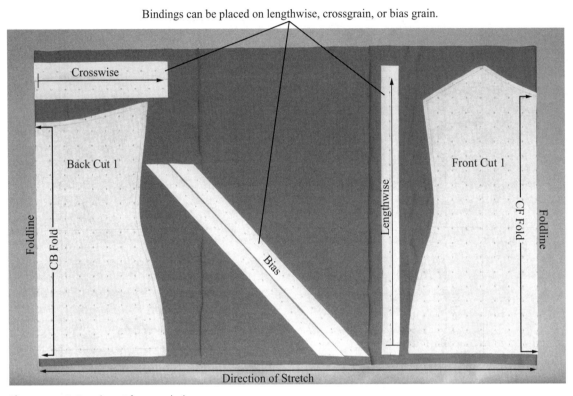

Figure 4.15 Pattern layout for a camisole

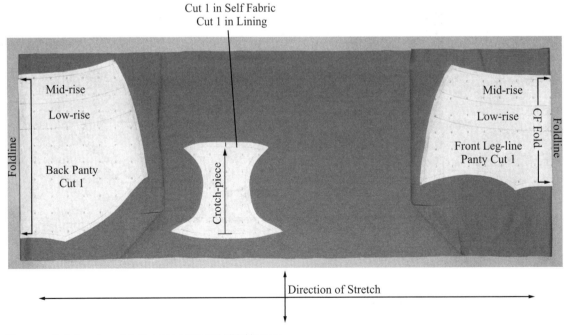

Figure 4.16 Pattern layout for leg-line panty and bikini bottom

Boy-cut Panty and Swim Shorts

To lay out panty or swim short patterns, follow the layout in Figure 4.17. For swim shorts, cut the crotch-piece from swimwear fabric or an alternative lightweight quick-dry fabric. Cut the panty crotch-piece from a breathable knit.

Bodysuit/Leotard

The bodysuit/leotard patterns are placed on double lengthwise folded fabric in Figure 4.18. You can use the same layout when cutting the swimsuit slopers in muslin to test the fit.

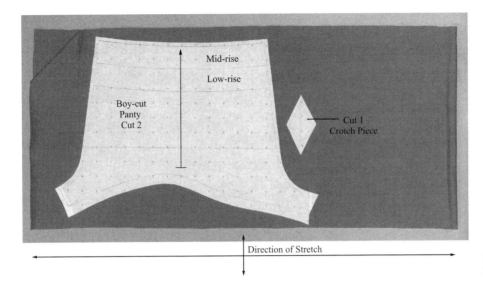

Figure 4.17 Pattern layout for boy-cut panty and swim short

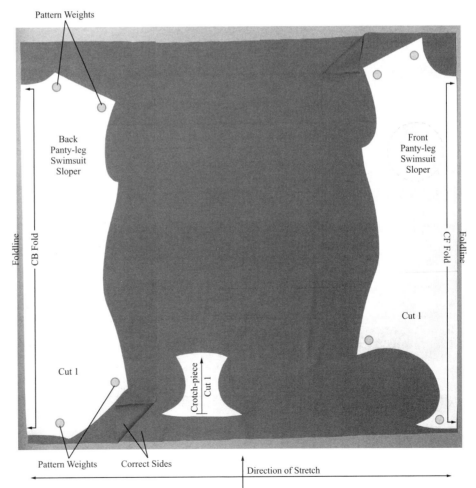

Figure 4.18 Pattern layout for swimwear slopers and bodysuit/leotard

One-piece Tank Swimsuit

In a one-piece tank swimsuit layout, only the front swimsuit pattern is placed on the fold because the back swimsuit has a shaped seam (see Figure 4.19).

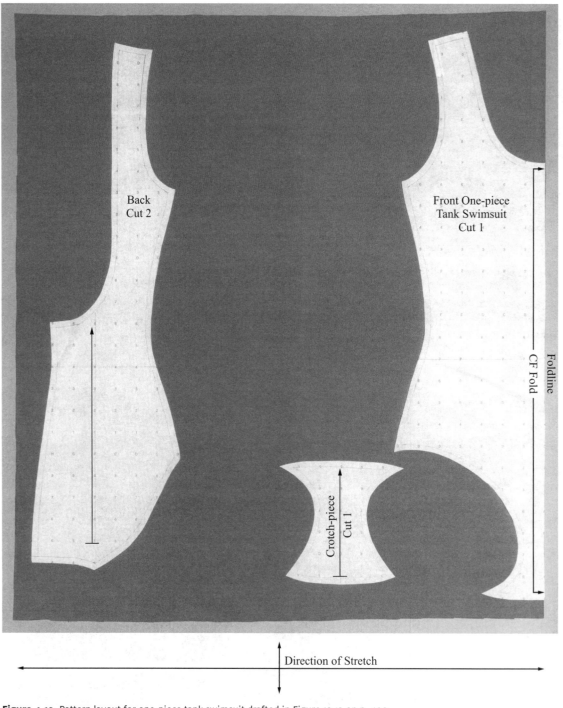

Figure 4.19 Pattern layout for one-piece tank swimsuit drafted in Figure 12.13 on p. 420

Bikini Top

To lay out and cut a bikini top, follow Figure 4.20. Notice that the strap and binding patterns are placed on the lengthwise grain for maximum stretch.

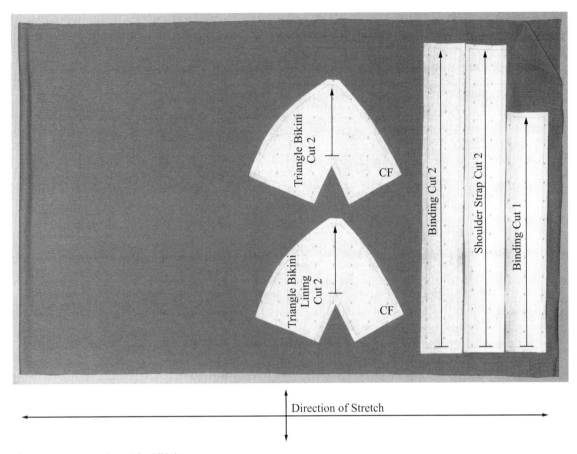

Figure 4.20 Pattern layout for bikini top

Stitching Knits

Seams in stretch knit fabrics must have built-in stretch. In Chapter 1, Donna Karan's advice was to listen to the fabric talk.[3] The fabric directs all the decisions that must be made about a design, including the interfacing machine needles, thread, and stitches you choose when constructing the garment (see Table 4.1). If the stitches do not stretch sufficiently, they will break when the garment is stretched onto the body.

3   Hal Rubenstein, "Designer Profile: Donna Karan," *InStyle*, November 2013, 149.

TABLE 4.1 Focus on the fabric

Whatever garment you are stitching, the machine needles, interfacing, thread, and stitches must suit the fabric.

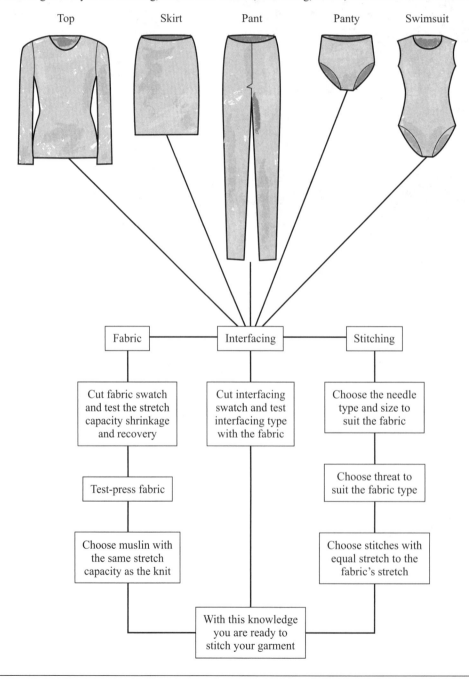

Sewing Machines, Needles, and Threads

Knits can be stitched on a mechanical (home) sewing machine if it has a zigzag stitch. Knits do not fray, so you don't need to serge the seams. However, serging is a quick and easy way to stitch knits, and the seams have better stretchability.

To stitch knits, you need these basic stitching tools: small scissors, thread clippers, a seam ripper, and tweezers for drawing threads through the loopers and needles of the serger.

An explanation of the sewing machines, thread, and sewing machine needles you need for stitching knits follows.

A **mechanical sewing machine** stitches straight stitches, zigzag stitches, and other decorative stitches (depending on the type of machine). It also stitches buttonholes. Some models have a variety of stretch stitches,

such as a stretch overlock stitch. The mechanical sewing machine in Figure 4.21 stitches stretchable seams and hems when the correct stitches and settings are used.

A **serger** (also known as an overlock machine; see Figure 4.22) is made up of loopers, tension dials (or discs), needles (left and right), a knife blade, feed dog presser foot, and flywheel (hand wheel). Sergers generally use two to four threads, which sit on spool pins. (You can use up to eight cones of thread for specialty stitches.) The looper threads interlock with the needle threads to form serging stitches.

As a seam is serged, the serger stitches the seam, overcasts the edge of the fabric, and trims any excess fabric from the seam. In addition, a serger can stitch a rolled hem, coverstitch, or flatlock stitch.

Differential feed is a standard feature on most sergers. It controls the movement of the front and back feed

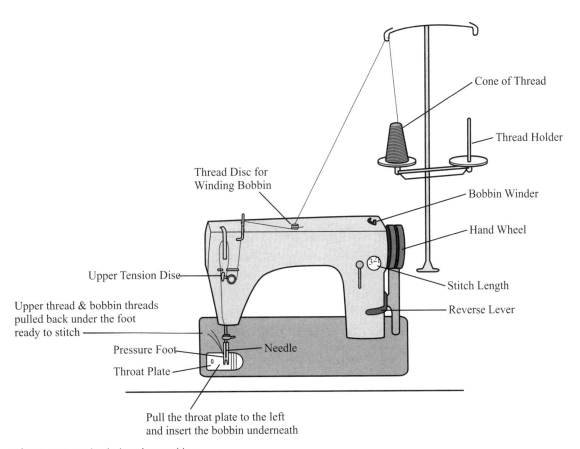

Figure 4.21 Mechanical sewing machine

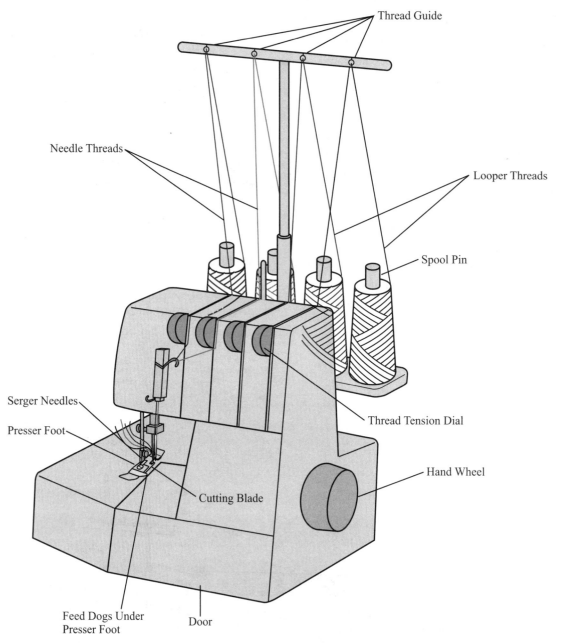

Thread Guide

Needle Threads

Looper Threads

Spool Pin

Serger Needles

Presser Foot

Thread Tension Dial

Hand Wheel

Cutting Blade

Feed Dogs Under
Presser Foot

Door

Figure 4.22 Serger

dogs, which work together to move the fabric through the serger without stretching or puckering the fabric. Consult your serger manual for detailed threading.

These machines use the following types of thread:

- *Sewing machine thread*—You can use all-purpose polyester thread to add strength and elasticity to the seams.
- *Serger thread*—Tex-27 is a perfect thread weight for serging light- to medium-weight knits. (Larger Tex numbers are heavier threads.) Cones are more

efficient and economical to use. Small reels of polyester thread can also be used.

You will use the following types of needles:

- *Sewing machine needles*—**Ballpoint needles** and **stretch needles** are made specifically for stitching knits. They have slightly rounded needle tips that slide between the loops and will not split them apart. Ballpoint and stretch needles can be **single**

needles or **twin needles**, as shown in Figure 4.23. Use a ballpoint needle to stitch heavier, looser knits; use a stretch needle to stitch highly elastic knits with spandex.

- A *single needle* has one shaft that stitches one row.
- *Twin needles* are two needles mounted on a single crossbar that simultaneously stitch two parallel rows. There are two numeric numbers to identify twin needles (e.g., 4.0/80). The first number indicates the space (in millimeters), and the second number is the needle size. Twin needles can be stretch or ballpoint.

- *Serger needles*—Consult your serger manual for the needle system that is required for your serger.
- *Hand sewing needles*—For hand sewing, you can use ballpoint needles because the slightly rounded point pushes the loops apart, and the needle will not snag the fabric. Use size 5–9 needles: the finer the fabric, the smaller the needle; the weightier the fabric, the larger the needle.

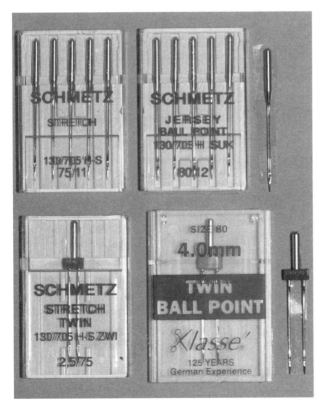

Figure 4.23 Sewing machine needles

IMPORTANT 4.1: SERGER THREAD

Use good-quality 100 percent polyester serger thread because it is strong, has a soft finish, and maintains the correct tension under the rigor of serging at high speed. Poor-quality thread can wreak havoc on the serger's tension system and will produce poor-quality stitching.

Stretchable Stitches

Knits *must* be stitched with **stretchable stitches**. Stretchable stitches are stitched with a *back-and-forth* motion, which gives them built-in stretch. However, all stretchable stitches do not stretch to the same amount. You must choose stitches that will allow seams and hems to stretch as much as the knit stretches.

IMPORTANT 4.2: STITCHING KNITS WITH A STRAIGHT STITCH

If a seam in knit fabric is stitched with a straight stitch, the stitches will "break" (see Figure 4.24). In some instances, straight stitches *are* the appropriate stitches to use. Here are three examples: staystitches, topstitches to a pocket on a garment, and topstitches to edges and hems of garments that do *not* need to stretch when they are worn. Table 4.2 describes a selection of stretchable stitches that you can stitch using a home sewing machine and a serger.

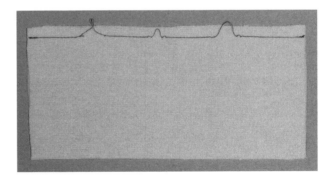

Figure 4.24 Straight stitches break when stretched

TABLE 4.2 Stretchable stitches chart

	Mechanical Sewing Machine	
Name of Stitch	Stitches	Where to Use
Zigzag Stitch	Narrow ‹‹‹‹‹‹‹‹‹‹‹‹‹‹‹‹‹‹‹‹ Wide WWWWWWWWWW	*Do not* use for seam stitching *Use for:* Overcasting seam and hem edges Edgestitch (use narrow only) Machine Basting (wide) Topstitching Applying elastic (wide only)
Crooked Straight Stitch The smallest of all zig zag stitches. Use .5 width and 2.5 stitch length	～～～～～～～～～～	*Do not* use on very stretchy and super stretchy knits *Use for:* Seam stitching on minimal to medium stretch knits only Stitching darts
3-stitch Zigzag	ᴧᴧᴧᴧᴧᴧᴧᴧᴧᴧᴧᴧᴧ	*Use for:* Applying clear elastic
Twin Needle Stitching Straight Stitches (Can also use zigzag stitches)	Correct Side – – – – – – – – – – – – – – – – – – – – – – – – Wrong Side WWWWWWWWWW	*Use for topstitching* Seams in stable knits Hems Neckline, armholes and other edges Use (4.0) spacing for heavyweight knits Use 2.0/2.5 spacing for lightweight knits
	Serger Stitches	
4-thread Serging (uses left and right needles and upper and lower loopers)	𝍱𝍱𝍱𝍱𝍱𝍱𝍱	*Use for:* Stitching seams in stretchy activewear knits
3-thread Serging	Narrow 𝍱𝍱𝍱𝍱𝍱𝍱𝍱 Wide 𝍱𝍱𝍱𝍱𝍱𝍱𝍱	Produce good-quality stretchable seams *Use for:* Stitching seams in lightweight or tissue-weight knits, stretch lace or sheer mesh Stitching seams in medium to heavyweight knits
Flatlock (two-sided stitch)	Ladder Stitch |||||||||||||||||| Loopers VVVVVVVVVV	Produces bulk-free *flat* visible seams that prevent chafing *Use for:* Seams of athletic garments and activewear that require excellent stretchability
2-thread Chain Stitch	Correct side – – – – – – – – – – Wrong side ∞∞∞∞∞∞∞∞∞	Produces a regular straight stitch on the correct side and chain-like stitch on the wrong side (disengage the knife) *Use for:* Understitching facings Topstitching elastic Single row of hem or edge stitching on minimal stretch knits
Coverstitch (two-sided stitch) (The cutting blade must be disengaged)	– – – – – – – – – – – – – – – – – – – – – – – – – – – – – – XXXXXXXXXX	Produces super-stretchy stitches *Use for:* Topstitching seams Attaching trims Hem stitching
Rolled Edge	𝍱𝍱𝍱𝍱𝍱𝍱𝍱𝍱𝍱	*Use for:* Stitching hem, neckline, wrist and other edge finishes on medium to lightweight knit

(continued

TABLE 4.2 Stretchable stitches chart (*Continued*)

Lettuce Edge (Same stitch as a rolled edge. Stretch from behind and in front to curl the edges)		*Use for:* Curly hem edges on lightweight knits such as mesh and lace
Hand stitches		
Catchstitch Invisible hand stitches		*Use for:* Excellent hem stitch to use on a classy knit garments

Stretchable Seams

A **stretchable seam** is one that stretches as much as the knit stretches. Before stitching your garment, stitch a sample seam. After stitching, stretch the seam. The seam must stretch to the extent the knit stretches. If the stitches break, then choose another type of stitch from Table 4.2 and repeat the process. Serged seams have the most stretch. For this reason, serging is the preferred method for stitching four-way stretch knits.

STITCHING TIP 4.1: MECHANICAL SEWING MACHINE

Keep in mind the following tips about stitching seams:
- Use a Teflon foot because it glides over the fabric surface as you stitch.
- Reduce the stitch length to add more built-in stretch.
- To stitch fine knits, place 2" wide strips of tissue wrapping paper under the seam or hem. Carefully tear away the paper after stitching.
- Hold the threads taut as you begin stitching; do not stretch the seam as you stitch. Let the fabric feed naturally into the machine.
- If the fabric begins to pucker, leave the needle down in your work; raise the presser foot to let the fabric relax. Then proceed to stitch again.
- Use a seam ripper or an awl to help ease the fabric under the presser foot as you stitch.

STITCHING TIP 4.2: SERGER

Keep in mind the following tips about serging seams:
A serger finishes fabric edges and stitches seams. Serged seams are *always* stretchable. For this reason, serging is the preferred method for stitching four-way stretch knits. Consult your serger manual for detailed threading.
- Use woolly nylon thread in the serger upper and lower loopers for better stretch.
- To avoid overstretched wavy seams/edges or puckered seams, adjust up the differential feed function so that the fabric is fed more quickly under the needles.
- Never cut the thread at the end of the fabric because the seam will unravel. Once the seam is serged, continue serging a few more inches of thread chain before clipping the thread.
- When serging, slowly guide the fabric with your hands.

Open Seam

Stitch weightier knits with minimal stretch (such as double knit) using open ½" seams (see Figure 4.25). Finish the seam edges first and then stitch, open, and press the seam.

Closed Seam

Most knits are stitched with ¼" closed seams (see Figure 4.26). When a closed seam is stitched, the two fabric pieces are stitched and finished together. The seam allowance is then turned to one side (with both ends of the seam facing the same direction). You can use a variety of stretchable seams to stitch knits. Refer to Figures 4.27, 4.28, and 4.29 to see each kind.

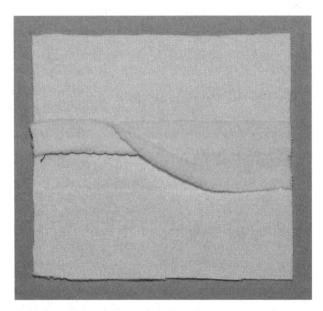

Figure 4.25 A ½" open seam

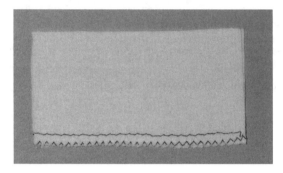

Figure 4.27 Crooked straight stitch with narrow zigzag edge finish

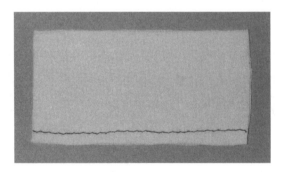

Figure 4.26 A ¼" unfinished seam

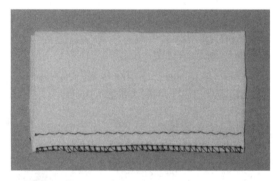

Figure 4.28 Crooked straight stitch with narrow serged edge finish

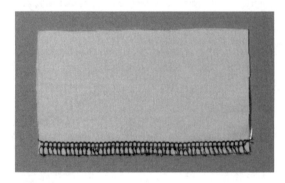

Figure 4.29 Four-thread serged seam

Elasticized Seams

Seams can be stabilized with elastic to prevent them from stretching out. Elastic can also help garment edges (and seams) cling to the body in places that would otherwise sag or gape. Elastic also can be used to gather a seam. In each of the stitching techniques described in Stitching Tip 4.3, you can stitch the elastic to the seam allowance using a home sewing machine or a serger.

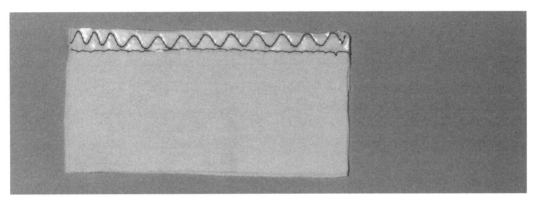

Figure 4.30 A ¼" clear elastic stitched to the seam allowance of a shoulder seam (*not stretched*) to prevent seams from stretching out

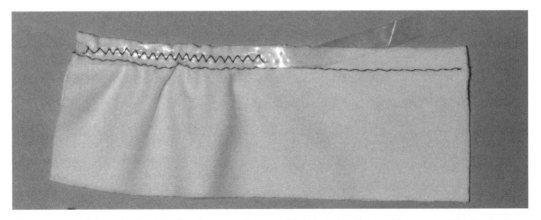

Figure 4.31 A ¼" clear elastic stitched to the seam allowance (*slightly stretched*) to enable a garment to cling to the body and to prevent gaping

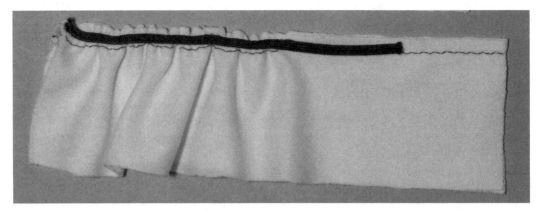

Figure 4.32 A ⅛" braided elastic stitched to the seam allowance (*fully stretched*) to create gathering

Stretchable Hems

A hem edge can be serged; machine-stitched using zig-zag stitches, twin needles, or a coverstitch; or serged with a lettuce edge or rolled edge. The hem can also be handstitched with a *catchstitch* or left raw (with the edge carefully cut using a rotary cutter). A twin needle topstitched hem is the stitching technique most widely used for hems in knit garments because it is stretchable (see Figure 4.33). You can use straight nonstretchable hem stitching if the hemline is wide enough for walking without needing to be stretched. To stabilize the hem in a lightweight knit, fuse a narrow strip of lightweight knit interfacing on the hem allowance before topstitching.

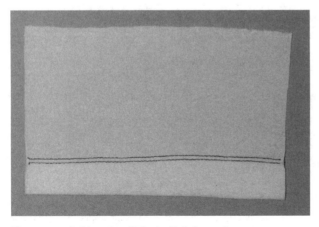

Figure 4.33 A 1" hem topstitched with twin needles

Knit It Together

This checklist summarizes what you have learned about laying out, marking, and cutting knits in this chapter.

- ✓ Preshrink knit fabric before cutting.
- ✓ Protect the fabric surface when pressing knits, or press from the wrong side.
- ✓ Knits need a nap layout to keep the color uniform.
- ✓ To place the pattern pieces on grain, follow the rib-line.
- ✓ The machine needles, thread, and stitches must suit the fabric type and weight.
- ✓ Seams must be stitched with stretchable stitches.
- ✓ Seams can be elasticized to stabilize and help the garment edges cling to the body and to prevent gaping.
- ✓ Knits can be topstitched with twin needles.

Stop: What Do I Do If . . .

. . . my fabric yardage is not enough to lay out my patterns using a napped layout? Can I place my pattern pieces up and down the fabric rather than placing them in one direction?

Before you lay out and cut the fabric pieces, drape the fabric on a form, as shown in Figure 1.7 on p. 10. Look down the fabric (from the top of the form) to see if there is any shading difference. If there is a shading difference, *do not* lay out the pattern pieces in both directions. If you cannot see any shading difference, you can lay out the pattern pieces in both directions.

. . . I can't see the rib-line? How can I place my patterns on grain?

Ask your instructor to help you identify the rib-line. Alternatively, use a magnifying glass to identify the rib-line. Chalk-mark the rib-line and use it as a guide.

Self-Critique

1. Why do knits need a napped layout?
2. How are grainlines drawn on the patterns to indicate a napped layout? (Refer to the "Grainlines" section in Chapter 3.)
3. What happens to the garment if the pattern pieces are not cut on grain?
4. What stitches would you use to stitch a T-shirt in a jersey two-way stretch knit with minimal stretch? (Refer to Table 4.2.)
5. What stitches would you use to stitch an activewear top constructed from a four-way stretch knit?
6. How do you choose the appropriate size of machine needle and stitches for a particular fabric? (Refer to Table 4.1.)
7. What sewing machine needles would you use to stitch a hem in a stretch knit?
8. What is the common factor required in a stretchable stitch?

Key Terms	
Ballpoint Needles	Rib-line
Differential Feed	Serger
Drop-match	Single Needles
Mechanical	Stretchable Seam
Sewing Machine	Stretchable Stitches
Nap Layout	Stretch Needles
	Twin Needles

5 Drafting the Hip and Top Foundations

Having a set of knit slopers is the starting point for drafting patterns for individual designs. Since knit fabric stretches to fit the body shape, slopers for woven fabric that incorporate ease, darts, and fitting lines are not appropriate to use. For this reason, you need to develop new slopers specifically for stretch knit fabrics.

This chapter discusses how to draft hip and top foundations for two-way stretch and four-way stretch knits. Figures 5.1a, b, and c show the comparison between the

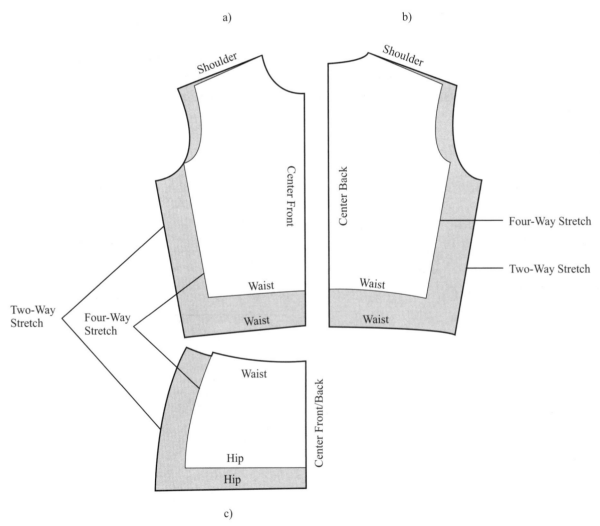

a)

b)

c)

Figure 5.1 Two-way and four-way stretch hip and top foundation comparison: **a)** front top foundations; **b)** back top foundations; **c)** hip foundations

two-way stretch and four-way stretch hip and top foundations. The foundations are *not* a garment but are *part* of a garment. The reason the foundations differ in size is that four-way stretch knits stretch in the width and length. In contrast, two-way stretch knits stretch only in the width. The foundations must reflect this difference (refer to Figures 1.2a and b on p. 2).

Setting up the hip and top foundations takes time, but an easier process will follow as the foundations transform into stretch knit slopers (or blocks). In due course, the foundations will evolve into slopers in various stretch categories (see Table 2.1 on p. 22). Refer to Table 2.2 on p. 17 to see the vast number of stretch knit garments that can be developed from the slopers that are built on the foundations.

Tools and Supplies

Before you draft hip and top foundations, it is important to have the patternmaking tools required and an understanding of the terminology of the pattern drafting techniques outlined in Chapter 3.

Taping the Form

To tape the form, you need a packet of ¼" wide black polyester twill tape (4 yards in packet) and Iris super fine pins (or silk pins).

The starting point for drafting the hip and top foundations is to measure the form. These measurements are used to draft the foundations. However, before you measure the form, you must tape it to indicate exactly where to measure. Taping the form also helps when fitting muslins and provides a guide when looking at the proportion of a garment.

You tape the form on the front bust and around the entire waistline and hipline. When taping the form, push the pins firmly into the form so that they are *flat*. Then the

knit will not snag when fitting muslins or garments. You *must* place the tape symmetrically on both sides of the form. This can be done only by measuring.

Tape the Bustline (Front Only)

Figure 5.2

1. Cut a length of tape long enough to tape the *front* bustline only (with 2" extra added).
2. Define the *apex* on one side of the form and pin-mark.
3. On one side, measure from mid shoulder down to the apex and pin-mark. Transfer this measurement to the other side of the form (to ensure the apex on both sides is symmetrical).
4. Pin the tape to the apex on both sides. Do not pin the tape to the center front of the form.

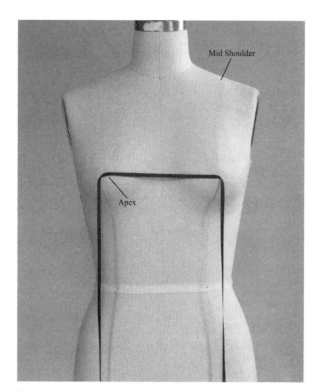

Figure 5.2 Tape apex to apex

Complete Taping the Bustline

Figure 5.3

1. Measure from the apex to the floor. Hold the tape *taut* and straight to the floor. Do not hold the tape at an angle. Jot down the measurement.

2. Transfer this measurement to both side seams. Hold the tape taut and straight up the side seam; then pin-mark this measurement on both sides of the form.

3. Pin both ends of the tape to the side seams. Fold the tape under ½" because twill tape frays.

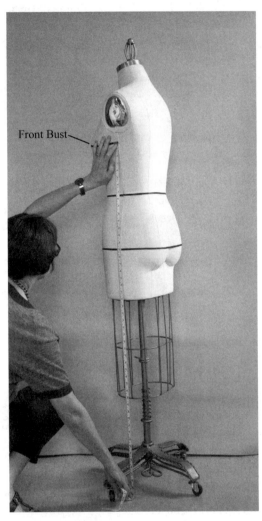

Front Bust

Figure 5.3 Complete taping the bustline

Tape the Waistline and Hipline

Figures 5.4a and b

The taped bustline, waistline, and hipline must be parallel to each other and to the floor.

1. Cut a length of twill tape for the full waist measurement with an extra 2" added.
2. To tape the waistline, begin at the side seam, extend the tape ½" past the side seam, and leave the tape flat (not folded). Measure from the bustline to the waistline. Use this measurement to tape the waistline parallel to the bustline.

3. After taping the entire waist, fold the other end of the tape under ½" to prevent fraying. Place the fold-line of the tape on the side seam and pin in place.
4. Cut a length of twill tape for the full hip measurement with an extra 2" added.
5. Tape around the *fullest* part of the hips. Depending on the size of the form, this measurement will be approximately 8" or 9" below the waistline.
6. Tape the hipline parallel to the waistline.

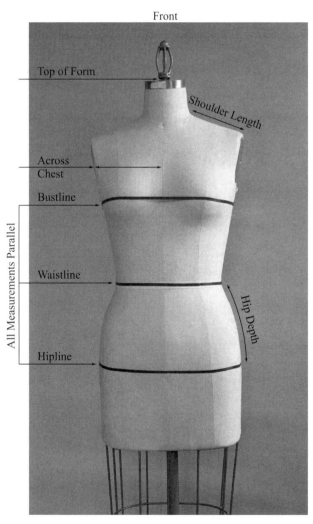

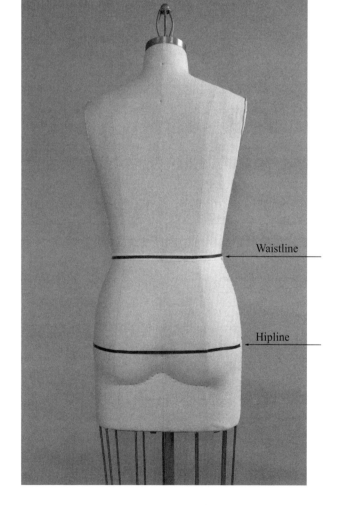

Figures 5.4a and b Tape the waistline and hipline

Taking Measurements

To measure accurately, measure on top of the tape and be sure to hold the tape measure taut as you measure. If you don't have accurate measurements, the garment won't fit properly. For measurements 1, 2, and 3 in the Form Measurements that follow, measure from the top metal plate of the form down the center front (see Figure 5.4).

Form Measurements

Measure and record the following measurements (in inches):

1. Top of front form to base of neck _____
2. Top of form to bust _____
3. Top of form to waist _____
4. Shoulder length (neck to shoulder edge) _____
5. Across chest (center front to mid armhole plate) _____
6. Apex to center front _____
7. Bust _____ (fullest part of the bust)
8. Waist _____
9. Hip _____ (largest part of the buttock)
10. Waist to hip depth _____ (measure down center front)

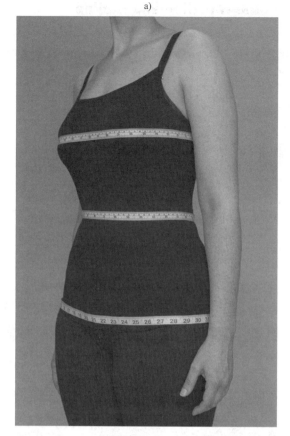

Figure 5.5a Measuring the bust, waist, and hip

Measure for a Custom Fit

Figures 5.5a and b

To measure someone for a custom fit, ask that person to wear undergarments to present a taut, smooth silhouette.

1. Define the person's waistline with twill tape pinned around the waistline as a guide for measuring.
2. Define the apex as a guide for measuring the bustline.
3. Measure around the *fullest* part of the bust and hips (see Figure 5.5a).
4. To measure the arm length, measure from the shoulder point and follow the contour of the back elbow to the wrist (see Figure 5.5b).

The next step is to draft the hip foundation and then the top foundation. Drafting the foundations accurately is the key to drafting stretch knit slopers with excellent fit.

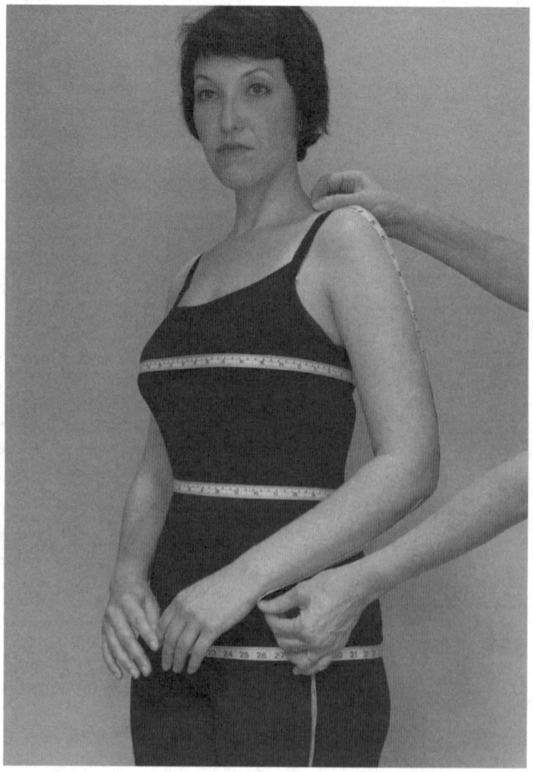

Figure 5.5b Measuring the arm length

Drafting the Hip and Top Foundations

The hip and top foundations are partial patterns drafted to the dress form measurements (or a person's measurements). Several steps are involved in drafting the foundations. The four-step process is outlined in Tables 5.1 and 5.2.

1. Step 1 *Drafting* Two-way Stretch Foundations
   The first foundations to be drafted are for a two-way minimal stretch knit. They are the **master foundations**. A master foundation is used to grade the other foundations.

2. Step 2 *Grading* Two-way Stretch Foundations
   After the master foundations have been completed (and made in oak-tag), you draft a complete set of foundations for each stretch category. The **minimal stretch foundation** is the first foundation to be drafted. It has the least amount of stretch. A minimal stretch foundation is used to grade the **moderate stretch foundations, very stretchy foundations**, and **super stretchy foundations**. The foundations represent each stretch category into which knits are grouped. As each stretch category of foundations is graded, the shape and scale become smaller but the style details remain the same.

3. Step 3 *Reducing* Two-way Stretch into Four-way Stretch
   After drafting and grading the two-way stretch foundations, you need to convert the very stretchy foundations for use with four-way stretch knits. You do this by reducing the length. Four-way stretch

TABLE 5.1 Hip foundation flow chart

Step 1—*Drafting* Two-way Stretch Hip Foundation				
Stretch Categories	**Minimal Stretch**	**Moderate Stretch**	**Very Stretchy**	**Super Stretchy**
The hip foundation is drafted from the dress form or body measurements	Master Foundation			
Step 2—*Grading* Two-way Stretch Top Foundation into Stretch Categories				
The hip foundation is graded smaller to decrease the dimensions for a knit with more stretch		2″ less in width than *minimal stretch*	2″ less in width than *moderate stretch*	2″ less in width than *very stretchy*
Step 3—*Converting* Two-way Stretch Top Foundation into Four-way Stretch				
Only the *very stretchy* foundation is reduced in the length			1″ shorter than two-way stretch	
Step 4—*Grading* Four-way Stretch Top Foundation into Stretch Categories				
Only the *super stretchy* foundation is graded				2″ less in width than very stretchy

foundations are required for drafting swimwear and panty slopers.

4. Step 4 *Grading* Four-way Stretch Foundations
Grading four-way stretch foundations is the last step in completing the hip and top foundations. Once you have converted the two-way very stretchy foundations into four-way stretch, these foundations are then graded to create options for use with super stretchy knits.

Refer to Figure 5.1 to see the hip and top foundations after completing the four-step process of making the foundations.

TABLE 5.2 Top foundation flow chart

Step 1—*Drafting* Two-way Stretch Top Foundation				
Stretch Categories	**Minimal Stretch**	**Moderate Stretch**	**Very Stretchy**	**Super Stretchy**
The top foundations are drafted from the dress form or body measurements	Back — Front — Master Foundations			
Step 2—*Grading* Two-way Stretch Top Foundation into Stretch Categories				
The top foundations are graded smaller to decrease the dimensions for a knit with more stretch		2″ less in width than *minimal stretch*	2″ less in width than *moderate stretch*	2″ less in width than *very stretchy*
Step 3—*Converting* Two-way Stretch Top Foundation into Four-way Stretch				
Only the *very stretchy* foundations are reduced in the length			1″ shorter than two-way stetch	
Step 4—*Grading* Four-way Stretch Top Foundation into Stretch Categories				
Only the *super stretchy* foundations are graded				2″ less in width than *very stretchy*

Step 1—Drafting Two-way Stretch Hip Foundation

The first hip foundation you draft is for a two-way minimal stretch knit. This is the master foundation that you will use to draft the top foundation in each stretch category.

Minimal Stretch

To draft the foundations, refer to the "Form Measurements" section earlier in this chapter on p. 70.

Draw the Hip-box

Figure 5.6

Begin by drawing a right angle on pattern paper. To draft the hip-box, you need measurements 8, 9, and 10 from the Form Measurements on p. 70.

1. Divide the waist and hip measurements by 4 and jot down the measurements:
   Waist measurement _____" ÷ 4 = _____"
   Hip measurement _____" ÷ 4 = _____"
2. X-W = ¼ hip measurement. Label waistline.
3. W-H = Waist to hip depth. Write "CF/CB" on the foundation.
4. H-H1 = Equal length to (W-X). Label the hipline.
5. X-H1 = Equal length to (W-H).
6. Mark ¼ waist measurement from (W) along the waistline.
7. W1-= Draw a guide mark (squared line) ⅝" up from the waistline.

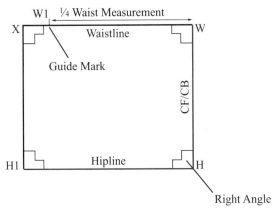

Figure 5.6 Draw a hip-box

Draw the Side Seam Curve

Figures 5.7a and b

1. H1-Y = 1".
2. W1-Y = Use a hip curve to draw a curved side seam, blending a smooth line from (Y). You can modify the shape when the muslin is fitted.
3. Place a graph ruler along the side seam and draw a ¼" squared line at (W1).

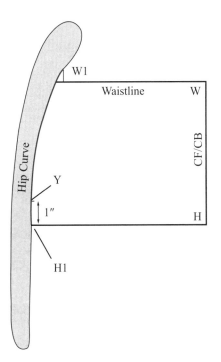

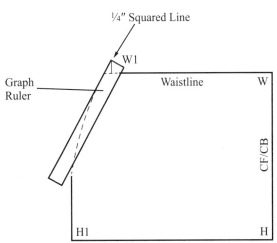

Figure 5.7 a) Draw a side seam curve; **b)** Draw a ¼" squared line

Draw the Waistline Curve (Figure 5.8)

Figure 5.8

Use the hip curve to draw a smooth waistline curve from the squared line (W1) to (W).

Trueing the Seams

1. Trace one copy of the hip foundation onto pattern paper with the waistline drawn.
2. Align the side seams/waists together to check that the waistline has a smooth continuous curve (see Figure 3.6b on p. 25).

Fabric You'll Need

Purchase 1/3 yard of two-way minimal stretch double knit. (A perfect fabric is Ponte, which is a medium weight.)

Cut and Stitch

Figure 5.9

1. Cut two hip foundations from single lengthwise folded fabric. Trace one side of the foundation and then flip the foundation to the other side and trace.
2. Add ½" seam allowance to the side seams only and cut the muslin (the waist and hip *do not* need seam allowances).
3. Stitch the side seams with a *crooked straight stitch*. (Refer to Table 4.2 for instructions.) Do not serge the seams together because the seams need to be pressed open so that they are flat and bulk free for an accurate fitting.

Test the Fit

Figure 5.10

Place the hip foundation on the form to test the fit. Pin any fitting adjustments as needed. Mark these adjustments on the hip foundation pattern before transferring into oak-tag.

What to look for:
- ✓ Check that the waistline and hipline align perfectly with the taped form.
- ✓ Check that the shape of the hipline contours the form. Reshape if necessary.
- ✓ Check the fit of the waist. Do not pin the waist tighter because skirts and pants (made from the hip foundation) must have enough room at the waist to stretch over the hips.

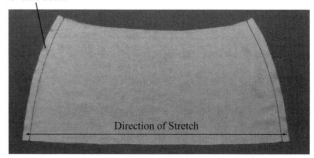

½" Side Seam

Direction of Stretch

Figure 5.9 Cut and stitch the muslin hip foundation

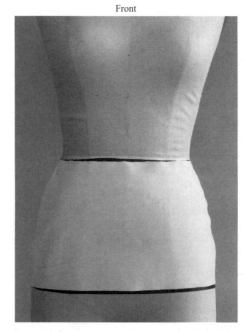

Front

Figure 5.10 Two-way stretch muslin hip foundation fitted on the form

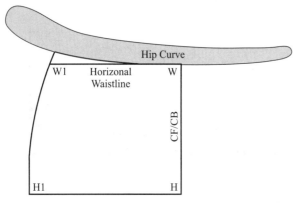

Hip Curve

W1   Horizonal   W
Waistline

CF/CB

H1   H

Figure 5.8 Draw a waistline curve

Finalize the Foundation

Figure 5.11

1. Transfer the hip foundation to oak-tag.
2. Write the pattern name "Two-way Stretch Hip Foundation" and "Minimal Stretch" on the foundation.
   - Draw the waistline and record the codes (W-W1-H-H1).
   - Write "CF/CB" on the foundation.

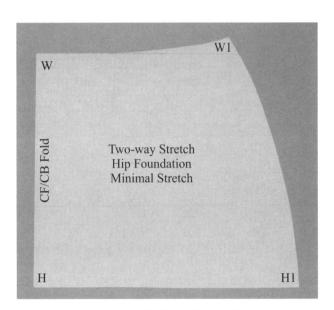

Figure 5.11 Two-way stretch hip foundation in oak-tag

Step 2—Grading Two-way Stretch Hip Foundation into Stretch Categories

The second step is to grade the two-way minimal stretch hip foundation into *moderate stretch*, *very stretchy*, and *super stretchy* foundations. (Refer to Chapter 3, which explains the grading system.)

Prepare the Grading Grid

Draw the grading grid on oak-tag. Mark (D) and ½" increments (A-B-C) in a *negative* direction on the horizontal line of the grading grid (see Figure 5.12).

Minimal Stretch

Figure 5.12

Figure 3.17a on p. 37 illustrates that the horizontal balance line (HBL) is the hipline of the hip foundation.

1. Place (W-H) on (D) with HBL on the horizontal line.
2. Trace the minimal stretch hip foundation on the grading grid.

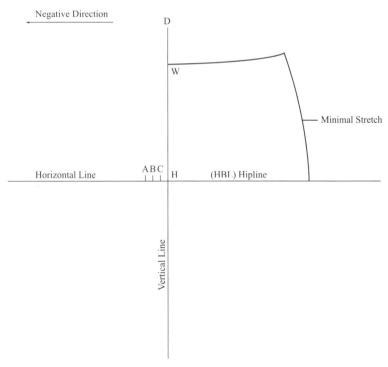

Figure 5.12 Trace minimal stretch

Moderate Stretch

Figure 5.13

Grading is done in a *negative* direction. As you grade, make sure that (HBL) is perfectly aligned on the horizontal line of the grading grid.

1. Move (W-H) on (C) with HBL on the horizontal line.
2. Trace the moderate stretch foundation onto the grading grid.

Very Stretchy

Figure 5.14

1. Move (W-H) on (B) with HBL on the horizontal line.
2. Trace the very stretchy foundation onto the grading grid.

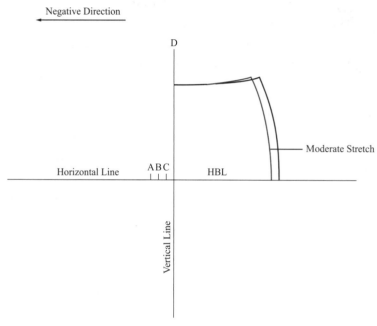

Figure 5.13 Grade moderate stretch

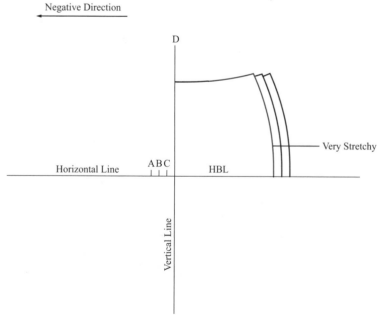

Figure 5.14 Grade very stretchy

Super Stretchy

Figure 5.15

1. Move (W-H) on (A) with HBL on the horizontal line.
2. Trace the super stretchy foundation onto the grading grid.
3. When the grading is completed, draw a horizontal line with an L-square ruler across the tip of the waist/side seam. If the grading has been done correctly, the waist/side seam will touch the squared line for each stretch category.

Cut Waist/Side Seams

Figure 5.16

1. Cut the moderate stretch foundation from the grading grid. (The minimal stretch foundation was drawn on the grid to differentiate between each stretch category; it does not need to be cut.)
2. Cut the waist/side seams in stretch categories at (W1).

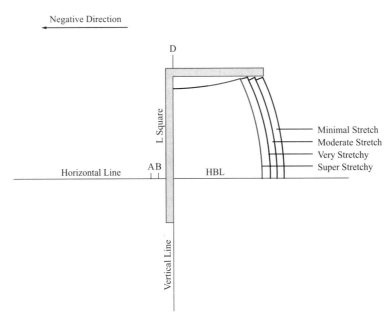

Figure 5.15 Grade super stretchy

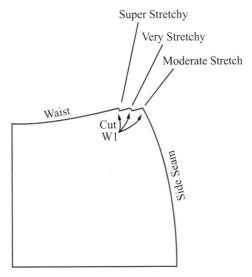

Figure 5.16 Cut the waist/side seams

Draw the Waistline Curve

Figure 5.17

1. Trace the moderate stretch foundation onto oak-tag. Draw the waistline from the center front for all stretch categories.
2. Then mark the waist/side seam only for the moderate stretch.
3. Place the minimal stretch foundation on top of the moderate stretch foundation. Align the waistlines/side seams together, and use a tracing wheel to transfer the remaining waistline onto the moderate stretch foundation as shown. Finish cutting the foundation.
4. Trace the very stretchy foundation onto oak-tag. Then transfer the waistline as you did for moderate stretch and cut the foundation.
5. Repeat the same process for super stretchy.

Finalize the Foundations

Figure 5.18

1. Write the pattern name "Two-way Stretch Hip Foundation" on the foundations.
2. Write the stretch category (moderate stretch, very stretchy, and super stretch) on each foundation.
3. Record codes (W-W1-H-H1) on each foundation.
4. Draw the waistline on all foundations.
5. Write "CF/CB" on the foundation. (See Figure 5.18.)

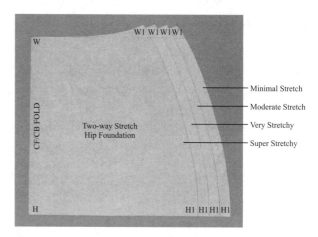

Figure 5.18 Two-way stretch hip foundations in oak-tag for each stretch category

Step 3—Reducing Two-way Stretch Hip Foundation into Four-way Stretch

The foundation *must* be reduced in the length to convert the two-way stretch hip foundation for use in four-way stretch knits. The four-way stretch hip foundation is required to draft panty slopers and the lower section of the swimwear slopers (see Table 2.1 on p. 16).

Length Reduction

Figure 5.19

Now you reduce the very stretchy hip foundation in length.

1. Draw a guideline halfway between (W1-H1) (W-H).
2. Draw parallel lines ½" on each side of the guide mark (1" in total).
3. Label this section "REDUCTION."

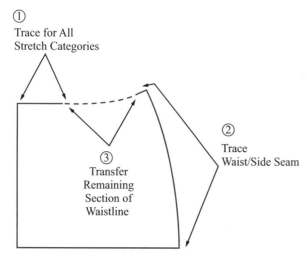

Figure 5.17 Draw the waistline curve

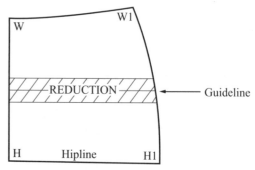

Figure 5.19 Length reduction

Fold the Reduction and Draw a New Hip Curve
Figure 5.20

1. Fold "REDUCTION" by aligning the parallel lines together to shorten the length of the foundation. Then secure with masking tape.
2. Remove ⅛" from the side seam at (H1). Draw a ½" squared line up from (H1).
3. Draw a new hip curve from (W1) to the squared ½" line. Equalize the difference (from folding the reduction) on the side seam.

Test the Fit
Figure 5.21

1. Cut two hip foundations from a four-way very stretchy knit. (Follow the same cutting directions as you did for testing the two-way stretch hip foundation.)
2. Add ½" seam allowance to the *side seams* only. The waistline and hipline *do not* need seam allowances.
3. Stitch the side seams as you did for two-way stretch.
4. Fit the four-way stretch hip foundation on the form. What to look for:
   - ✓ Check that when the knit is stretched downward it reaches the hipline of the form.

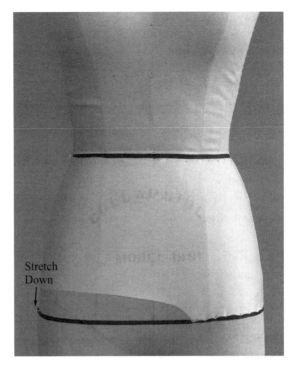

Stretch Down

Figure 5.21 Four-way stretch hip foundation in muslin fitted on the form

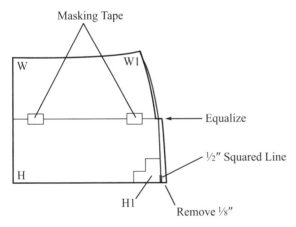

Masking Tape

W   W1

Equalize

½" Squared Line

H

H1

Remove ⅛"

Figure 5.20 Fold the reduction and draw a new hip curve

Finalize the Foundation

1. Align side seams and check that you have a smooth, continuous waistline curve.
2. Transfer the hip foundation into oak-tag.
3. Write down pattern information, mark the pattern name "Four-way Stretch Hip Foundation," and record the stretch capacity.
4. Write "CF/CB" on the foundation.
5. Draw the waistline and document codes.

Step 4—Grading Four-way Stretch Hip Foundation

In this step, you grade the four-way very stretchy hip foundation into a super stretchy foundation. It is the last step in making the hip foundations. You grade using the same grading grid and method you used to grade the two-way stretch hip foundation into each stretch category.

Super Stretchy

Figure 5.22

Grading is done in a *negative* direction.

1. Draw the grading grid on oak-tag. Mark (C) ½" from (D) in a *negative* direction on the horizontal line of the grading grid.
2. Place (W-H) on (D) with HBL on the horizontal line. Trace the very stretchy foundation onto the grading grid as shown.
3. Move (W-H) on (C) with HBL on the horizontal line. Draw the super stretchy foundation on the grading grid.
4. Cut only this foundation because you already have the very stretchy foundation.

Finalize the Foundations

1. Write the pattern information "Four-way Stretch Hip Foundation" and stretch capacity.
2. Draw the waistline, write "CF/CB" on the foundation, and record codes on each foundation (see Figure 5.23).

Drafting the Top Foundations

Now you're ready to draft the top foundations. Refer to Table 5.2 to see the four-step process that is involved in making the two-way and four-way stretch top foundations.

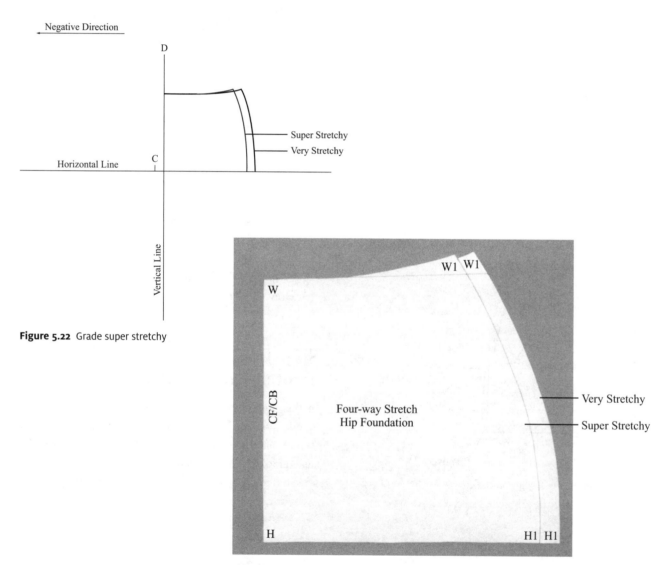

Figure 5.22 Grade super stretchy

Figure 5.23 Four-way hip foundations in oak-tag in each stretch category

Step 1—Drafting Two-way Stretch Top Foundations

The top foundation is drafted from the shoulder to the waist (see Figure 5.30). Using the two-way stretch top foundations, you can draft four-way stretch top foundations.

Minimal Stretch

The first top foundation to be drafted is for a two-way minimal stretch knit. This is the master foundation that you will use to draft the foundation in each stretch category. To draft the top foundation, refer to "Form Measurements" section earlier in this chapter.

Draw the Top-box

Figure 5.24

You need measurements 3 and 7 from the Form Measurements on p. 70.

1. Begin by drawing a right angle on pattern paper.
2. T-W = Top of form to waist.
3. T-T1 = ¼ bust measurement.
4. W-X = Equal length to (T-T1). Label the waistline.
5. T1-X = Equal length to (T-W1).
6. Label "Top of Form" and "(CF/CB)."

Draw a Guide Mark/Guideline

Figure 5.25

Now you need measurements 1 and 2 from the Form Measurements on p. 70.

1. Guideline = Draw a parallel line 1¼" below "Top of Form."
2. Guide mark = Draw a short parallel line 2" below the guideline.
3. N = Back neck depth ½" below the guideline. Draw a ¾" squared line.
4. T-N1 = Top of form to front base of neck.
5. N1-N2 = 2⅜". Draw a squared line at CF/CB.
6. N2-S1 = Draw a squared line from (N2) to the guideline.
7. U = Armhole depth 6¾" below the guide mark. Draw a parallel to (T-T1) from (U) to CF/CB.
8. Y = Chest line, halfway between the guide mark and (U).
9. C-C1 = Halfway across chest measurement drawn parallel to (T1-T) and squared at CF/CB.

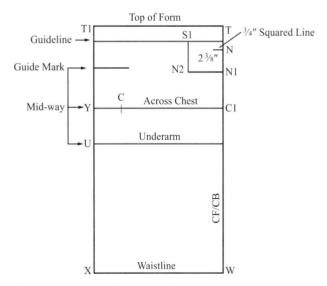

Figure 5.25 Draw a guide mark/guideline

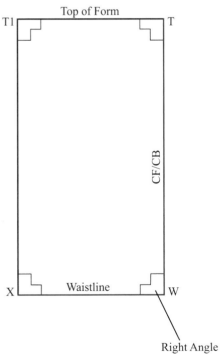

Figure 5.24 Draw the top-box

Draw the Front Neckline, Shoulder Slope, Armhole, and Bustline

Figure 5.26

1. S-S1 = Shoulder length. Place a graph ruler on (S1) and slant the ruler until the shoulder length measurement touches the guide mark. Draw the shoulder slope and ¼" squared-off angle at (S) to mark the shoulder/armhole tip.
2. Draw a squared-off angle at (U). When you employ the pattern drafting principle of drawing squared-off angles, you will *always* have smooth continuous lines.
3. S-C-U = Position the French curve on the squared-off angle at (U) and the other points to draw the *front* armhole curve. You may find that the armhole curve needs to be drawn in two stages. For example, draw (S-C) first and then realign the French curve and draw (C-U).
4. T-B = Draw the *bustline* parallel to the underarm line. Use measurement 2, "Top of Form to Bust."
5. Mark apex on the bustline (B) with a cross-mark. Use measurement 6, "Apex to Center Front." Marking the apex provides a guide when you are pattern plotting an empire waist or princess line, or creating a dart. (See Figure 5.26.)

Draw the Side Seam, Waistline, Back Armhole, and Neckline

Figure 5.27

1. Mark ¼ waist measurement from (W) along the (W-X) line. (This is the same waist measurement that you used to draft the hip foundation in Figure 5.6).
2. Draw a ⅜" squared guide mark down from the waist measurement. Label (W1).
3. Position the hip curve on W1 and (W), and draw the waistline curve.
4. At (W1), draw a squared-off angle.
5. Position the French curve on (S1) and squared line (N). Draw the *back neckline* curve.
6. Mark two short guide marks ½" down the armhole from the shoulder tip (S) and ½" up from (U).
7. C-C3 = ¼".
8. S-C3-U = Place the French curve on guide marks and draw the *back armhole* curve.
9. U-W1 = Draw a straight side seam.

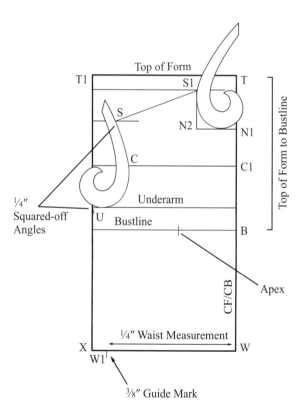

Figure 5.26 Draw the front neckline, shoulder slope armhole, and bustline

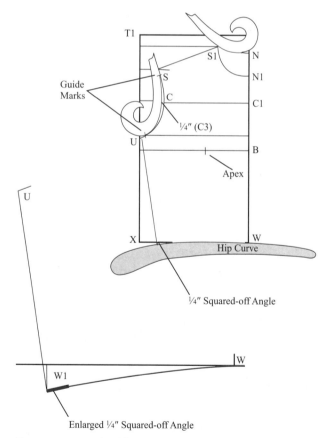

Figure 5.27 Draw the side seam, waistline, back armhole, and neckline

Measure Armholes

The armhole measurements are required for drafting the sleeve sloper. Measure and record the length of the front and back armholes (separately) on the foundations. The front armhole should be approximately ¼" *longer* than the back armhole. To measure, walk the tape measure around the curve, as illustrated in Figure 3.3 on p. 21.

Trueing the Seams

Figure 5.28

1. Make sure the the hip and top waistline measurements are equal lengths. Align the top front and back waistlines (W-W1) to the hip foundation waistline (W-W1). Adjust if necessary to make the waistlines the same length.
2. Check that the front and back side seams and shoulder seams are equal lengths.
3. Check that the foundations have smooth continuous armhole, underarm, shoulder, and waistline curves.

Fabric You'll Need

Purchase ⅝ yard of lightweight two-way minimal stretch knit. (This is not the same knit that was used to test-fit the hip foundation. The hip foundation was made in a heavier double knit.)

Cut and Stitch

Figure 5.29

1. To cut the muslin top foundation, prepare double lengthwise folded fabric (see Figure 4.10 on p. 48).
2. Place the center front and back patterns on the foldlines and pin.
3. Add ¼" seam allowances to the side and shoulder seams only.
4. Cut the foundations.
5. To stitch the foundation, place the correct sides of the front and back pieces together, and serge or crooked straight stitch ¼" shoulder and side seams.

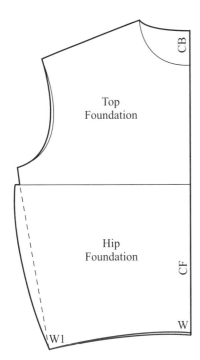

Figure 5.28 Trueing the seams

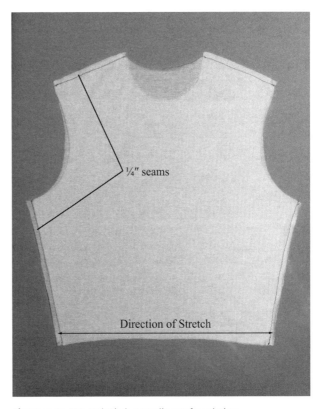

Figure 5.29 Cut and stitch a muslin top foundation

Test the Fit

Figures 5.30a and b

To test the fit, place the top foundation on the form. Pin any fitting adjustments as needed. Mark these adjustments on the foundation pattern before finalizing it in oak-tag.

What to look for:

✓ Check that the apex is aligned to the form apex. Remark the position if it is not aligned.

✓ Check the fit of the waist. Do not tighten the waist because it must be the same waist measurement as the waist of the hip foundation.

Front

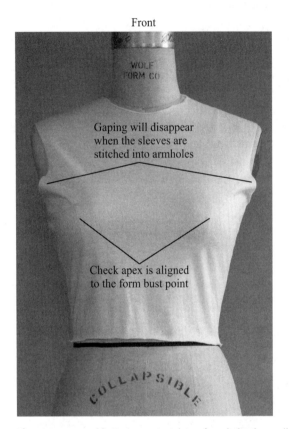

Gaping will disappear when the sleeves are stitched into armholes

Check apex is aligned to the form bust point

Back

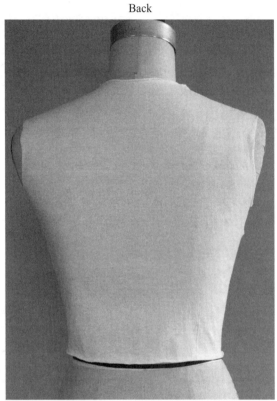

Figures 5.30a and b Two-way stretch top foundation in muslin fitted on the form

Finalize the Foundations

1. Transfer the front and back top foundations onto oak-tag.
2. Write the pattern name "Two-way Stretch Front/ Back Top Foundation" on the foundations.
3. Write the stretch category (minimal stretch) on the foundation.
4. Draw the waistline (W1-W) and underarm (U).
5. Mark the apex and label (X).
6. Notch the front armhole.
7. Record codes (S-C-C3-U-W-W1) on the foundations.
8. Write "CF/CB" on each foundation.
9. Pierce the apex with an awl. (See Figure 5.31.)

Step 2—Grading Two-way Stretch Top Foundation into Stretch Categories

Now you grade the front and back top foundations into moderate stretch, very stretchy, and super stretchy categories. These knits have *more* stretch than a minimal stretch knit. The grading is done in a *negative* direction to make the foundation 2" smaller as each stretch category is graded. Refer to Table 5.2 to see how you use the minimal stretch master foundation to grade the top foundations in each stretch category.

Prepare the Grading Grid

Refer to Figures 3.15 and 3.16 on pp. 35 and 36 to see the grading grid and the measurements marked on the grid.

1. Prepare the grading grid on oak-tag and label (D).
2. From (D), mark (A-B-C) in ½" increments in a *negative* direction on the horizontal line.
3. Mark C2 and B2 in ¼" increments from (D).

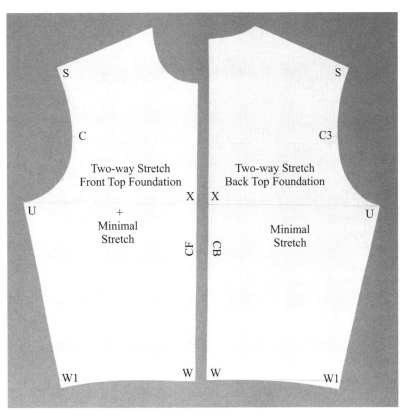

Figure 5.31 Two-way stretch top foundation in oak-tag

Minimal Stretch

Figure 5.32

The minimal stretch master foundation is used to grade the foundations into each stretch category. The grading method used is the same for the front as for the back. Record the stretch capacity of each foundation as you grade. Figure 3.17b on p. 38 illustrates the horizontal balance line (HBL) on the underarm of the top foundation.

1. Label (X) on the foundation, as indicated in Figure 5.31.

2. Trace minimal stretch on the grading grid. Place (X) on the vertical line (D).

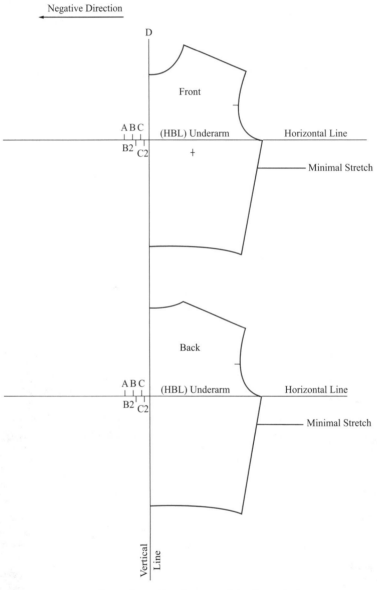

Figure 5.32 Prepare the grading grid and trace a minimal stretch sloper onto the grid

Moderate Stretch

Figure 5.33

You grade in a *negative* direction to reduce the foundation in size to accommodate a knit with more stretch. As you grade, (HBL) must be perfectly aligned on the horizontal line of the grading grid.

1. Move (X) on (C2) and mark the apex. Then draw the shoulder/armhole tip and outline to sloper mid armhole at (C and C3).
2. Move (X) to (C) and mark the underarm/side seam and outline the side seam/waist.

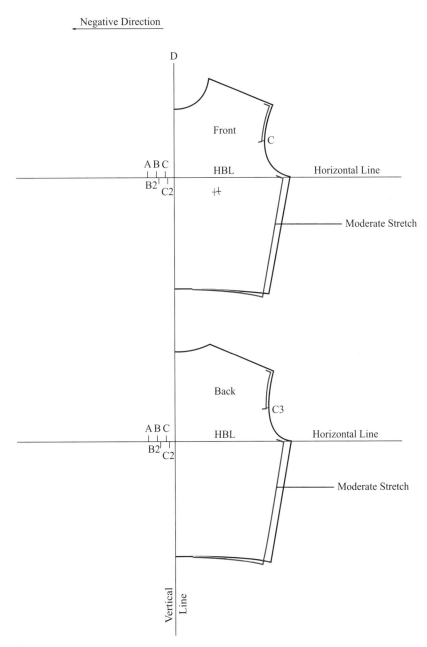

Figure 5.33 Grade moderate stretch

Very Stretchy

Figure 5.34

1. Move (X) on (C), and mark the apex and shoulder/ armhole tip. Then continue outlining to the sloper mid armhole at (C and C3).

2. Move (X) on (B), mark the underarm/side seam, and outline the side seam/waist.

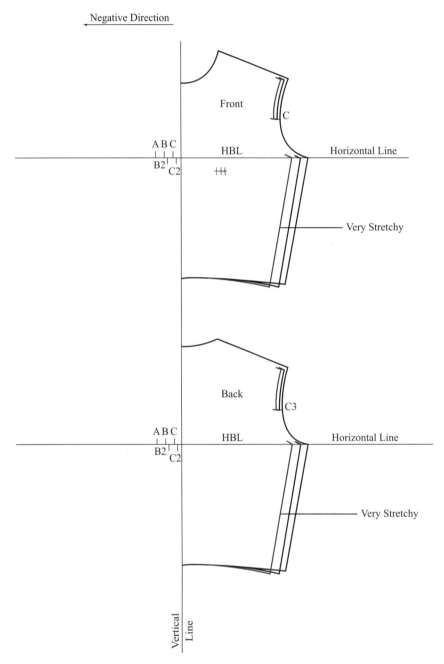

Figure 5.34 Grade very stretchy

Super Stretchy

Figure 5.35

1. Move (X) on (B2) and mark the apex and shoulder/armhole tip. Then continue outlining to the sloper mid armhole at (C and C3).
2. Move (X) on (A), mark the underarm/side seam, and outline the side seam/waist.

3. When the grading is completed, draw a horizontal line with an L-square ruler across the tip of the shoulder/armhole and the waist/side seam. If the grading has been done correctly, each of these points will align on the L-square for each stretch category.

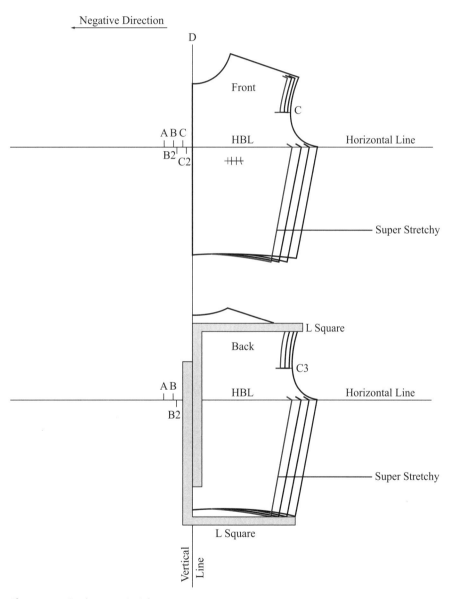

Figure 5.35 Grade super stretchy

Draw the Shoulder Line and Armhole Curve
Figure 5.36

On completion, you will have a graded nest of two-way stretch top foundations drawn on oak-tag in all stretch categories.

1. Draw a new front shoulder line from the neckline to the shoulder/armhole tip.
2. Position the French curve at the mid armhole (C and C3) and squared underarm (U) of the foundations. Finish drawing the front underarm curve for all stretch categories.
3. Repeat the process for the back.

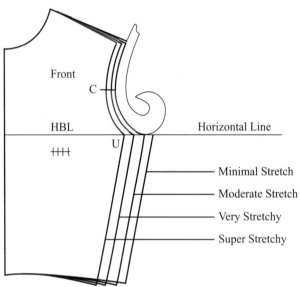

Figure 5.36 Draw the shoulder line and armhole curve

Cut Waist/Side Seams
Figure 5.37

The final grading process is to trace the foundations from the graded nest onto oak-tag.

1. Cut the moderate stretch front and back foundations from the grading grid. (The minimal stretch was drawn on the grading grid to differentiate between each stretch category; it does not need to be cut because you already have these foundations.)
2. Cut the side seam/waist at (W1) for each stretch category.

Draw the Waistline Curve
Figure 5.37

1. Trace the moderate stretch foundations onto oak-tag. Then place the minimal stretch foundation on top of the moderate stretch foundation. Align the side seam/waistlines together, and use a tracing wheel to transfer the waistline onto the moderate stretch foundation.

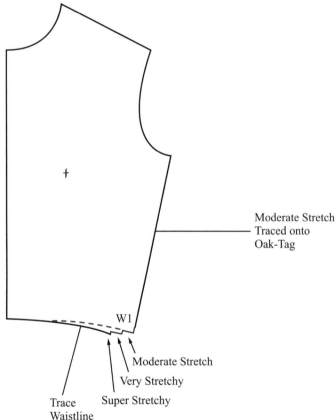

Figure 5.37 Cut waist/side seams

2. Transfer the apex to the front.
3. Cut the very stretchy front and back foundations. Then trace the front and back foundations onto oak-tag.
4. Transfer the waistline as you did for the moderate stretch. Also transfer the apex.
5. The super stretchy foundations are the remaining foundations.

Trueing the Seams

Align the foundations as you did for minimal stretch. It is important to have smooth continuous armhole, underarm, and waistline curves (see Figure 3.5 on p. 24).

Finalize the Foundations

Figure 5.38

1. Write the pattern name "Front/Back Two-way Stretch Top Foundation" on each graded foundation.
2. Write the stretch category (moderate stretch, very stretchy, and super stretchy) on each foundation.

3. Record codes (S-C-C3-U-W-W1) on each foundation.
4. Write "CF/CB" on each foundation.
5. Draw the waistline (W1-W) and underarm.
6. Pierce the apex with an awl.
7. Notch front armholes.

Step 3—Reducing Two-way Stretch Top Foundation into Four-way Stretch

The length of the foundation *must* be reduced when converting the two-way stretch top foundation for use in four-way stretch knits. In Tables 5.1 and 5.2 (*step 3*), notice that only the very stretchy and super stretchy foundations are reduced in the length. The four-way stretch top foundation will eventually be combined with the four-way stretch panty slopers and made into swimwear slopers (see Table 2.1 on p. 16). (They can also be used to draft patterns for a bodysuit and leotard.) Minimal stretch and moderate stretch foundations are not converted into four-way

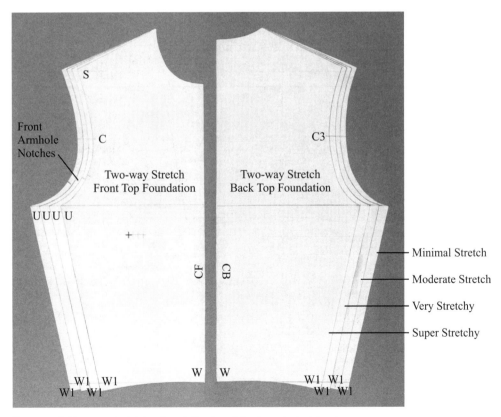

Figure 5.38 Two-way stretch top foundation in oak-tag in each stretch category

stretch because these knits will not create a streamline tight fit required for swimwear.

Length Reduction

Figure 5.39a

1. Draw a vertical line onto pattern paper.
2. Place the front and back two-way very stretchy foundations on each side of the vertical line and trace each one onto pattern paper.
3. Do not transfer the apex because it is marked at the fitting stage.
4. Draw a line squared at the center front/back across the shoulders, underarm, and waistline.
5. Draw guideline 1 = Halfway between shoulder and underarm. Mark ¼" (½" in total) on each side of the guideline. Label it "REDUCTION."
6. Draw guideline 2 = Midway between underarm and waist. Mark ½" (1" in total) on each side of the guideline. Label it "REDUCTION."

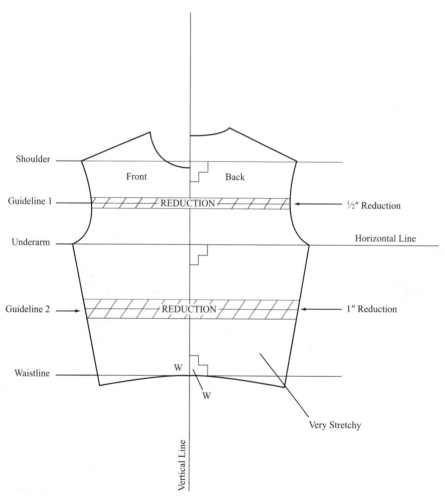

Figure 5.39a Length reduction

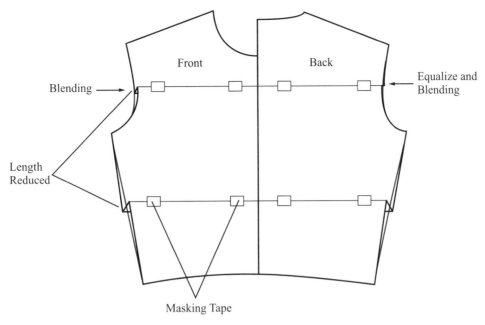

Figure 5.39b Fold reduction

Fold Reduction

Figure 5.39b

1. Fold "REDUCTION" by aligning the parallel lines together to shorten the length of the foundation and secure with masking tape.
2. Draw a straight line for the new side seam.
3. Draw a new blended armhole curve to equalize where the length was reduced.

Fabric You'll Need

Purchase ⅝ yard (light- to medium-weight) four-way very stretchy knit (swimwear fabric can be used).

Cut and Stitch

Figure 5.40

Next, cut and stitch the top foundation. Add ¼" seams to the shoulders and side seams. Then stitch the seams using serging. (To stitch the foundation, refer to Figure 5.29.)

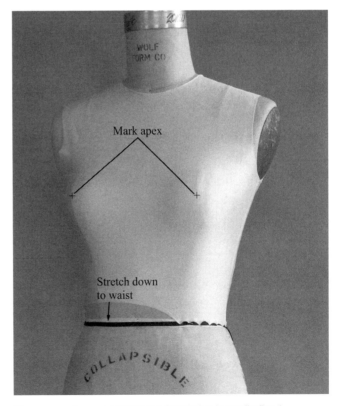

Figure 5.40 Four-way stretch top foundation in muslin fitted on the form

Test the Fit

To test the fit, place the foundation on the form. Stretch the muslin waist to the form waistline and pin in place. Cross-mark the apex and transfer to the foundation patterns.

What to look for:

✓ Check whether the length of the foundation is correct. If the length does not stretch to the taped waistline, you may not have chosen a knit with an appropriate stretch capacity.

Step 4—Grading Four-way Stretch Top Foundation

Now you grade the very stretchy top foundations into super stretchy foundations. In Table 5.2, notice that step 4 is the last step in the process of making the twin foundations.

Super Stretchy

Figure 5.41

Grading is done in a *negative* direction.

1. Prepare the grading grid on oak-tag and label (D).
2. Mark increments (C2) ¼" from (D) and (C) ½" from (D) in a negative direction.
3. The horizontal balance line (HBL) is the underarm of the sloper (see Figure 3.17 on p. 37).
4. Make sure (X) is recorded on the foundation, as indicated in Figure 5.31.
5. Place (X) of the very stretchy top foundations on the vertical line (D) with HBL lined up on the horizontal line. Trace the foundation onto the grading grid.
6. Move (X) on (C2), mark the shoulder/armhole tip, and outline to the sloper mid armhole at (C and C3).
7. Move (X) on (C), mark the underarm/side seam, and continue outlining the waist.
8. Place a French curve at the mid armhole and draw the underarm curve.
9. Draw a new shoulder line.

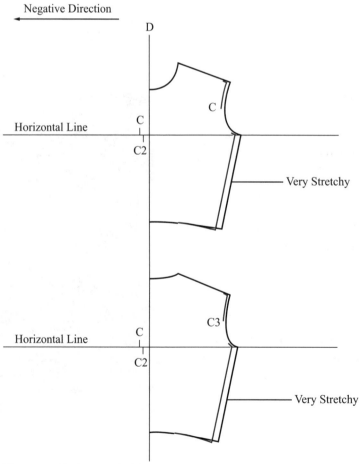

Figure 5.41 Grade super stretchy

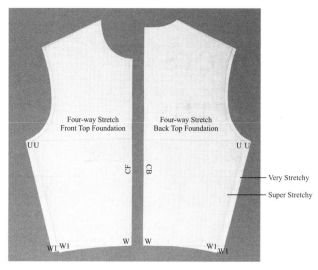

Figure 5.42 Four-way stretch top foundations in oak-tag

Finalize the Foundations

Figure 5.42

After the fitting is completed, transfer the foundations into oak-tag.

1. Write the pattern name "Four-way Stretch Front/ Back Top Foundation."
2. Write the stretch category (very stretchy and super stretchy) on each foundation.
3. Draw the waistline and underarm (U).
4. Record only the codes (U-W-W1) on each foundation.
5. Write "CF/CB" on each foundation.
6. Pierce the apex with an awl.
7. Notch front armholes.

Knit It Together

This checklist summarizes what you have learned about drafting the hip and top foundations in this chapter.

✓ The hip and top foundations are drafted from the form measurement or from a person's body measurements.

✓ The hip and top foundations are used to create the top slopers.

✓ The hip and top foundations are drafted for two-way stretch knits and four-way stretch knits.

✓ The hip and top foundations are drafted in stretch categories (minimal stretch, moderate stretch, very stretchy, and super stretchy) to match the stretch categories in the stretch gauge shown in Figure 1.4.

Stop: What Do I Do If . . .

. . . my four-way stretch top foundation was too big for the form? I'm not sure what stretch category of knit I used.

Repurchase the exact four-way stretch knit in the correct stretch category. Next, restitch and refit the muslin. There is no room for guesswork!

. . . my two-way stretch top foundation does not fit on my form?

Remeasure the form to check that the measurements you took were accurate. Next, check the patterns because you may need to correct a drafting error. It is important that the top foundations (and hip foundations) fit your form because all the slopers are created from these partial patterns.

Self-Critique

1. Why is it important to have the correct patternmaking tools and an understanding of pattern drafting terminology?
2. Why is it important to tape the form?
3. Why is it important to measure the form accurately?
4. Explain why the two-way and four-way stretch foundations are different dimensions in Figure 5.1.
5. What three main actions are found in Tables 5.1 and 5.2?
6. In certain locations on the top foundation in Figures 5.26 and 5.27, squared-off angles are drawn. Why is drawing these angles an important pattern drafting principle? (Refer to the "Pattern Drafting Principles" section in Chapter 3.)
7. Why is it important to test-fit foundations in the correct Foundations category?
8. How do you prepare the grading grid and determine what measurements to use to grade the foundations?

Key Terms	Super Stretchy
Master Foundations	Foundations
Minimal Stretch	Very Stretchy
Foundation	Foundations
Moderate Stretch	
Foundations	

6

Top Slopers
and Patterns

This chapter teaches you how to create top slopers from the hip and top foundations drafted in Chapter 5. By using the basic top sloper and modifying it, you can design your own chic T-shirt. Karl Lagerfeld, the German fashion designer, remarked, "There's no modern wardrobe without T-shirts."[1]

1 Anne Monoky, "Designers Like Lagerfeld Showcase a Cult of Personali-Tee," *Harper's Bazaar*, August 11, 2011. Retrieved from http://www.harpersbazaar.com/fashion/trends/a7267 /designers-showcase-cult-of-personali-tee-081711/

This chapter explains how to transform the basic top slopers into your own pattern design by introducing a new silhouette, restyled neckline, or modified sleeve. As the chapter progresses, you learn stitching techniques that relate to neckline finishes. Many of these elements are part of the T-shirt designs and other popular tops featured in Figures 6.1a through g.

a)   b)   c)   d)

e)   f)   g)

Figure 6.1 a) Crew-neck T-shirt with rib bands; **b)** V-neck sweater with raglan sleeves and bands; **c)** tunic with circular hem and turned and topstitched edge finish; **d)** flared top with cap sleeves, yoke, and turned and topstitched edge finish; **e)** sleeveless gathered top with binding; **f)** asymmetrical draped lined top; **g)** polo top with placket, collar, and narrow facing

Converting Two-way Stretch Hip and Top Foundations into Top Slopers

In this chapter you make a set of top slopers to match each stretch category. You also draft and grade a sleeve sloper into each stretch category to fit the armholes (armscye) of the top slopers.

The top slopers are created from the hip and top foundations that were drafted in Chapter 5. Look back at the "Knit Family" in Table 2.1 on p. 16 to see how the slopers evolve from the hip and top foundations. In addition, Table 2.2 on p. 17 lists the garments that you can draft from the top slopers.

The top slopers have a curve-hugging fit and can be constructed from two-way and four-way stretch knits. Tops do not need the lengthwise stretch; however, having it does not affect the fit. Even though each set of slopers is made to match a knit stretch category, you can choose a different fit. (To find out more about this idea, refer to the section "Fit-Flexibility: Adding Extra Room into Garments" in Chapter 2.)

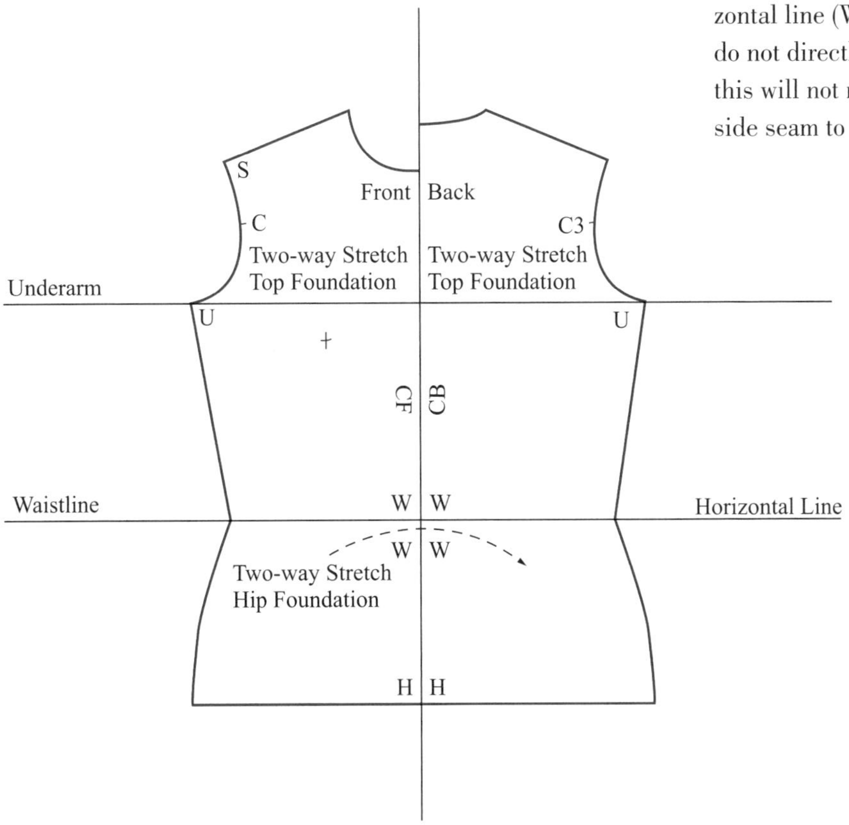

Minimal Stretch

Figure 6.2

The **minimal stretch slopers** are the master slopers. A **master sloper** is the first sloper to be drafted. You form the top slopers by joining together the hip and top foundations and converting them into slopers.

1. Draw intersecting lines on oak-tag.
2. Place the center front (CF) and center back (CB) of the two-way minimal stretch top foundations on each side of the vertical line, and place the waistline on the horizontal line and trace (do not draw *below* the waistline). Record codes (S-C-C3-U). You will use these codes to draft the sleeve sloper and sweater and cardigan slopers in Chapter 8.
3. Draw a line across the underarms (parallel to the waistline) and cross-mark the apex. Even though the apex may not be needed for darts, it acts as a guide for the placement of style lines.
4. Position (W-H) CF/CB of the two-way minimal stretch hip foundation on each side of the vertical line with the waistline placed directly on the horizontal line. (The hip foundation does *not* have a front and back.) Trace onto the grid from the horizontal line (W) down to the hipline. If the waistlines do not directly connect at the waistline/side seam, this will not matter because you will draw a shaped side seam to join the hip and top foundations.

Figure 6.2 Draft minimal stretch

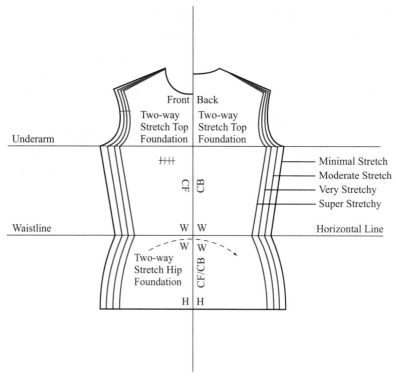

Figure 6.3 Draft moderate stretch, very stretchy, and super stretchy slopers

Moderate Stretch, Very Stretchy, and Super Stretchy

Figure 6.3

Next, you develop the **moderate stretch slopers**, **very stretchy slopers**, and **super stretchy slopers**. These slopers are used to draft the patterns for tops constructed from each stretch category of knit represented.

1. Trace the front and back top foundations in each stretch category onto the grid just as you did for minimal stretch.
2. Every side seam/underarm should touch line (U).
3. Transfer the apex. From the minimal stretch, the apex moves in ¼" increments toward the center front for each stretch category.
4. Trace the hip foundation onto the grid just as you did for minimal stretch.

Draw Minimal Stretch Front Side Seam
Figure 6.4

1. Draw a short guide mark halfway between the underarm and *waistline*.

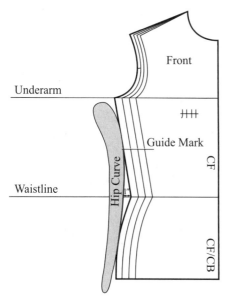

Figure 6.4 Draw a minimal stretch front side seam

2. Position the hip curve on the guide mark and upper hip with a gap of approximately ¾" to 1" at the waistline. Draw a curved side seam to join the hip and top foundations together.

Draw Moderate Stretch, Very Stretchy, and Super Stretchy Front Side Seams
Figure 6.5

1. Draw the *front* side seams for each stretch category in ½" increments inside the minimal stretch side seam. Then use the hip curve to join the dash lines.
2. Do not draw the back side seam yet; you will do this in the following section.

Cut Slopers and Draw Back Side Seams
Now you can trace the slopers onto oak-tag and cut in each stretch category.

1. Cut the center front/back vertical line to separate the front and back slopers.
2. Trace and cut the minimal stretch front sloper onto oak-tag.
3. Cut the front moderate stretch sloper and trace onto oak-tag. Follow on to cut and trace the very stretchy and super stretchy slopers.

4. Place the front sloper onto the corresponding back sloper and draw the side seam so that they are exactly the same shape and length.
5. Trace and cut each sloper stretch category as you did for the front.

Trueing Seams
✓ Check that the front and back shoulder and side seams are equal lengths.
✓ Check that the front and back slopers have squared-off angles (see Figure 3.5 on p. 24).
✓ Check that underarms and armholes have smooth transitioning curved lines (see Figure 3.5 on p. 24).

Finalize Slopers
Figure 6.6

1. Write the pattern name "Front/Back Two-way Stretch Top Sloper (with Sleeves)" and document the stretch category on each sloper.
2. Write "CF/CB" on the sloper.
3. Draw the waistline and underarm, notch the armholes, and pierce the apex with an awl.
4. Record the codes as shown.
5. Measure each armhole length in preparation for drafting the sleeve slopers and record.

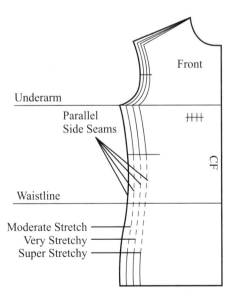

Figure 6.5 Draw moderate stretch, very stretchy, and super stretchy front side seams

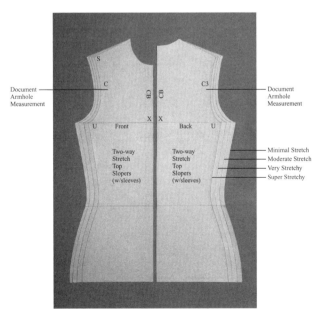

Figure 6.6 Front/back two-way stretch top slopers (with sleeves)

Drafting Two-way Stretch Long-Sleeve Sloper

The sleeve sloper must perfectly fit into the armholes and not look either tight or puckered. The sleeve must also hang correctly and feel comfortable when the garment is worn. Short, elbow, and three-quarter length sleeves can be drafted from the long-sleeve sloper.

Minimal Stretch

Figure 6.7a
Now draft the minimal stretch long-sleeve sloper from the front minimal stretch top sloper.

1. Cut a piece of pattern paper 3" longer than and twice as wide as the top sloper.
2. Fold the paper in half lengthwise.
3. Position the front minimal stretch top sloper onto the pattern paper with the (U) underarm/side seam placed on the folded edge.

4. Align the center front parallel to the folded edge. In some cases, the hip may go beyond the folded edge. Some dress forms (and bodies) have larger hips than bust.
5. Mark the shoulder and trace the *front* armhole.
6. Write the codes (S, C, and U) on the sloper outline.

Add Guide Marks/Guidelines

Figure 6.7b

1. X-S = Draw a squared line from (S) to the folded edge.
2. X-S1 = 1¼". Draw a ¼" squared line at (S1).
3. A = Halfway between (X-U). Draw a squared line beyond (C).
4. A-C1 = Mark the measurement according to the dress form size (Size 8 = ⅝", Size 10 = ¾", Size 12 = ⅞"). You may need to adjust this measurement (slightly wider or narrower) when the sleeve capline is drawn.

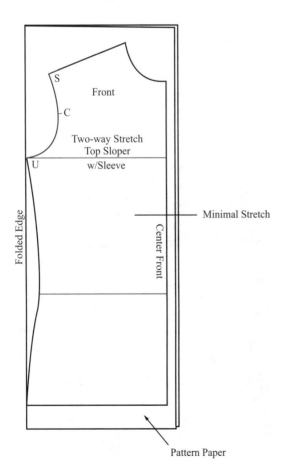

Figure 6.7a Draft minimal stretch

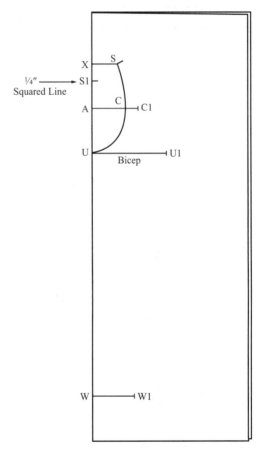

Figure 6.7b Add guide marks/guidelines

5. U-U1 = Bicep. Draw a squared line across the underarm. Mark half the total bicep length according to the dress form size (Size 8 = 10½", Size 10 = 11", Size 12 =11½").

6. S1-W = Sleeve length is 24" or to your own length. When you measure the length, the arm must be slightly bent (see Figure 5.5b on p. 70). Subtract the shoulder length to calculate the sleeve length.

7. W-W1 = Wrist length. Draw a squared line across wrist. Mark half the total length according to dress form size (Size 8 = 7¼" Size 10 = 7½", size 12 = 7¾").

Draw the Sleeve Capline and Under-sleeve Curve

Figure 6.7c

1. U1-W1 = Draw the underarm and extend (W1) 1/8" below the wrist.
2. Draw a ¼" squared-off angle at (U1 and W1).
3. Guideline = Halfway between U and W.
4. Elbow = 1" above the guideline.
5. Position a French curve at ¼" squared line (S1) and (C1). Draw the curved capline.
6. Position the French curve at (C1) and ¼" squared-off angle at (U1). Draw the under-sleeve curve. Reposition the French curve if you do not have a smooth connecting line at (C1) and redraw the curve.
7. W-W1 = Draw the hemline using the hip curve. (See Figure 6.7c.)

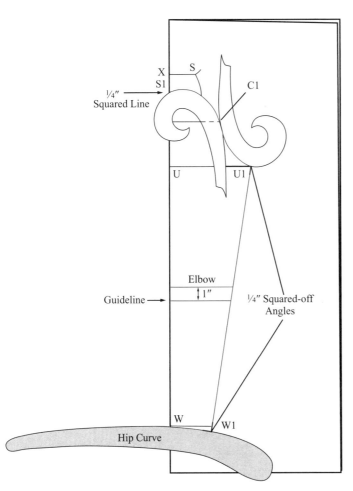

Figure 6.7c Draw the sleeve capline and under-sleeve curve

Align the Sleeve to the Armhole
Figure 6.8

Sleeves in knits *do not* need any cap ease due to the stretchability of the fabric. The sleeve will stitch beautifully into the armhole when the armhole/sleeve capline ratio is correct. If the capline length is too long for the armhole, the sleeve will look puckered when stitched. If the seam length is shorter than the armhole length, the sleeve will look tight when stitched. To determine the sleeve cap and front/back armhole ratio, you must measure the seamlines. The ratio calculates the difference between the two lengths.

1. Fold the pattern and trace to create the whole sleeve pattern.
2. Open the pattern and draw the grainline on the center of the sleeve. At this point, both sides of the sleeves are exactly the same. Mark a notch to indicate the front sleeve.
3. Compare the front/back armhole lengths to the sleeve cap length. To do this, you need the minimal stretch front and back armhole measurements recorded on the slopers in Figure 6.6. Measure from the sleeve underarm to the cap, and mark the front and back armhole lengths.

Correct Capline/Armhole Ratio
Figure 6.8

1. If the capline and armhole seam lengths are the same, they have the correct ratio.
2. If the capline has ½" excess length, this is *ease* that can remain in the cap.
3. Notch the sleeve cap. In Figure 5.27 on p. 82, the top foundation, across the back armhole, was widened by ¼". This shortened the back armhole length by ⅛" to ¼". Consequently, the cap notch must be moved toward the back sleeve to reflect this adjustment.
4. You can now cut, stitch, and fit the top on the form if the sleeve capline/armhole ratio is correct. If the sleeve/capline ratio is incorrect, refer to the next section to make the adjustment.

Incorrect Capline/Armhole Ratio
Figure 6.9

If there is excess length in the sleeve cap (with more than the recommended ½"), an adjustment is necessary. Choose one of the following methods to make the adjustment so that the sleeve fits perfectly into the armhole. After the adjustment has been made, remeasure the sleeve capline length and compare to the armhole length.

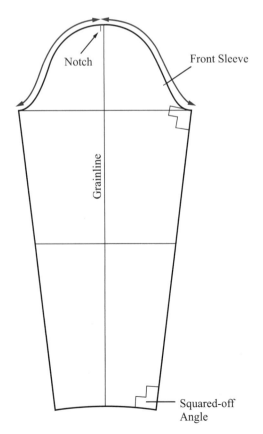

Figure 6.8 Correct capline/armhole ratio

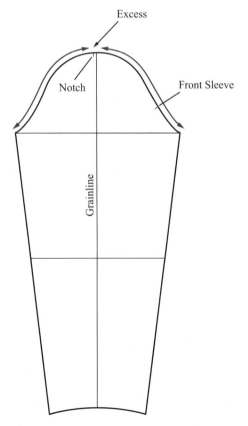

Figure 6.9 Incorrect capline/armhole ratio

Armhole Adjustment

Figure 6.10

Marking ⅟₁₆" to ⅛" increase/decrease to the shoulder height will increase the armhole length.

Capline/Bicep Adjustment

Figure 6.11

A capline/bicep adjustment will result in ¼" to ⅜" extra length in the sleeve capline. This adjustment can be done in the following ways:

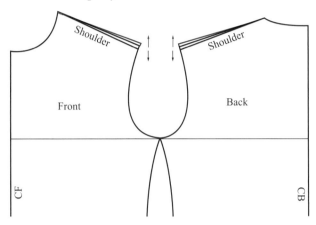

Figure 6.10 Armhole adjustment

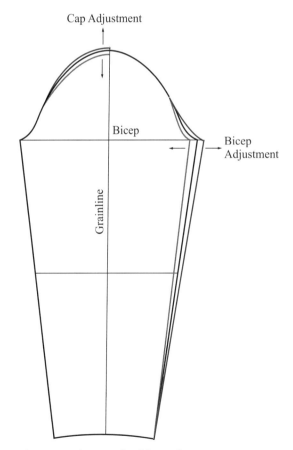

Figure 6.11 Sleeve capline/bicep adjustment

1. Mark ⅛" to increase or decrease the cap height. Use the sleeve sloper or a French curve to redraw the new capline.
2. Mark ⅛" equally on both sides of the bicep to extend or reduce the sleeve cap seam length.

Fabric You'll Need

Purchase 1½ yards of 58" to 70" wide light- to medium-weight minimal stretch knit fabric. Do not use a heavyweight double knit because it will be too bulky. It is important to do a stretch test using a stretch gauge, as shown in Figure 1.4.

Cut and Stitch

1. You can cut the top from double lengthwise folded fabric, as shown in Figure 4.10 on p. 53. (The layout is the same for short- or long-sleeve tops in plain or stripe fabric.) The top can also be cut from a single spread of fabric. (Refer to Figure 4.9 on p. 52.)
2. Add ¼" seam allowances to the shoulders, armholes, and side/underarm seams. (There is no need to add a seam allowance to the neckline or a hem allowance.)
3. Cross-mark the apex on the correct side of the muslin.
4. Stitch the muslin top following the stitching order in Table 6.1. Refer to Table 4.2 on p. 65 to see a variety of stretchable stitches. Serging the seams is the fastest stitching method. If you do not have a serger, stitch the seams with a crooked straight stitch.

STITCHING TIP 6.1: STITCHING ORDER

The **stitching order** refers to the steps involved to stitch a top following a logical order. Tables 6.1 and 6.2 outline how to stitch a sleeveless top, a top with set-in sleeves, and a top with raglan sleeves.

The shoulder seams are stitched and stabilized with clear elastic (see Figure 4.30 on p. 63). The sleeve is stitched into the armhole using the flat insertion method. This is the appropriate stitching method to use for stitching sleeves without cap ease. Place the top over the sleeve, pin underarms together, and pin the shoulder seam to the sleeve cap notch and carefully serged into the armhole. (If the sleeve has a small amount of ease, gently stretch the armhole as you serge to accommodate the ease.)

TABLE 6.1 Stitching order for sleeveless top and top with set-in sleeves

Step1 1. Stitch any style details to complete a garment piece before stitching the garment pieces together **Gathers**  **Placket** **Pockets and seams**	

Step 2 1. Stitch the shoulder seams 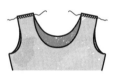	**Step 3** 1. Stitch the neckline finish so it's circular 2. Stitch the neckline finish to the neck edge **Suitable Finishes** 1. Rib Band 2. Binding 3. Narrow Facing 4. Turtleneck 5. Turned and Topstitched  *Go to Step 6 to stitch a sleeveless top*
Step 4—Top w/sleeves 1. Stitch the sleeves (*Stitched flat*) 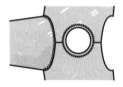	**Step 5** 1. Stitch side the seams (w/sleeves and sleeveless)  *Go to Step 7 to complete the top*
Step 6—Sleeveless Top 1. Stitch the armhole finish so it's circular 2. Stitch the armhole finish to armhole edge 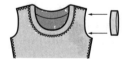	**Step 7** 1. Stitch the hem 

TABLE 6.2 Stitching order for top with raglan sleeves

Step 1
1. Stitch any style details to complete a garment piece before stitching the garment pieces together

Gathers	Pocket	Seams

Step 2	Step 3
1. Stitch the raglan sleeves to front and back garment 2. Turn the seams toward shoulders	1. Stitch the neckline finish so it's circular 2. Stitch the neckline finish to the neck edge
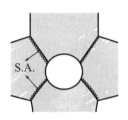	**Suitable Finishes** 1. Rib Band 2. Binding 3. Narrow Facing 4. Turtleneck 5. Turned and Topstitched 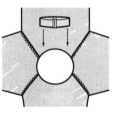

Step 4	Step 5
1. Stitch the side seam/and sleeve underseam from wrist to hem	1. Stitch the hems
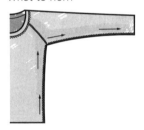	

Test the Fit

Figures 6.12a and b

Place the top on the dress form and review the fit. Also ask someone to wear the top to make sure the sleeves feel comfortable (i.e., the arms can bend and hands fit comfortably through the wrist opening). Pin any fitting adjustments as needed. Mark these adjustments on the sloper.

What to look for:

✓ Check that the top fits correctly; make sure that the waist is not too tight or too loose.

✓ Check that the apex is positioned correctly.

✓ Evaluate the hang of the sleeve. If the sleeve cap height is too short, drag lines will show from the underarm to the sleeve cap. To rectify this issue, increase the cap height (see Figure 6.11).

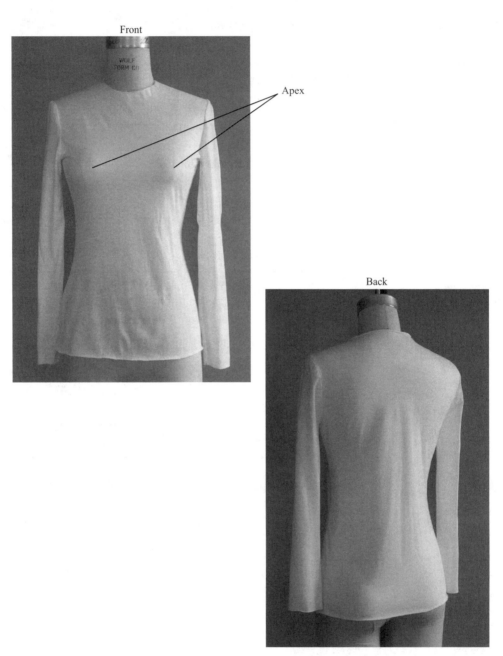

Figures 6.12a and b Two-way stretch muslin top (with sleeves) fitted on the form

Grading Two-way Stretch Long Sleeve into Stretch Categories

Now you can grade the long sleeves into each stretch category.

Long-sleeve Template

Figure 6.13a

A long-sleeve template is a half pattern made in *minimal stretch* and is used for grading the sleeve. Both sides of the sleeve are identical (only the cap notch differs). Once the sleeve grading is completed, you will trace each stretch category of sleeve and cut it in oak-tag.

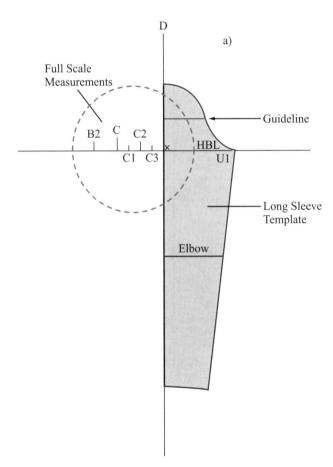

1. Trace and cut the minimal stretch half sleeve in oak-tag. (Refer to Figure 6.13a to see the oak-tag half sleeve.)
2. Draw HBL (bicep).
3. Label (X and U1).
4. Draw a guideline (squared at the grainline) halfway between HBL and the sleeve cap.
5. Write "Long-sleeve Template" on the pattern.

Prepare Grading Grid

Figure 6.13a

In Figure 6.13a, the grading measurements are marked on the grid for a full-scale grade. The sleeve template is ¼ scale. In Figure 6.13b, the grading measurements are marked on the grading grid for ¼ scale.

1. Draw the grading grid onto oak-tag.
2. Label (D) and mark grading increments (C3, C2, C1, C, and B2). (Refer to Table 3.4 on p. 37 for grading measurements.)

Minimal Stretch

Figure 6.13a

1. Place the sleeve template on vertical line (D) with HBL (X) placed on the horizontal line.
2. Trace the minimal stretch sleeve onto the grid.
3. Transfer the elbow.

Figure 6.13a Prepare the grading grid

Moderate Stretch

Figure 6.13b

The grading for moderate stretch, very stretchy, and super stretchy is done in a *negative* direction.

1. Move (X) on (C3) and draw the sleeve capline to the template guideline, mark the wrist, and draw the hemline.
2. Move (X) on (C2) and draw a squared-off angle at the underarm.

Very Stretchy and Super Stretchy

Figure 6.13c

1. Move (X) on (C2) and draw a very stretchy sleeve capline to the template guideline, mark the wrist, and draw the hemline.
2. Move (X) on (C) and draw a squared-off angle at the underarm.
3. Move (X) to (C1) and draw a super stretchy sleeve capline to the guideline, mark the wrist, and draw the hemline.
4. Move (X) to (B2) and draw a squared-off angle at the underarm.

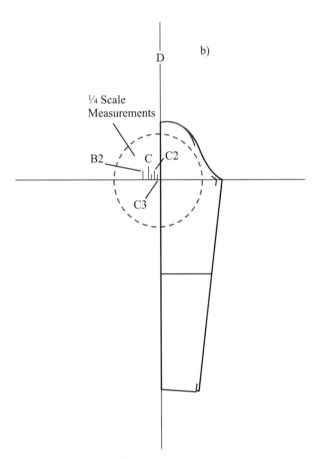

Figure 6.13b Grade moderate stretch

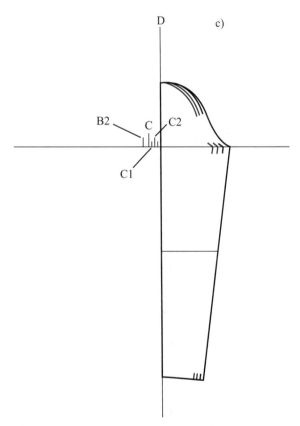

Figure 6.13c Grade very stretchy and super stretchy

Draw the Under-sleeve Curve

Figure 6.13d

1. Position the French curve at the guideline point and ¼" underarm mark.
2. Draw the under-sleeve curve for each stretch category.

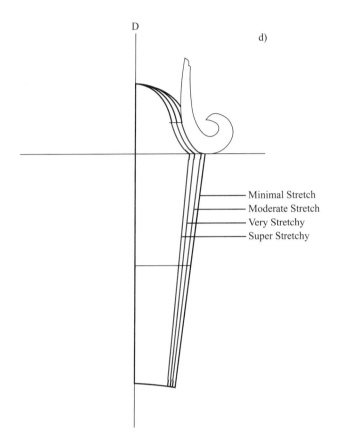

Figure 6.13d Draw the under-sleeve curve

Cut Slopers

Figure 6.14

Now you're ready to trace the sleeve sloper onto oak-tag.

1. Cut the minimal stretch half-sleeve.
2. Prepare a piece of oak-tag a few inches longer and wider than the entire sleeve.
3. Draw intersecting lines on oak-tag. The vertical line is the sleeve grainline.
4. Place the half-sleeve template on the vertical line with the elbow placed on the horizontal line. Trace both sides of the sleeve as shown. Cut and label the sleeve sloper. Notch the front sleeve.
5. Cut the moderate stretch half-sleeve and trace onto oak-tag as you did for minimal stretch. Repeat this process for very stretchy and super stretchy sleeve slopers.
6. You will notch the sleeve cap in the following section.

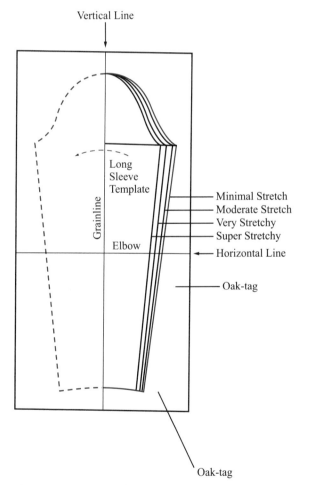

Figure 6.14 Cut sleeve slopers

Finalize Slopers

Figure 6.15

1. Stack the moderate stretch, very stretchy, and super stretchy sleeve slopers (largest to smallest). To do this, accurately line up all the grainlines, under-arms, and elbows.
2. Place the minimal stretch paper sleeve pattern on top of the graded sleeves with the grainline also aligned. Use pattern weights to keep the slopers stable.
3. Transfer the cap notch (with a tracing wheel) onto every sloper (mark in pencil only.)
4. Notch the front sleeves.
5. Measure the front and back sleeve capline *separately*, and document the measurement on each sloper. Compare the capline length to the armhole length for each stretch category. Adjust if necessary (refer to Figures 6.10 and 6.11). Then notch each sleeve cap.
6. Label each sloper and document the stretch capacity.

Reducing a Two-way Stretch Sleeve into Four-way Stretch

The next task is to reduce the two-way super stretchy sleeve in length and convert it into a four-way stretch sleeve for use in a bodysuit, leotard, or catsuit. The sleeve length from underarm to wrist is not reduced. You can adjust the arm length when the sleeve is fitted.

Mark the Reduction

Figure 6.16a

You reduce the length between the sleeve cap and bicep. This corresponds to the reduction (between the shoulder and underarm) of the two-way stretch top foundation in Figure 5.39a on p. 92. Here, you reduce the very stretchy and super stretchy sleeve slopers in length.

1. Trace the sleeve sloper onto pattern paper. Draw the bicep and elbow lines.
2. Draw a guideline midway between the sleeve cap and bicep.
3. Draw two horizontal lines ¼" on each side of the guideline. Label it "REDUCTION."

Figure 6.15 Two-way stretch long-sleeve slopers

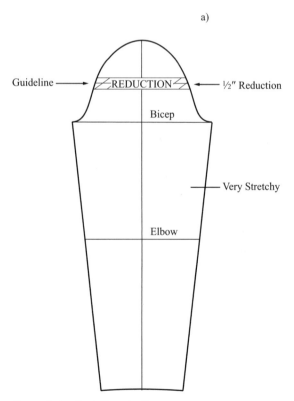

Figure 6.16a Mark the reduction

Fold the Reduction

Figure 6.16b

1. Fold "REDUCTION" by placing the horizontal lines together to reduce the sleeve cap length. Secure with masking tape.
2. Draw a blending capline and under-sleeve curve to equalize.

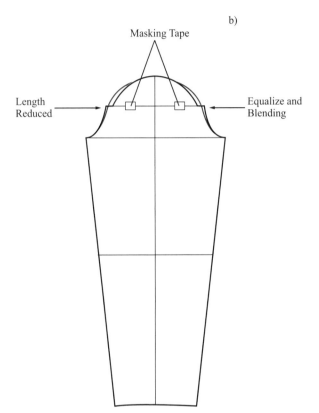

Figure 6.16b Fold the reduction

Align the Sleeve to the Armhole

1. Measure and record the front and back armhole lengths. Measure and record the front and back sleeve capline.
2. If there is a length discrepancy, an adjustment is necessary. (Figures 6.10 and 6.11 specify how to do this.)

Finalize the Slopers

Figure 6.17

To fit the sleeve, you must stitch it into the armhole of a four-way stretch garment such as a unitard (Chapter 10) or a bodysuit/leotard (Chapter 12) and then fit it. After fitting, you can transfer the paper sleeve pattern onto oak-tag.

1. Mark notches, record the stretch capacity, and draw the grainline.
2. Label the pattern as shown.

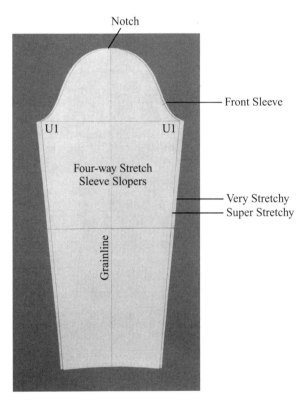

Figure 6.17 Four-way stretch long-sleeve slopers

Sleeveless Top Slopers

Next, you *raise* and *reduce* the armhole/underarm to change the top slopers (with sleeves) into sleeveless top slopers.

Minimal Stretch

Figure 6.18a

Use the same pattern drafting technique to change the minimal stretch, moderate stretch, very stretchy, and super stretchy slopers (with sleeves) into sleeveless slopers for sleeveless garments.

1. Draw intersecting lines on oak-tag.
2. Place the center front/back top slopers in each stretch category on each side of the vertical line with the underarm (U) placed on the horizontal line. Trace the slopers, draw the waistline, and crossmark the apex.
3. Draw a guideline ¼" above and parallel to the horizontal line.

4. On the front guideline, draw a short squared perpendicular guide mark up at (U).
5. On the guideline, mark ¼" in from the guide mark and label it (B).

Draw a New Side Seam and an Armhole
Figure 6.18b

1. Use the front sloper (with sleeves) to draw the new side seams. Place the sloper underarm (U) at (B) and the side seam just above the waistline of the sleeveless sloper. Draw the new side seam, blending it to the original side seam.
2. Make sure a squared line is drawn on the underarm at (B).
3. Line up the French curve at (B) and mid armhole, and draw the underarm curve.

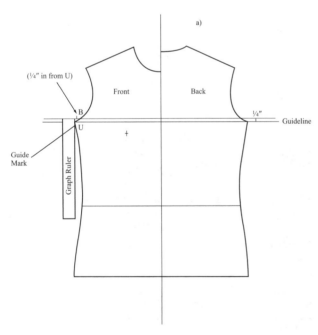

Figure 6.18a Trace slopers on the grid and draw a guideline

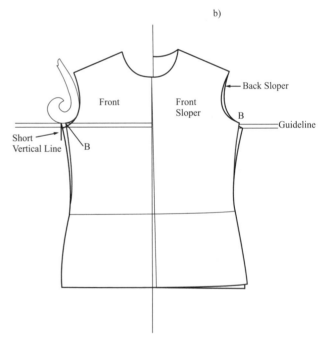

Figure 6.18b Draw a new side seam and an armhole

Test the Fit

Figures 6.19a and b

Cut and stitch the sleeveless top. Place it on the dress form and pin any fitting adjustments as needed to make the top fit correctly.

What to look for:

✓ Check the armholes; this should be the only adjustment. Do not be concerned if the armholes gape. When you stitch the armhole finish, the armholes will pull in.

The gaping armhole will "pull in" after the finish is stitched in place.

Front   Back

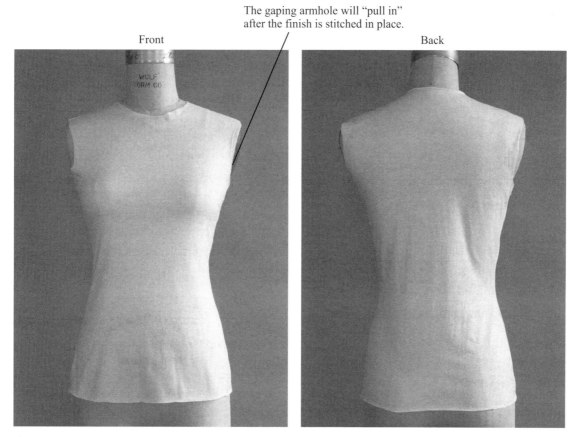

Figure 6.19a and b Sleeveless two-way stretch muslin top fitted on the form

Figure 6.20

1. Label the patterns as shown.
2. Draw the waistline and underarm line (U).
3. Pierce the apex with an awl.

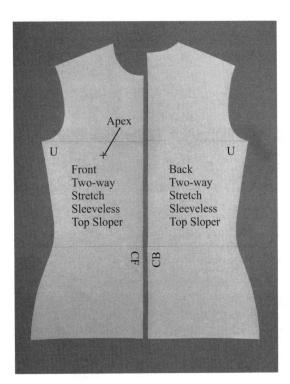

Figure 6.20 Two-way stretch front/back sleeveless top slopers

Sweater Slopers

Sweaters can be made from fine knits or bulky sweater knits. They can be *fitted*, *loose-fit*, or *oversized*; there is no rule to the dimensions of a sweater. You can use the top slopers to draft patterns for tightly fitted sweaters. However, the majority of sweaters have ease incorporated for a roomier fit. In Chapter 8, the two-way stretch top slopers are enlarged varying amounts and graded into sweater slopers. Follow the instructions outlined in the "Slopers for Cardigans, Sweaters, and Sweater-Jackets" section in Chapter 8 to draft fitted, loose-fit, or oversized slopers to match with the fit of your sweater design.

Pattern Drafting Tops

To pattern draft tops, begin by conducting a stretch test (see Figure 1.6 on p. 9). Next, choose the appropriate slopers. Even though a set of slopers is drafted to match each stretch category of knit, you can choose a different stretch category of sloper to fashion a more generous fit. (Refer to the "How to Choose Slopers" section in Chapter 2.) Table 2.3 on p. 18 demonstrates how you can use the minimal stretch slopers to draft the patterns for a top made from a super stretchy knit. (To find out more about this idea, refer to the section "Fit Flexibility: Adding Extra Room into Garments" in Chapter 2.) Also, you can use the sweater slopers (drafted in Chapter 8) to draft the patterns for a loose-fit or oversized top.

Begin by tracing the appropriate slopers onto pattern drafting paper in preparation for drafting the patterns. (For helpful pattern drafting tips, refer to Pattern Tip 3.1 in Chapter 3.)

Symmetrical and Asymmetrical Designs

A *symmetrical top* is identical on both sides of the garment (see Figures 6.1b, c, e, and g). When the design is symmetrical, trace *half* slopers onto pattern paper. Many of the pattern pieces will be labeled "Cut 1" and are cut on the fold of the fabric.

An *asymmetrical top* looks different on both sides of the garment (see Figure 6.1f). When the design is asymmetrical, trace *both sides* of the sloper onto pattern paper to make one complete front/back pattern. (This is the case even when a garment has a pocket on one side.) After finalizing the patterns, label right side up (R.S.U.) for layout instructions. (For more information, refer to Chapter 4, "Laying Out, Cutting, and Stitching Knits.")

Top Length Variations

Tops are worn on the upper body and can be varying lengths (see Figure 6.21). For example, a T-shirt can be cropped, high-hip, or torso length. A sweatshirt can also be cropped or torso length. A tank top can also vary in length. Variations include the following:

- *Midriff*—Above the waistline
- *Cropped*—Shoulder to waistline
- *High-hip*—Midway between waistline and hipline
- *Torso*—Shoulder to hipline
- *Tunic*—Thigh length

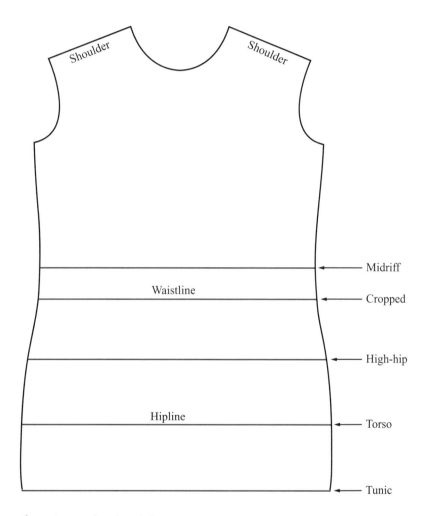

Figure 6.21 Top length variations

Neckline Variations

The top slopers have been drafted to contour the form neckline. Many popular necklines—for example, round, scoop, square, and V-shape—can be created from the base neckline of the top slopers (see Figures 6.22a through g).

When you sew a top, the neckline must have a finish stitched to the edge, such as a band, binding, narrow facing, or a turned and topstitched edge (or another type of finish). (The "Neckline Finishes" section later in this chapter discusses how to draft the patterns for finishes with stitching instructions.)

PATTERN TIP 6.1

As each pattern is drafted, align shoulder lines together and draw a blending neckline to round any angular line. (See Figures 6.23, 6.24, and 6.25.)

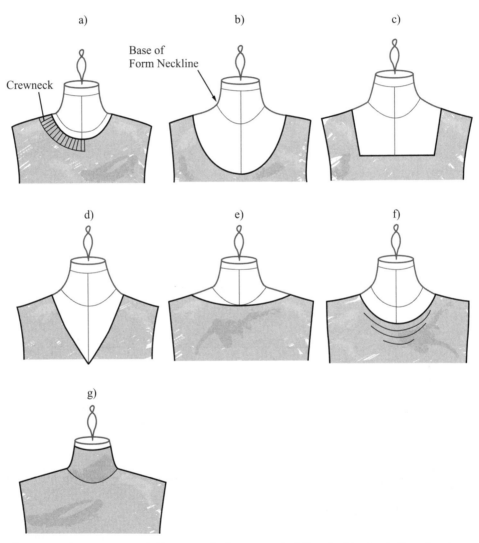

Figure 6.22 a) Round crew neck; **b)** scoop neck; **c)** square neck; **d)** V-neck; **e)** boatneck; **f)** cowl-neck; **g)** turtleneck

Round Crew Neck

Figure 6.23

For a round crew neck, the sloper neckline must be lowered on the center front so that the neckline opening fits comfortably over the head. (Refer to Figure 6.23 to draft the patterns.)

1. Lower/widen the neckline from the sloper neckline. At the center front/back, you must draw the outline from a squared line.

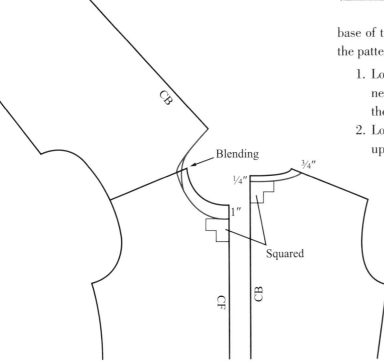

Figure 6.23 Draft a round crew neck

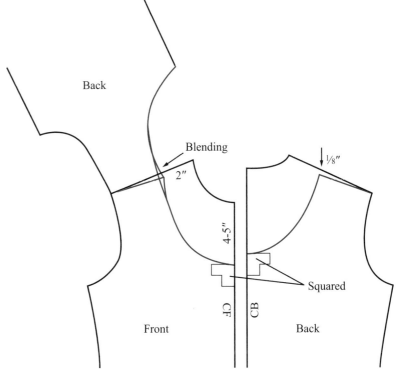

Scoop Neck

Figure 6.24

A scoop neck is a rounded low-cut neckline that is dropped 4" to 5" below the base of the form neckline. (Refer to Figure 6.24 to draft the patterns.)

1. Lower/widen the neckline as shown. The front neckline depth is lower than the back. You draw the center front/back from a squared line.
2. Lower the neckline/shoulder point ⅛" to tighten up the neckline. Redraw the shoulder seams.

Figure 6.24 Draft a scoop neck

Square Neck

Figure 6.25

A square neckline isn't technically a square, but it forms a square-like shape around the neckline. (Refer to Figure 6.25 to draft the patterns.)

1. Draw the neckline shape so the front neckline depth is approximately ½" lower than the back neckline.
2. Lower the neckline/shoulder point ⅛". Draw a new shoulder seam.

V-neck

Figure 6.26

A V-neck comes down to a point in the shape of the letter *V.*

1. Draw the front V-neckline (to the depth you require).
2. Draw a round back neckline.

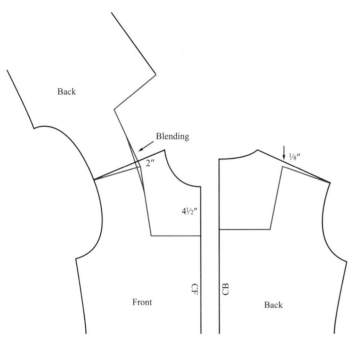

Figure 6.25 Draft a square neck

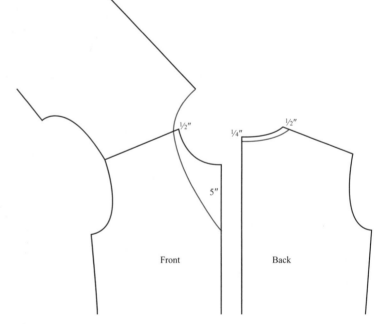

Figure 6.26 Draft a V-neck

Boatneck

Figure 6.27a and b

A boatneck is a wide neckline that runs horizontally following the curve of the collar bone. The width of the neckline can almost be at the shoulder point. (Refer to Figure 6.27a to draft the pattern.)

1. Do not raise the center front above the body's neckline because it will feel uncomfortable. Draw the back neckline from the shoulder point at right angles to the center back.

2. The neckline does not need trueing because it remains angled. Mark matchpoints (for stitching) at the neck/shoulder point (see Figure 6.27a).

3. Add a 1" facing to the neckline, and draw directional seamlines on the shoulder seams of the facing. Directional seamlines ensure that the facing, when turned back and topstitched, will lie flat underneath the neckline (see Figure 6.27b).

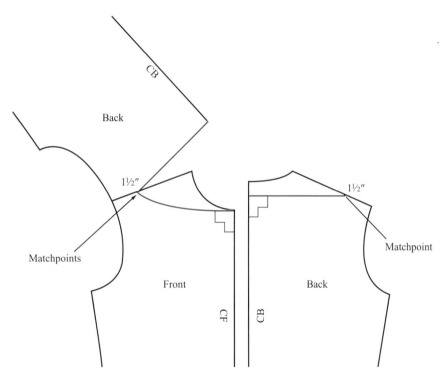

Figure 6.27a Draft a boatneck

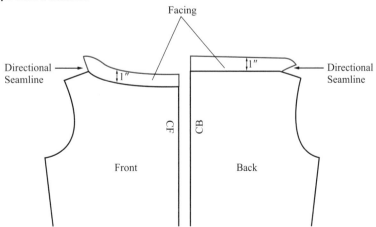

Figure 6.27b Add facings to the neck edge

1. Clip into the matchpoints on the back only.
2. Place correct sides of the top together.
3. Stitch the shoulder seam from the armhole to the matchpoint, clip into the front matchpoint, pivot and stitch the facing.
4. Press shoulder and facing seams open as shown in Figure 6.28.
5. Fold the facing to the wrong side and topstitched ½" to ¾" from the edge with straight stitches or with twin needles. (A wide neckline does not need to stretch, so straight stitches will not break.)

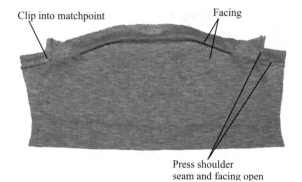

Figure 6.28 Stitching the boatneck shoulder/facing seam

Cowl-neck

Figure 6.29

A cowl-neck drapes beautifully when constructed from a lightweight knit. After the pattern is drafted, cut the front muslin to perfect the drape. In a knit, you can cut the cowl-neck pattern piece from fabric on the straight grain. (You can also cut it on the bias.) (Refer to Figure 6.29 to draft the patterns.)

1. Trace the front/back two-way stretch slopers and label (C) at the hem.
2. A and E = Mark neckline points on the shoulder line for medium or low-cut.
   - *Medium cowl-neck*—Position an L-square ruler on (A and C), and draw a right angle. Label (B).
   - *Low-cut cowl*—Position the L-square ruler on (E and G), and draw a right angle. Label (F).
3. Draw the back neckline.
4. C-D and G-D = Draw a squared hemline. Draw a back hemline at height (D).
5. Add a large facing beyond the neck edge. Fold the pattern paper along the neck edge, and trace the shoulder line and 3" of the armhole to form the facing. Draw a curved facing edge as shown.

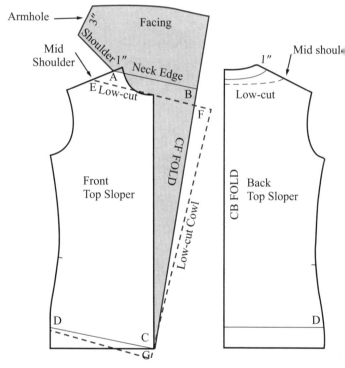

Figure 6.29 Draft a cowl-neck

Turtleneck

A turtleneck can be designed as a *single* or *double* turtleneck (see Figure 6.22g). A *single* turtleneck is one layer of fabric that can be cut as wide as 12". In a tissue-weight knit, this width scrunches beautifully around the neck. A *double* turtleneck is two layers of fabric. The finished width can be as narrow as 2" in a medium-weight knit or as wide as 8" in a lightweight knit. (Refer to Figure 6.30 to draft the patterns.)

1. Lower the neckline, as shown in Figure 6.23. Lowering the neckline prevents the collar from feeling too tight.
2. Measure the front and back neckline length, and double this measurement for the total length. The length must be approximately 18". The turtleneck opening needs to stretch to 22" (the average head circumference) to comfortably pull on over the head. To create a larger turtleneck opening, lower the neckline another ⅛" to ¼".
3. A-B-C-D = For the turtleneck pattern, draw a rectangle to the required width and length.
   - For a *single turtleneck*, add a 1" **edge allowance**. The edge allowance is for turning a folded edge.
   - For a *double* turtleneck, mark double the finished height of the band, and draw the foldline midway.
4. Add ¼" seam allowances, draw a grainline, and label the pattern.
5. Cut the turtleneck on the crosswise stretch of the fabric in the same way the next finish is cut in Figure 4.10 on p. 48.
6. Stitch a turtleneck sample and slip it on to make sure it glides easily over your head.

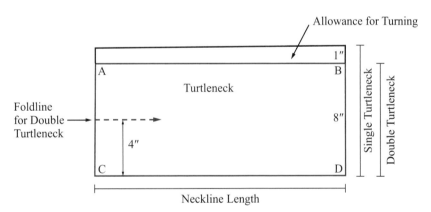

Figure 6.30 Draft the pattern

STITCHING TIP 6.3: STITCHING A SINGLE TURTLENECK

1. Fold the length of the turtleneck in half with correct sides together. Serge the seam and press to one side.
2. Press the 1" edge allowance to the wrong side, and topstitch with twin needles.
3. Quarter **pin-mark** the neckline opening into four equal sections.
4. Align the seam join to the shoulder seam, and serge the turtleneck to the neckline opening. (See Figure 6.58b.)

STITCHING TIP 6.4: STITCHING A DOUBLE TURTLENECK

1. Fold the length of the turtleneck in half with correct sides placed together, stitch a ¼" seam using a crooked straight stitch, and press open.
2. Fold the turtleneck with the neckline edges placed together.
3. Quarter pin-mark the neckline opening. Serge the turtleneck to the neckline.
4. The turtle neck in Figure 6.32 is wide enough to fold over into a 2" collar.

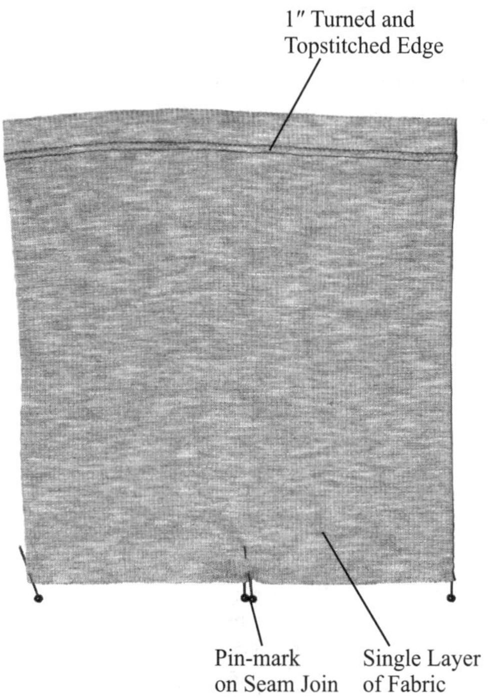

1" Turned and
Topstitched Edge

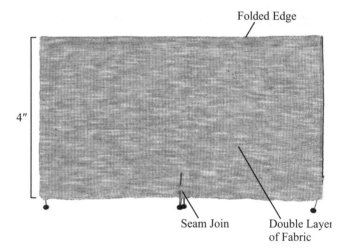

Folded Edge

4"

Seam Join

Double Layer
of Fabric

Figure 6.32 Stitching a double turtleneck

Pin-mark
on Seam Join

Single Layer
of Fabric

Figure 6.31 Stitching a single turtleneck

Silhouette Variations

Tops can have a variety of silhouettes. They can be straight, flared, gathered, tucked, or draped. One universal way to change the silhouette of a top pattern is to manipulate it using the slash/spread and slash/separate pattern drafting techniques. You can use these simple techniques to add width or length (fullness) to the pattern.

Flared

Figure 6.33a and b

A flared garment hangs beautifully when constructed from a knit with excellent drape.

1. Draft an A-line side seam; then draw the yoke line and slash lines (evenly spaced). Label the pattern (see Figure 6.33a).

PATTERN TIP 6.2: SLASH/SPREAD AND SLASH/SEPARATE PATTERN TECHNIQUES

The *slash/spread* pattern drafting technique adds fullness to *one* pattern edge to create volume and flare (see Figure 6.33b). The *slash/separate* pattern technique adds fullness to *both* pattern edges in equal or unequal proportions (see Figure 6.39b). (The fullness can be for flaring, gathering, tucking, or pleating.) You can slash and open the pattern at one or several points to evenly distribute the fullness. Finally, you can true the patterns by drawing a blending line to correct uneven line lengths and angular lines.

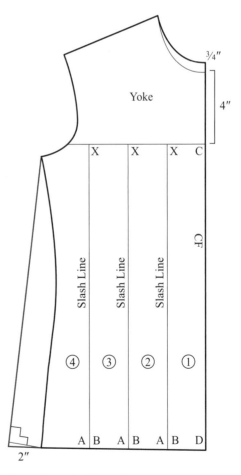

Figure 6.33a Draft the pattern

2. Slash/spread the pattern, as shown in Figure 6.33b.
3. Repeat these instructions to draft the back.

Circular

Figures 6.34 and 6.35
The top in this design has a circular hip piece. You use the same pattern drafting technique to draft a circle skirt.

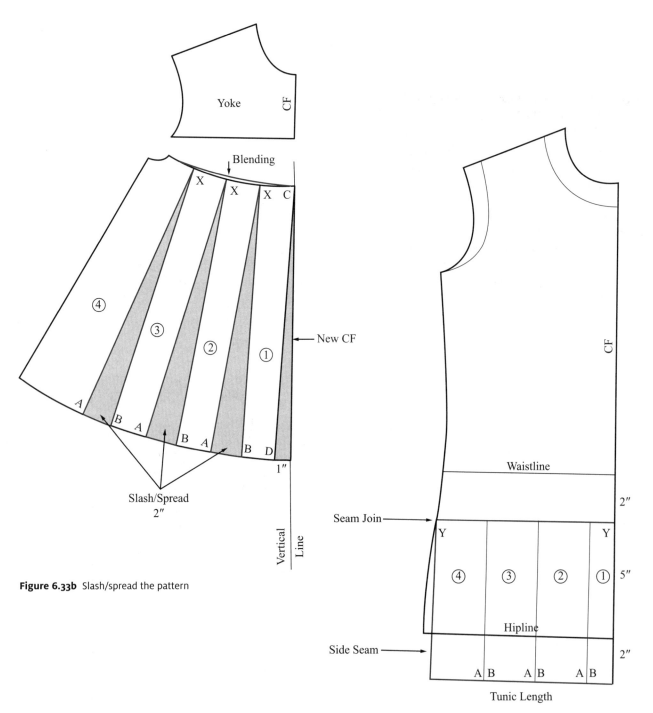

Figure 6.33b Slash/spread the pattern

Figure 6.34 Draft the pattern

1. Plot the front/back neckline, which is lowered ¾˝.
2. Plot the armholes, hem length (which in this case is tunic length), and the hipline (see Figure 6.34).
3. Slash/spread the pattern, as shown in Figure 6.35.

Finalize the Pattern

Figure 6.36

1. Fold the pattern paper along the CF and trace the other side of the circular pattern.
2. Repeat instructions to draft the back pattern.

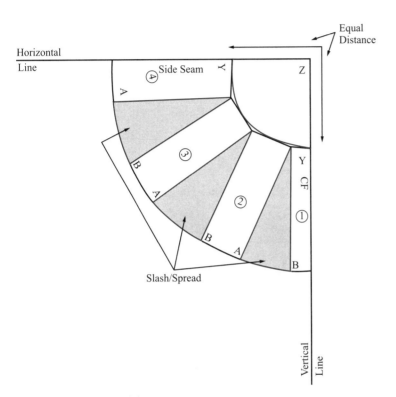

Figure 6.35 Slash/spread the pattern

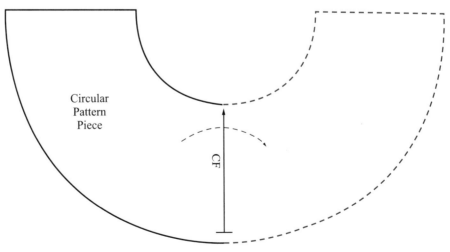

Figure 6.36 Finalize the pattern

Gathered

Tops with gathering are best constructed from soft knits with excellent drape. The top you draft in this section is the one shown in Figure 6.1e with the gathered neckline.

1. Draw the scoop neckline, as in Figure 6.24. Plot the armholes and hem length.
2. Mark the mid-neck point where gathering will begin.
3. Extend the CF neckline 1". Draw a squared line at (C) and connect to (D) (see Figure 6.37).
4. Slash/spread the pattern, as shown in Figure 6.38.

Draped

For the design of the asymmetrical draped top in Figure 6.1f, the drape is created from one gathered shoulder and side seam. To create the drape, you use the slash/separate technique and incorporate fullness (for gathering) into the pattern. This top would benefit from having a lining.

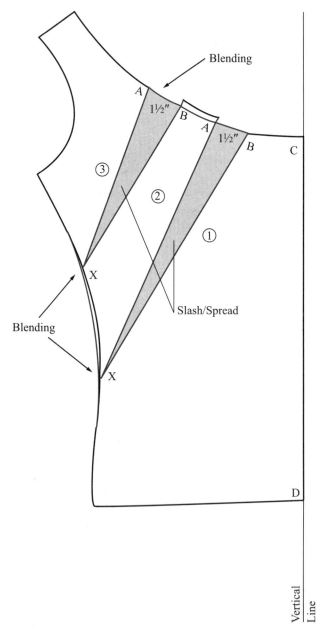

Figure 6.38 Slash/spread the pattern

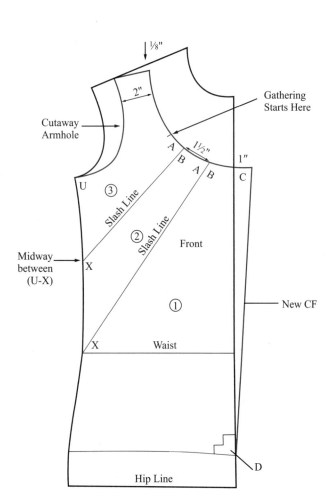

Figure 6.37 Drafting the gathered top

IMPORTANT 6.1: STYLE AND FABRIC

The draped top in Figure 6.1f *must* be made in a light-weight knit to be successful. It must be emphasized that this style will not be successful constructed in the wrong type or weight of knit.

1. Align the neckline of the front sloper (A-B) 19" out from the vertical line with (D) on the vertical line. Trace both sides of the sloper onto pattern paper.
2. Plot the silhouette, mark the waistline, and draw a new hemline.
3. Draw two slash lines from the shoulder to the side seam and label (see Figure 6.39a).

4. If the top is lined, trace another copy of the pattern and label it "Front Lining." (To stitch a lining, refer to Chapter 7.)
5. Draw a vertical line on pattern paper (see Figure 6.39b).
6. Align center front of panels 1, 2, and 3 on the vertical line as you separate each pattern piece and trace.
7. Draw smooth blending lines on the curved shoulder seam and side seam (see Figure 6.39b).
8. Mark notches for the length of gathering.

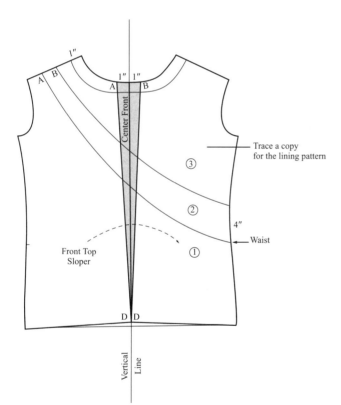

Figure 6.39a Draft the pattern

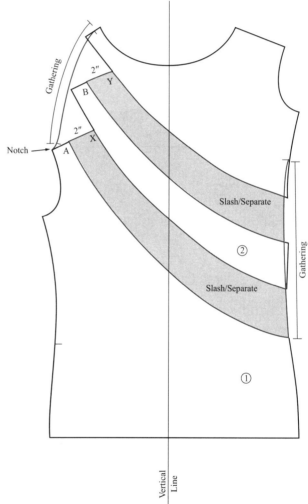

Figure 6.39b Slash/separate the pattern

Pattern Drafting Sleeves

Sleeves can be a separate component of the design or joined to the bodice and both components cut as one piece (see Figures 6.40a through i). You can design sleeves in a variety of lengths and in a variety of styles. All of these sleeves can be an element of a T-shirt, dress, sweater, cardigan, or jacket. Sleeves can also be dolman and loose fitting.

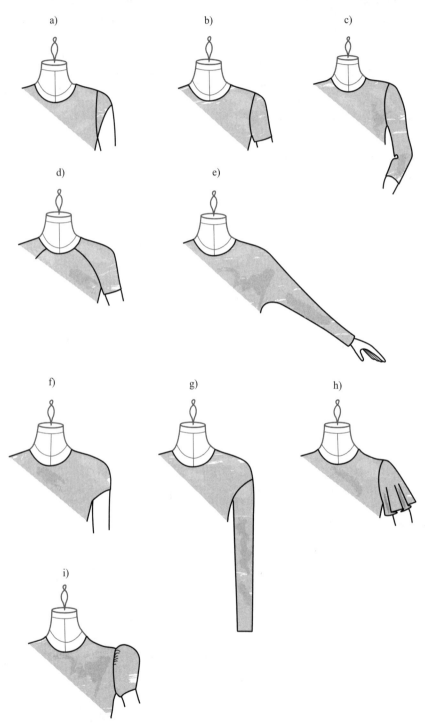

Figure 6.40 a) Cap sleeve; **b)** short set-in sleeve; **c)** three-quarter sleeve; **d)** raglan sleeve; **e)** dolman sleeve; **f)** dropped shoulder; **g)** dropped shoulder with sleeve; **h)** flared sleeve; **i)** puff sleeve

Sleeve Length Variations

Sleeves also can be designed in a variety of lengths. They can be wrist length, above or below the elbow, or anywhere in between. To draft the sleeves in this section, trace *half* of the sleeve on a piece of pattern paper large enough for the whole sleeve. Then draw the grainline and horizontal line (U1) where indicated. To complete the sleeve pattern, fold the pattern along the grainline, and trace to create the whole sleeve pattern. Finally, notch the sleeve cap and front sleeve.

Cap Sleeve

Figure 6.41
A cap sleeve is a small fitted sleeve that conforms to the shape of the upper arm. Refer to Figure 6.41 to draft the cap sleeve.

1. On the guideline, mark ¼" in from the sleeve underseam.
2. Mark 3½" for the sleeve length from cap to hem and 1" on the underseam.
3. Draw a curved hemline to the grainline.

Short Sleeve

Figure 6.42
The sleeve length can vary from 1" to above the elbow. Refer to Figure 6.42 to draft the short sleeves.

1. Draw the hemline parallel to (UI). Reduce ¼" and draw a curved hemline to the squared line at (S).
2. Add a 1" hem allowance parallel to the hemline.
3. Draw directional seamlines on the hem allowance on the underseam.

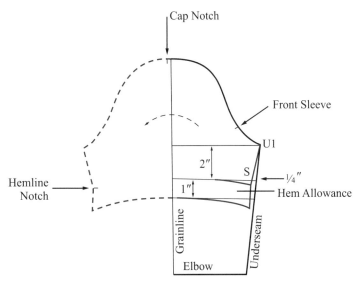

Figure 6.42 Draft a short sleeve

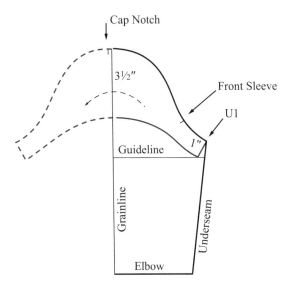

Figure 6.41 Draft a cap sleeve

Three-quarter Sleeve

Figure 6.43

A three-quarter length sleeve falls halfway between the elbow and wrist (see Figure 6.40c). Add a hem allowance (see Figure 6.43) following the same directions for adding a hem allowance to a short sleeve in Figure 6.42.

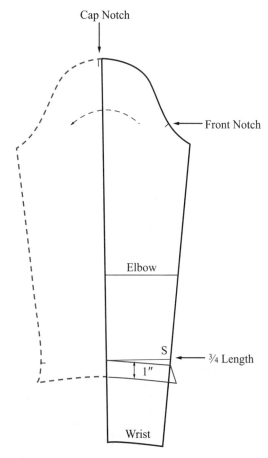

Figure 6.43 Draft a three-quarter length sleeve

Sleeve Variations

A sleeve can be set into the armhole, or it can be partly or fully combined with the front and back bodice.

Set-in Sleeves

A set-in sleeve is drafted to fit the armhole (armscye) of the top slopers (Figure 6.7). Examples include cap sleeve and flared or puff sleeves, as shown in Figures 6.40a, b, c, h, and i.

Based on the Stitching Order in Table 6.1, a set-in sleeve is stitched into the armhole while lying flat rather than stitched into a circular armhole.

Sleeve/Bodice Combination

A sleeve bodice/combination combines part or all of the sleeve with the bodice. Examples include the raglan sleeve, dolman sleeve, and dropped shoulder with sleeve, as shown in Figures 6.40d through g.

Raglan Sleeve

Figure 6.44a and 6.44b

Raglan sleeves are joined to diagonal seams on the bodice from the underarm (or armhole) to the neckline.

1. Trace the front sloper onto pattern paper. Align the back shoulder to the front shoulder and trace. Label (U) (see Figure 6.44a).
2. Draw the neckline and hem length.
3. A-C = Extend the shoulder line a few inches longer than the sleeve length.
4. Place the two-way stretch sleeve sloper underseam (U1) on the front/back underarms (U), and align the sleeve grainline on the (A-C) line. Trace the sleeve sloper.
5. Add the width of the sleeve cap overlap at (B) to the sleeve length, as shown in Figure 6.44a.
6. Draw raglan style lines from the neckline to the intersection (U-U1). Mark front and back notches.

7. Draw a curved sleeve underseam to the hemline (D) on the *front* only.
8. Fold the pattern along the sleeve grainline, and align the front/back underarms (U-U1) together. Trace the *front* sleeve underseam/side seam to the back pattern. The raglan seamlines at (X) must perfectly match together.
9. Trace each pattern, label, and mark notches.
10. Reshape the under-sleeve curve on each raglan seamline, as shown in Figure 6.44b.

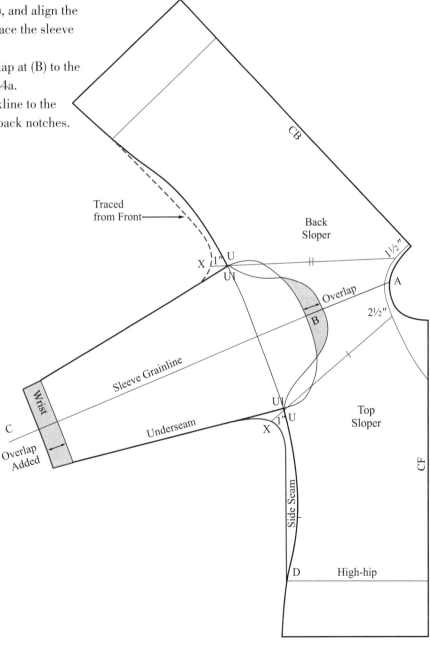

Figure 6.44a Draft a raglan sleeve

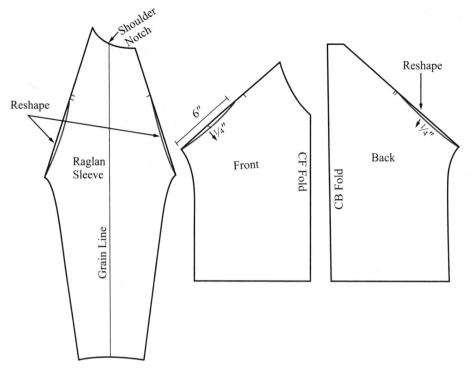

Figure 6.44b Trace patterns and reshape the under-sleeve curve

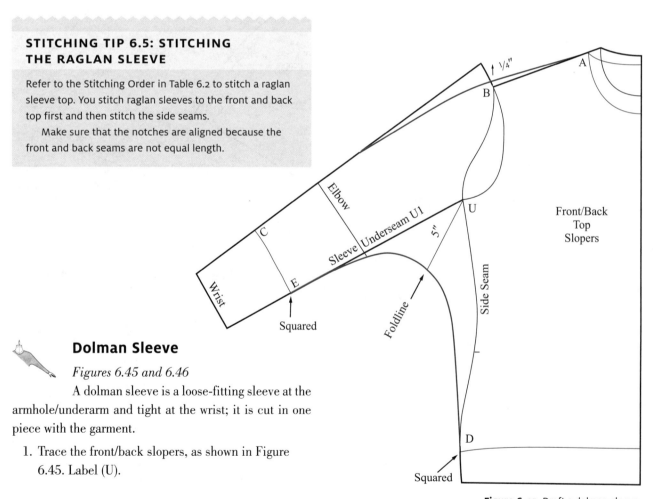

Dolman Sleeve

Figures 6.45 and 6.46

A dolman sleeve is a loose-fitting sleeve at the armhole/underarm and tight at the wrist; it is cut in one piece with the garment.

1. Trace the front/back slopers, as shown in Figure 6.45. Label (U).

Figure 6.45 Draft a dolman sleeve

2. Place the sleeve underarm (U1) to the top underarm (U) and align the sleeve cap to the shoulder. Trace the sloper. Outline the neckline, hem, and sleeve lengths. In this draft, the sleeve is ¾" length. Label (A-C-E-D).

3. Raise the shoulder tip ¼" and label (B).

4. Fold the pattern by placing the sleeve underseam and side seam together, and then crease a foldline. Mark a 5" length on the foldline.

5. E-D = Draw a curved sleeve underseam/side seam. Draw squared lines at (E and D).

6. For a more expansive sleeve, refer to the "Stop: What Do I Do If. . ." section.

7. Trace the pattern pieces, as shown in Figure 6.65.

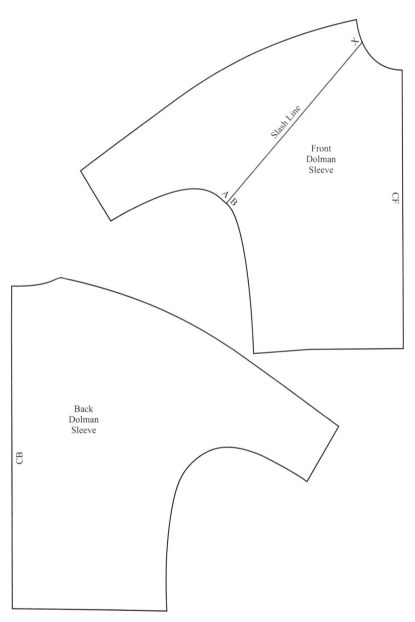

Figure 6.46 Trace and separate patterns and then slash/spread to expand the dolman sleeve

Dropped Shoulder

Figure 6.47

In the dropped shoulder style, the armholes of the garment are positioned on the upper arm rather than placed on the shoulder.

1. Trace the front/back slopers, as shown in Figure 6.47. Label (U).
2. Place the sleeve underarm (U1) to the top underarm (U), and align the sleeve cap to the shoulder. Trace the sloper.
3. Outline the neckline shape and hem length.
4. Mark the length of the dropped shoulder down from the sleeve cap. Label (C).

5. Raise the shoulder tip ¼". Label (B-C-E-D) = Draw the dropped shoulder line and curved side seam.
6. Trace the front/back and pattern pieces from the working patterns.

Dropped Shoulder with Sleeve

To further develop the dropped shoulder, you can add a sleeve. The sleeve can be short, three-quarters, or long.

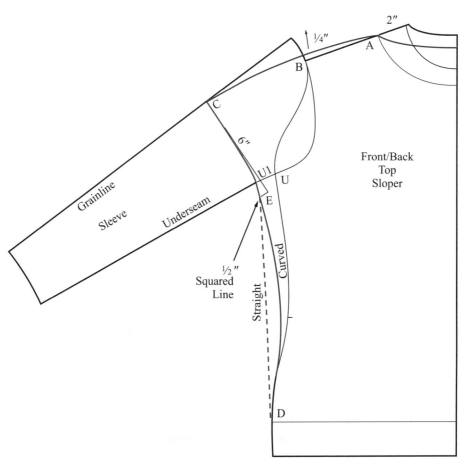

Figure 6.47 Draft a dropped shoulder

Draft the Pattern

Figure 6.48

1. Trace the "sleeve" section from the working pattern in Figure 6.48.
2. Fold a piece of pattern paper in half. Place the half sleeve grainline on the folded edge and cut a full sleeve pattern. Unfold the sleeve and notch the sleeve.

Silhouette Variations

Various sleeve designs can be drafted from the basic sleeve sloper. Two popular styles are puffed and flared sleeves.

Flared Sleeve

Figures 6.49a and 6.49b

A flared sleeve (at any length) adds fullness outward toward the bottom edge.

1. Trace the *half* sleeve pattern and draw line (U1).
2. Draw the hem length parallel to (U1).
3. Draw slash lines (evenly spaced) from the capline to the hem and label (see Figure 6.49a).
4. Slash/spread the pattern, as shown in Figure 6.49b.
5. Draw a blending capline to round any angular lines.
6. Fold the pattern in half along the grainline, and trace the pattern to create the entire sleeve pattern. Mark the cap and front sleeve notches.

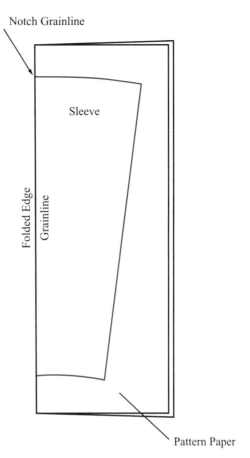

Figure 6.48 Draft the pattern

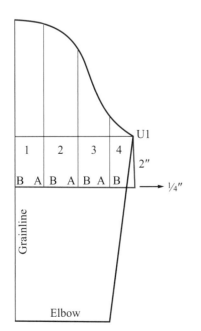

Figure 6.49a Draft a flared sleeve

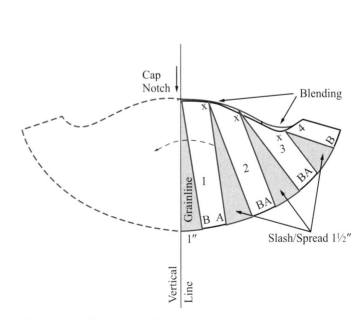

Figure 6.49b Slash/separate the pattern

Puff Sleeve

Figures 6.50a and 6.50b

A puff short sleeve is gathered at the capline to add roundness. The bottom edge of the sleeve can be fitted or gathered and joined to a band. A binding is also an ideal way to finish the sleeve edge.

1. Trace the *half* sleeve sloper and draw line (U1).
2. Draw the hemline parallel to (U1).
3. Reduce the top front/back shoulder length in from the armhole to accommodate the gathering. Draw the armhole curve, as shown in Figure 6.50a. Determine where the gathering will begin on the armhole and notch.

4. Draw two evenly spaced slash lines. (Draw one slash line from the armhole notch 4" around the under-sleeve curve.) Label the sleeve pattern.
5. Slash/spread the pattern, as shown in Figure 6.50b.
6. Raise the cap 2" and draw a blending capline and hemline.
7. Fold the pattern along the grainline, and trace to create the whole sleeve pattern.

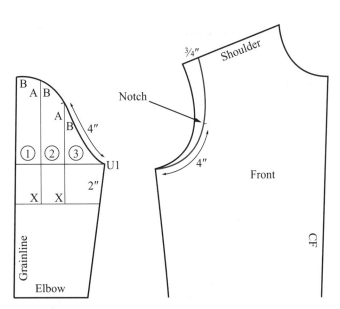

Figure 6.50a Draft the pattern

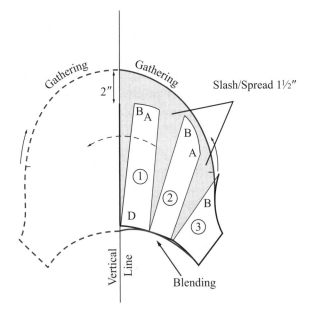

Figure 6.50b Slash/separate the pattern

Neckline Finishes

Numerous edge finishes can be stitched to the neckline openings of tops. An **edge finish** can be a strip of fabric, lace, or elastic stitched to a garment neckline (armholes or wrist) to finish the openings. All the finishes discussed here can also be stitched to the armhole wrist of a top, sweater, or cardigan; or to the hem edge. It is important that the neckline opening stretches adequately to fit over the head after the finish is applied. The edge finishes discussed in the following sections are bands, binding, a narrow facing, and a turned and topstitched edge (see Figures 6.51a through d). For the finish to be successful, you must draft the patterns accurately.

Length of Finish

To determine the length to cut the finish, first you must measure and record the seam length of the garment openings, where the finish will be stitched.

a)

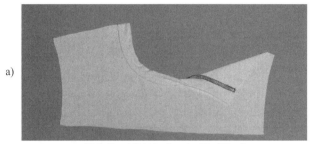

"Rib Band Stitched to the Neckline"

b)

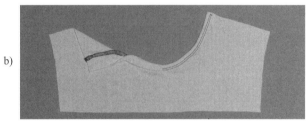

"Binding Stitched to the Neckline"

c)

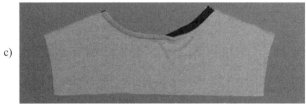

"Narrow Facing Stitched to the Neckline"

d)

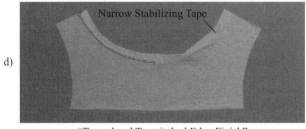

"Turned and Topstitched Edge Finish"

Figure 6.51 a) Rib band stitched to the neckline; **b)** binding stitched to the neckline; **c)** narrow facing stitched to the neckline; **d)** turned and topstitched edge stitched to the neckline

Measure the Seam Length

Figure 6.52

1. Measure the front and back patterns *on* the seamline; do not include the seam allowances in the measurement.
2. Double this measurement for the total seam length.

Reduce the Length

Figure 6.53

When you reduce the finish length, the shorter length (when stretched and stitched) changes to the neckline shape and lies flat after stitching.

1. Draw a line the total length of the seamline.
2. Reduce this length to determine the length of the finish. Reducing the length ensures that the finish sits nice and flat against the body after it is stitched.

3. There is *no set* measurement for reducing every type of finish because of the differences in the stretchability of the finish. In the section on each finish, you learn how to determine the length of the finish. You *must* then stitch the finish (as a sample) to the garment edge to fine-tune the reduction. In some cases, the finish is not reduced.

Divide the Garment Edge and Finish into Equal Sections

Before stitching the finish, you divide the garment openings (whether neckline, armhole, wrist, or hem) into equal sections that are defined by a pin-mark (or chaco-mark). The finish is also divided into equal sections. You then pin together the garment and finish markings and stitch the finish to the garment opening. This method provides uniform tension when the finish is stitched.

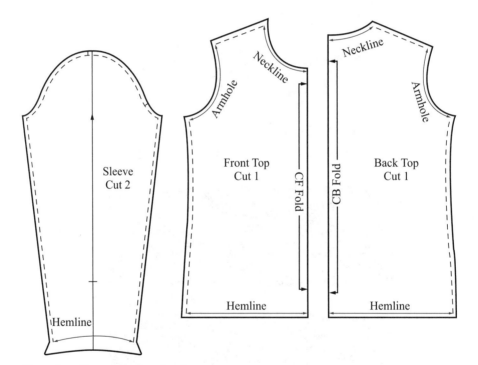

Figure 6.52 Measure the seam length

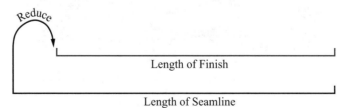

Figure 6.53 Reduce the length

Pin-mark the Neckline Opening into Equal Sections

Figure 6.54

In this step of the process, you divide the garment opening into fourths and pin-mark the divisions.

1. Stitch the shoulder seams.
2. Pin-mark *one* shoulder seam (1).
3. Fold the garment in half (with wrong sides together) at the pin-marked seam. Smooth the neckline so that it lies flat, and pin-mark the foldline (2).
4. Align two pin-marks (1 and 2) together and line up the neck edges. Pin-mark the other two foldlines (3 and 4). When the neckline is opened, the pin-marks are not symmetrical.

Bands (Rib Knit or Self Fabric)

Bands can be stitched to any shape neckline, whether round (crewneck), wide, scoop, or V-neck. Bands are also an excellent finish for armholes, wrists, and hem edges. Use a rib knit or self fabric with 50 percent more stretch than the original length. The patternmaking technique used to determine the length of the band pattern is the same principle whether the band is stitched to the neckline, armhole, or hem.

All bands are cut on the crosswise stretch of the fabric (see Figure 4.10 on p. 48).

Measure the Seam Length

Figure 6.55

1. Draw the neckline outline on the pattern.
2. Draw a second line, parallel to the outline, to indicate the width of the band.
3. Measure the length of the band seamline.

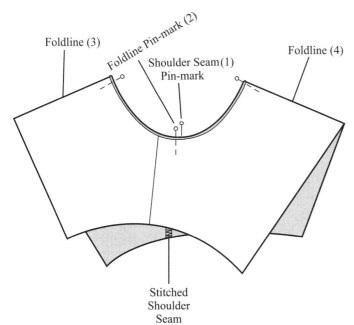

Figure 6.54 Pin-mark the neckline into equal sections

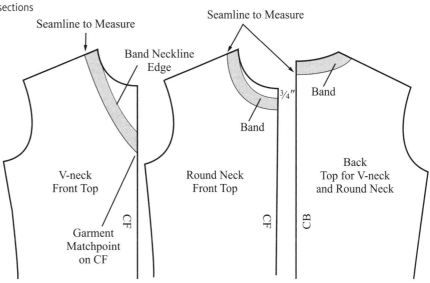

Figure 6.55 Measure the seam length

Draft a Band
Figure 6.56

1. Draw a line the *total* length of the seamline as shown.
2. Reduce length by $\frac{1}{7}$.[2] For example, if the seam length is 21", then divide by 7 (21" ÷ 7 = 3"). The band length would be 18" (or 21" − 3" = 18").
3. Decide on the finished width. Neckline and armhole bands are approximately ¾" to 1¼" when finished. Wrist and hem bands can be as wide as 4" to 5". Bands in lightweight knits can be as narrow as ½".
4. Double this width and add ¼" seam allowances, draw the grainline, and label the pattern, as shown in Figure 4.10 on p. 48.

Draft a V-neck Band
Figure 6.57

1. Draft the V-neckline following the pattern drafting steps in Figure 6.57.
2. Outline the width of the band on the pattern.
3. Draft the band pattern with an angled center front seam as shown. (Trace the center front V-neck from the pattern in Figure 6.26 to establish the angle on the band.)
4. Draw directional seams on the ¼" center front seams as indicated.

---

2   Keith Richardson, *Designing and Patternmaking for Stretch Fabrics* (New York: Fairchild Books, 2008), 71.

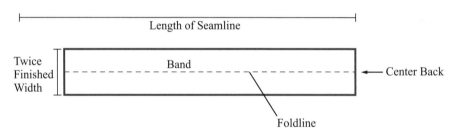

Figure 6.56 Draft a band

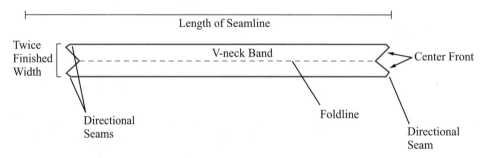

Figure 6.57 Draft a V-neck band

STITCHING TIP 6.6: STITCHING THE BAND TO A ROUND NECK

1. Join the seam and finger press open.
2. Fold the band in half with wrong sides together, and quarter pin-mark with one pin-mark on the seam (see Figure 6.58a).
3. Quarter pin-mark the neckline opening (see Figure 6.58b).
4. Slip the band inside the neckline opening with correct sides placed together. Align the band seam to one shoulder seam. Align remaining markings together, and pin the band to the neck opening (see Figure 6.58b).
5. With the band facing up, stitch the band to the opening. Stretch the band to fit between markings as you stitch (see the Stitching Order in Table 6.1).
6. Press the seam allowance toward the garment. The band can stay as it is or be topstitched.

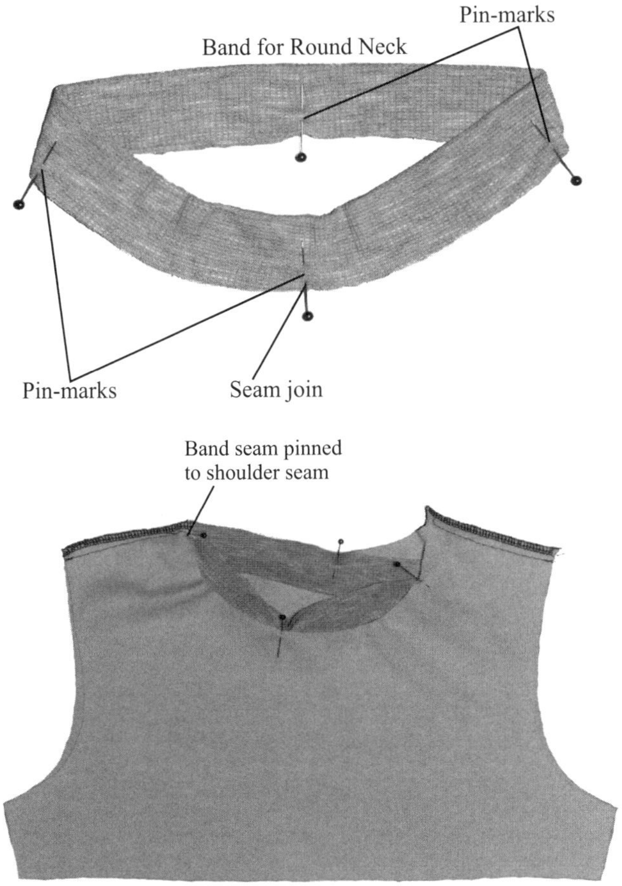

STITCHING TIP 6.7: STITCHING THE BAND TO A V-NECK

1. Join the seam and finger press open.
2. Fold the band in half with wrong sides together (see Figure 6.59a).
3. Quarter pin-mark the band with pin-marks on the center back and center front seam. Quarter pin-mark the neckline opening.
4. Slip the band over the neckline opening with correct sides placed together. Align the band seam to the center front. Align the remaining markings together, and pin the band to the neck opening (see Figure 6.59b).
5. Begin stitching from the center front and stitch to the center back; stretch the band to fit the garment edge between markings. Clip into the center front match-point. Stitch the other side of the band in the same way (see Figure 6.59b).

Pin-marks

Band for Round Neck

Pin-marks   Seam join

Band seam pinned to shoulder seam

Figures 6.58a and b Band for a round neck: cut, stitch, pin-mark the band, and pin to the neck opening

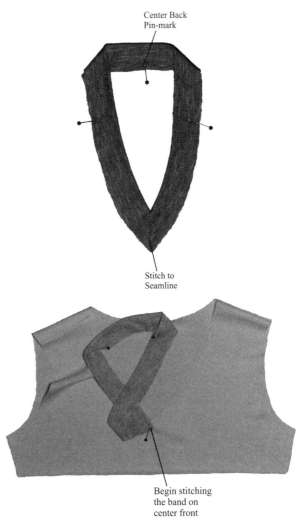

Center Back Pin-mark

Stitch to Seamline

Begin stitching the band on center front

Figures 6.59a and b Band for a V-neck: cut, stitch, pin-mark the band, and pin to the neck opening

Binding

A narrow binding is a popular finish for the neckline and armholes of casual everyday tops, dresses, and workout gear. Self fabric, contrasting fabric, or rib knit can be used for the binding.

The garment opening will have minimal stretch after a binding is applied. For that reason, the scoop neckline in Figure 6.1e is the perfect neckline opening for a binding. Use a lightweight fabric for the binding because it has two layers of fabric.

Draft the Front and Back Patterns

Figure 6.60

Seam allowance *is not* added to any pattern edge where a binding is applied because the binding encases the raw edge.

1. Draw the outline of the neckline on the pattern.
2. Draw a second line, parallel to the outline, to indicate the width of the binding. The finished width of the binding can be ¼", ⅜", or ½".
3. Measure the length of the second line (this is the stitching position of the binding).

Draft the Binding

Figure 6.61

1. Draw a line the *total* length of the seamline as shown.
2. Reduce the length according to the stretch of the knit being used for the binding:

- *Minimal stretch*—Reduce by ⅐ the total seamline length.
- *Moderate stretch*—Reduce by ⅙ the total seamline length.
- *Very stretchy*—Reduce by ⅕ the total seamline length.
- *Super stretchy*—Reduce by ¼ the seamline length.

3. Multiply the finished width of the binding by *four* and double this width. Then add ¼" *ease* for turning. For example, a ¼" finished binding will be cut 2¼" wide (¼" × 4 = 1" × 2 = 2" + ¼" = 2¼").
4. Add a ¼" seam allowance to each end of the binding for joining, and draw the grainline.

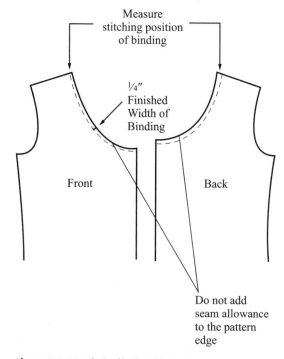

Figure 6.60 Draft the front and back patterns

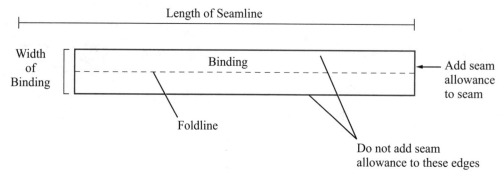

Figure 6.61 Draft the binding

5. Cut the binding on the crossgrain of two-way or four-way stretch knits, or for more stability, cut the binding on the lengthwise grain of a two-way stretch knit. The binding can also be cut on the crossgrain (see Figure 4.15 on p. 52).

STITCHING TIP 6.8: STITCHING THE BINDING

Refer to Figure 6.51b to stitch the binding.
1. Fold the binding in half with wrong sides together and press.
2. Place correct sides of the garment and binding together, align markings and pin.
3. With the binding facing up, stitch to the neck edge. The position to stitch the binding is the finished width of the binding.
4. Press the seam allowance toward the binding.
5. Fold the binding over the raw edge to the wrong side, pin, and topstitch from the correct side.

Narrow Facing

A narrow facing is used to finish raw edges of a neckline or the armholes. You can stitch the facing to the *entire* neckline or to *part* of the neckline. The facing is cut from a narrow strip of lightweight knit; bias-cut woven fabric or bias binding also can be used. The polo top in Figure 6.1g has a narrow facing stitched to the back neckline.

Draft the Facing
Figure 6.62

1. Draw the neckline/armhole outline on the pattern. Add ¼" seam allowances to these edges for stitching the facing.
2. Measure the length of the seamlines where the facing will be applied.
3. Draft the facing pattern 1¼" wide and the total length of the neckline.
4. You *do not* need to reduce the length of the facing.
5. Add ¼" extra seam allowance to both ends of the facing.

STITCHING TIP 6.9: STITCHING THE NARROW FACING

Refer to Figure 6.51c to stitch the narrow facing.
1. Fold the facing in half with wrong sides together and lengthwise edges aligned and then press.
2. Place correct sides of the garment and facing together and stitch a ¼" seam.
3. Turn the facing inside the garment, understitched and topstitched.

Figure 6.62 Draft the facing

Turned and Topstitched

Turned and topstitched is a versatile and simple edge finish to use on necklines, armholes, and hems.

Draft the Patterns

Figure 6.63

1. Draw the outline of the garment on the pattern.
2. Add a ½" edge allowance beyond the seamline for turning the folded edge.
3. Draw directional seamlines at the armhole/shoulder, neckline/shoulder, and armhole/underarm points.

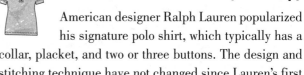

Collar and Box Placket (Polo Top)

American designer Ralph Lauren popularized his signature polo shirt, which typically has a collar, placket, and two or three buttons. The design and stitching technique have not changed since Lauren's first men's polo shirt was produced in 1972.[3]

To stitch a placket, you need to cut away (or slit) a section to allow space for the placket to be stitched (see Figure 6.1g). The amount to cut away on the center front is determined by the width of the placket.

---

3 The Cut, "Ralph Lauren," accessed October 28, 2014, http://nymag .com/fashion/fashionshows/designers/bios/ralphlauren/

STITCHING TIP 6.10: STITCHING THE TURNED AND TOPSTITCHED EDGE

Refer to Figure 6.51d to stitch the turned and topstitched edge.

1. Press narrow stabilizing tape cut from four-way stretch knit interfacing to the neckline for stability. Then join the shoulder seams, but do not serge the neck edge.
2. Press the allowance to the wrong side, stretching as you press so that the turning lies flat. If the fabric is springy, loosely hand baste the turning and then press.
3. Topstitch the edge with narrow (2.00–2.5) twin needles. Begin stitching on a seamline.

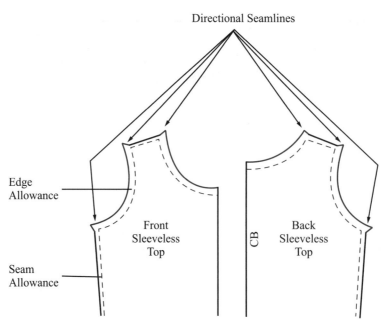

Figure 6.63 Draft the pattern

Draft a Cutaway Section and Placket

Figures 6.64a, b, and c

1. Draw the placket *width* and *length* on the front pattern.
2. Add a ¼" seam allowance to the three edges of the placket. Notice the cutaway section on the front pattern in Figure 6.64a.
3. Fold a piece of pattern paper in half, and trace the placket outline from the folded edge of the paper. Add ¼" seam allowances (see Figure 6.64b).
4. Open the pattern, label and document the number of pieces to cut, draw the grainline on the foldline, and indicate matchpoints (see Figure 6.64c).
5. Draft the collar pattern.

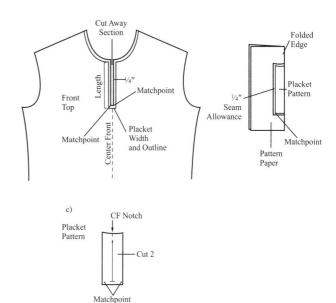

Figures 6.64a, b, and c Draft a cutaway section and placket

Knit It Together

This checklist summarizes what you have learned about drafting the top slopers and patterns in this chapter.

- ✓ The hip and top foundations are the base of forming the top slopers.
- ✓ The hip and top foundations in each stretch category are used to draft the top slopers in each stretch category.
- ✓ A sleeve sloper is drafted to fit the armholes of the top slopers.
- ✓ The sleeveless top slopers are developed from the top slopers with sleeves.
- ✓ The neckline finishes can be stitched to the armhole, wrist, or hemline.
- ✓ In nearly all cases, the length of the neckline finish must be cut shorter than the neckline it is stitched to.

Stop: What Do I Do If . . .

. . . the top I've designed with a dropped shoulder has a band like the polo top in Figure 6.1g? How do I draft the pattern?

A band or turned-back cuff can be stitched to the edge of the sleeve opening. For the *band*, draft the pattern twice the finished band width. For the *turned-back cuff*, draft the pattern four times the finished band width.

. . . the dolman sleeve pattern under the arm does not have enough length?

Slash/spread the pattern for a more expansive sleeve. Refer to Figure 6.46 to draw the slash line. Refer to Figure 6.65 to slash/spread the pattern.

Self-Critique

1. How are the top slopers formed?
2. Does the sloper sleeve cap need ease?
3. How important is it to have the sleeve capline and armhole seamlines the correct length ratio?
4. If the sleeve capline/armhole ratio is *incorrect*, how would you correct the patterns?
5. What pattern drafting techniques are used to change the silhouette of the slopers to create a new design? Explain these drafting techniques.
6. For the finish to lie flat around the neckline or armhole after it is stitched, the pattern must be drafted the correct length. How do you determine the length of the finish?
7. How do you stitch a rib band to the neckline of a top?

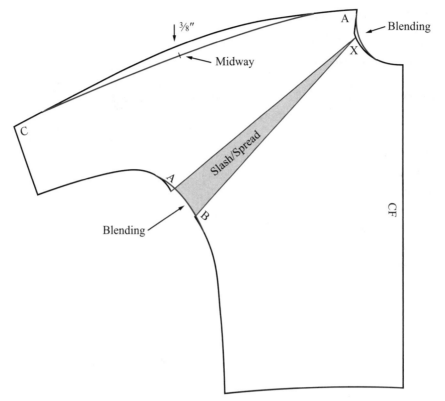

Figure 6.65 Slash/spread the pattern

8. How would you draft a flounce pattern to add to the three-quarter length sleeve in Figure 6.40c?
9. The polo top in Figure 6.1g has a narrow facing stitched as the neckline finish. What other styles in Figure 6.1 could also have a narrow neckline facing? (Keep in mind that the facing does not have a lot of stretch when completed.)

Key Terms	Master Sloper	Pin-mark	Very Stretchy Slopers
Edge Allowance	Minimal Stretch Slopers	Stitching Order	
Edge Finish	Moderate Stretch Slopers	Super Stretchy Slopers	

7 Dress Slopers and Patterns

In 1970, Diane von Furstenberg arrived in New York and began designing jersey wrap dresses for women. Her dresses left an imprint on the fashion world because stretchable dresses are versatile and comfortable.[1] Nowadays a jersey knit dress can be a great suit alternative when paired with the right complementary garment.

Stretch knit dresses also look sophisticated worn for an evening out; they are perfect to wear for every occasion.

This chapter outlines how to draft a "dress-piece." The top slopers, when combined with the dress-piece, create the dress slopers. From the dress slopers, you can draft numerous dress patterns. Halter, strapless, one-shoulder, princess line, and classic wrap dress patterns are covered in this chapter (see Figure 7.1).

1 DVF, accessed November 14, 2014, http://www.dvf.com/timeline-70s.html.

Figure 7.1 a) Tank dress with princess style lines; **b)** halter dress; **c)** strapless dress; **d)** wrap dress; **e)** blouson dress with casings; **f)** draped one-shoulder asymmetrical dress; and **g)** lined shift

Drafting the Dress-piece

A **dress-piece** is a partial pattern extending from the hipline to knee length in each stretch category. Table 2.2 on p. 17 indicates that dresses are drafted from the top slopers. You add the dress-piece to the hipline of the top slopers to create the dress slopers.

> ### PATTERN TIP 7.1: CHOOSING THE SLOPERS
>
> Before choosing the stretch category of sloper to use, begin by conducting a stretch test (using the stretch gauge in Figure 1.6 on p. 9). The test determines the "stretchiness" of a particular knit. There are two ways you can choose the slopers. Refer to "How to Choose Slopers" in Chapter 2 to learn more about the methods for choosing slopers. Furthermore, you can enlarge the slopers for a more generous fit. Figures 8.8, 8.9, and 8.10 demonstrate how to grade the minimal stretch top slopers into fitted and loose-fit cardigan and sweater slopers. These generous-sized slopers can also be used to draft dress patterns.

Minimal Stretch

Figure 7.2

1. Trace the minimal stretch hip foundation onto oak-tag.
2. Mark waist to knee length (22") or to your own length: short = 16" and above knee = 19". Label (L).
3. At (L), draw a squared line (parallel to the *hipline*) equal to (H-H1). Label it "Hemline."
4. H1-L1—draw a straight line for the side seam.
5. Label "CF/CB."

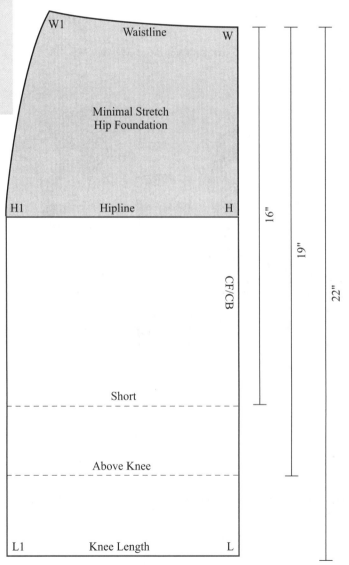

Figure 7.2 Draft minimal stretch

Moderate Stretch, Very Stretchy, and Super Stretchy

Figure 7.3

1. Place the hip foundations for each stretch category on the hipline of the minimal stretch dress-piece. Mark each side seam. (Refer to Figure 5.15 on p. 77 to see the hip foundation stretch categories.)
2. At (L1), mark ½" increments for each stretch category.
3. H1-L1—draw straight lines for the side seams for each stretch category.

Finalize the Dress-piece

Figure 7.3

1. Cut the minimal stretch dress-piece and trace onto oak-tag.
2. Cut and trace the other dress-pieces in each stretch category.
3. Write the pattern name "Dress-piece" and document the stretch category on each pattern.
4. Indicate "CF/CB" on each dress-piece.

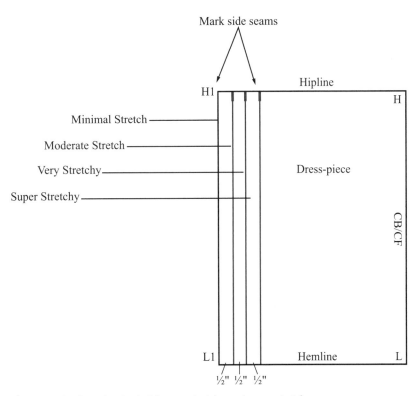

Figure 7.3 Draft moderate stretch, very stretchy, and super stretchy

Pattern Drafting Dresses

The dress-piece and the two-way stretch top slopers are joined on the hipline to form the dress slopers (see Figure 7.4). Dress slopers with bust and elbow darts (for sleeves) may be necessary for drafting patterns for dresses constructed from a double knit with minimal stretch. Unappealing folds become visible under the arms when a knit does not have adequate stretch to fit smoothly over the bustline. Chapter 8 outlines how to adapt slopers for woven fabric into stretch knit slopers.

Dresses can be constructed from two-way and four-way stretch knits. Most dresses do not require the lengthwise stretch; however, having it will not affect the fit of the dress.

Symmetrical and Asymmetrical Patterns

Whether a dress is symmetrical or asymmetrical influences how you draft and label the patterns. *Symmetrical patterns* can be drafted as half pattern pieces because both sides of the garment are the same (see Figure 3.12 on p. 31). *Asymmetrical patterns* are drafted as full pattern pieces for both sides of the garment. The patterns are labeled right side up (R.S.U.) so that they are placed on the fabric correctly, according to the asymmetrical design (see Figure 3.13 on p. 32).

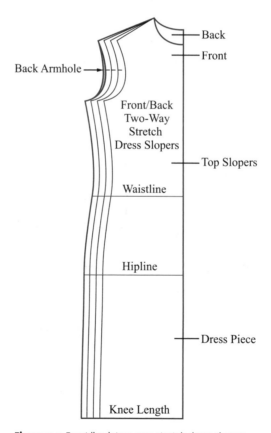

Figure 7.4 Front/back two-way stretch dress slopers

Length Variations

Dresses (and skirts) can be cut at various lengths (see Figure 7.5):

- *Mini*—Very short mid-thigh hemline
- *Short*—Above knee (falls anywhere between mini and knee length)
- *Knee*—Middle of knee
- *Midi*—Mid-calf length
- *Calf*—Point between knee and ankle
- *Maxi*—Anywhere between mid-calf and ankle length
- *Ankle*—A few inches above the floor
- *Asymmetrical hem*—Hemline cut longer on one side than the other

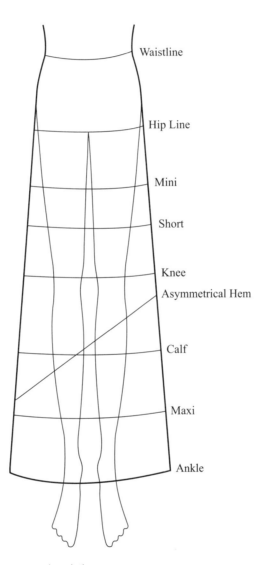

Figure 7.5 Length variations

Silhouette Variations with Design Lines

Dresses can have a variety of neckline shapes, which are illustrated in Figure 7.1. Refer to Figure 6.22 on p. 116 to see other neckline variations. Dresses also can be sleeveless or have set-in raglan or dolman sleeves. They may have the following silhouette variations (see Figure 7.6):

- *Sleeveless*—This garment has no sleeves. The armholes can be cut low on the underarm or cut away on the shoulders to create wide shoulder straps.
- *A-line*—The side seam gradually points out from the hip to the hem. The silhouette resembles the letter *A*.
- *Pegged*—The side seam gradually narrows from the hip to the hemline.
- *Flared*—Fullness is added, which spreads the side seams outward toward the hemline of the garment.
- *Empire waist*—The waistline sits below the bustline and above the natural waistline.
- *Waist*—The waistline sits on the natural waistline.
- *Drop waist*—The waistline falls below the natural waistline.
- *No definite waistline*—The garment is loose fitting around the waist.
- *Princess line*—Vertical seamlines extend from the armhole or shoulder to the hemline.

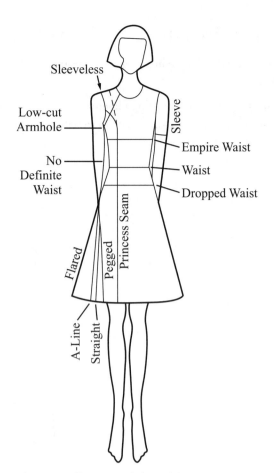

Figure 7.6 Silhouette variations with design lines

Sleeveless Tank Dress

A **tank dress** is sleeveless with a low neckline and wide shoulder straps (see Figure 7.1a). In this draft, the silhouette of the dress is a slim, close-fitting **sheath** with pegged side seams to create a svelte fit.

Draft the Patterns

Figure 7.7a

In this section, you draft a basic tank dress. Later in the chapter, you draft a tank dress with princess style lines. Front and back patterns are drafted from the front sloper.

1. Trace the *front* dress sloper in the appropriate stretch category onto pattern paper.
2. Mark a short guideline at (C) on the front armhole. (Refer to the top foundation in Figure 5.31 on p. 85.)
3. Adjust into a sleeveless sloper, as shown in Figures 6.18a and b on pp. 112.
4. Draw an underarm line (U) as a guide for the neckline depth.

Front

Figure 7.7a

1. D = Mark the front neckline depth.
2. B = Mark the position of the neckline on the shoulder. Lower this point ⅛".
3. B-D = Draw an angled guideline to facilitate the "U" shape. Draw the front neckline.
4. A-B = Mark the shoulder width and draw a shoulder line.
5. A-C-U = Draw an armhole parallel to the neckline shape to create shoulder straps and curve to the underarm (U).
6. Measure ¾" in from the side seam/hemline point. Draw a new side seam with a squared-off angle at the hemline.

Back

Figure 7.7b

1. D-E = Mark the back neckline 1" higher than the front neckline.
2. B-E = Draw the back neckline.
3. C1 = Mark the *back* armhole ¼" wider than the front armhole (C).
4. A-C1-U = Draw the back armhole and curve to the underarm (U).

Finalize the Patterns

1. (U-C-A-B-D) = Trace the *front* pattern.
2. (U-C1-A-B-E) = Trace the *back* pattern.
3. Align front and back shoulder lines together and draw a smooth blending neckline. (Figure 6.24 illustrates how to round an angular shoulder line.)

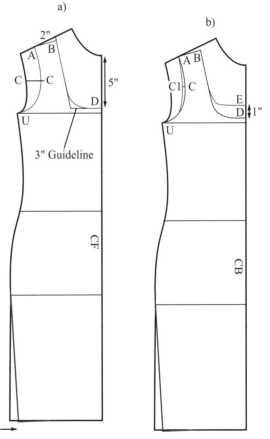

Figure 7.7a Draft a front tank dress

Figure 7.7b Draft a back tank dress

Halter

A **halter** dress leaves the arms, shoulders, and back of the garment bare. The garment is held in place by straps that tie around the back neckline, as illustrated in Figure 7.1b. The dress you draft in this pattern has an empire waist with bust darts.

Draft the Patterns

Figure 7.8

1. Trace the *front* dress sloper (with sleeves) onto pattern paper. Cross-mark the apex. Draw the underarm (U). Determine the length. Label the neck/shoulder tip (B).
2. E-F = Draw an empire line 3" below the apex. Draw a vertical line from the apex to the empire line (parallel to CF/CB).
3. C = Lower the underarm ½" and reduce the width ½".
4. C-E = Draw a new side seam parallel to the outline.

5. At the neck/shoulder tip, draw a 1½" line (squared to CB/CF).
6. A-C = Draw an inward curved *front* armhole.
7. F-V = 1". Draw a curved front empire line to the center front.
8. B-V = Draw the front neckline (straight or curved).
9. C-D = Draw a back strapless line.
10. Extend line (E) to the side seam.

Trace the Front Pattern and Draw a Slash Line/Grainline

Figure 7.9a

1. C-A-B-V-E = Trace the front halter pattern and vertical line.
2. From the apex, draw a slash line to the armhole. Label (X).
3. Extend the vertical line; then label the grainline and sections 1 and 2.

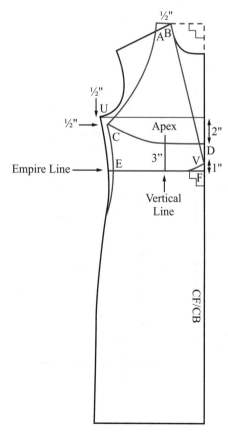

Figure 7.8 Draft the halter dress

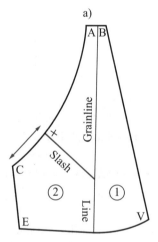

Figure 7.9a Trace the front pattern and draw a slash line/ grainline

Slash/Spread the Pattern and Insert a Dart

Figure 7.9b

In a garment with an empire waist, incorporating bust darts enhances the fit because the darts contour the bust area.

1. Cut the slash line to the pivot point (X).
2. Trace panel (1) onto pattern paper.
3. Move panel (2) and allow 1¼" for the dart intake and trace.

Draw the Dart Legs

Figure 7.9c

1. Draw a horizontal guideline. Extend the grainline to this line.
2. Mark a dart point ⅜" below the apex. Draw dart legs ⅝" on each side of the grainline to the dart point.

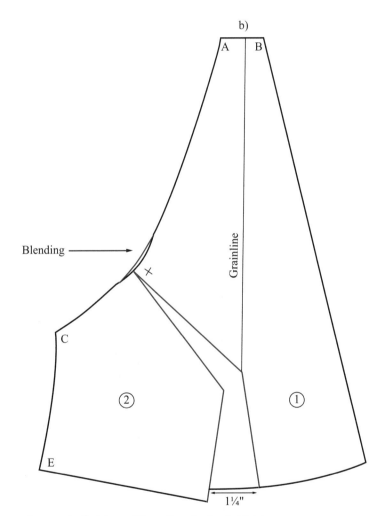

Figure 7.9b Slash/spread the pattern for the dart intake

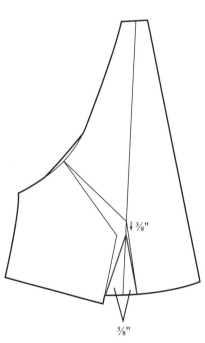

Figure 7.9c Draw Dart Legs

Fold the Dart and True the Patterns

Figures 7.9d and e

1. Trace the back pattern (C-D-F-E).
2. Align (C-E) front/back side seams together. (See Figure 7.9d.)
3. Add a strap to (A-B). Draw a blending line to round the angular line.

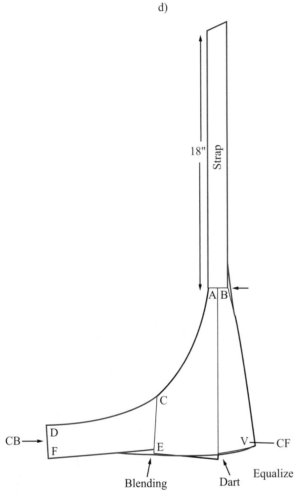

Figure 7.9d Trueing the Pattern

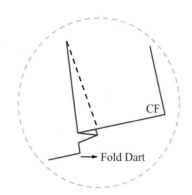

Figure 7.9e Folding the dart

4. Fold the bust dart toward the center front, as shown in Figure 7.9e.
5. F-E-V = Draw a smooth transitioning empire line and equalize between the two dart legs.

Finalize the Patterns

Figure 7.10

The simplest way to stitch the halter top is to line the front and back top sections. For cutting instructions, the pattern is labeled accordingly as shown.

1. Trace the *front* skirt from the working pattern. Follow the empire line (E-V). Mark the matchpoint on (V).
2. Trace the *back* skirt from the working pattern. Follow the empire line (E-F).
3. Add seam allowances and a hem allowance. (Add ½" seam allowance to the empire line.)
4. Compare the top and skirt empire seamlines together. They must be the same length. Adjust the length if necessary.
5. Draw directional grainlines.
6. Label patterns and the number of pattern pieces to cut.

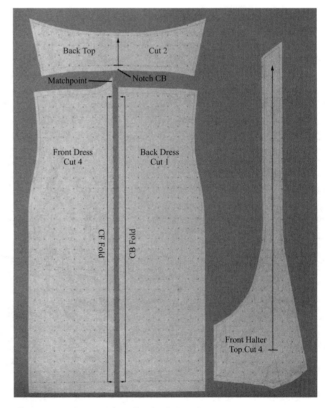

Figure 7.10 Final patterns for the halter dress

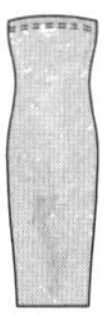

Strapless Dress

A **strapless** dress exposes the shoulders (see
Figure 7.1c). It can be short or knee length, midi,
maxi, or ankle length (see Figure 7.5). If the
dress is constructed from a medium- or lightweight knit,
it would benefit from the insertion of a **cut-in-one self
lining**. In this case, the outer and lining patterns are cut
as one pattern, and the hemline is a folded edge. (Refer to
the "Lined Dresses" section later in this chapter to draft
the strapless dress with a cut-in-one self lining.)

Before drafting the patterns, choose the type and width
of elastic you will use because your choice affects the facing width added to the strapless edge. (Refer to Table 3.2
on p. 28.)

Draft the Patterns

Figure 7.11a

1. Trace the *front* dress sloper onto pattern paper. Adjust
   into a sleeveless sloper, as shown in Figures 6.18a
   and b on p. 112. Draw the underarm (U) as a guide
   for the placement of the front and back strapless line.
   Then determine the dress length.
2. C = Lower the underarm ¾".
3. A-C = Contour the front strapless line.
4. B-C = Contour the back strapless line.
5. Trace the front pattern; follow strapless line (A-C).
6. Trace the back pattern; follow strapless line (B-C).
7. Align front and back side seams together as shown
   and draw a smooth blending strapless line.

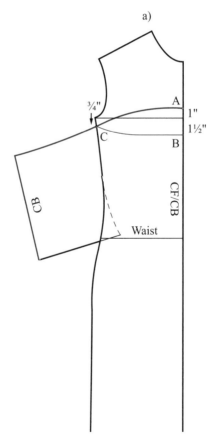

a)

Figure 7.11a Draft the strapless dress

Add Facings

Figure 7.11b

1. Add a facing (⅛" wider than the elastic width) above the strapless line. In this case, the facing is 1⅛" wide for a 1" wide elastic.
2. Make sure that the facing length is the same length as the strapless line (A-C and B-C).

Finalize the Patterns

Figure 7.12

1. Add seam allowances (including ¼" to the facing edge).
2. Add a hem allowance (for an unlined dress).
3. Draw directional grainlines.
4. Label patterns and the number of pattern pieces to cut.

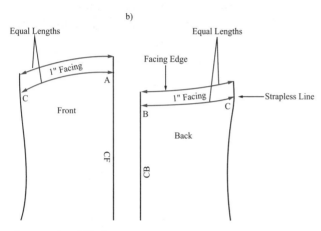

Figure 7.11b Add facings

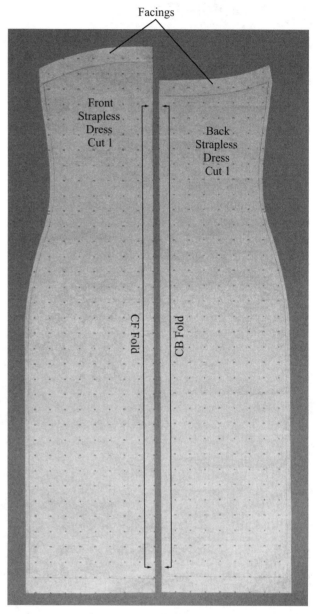

Figure 7.12 Final patterns for the strapless dress

Wrap Dress

The wrap dress, which is a signature style of Diane Von Furstenberg, is still popular today (see Figure 7.1d). It has a crossover bodice that forms a flattering V neckline. A tie belt wraps around the waistline as the closure. The wrap dress (with waistline) is drafted from the top foundation, hip foundation, and dress-piece

in the same stretch category. The skirt silhouette can be straight, pegged, flared, or circular. Any type of sleeve shown in Figure 6.40 on p. 128 can be an element of the dress.

Draft the Top Patterns

Figure 7.14

1. Trace both sides of the *front* top foundation onto pattern paper. Draw the underarm (U) as a guide for the neckline depth. Label the waist/side seam (A).
2. Trace the *back* top foundation onto the working pattern, as shown in Figure 7.14. Label the center back (B).
3. Determine the front neckline depth. (In this pattern, it is 4½".)
4. D = Mark the point where the top will wrap on the waistline. Draw a ¾" squared line up from (D). (The tie belt is stitched here.)
5. E-D = Draw the front neckline.
6. E-F = Draw the back neckline.

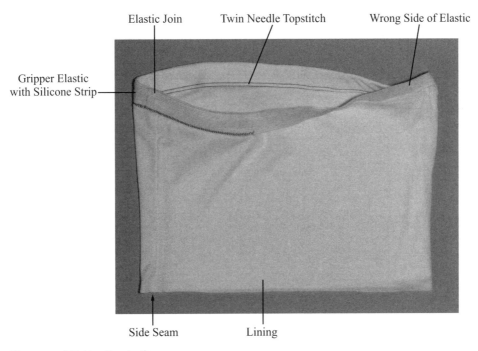

Elastic Join   Twin Needle Topstitch   Wrong Side of Elastic

Gripper Elastic
with Silicone Strip

Side Seam   Lining

Figure 7.13 Stitching the elastic

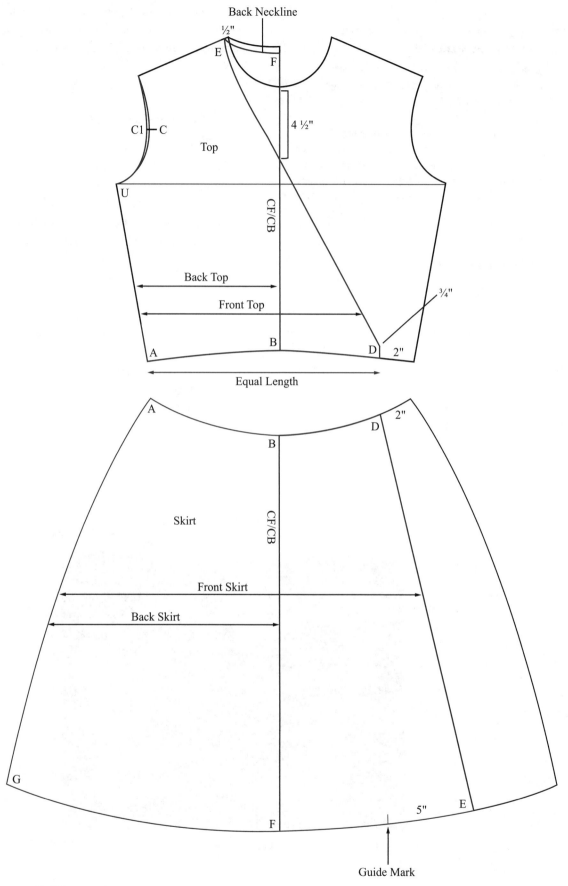

Back Neckline

½"

E

F

C1 — C

Top

4 ½"

U

CF/CB

Back Top

Front Top

¾"

A

B

D

2"

Equal Length

A

D

2"

B

Skirt

CF/CB

Front Skirt

Back Skirt

G

5"

E

F

Guide Mark

Figure 7.14 Draft the wrap dress

Draft the Skirt Pattern

Figure 7.14

1. Trace both sides of the hip foundation onto pattern paper. Align the dress-piece to the hip foundation and trace both sides (see Figure 7.2). Draft the skirt pattern according to the silhouette (see Figure 7.6). (Refer to Chapter 9 to draft an A-line or flared skirt.) Label the center back (B-F) and side seam (A-G).
2. A-D = Mark the waistline to match the same length as (A-D) top waistline.
3. Mark a guidemark on the hemline an equal width to (B-D).
4. E = Mark the point where the skirt will wrap on the hemline.
5. D-E = Draw a straight line.

Draft the Tie Belt

The tie belt is stitched to the front dress and then wraps around the back waist and ties in the front. It is important to draft the ties to the correct length so that the belt aligns perfectly on the side of the asymmetrical dress. (Refer to Figure 7.15 to see the tie belt and short tie patterns for the wrap dress.)

1. Draft two tie belts 3" wide. The tie belt that wraps around the back is 55" long. The other tie belt is 28" long.
2. Draft two short ties 10" long and ¾" wide.
3. Add ¼" seam allowances around the edges.
4. You can cut the tie belt and short tie patterns in either direction (lengthwise or crossgrain).

Finalize the Patterns

Figure 7.15

To see the patterns that must be traced from the working pattern (front top, back top, front skirt, and back skirt patterns), refer to Figure 7.15. To trace each pattern piece from the working pattern, follow these codes:

1. A-U-C-E-D = Front top.
2. A-U-C1-E-F-B = Back top.
3. A-D-E-G = Front skirt.
4. A-B-F-G = Back skirt.

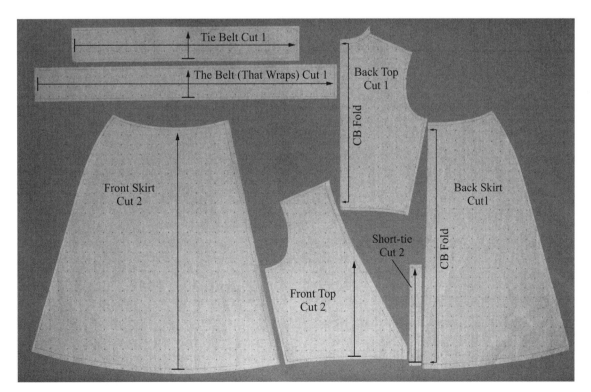

Figure 7.15 Final patterns for wrap dress

5. Align front and back shoulder lines together and draw a smooth blending neckline. (Figure 6.26 on p. 118 illustrates how to round an angular line.)
6. Draw grainlines and label patterns as shown.
7. Add the appropriate seam allowance to the patterns.
8. Add an edge allowance to the neckline, skirt opening, and hem edge. (Refer to Figure 6.63 on p. 144.)

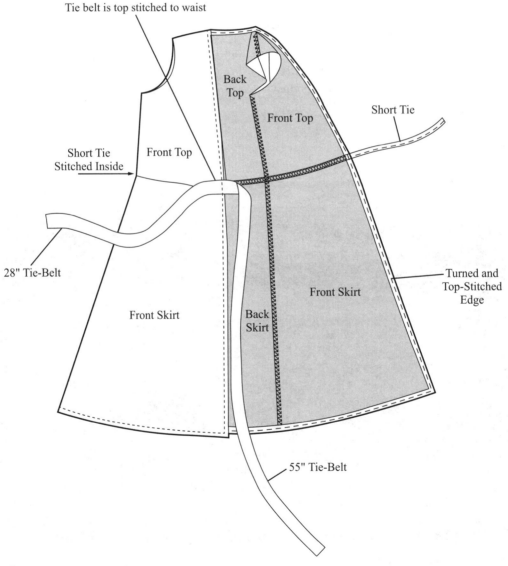

Figure 7.16 Stitched wrap dress

Blouson Dress with Casing

A **blouson** dress has extra length and width incorporated into the patterns (see Figure 7.1e).

An elasticized waist casing causes the garment to blouse and hang in loose folds over the casing. Designing the dress with a waist seam makes the casing easier to stitch. Use a soft, drapey two-way or four-way stretch knit for this dress. Choose the type and weight of elastic. (Refer to Table 3.2 on p. 28.) Use elastic at least 1" wide or wider to support the weight of the long dress. The blouson dress also features a hemline that is longer in the back than the front. To expand the hemline, you can use the slash/spread pattern technique to add fullness.

Draft the Top Patterns

Figure 7.17a

You draft the front and back top patterns from the top foundation.

1. Trace the top foundation in the appropriate stretch category. Draft a round neckline (see Figure 6.23 on p. 117).
2. Adjust the underarm for a sleeveless garment, as shown in Figures 6.18a and b on p. 112. Draw the underarm line. Label (U-Y).

3. Draw a parallel line 2" beyond CF/CB. Extend the front/back neckline and label (I and H).
4. Mark the length of front split down from (H).
5. Extend the CF/CB line 2" below the waistline for blousing. At the 2" mark, draw a squared parallel line to and the same length as (U-Y). Label (C). Extend the base line and label (D).
6. Relabel CF/CB on the (I-D) line and waistline on the (C-D) line.
7. G = Lower the underarm.
8. G-E = Draw a straight line from the front armhole to the front neckline.
9. G-F = Draw a straight line from the back armhole to the back neckline.
10. Draw a slash line (X) and (A-B).

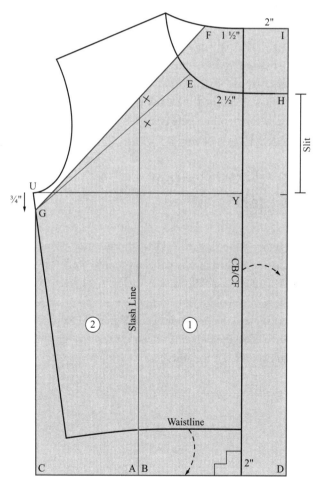

Figure 7.17a Draft the blouson dress with casings

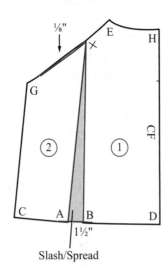

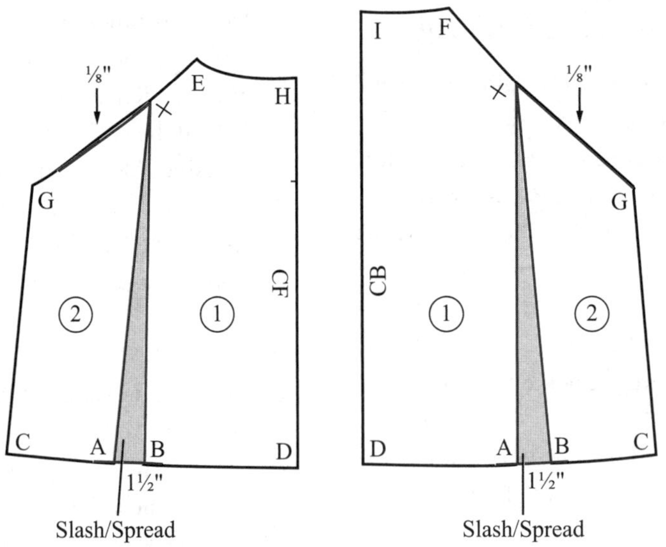

Figure 7.17b Slash/spread the pattern

Slash/Spread the Pattern

Figure 7.17b

1. G-E-H-D-C = Trace the front pattern and slash line.
2. G-F-I-D-C = Trace the back pattern and slash line (gray area).
3. Slash/spread the front/back patterns as shown.
4. Draw the hemline between (A-B).
5. G-X = Draw a curved line.

Draft the Skirt Pattern

Figure 7.18a

1. Use the (waist to knee) section of the dress sloper in Figure 7.4 to draft the skirt pattern. Draw a vertical line on pattern paper. Label it "side seam."
2. Place the waist/side seam extended to the length of the hipline on the vertical line as shown. For an A-line skirt, place the hem/side seam 2" from the vertical line. Trace the front and back skirt onto pattern paper.
3. Draw a curved waistline.

Draw the New Center Front/Back and Hemline

Figure 7.18b

1. Extend CF/CB so the skirt waist length is equal to (C-D) top waist length.
2. Mark the front and back hem lengths (mid-calf and ankle).
3. Draw the hemline in one smooth continuous line as shown.

Add the Casing

Figure 7.18c

1. Above the waistline (C-C), add a casing (width of elastic plus ¼").
2. Trace the front/back skirt patterns from the working pattern.

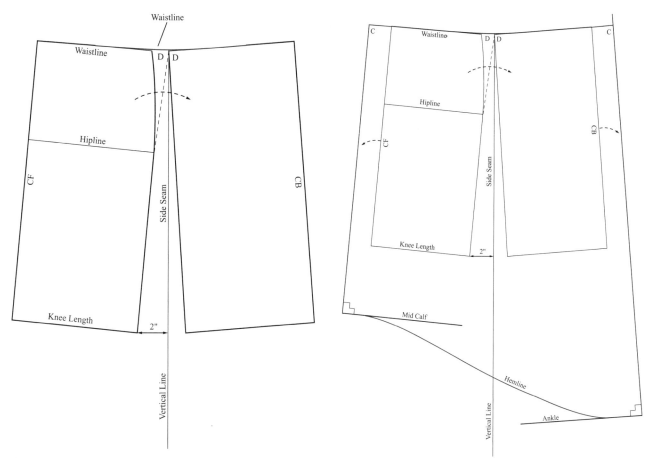

Figures 7.18a Position skirt slopers on the vertical line and trace.

Figure 7.18b Draw a new center front/back and hemline.

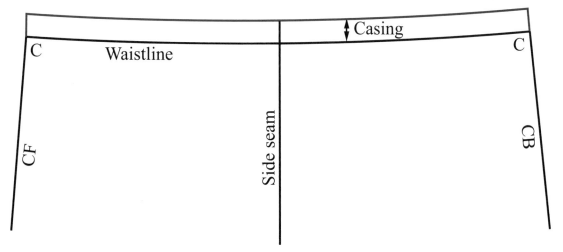

Figure 7.18c Add casing.

Finalize the Patterns

Figure 7.19

1. Draft a drawstring pattern ¾" wide × 47" long for the neck tie.

2. Add the seam allowance to the patterns. (Also add a ¼" seam allowance to the casing edge.) For a shaped hem, add ½" allowance.

3. On the diagonal armhole seams, add ½" seam allowances for a turned and topstitched edge. Draw directional seamlines as shown in Figure 6.63 on p. 114.

4. Draw grainlines and label patterns as shown.

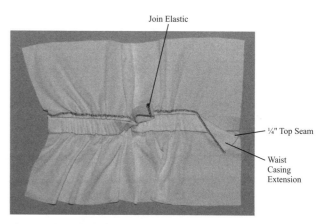

Join Elastic

¼" Top Seam

Waist Casing Extension

Figure 7.20a Stitched waist casing

STITCHING TIP 7.5: STITCHING THE CASINGS

1. Stitch side seams of the top and skirt.
2. Join waists together and stitch the waist casing. Leave a 1" opening at the side seam for threading elastic into the casing (Figure 7.20a).
3. Stitch a narrow facing for the neckline casing, and then understitch. Use 1⅛" wide bias-cut strips in a lightweight woven fabric for the casing. Thread a drawstring through the casing (Figure 7.20b).
4. Insert elastic and tighten to a comfortable fit. Pull elastic out of the casing and join. Then topstitch the opening.

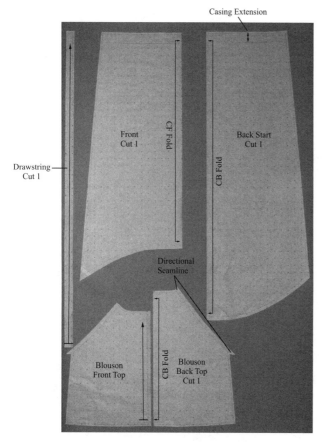

Casing Extension

Front Cut 1

CF Fold

Back Start Cut 1

CB Fold

Drawstring Cut 1

Directional Seamline

CB Fold

Blouson Front Top

Blouson Back Top Cut 1

Figure 7.19 Final patterns for blouson dress with casings

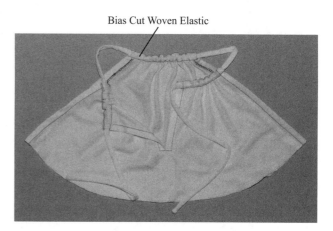

Bias Cut Woven Elastic

Figure 7.20b Stitched neck casing

Princess Line Dress

The **princess line** dress is figure flattering because style lines create clean lines that slim the body (see Figure 7.1a). The dress can be sleeveless or with sleeves, and can be any length. Here, you draft the front/back tank dress patterns in Figure 7.7 and plot the princess style line.

Draft the Patterns

Figure 7.21

1. Cross-mark the apex on the pattern.
2. Draft the front/back panel.

3. A-B = Plot a bust curve from the armhole to or close to the apex.
4. B-C = Plot the apex to the waist.
5. C-D-E = Plot the waist to the hip and extend to the hem.
6. To create the side panel (for front and back), divide the style line from approximately 2" below the apex and remove ⅜" to ½" at the waist. Draw a curved style line to the hip.

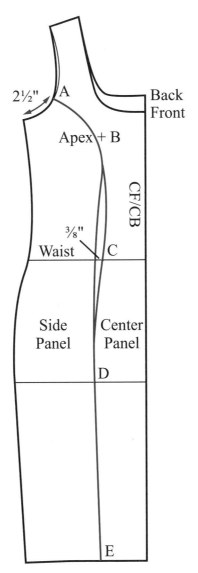

Figure 7.21 Draft the princess line dress

Finalize the Patterns

Figure 7.22

1. Trace the front and back center panels and notch the waist.
2. Trace the side panel and notch both sides of the waist.

3. Add a seam/hem allowance to the patterns.
4. Draw grainlines.
5. Label the side panel as "Cut 4" because you will use the pattern for the front and back dress.

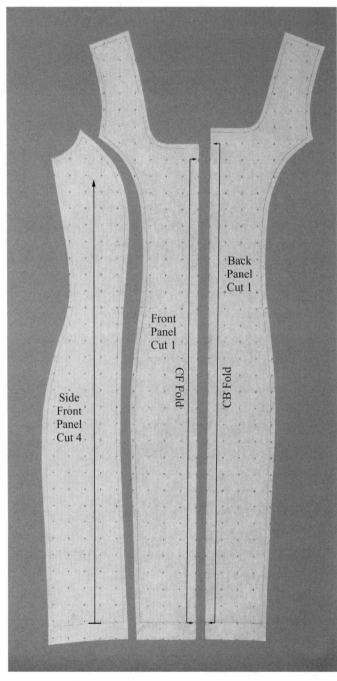

Figure 7.22 Final patterns for the princess line dress

Princess Line Front Gathered Panel

The princess line dress is a classic style. To accentuate the front panel, slash/separate the pattern to add gathering to create a different look for the dress. The amount to slash/spread the pattern will vary according to the weight of the fabric. Trace the princess line center front panel, as shown in Figure 7.23.

Slash/Separate the Pattern

Figure 7.23

1. Draw slash lines and label sections. The first slash line is on the apex (see Figure 7.23).
2. Slash/separate the pattern. As a guide, spread the pattern *half* of the length of the front panel (from shoulder tip to hem). Divide this length by 7 to determine the amount to add between the slash lines.
3. Draw the new princess style line and equalize as shown in the figure.
4. Notch the halfway point on the front panel and side panel.

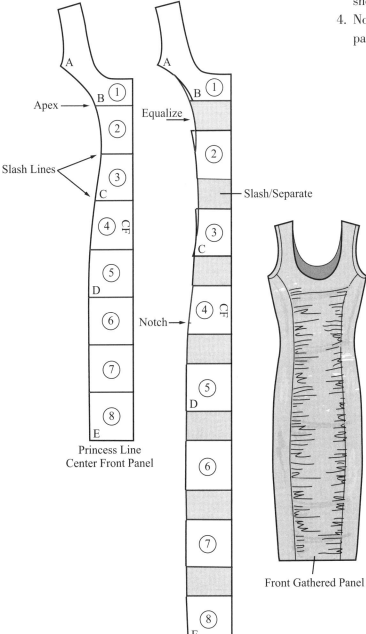

Figure 7.23 Trace the princess line center front panel; draw slash lines; and slash/separate the pattern

Godet

Figure 7.24

A **godet** is a triangular piece of fabric inserted to expand the hemline. Six godets in total are stitched to each seamline of the princess line dress.

1. Determine the length and width of the godet.
2. Draw the godet pattern in the position it will be stitched to the seam. Mark a notch on the seamline at the tip of the godet.

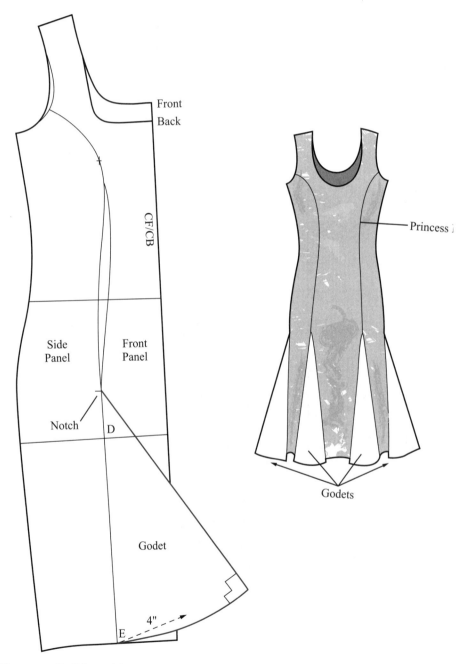

Figure 7.24 Draft the godet

Finalize the Pattern

Figure 7.25

1. Add seam and hem allowances and mark the matchpoint.
2. Draw a grainline.
3. Label the pattern "Cut 6."

Matchpoint

¼"

Godet
Cut 6

½" Hem Allowance

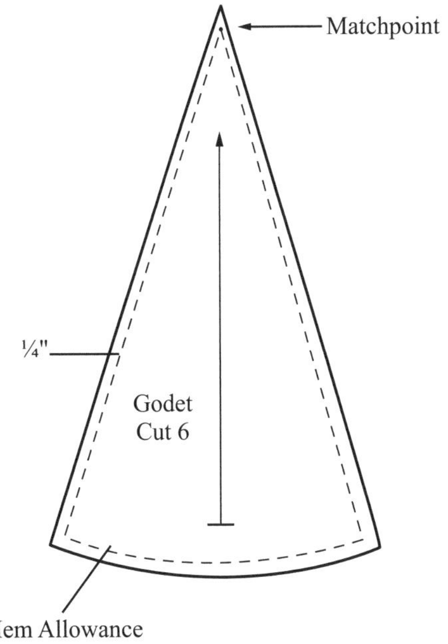

Figure 7.25 Final godet pattern

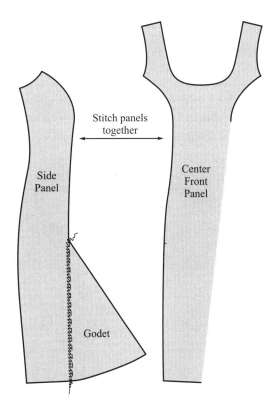

Stitch panels together

Side
Panel

Center
Front
Panel

Godet

Figure 7.26 Stitching the godet

Draped One-shoulder Asymmetrical Dress

A **one-shoulder dress** is asymmetrical (see Figure 7.1f). The neckline starts from one shoulder and extends diagonally to the other underarm. The dress must be constructed from a four-way stretch knit because the front is cut lengthwise and on the crossgrain of the fabric. Look ahead to Figure 7.27b on p. 117 to see how the pattern curves after the slash/spread technique has been used.

sloper, as shown in Figures 6.18a and b on p. 112. Draw the underarm (U). Then determine the dress length.

2. C = Lower the *left front* underarm ½" and reduce the width ½". Draw a new side seam and a 1" squared line at (C).

3. A-C = Contour the diagonal neckline from the squared line to the shoulder.

4. On the *right front*, mark the length of the gathering on the side seam.

5. Draw slash lines and label sections.

Draft the Patterns

Figure 7.27a

1. Trace front pattern pieces for both sides of the garment as shown. Draw the back armhole (the back neckline is not required). Adjust to a sleeveless

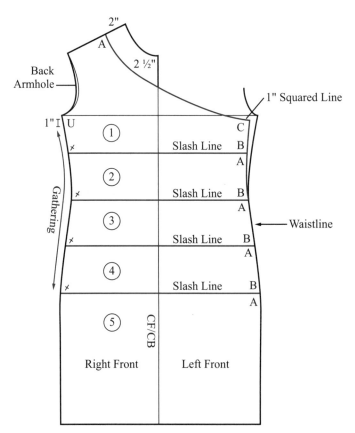

Figure 7.27a Draft the draped one-shoulder asymmetrical dress

Slash/Spread the Pattern

Figure 7.27b

The length to spread the pattern can vary according to the weight of the fabric. In this draft, you spread the pattern twice the length of the gathered section. This would be the perfect amount for gathering mesh or a tissue-weight knit. Divide this length by 4 to determine the amount to add between (A-B) slash lines.

1. Trace the front/back patterns from the working pattern. The front pattern can be used for a lining pattern. (This may be the simplest way to stitch the dress.)
2. Cut slash lines and trace panel (5) onto pattern paper. Transfer the grainline.
3. Spread the pattern to add fullness as shown. Draw smooth continuous lines to round angular lines.

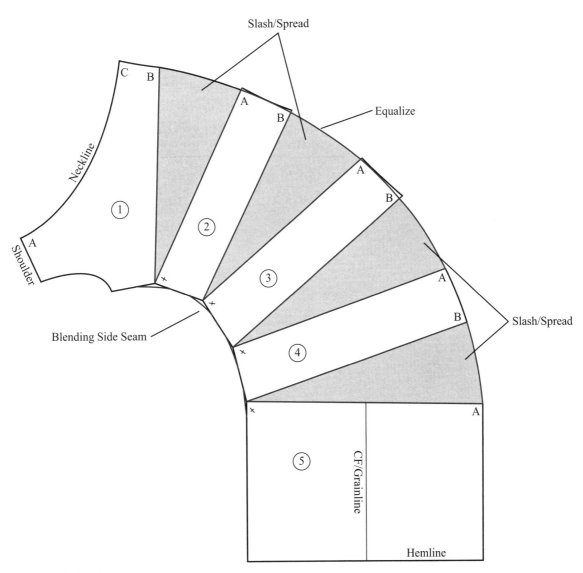

Figure 7.27b Slash/spread the pattern

Finalize the Patterns

Figure 7.28

1. Add seam and hem allowances.
2. Draw directional grainlines.
3. Label patterns (R.S.U.) so that they are placed on the fabric correctly according to the asymmetrical design (see Figure 3.13 on p. 32).

4. Notch the length of the gathering on the front side seam. Notch the finished length of the gathering on the back side seam.

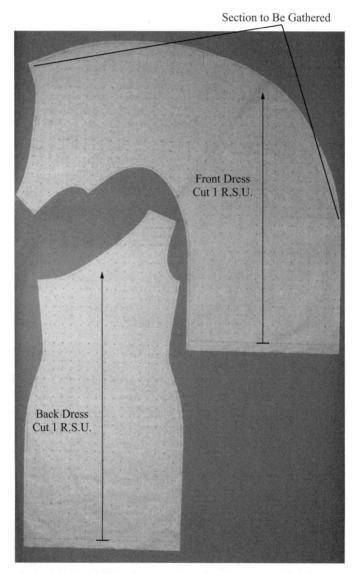

Figure 7.28 Final patterns for draped one-shoulder asymmetrical dress

Dress with Facings

A facing finishes the neckline and/or armholes with a clean edge. Now you're ready to draft front and back facings the full width of the shoulders and stitch them to the V-neck dress in Figure 7.29. You attach the facings to the armholes to prevent them from flipping out to the correct side.

Draft the Facings

Figure 7.29

You draft the patterns slightly smaller than the outer garment patterns so that the facings will fit perfectly underneath the garment when they are stitched in place.

1. Trace the front and back pattern outline.
2. Outline the lower edge of the facing.
3. S-U = Remove ⅛" at the shoulder tip and draw a curved line to the underarm.
4. U-E = Remove ⅛" from the facing/side seam. Draw a straight line.

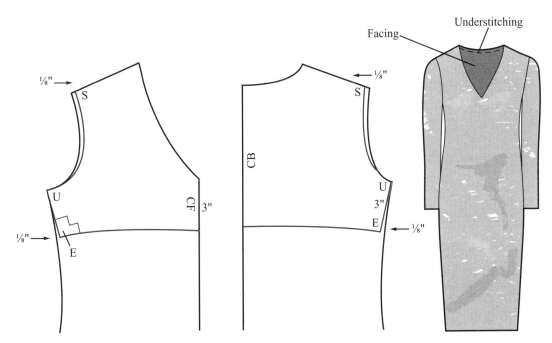

Figure 7.29 Draft the facings

Finalize the Patterns

Figure 7.30

1. Add seam allowances.
2. Draw grainlines.
3. Label the patterns.

Lined Dresses

You are able to draft lining patterns from outer garment patterns. If the dress is sleeveless, make the same armhole pattern adjustment that you did on the facing patterns in Figure 7.30.

STITCHING TIP 7.7: STITCHING THE FACINGS

1. If the dress is constructed from a double knit, use a lightweight knit for the facings.
2. Press narrow ⅜" strips of four-way stretch interfacing to the neckline edge to stabilize. (Refer to Figure 6.51d on p. 137.)
3. You can leave the bottom edge of the facing with a raw edge to prevent serging showing a ridge on the correct side of the garment.
4. Stitch the facing in place, understitch, turn the facing to the wrong side, and attach to the armholes.
5. Stitch the side seams (see Figure 7.31).

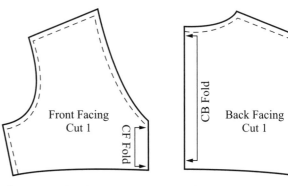

Figure 7.30 Final facing patterns

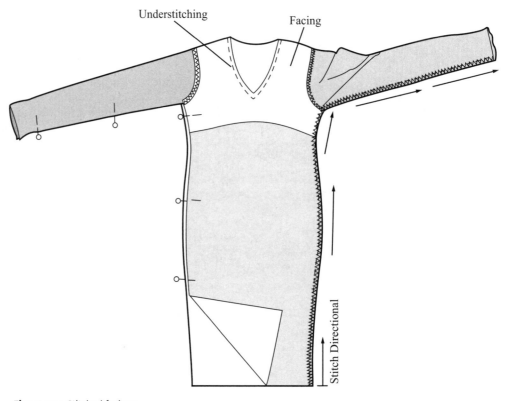

Figure 7.31 Stitched facings

Separate Lining

Figure 7.32

In this section, you draft a **shift** dress pattern with a **separate lining**. A shift is a short, loose-fitting dress with no definite waistline.

1. Draft the dress pattern as shown.
2. Draw the lining length ¾" shorter.

STITCHING TIP 7.8: STITCHING THE SEPARATE LINING

You stitch the lining edge to edge with the outer fabric to create a clean finish on the neckline (and armholes if sleeveless).

1. Press narrow ⅜" strips of four-way stretch interfacing to the neckline (and armhole) edges to stabilize the seams and to prevent the seams from stretching when stitched. (Refer to Figure 6.51d on p. 137.)
2. Stitch the outer fabric and lining shoulder seams.
3. Stitch the neckline and armholes of the outer fabric and lining together and understitch. (If the dress has sleeves, do not stitch the armholes.)
4. Stitch the side seams in one long length from the front hemline to underarm to back hemline.
5. Insert the sleeves.
6. Stitch the garment and lining hems separately.
7. Secure the lining and outer fabric side seams together, as shown in Figure 7.33.

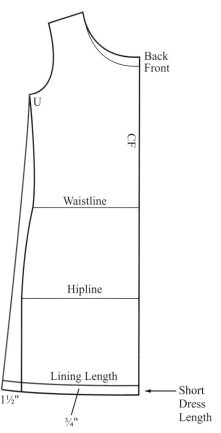

Figure 7.32 Draft the separate lining

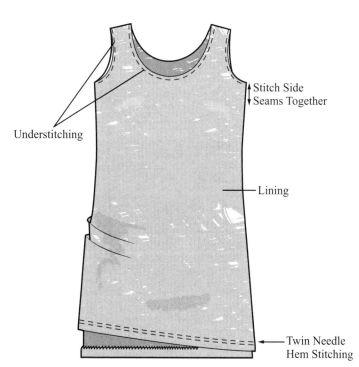

Figure 7.33 Stitched separate lining

Cut-in-one Self Lining

Figure 7.34

The strapless dress in Figure 7.1c has a self lining. The front and back patterns are drafted in Figures 7.11a and b. Follow on to draft the outer pattern and lining pattern as a one-pattern piece. This pattern drafting technique can be employed to draft the patterns for other dresses with a self lining.

1. Remove the hem allowance from the final patterns in Figure 7.13.
2. Trace both sides of the pattern on the fold.
3. Fold the pattern along the hemline (foldline) and trace the identical pattern again as shown.
4. Add a seam allowance to the side seams (and the facing edge in this case).

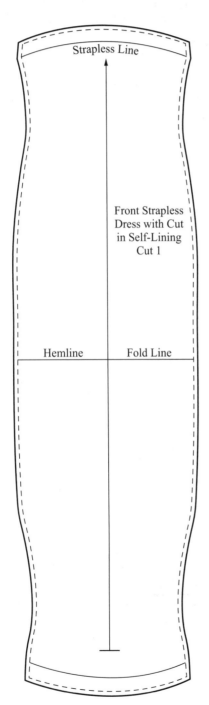

Figure 7.34 Draft the cut-in-one self lining

STITCHING TIP 7.9: STITCHING THE SELF LINING

1. Stitch the front and back side seams and press the seams open.
2. Fold the dress so that wrong sides are placed together and attach the strapless neckline edges together.
3. Apply elastic to the strapless edge (see Figure 7.13).

Slip Dress

To draft a slip dress, refer to Chapter 11 and draft front and back cami patterns. Then lengthen the patterns to the dress length of your choice.

Zippers in Dresses

Dresses in knits don't usually require a zipper opening because most knits stretch onto the body. However, some stable knits may not have sufficient stretch, or if the neckline opening is high cut, a dress will not fit onto the body without a zipper.

Before stitching the zipper, stabilize the seam where the zipper will be stitched with ¾" wide strips of interfacing or stay tape. If you neglect to use a stabilizer, the seam can look wavy because it has stretched out as the zipper was inserted.

Knit It Together

This checklist summarizes what you have learned about drafting dress patterns in this chapter.

✓ A dress-piece is drafted as a partial pattern.

✓ The dress-piece and top slopers are joined together to form the dress slopers in each stretch category.

✓ A dress pattern can be drafted for any stretch category of knit from the dress slopers.

✓ Any of the sleeve designs in Chapter 6 can be part of a dress.

✓ The neckline finishes described in Chapter 6 can be stitched to dresses as a finish.

Stop: What Do I Do If . . .

. . . I want to draft a dress with a dolman sleeve? I can't find any instructions.

You can draft the dolman sleeve from Chapter 6 and Figure 6.45 on p. 132 as a dress pattern as well as a top pattern. First, decide on the fit you want to create. For a fitted dress, use the dress slopers outlined in this chapter. For a dress with design ease (or wearing ease), you can use the fitted, loose-fit, or oversized cardigan/sweater slopers in Chapter 8.

. . . I want to create a dress with a cowl neckline? In Figure 6.29 on p. 120, the cowl neckline is drafted on a top pattern. How do I modify the top pattern into a dress pattern?

There are two options for drafting the cowl neckline on a dress pattern:

- For a *fitted* dress, you must draw the center front cowl neckline to a seamline. It can be the hipline

(as shown in Figure 6.31), empire waist, or the natural waistline. (The front dress will have *two* pattern pieces: top and base pattern pieces.)

- For a *loose-fit* dress, you draw the center front cowl neckline to the hemline. The front dress pattern is cut as *one* piece.

Self-Critique

1. What slopers do you use to draft dress patterns?

2. Can a dress be constructed from a four-way stretch knit?

3. What seams would you elasticize on the halter dress in Figure 7.1b?

4. What type or width of elastic would you stitch to the neckline of the strapless dress in Figure 7.1c? (Refer to Tables 3.2 and 3.3 on p. 27 and p. 28.)

5. How would six godets be incorporated into the hemline of the strapless dress in Figure 7.1c? Sketch the design and discuss the pattern drafting that would be required.

6. The shift dress in Figure 7.1g has a separate lining. What other method of lining could you use to line the dress?

7. Refer to the shift in Figure 7.1g. How would you alter the dress patterns in Figure 7.32 to cater to a larger-busted woman?

8. Why is the hem of the dress in 7.1a stitched with twin needle stitching and the hem of the dress in Figure 7.1e stitched with a single row of stitching? (Refer to the "Stretchable Hems" section in Chapter 4.)

Key Terms	Godet	Separate Lining	Tank Dress
Blouson	Halter	Sheath	
Cut-in-one Self Lining	One-shoulder Dress	Shift	
Dress-piece	Princess Line	Strapless	

8 Jacket, Cardigan, Sweater, and Sweater-Jacket Slopers and Patterns

Jackets, cardigans, sweaters, and sweater-jackets made in stretch knits are practical additions to a woman's wardrobe because they are comfortable and add an extra layer of warmth. A jacket contructed in a double knit can be tailored with a collar and style lines. Cardigans can be cropped, rest on the hip or knee, be three-quarter or ankle length, hang unfastened, or have a tie-belt closure. Sweaters can be soft and lightweight or warmly wrapped around the body. A sweater-jacket is a short cropped jacket with a zip closure and frequently designed with a hood. Jackets and cardigans can be constructed from two-way or four-way stretch knits.

This chapter outlines how to develop slopers for cardigans, sweaters, and sweater-jackets. The pattern designs for the garments featured in Figures 8.1a through g and 8.2a and b are also outlined.

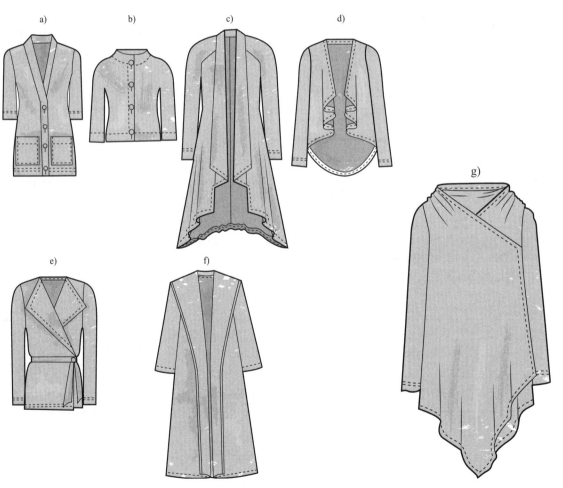

a) b) c) d) e) f) g)

Figure 8.1 a) V-neck button-front cardigan with band and patch pockets; **b)** high-neck button-front cardigan with dolman sleeves; **c)** flared cardigan with collar; **d)** draped cardigan; **e)** wrapped cardigan with tie belt; **f)** loose-fit cardigan with shawl collar and in-seam pockets; **g)** wrap-around-the-body cardigan

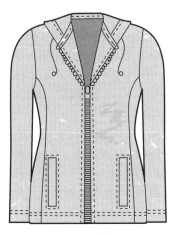

Figure 8.2a Zip-up sweater-jacket with welt pockets and hood

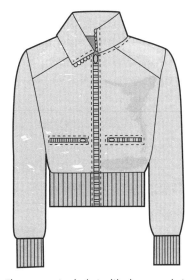

Figure 8.2b Zip-up sweater-jacket with zip-up pockets and collar

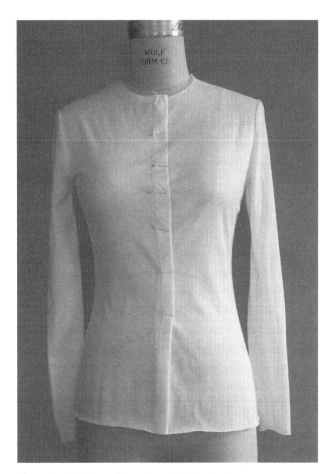

Figure 8.3 Fitted muslin cardigan fitted on the form

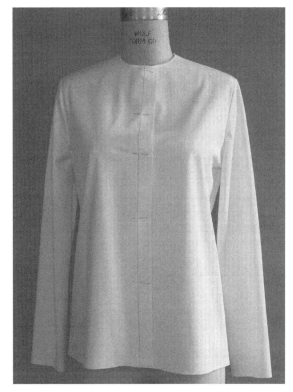

Figure 8.4 Loose-fit muslin cardigan fitted on the form

Slopers for Jackets, Cardigans, and Sweater-Jackets

In this chapter, you develop slopers for jackets, cardigans, and **sweater-jackets**. They can be *fitted, loose-fit,* or *oversized.* You must use the appropriate slopers to suit the type of knit, style, and fit you envision for your design. Fitted and loose-fit cardigan muslins have been cut, stitched, and placed on the form in Figures 8.3 and 8.4. For the opening, a 1" extension is added to the center front.

This chapter outlines how to draft four different types of slopers:

1. Jacket Slopers for Stable Knits
   Slopers for drafting patterns for jackets made in stable double knits require darts/or fitting lines because these knits have minimal stretch. These knits do not mold to the body as stretchier knit will. The darts enable the fabric to mold to the body shape. Jacket slopers for woven fabric are graded in a *negative* direction to remove 2" of ease. This converts the slopers into stretch knit slopers.

2. Fitted Slopers
   Fitted slopers are used for drafting patterns for cardigans, sweaters, and sweater-jackets constructed from stretchy knits. Two-way minimal stretch top slopers (with sleeves) are graded in a *positive* direction to incorporate an additional 2" to 3" (see Table 8.1).

3. Loose-fit Slopers
   Loose-fit slopers are used for drafting patterns for cardigans, sweaters, and sweater-jacket styles made from weightier knits with less stretch or when a loose fit is required. (This does not discount their use for styles made in lightweight knits.) Minimal two-way stretch top slopers with sleeves are graded in a *positive* direction to incorporate an additional 6" (see Table 8.1).

4. Oversized Slopers
   Oversized slopers are used for drafting patterns for cardigans and sweaters to give your customers that extra bit of room they desire. Minimal two-way stretch top slopers with sleeves are graded in a *positive* direction to incorporate an additional 7" to 10". A dropped shoulder is created and the appropriate sleeve sloper is drafted to synchronize with the additional room in the armscye. There is no limit to the kind of knit that you can use. However, the type and weight of knit you use *must* suit the design (see Table 8.1).

TABLE 8.1: Grading measurement chart

Grading Fitted, Loose-fit, and Oversized Slopers					
Total Body Increase	Quarter Body Increase	Shoulder Increase	Horizontal Line to Guideline ¼ of Total Body Increase	Sleeve Cap Increase	Bicep Increase
Grading in a Positive Direction					
Fitted					
2"	½" (E)	¼" (D2)	½"	¹⁄₁₆"	¼" (D2)
3"	¾" (E1)	⅜"(D3)	¾"	⅛" (D1)	⅜" (D3)
Loose-fit					
4"	1" (F)	½" (E)	1"	¼" (D2)	½" (E)
5"	1¼" (F2)	⅝" (E1)	1¼"	³⁄₁₆"	⅝" (E1)
6"	1½" (G)	¾" (E2)	1½"	⅜" (D3)	¾" (E2)
Oversized					
7"	1¾" (G2)	⅞" (E3)	1¾"	A separate sleeve is drafted to match the armscye (armhole) measurement.	
8"	2" (H)	1" (F)	2"		
9"	2¼" (H2)	1⅛" (F1)	2¼"		
10"	2½" (I)	1¼" (F2)	2½"		

Jacket Slopers for Stable Knits

Figure 8.5a

You grade jacket slopers for woven fabric in a *negative* direction to remove 2" of ease. The waistline represents the horizontal balance line (HBL). Mark (X) on the waistline as shown.

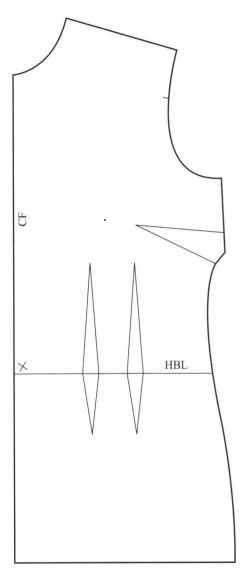

Figure 8.5a Prepare woven jacket slopers

Prepare the Grading Grid for Front/Back

Figure 8.5b

Refer to Figures 3.15 and 3.16 on p. 35 and p. 36 to see the grading grid and grading measurements marked on the grid.

1. Draw a grading grid and label (D). Mark grading measurements (C2) ¼" and (C) ½" from (D) on the horizontal line in a *negative* direction.
2. Place the center front/back sloper on the vertical line and (X) waistline on the horizontal line. Trace the sloper onto the grid.
3. Move sloper (X) on (C2) and draw the shoulder point, armhole curve, and notches to the underarm. Also, mark the dart points, apex, waist, and back shoulder darts.

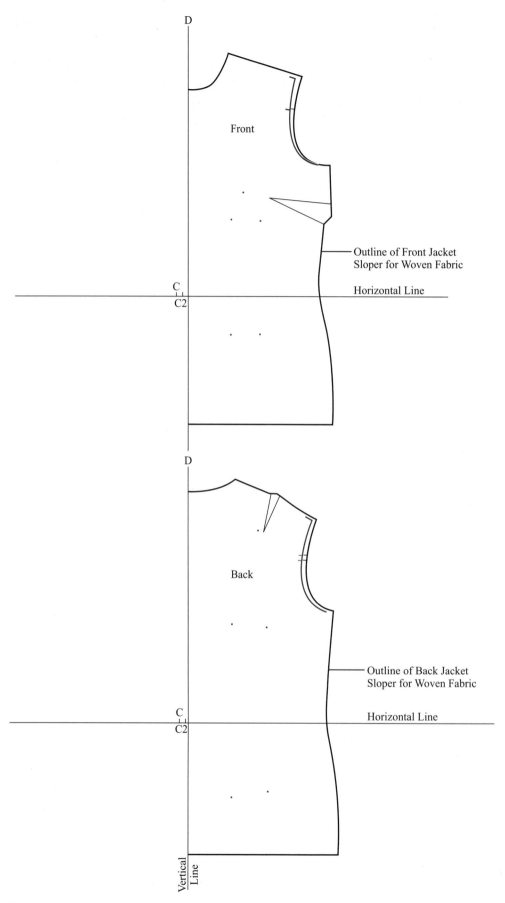

Figure 8.5b Grade the armhole

Grade the Side Seam

Figure 8.5c

1. Move (X) on (C). Draw the underarm and side seam. Then ensure the underarm/side seam is squared (as shown on the back).
2. Draw a new shoulder line and darts.
3. Measure the length of the front/back armholes (separately) and record.

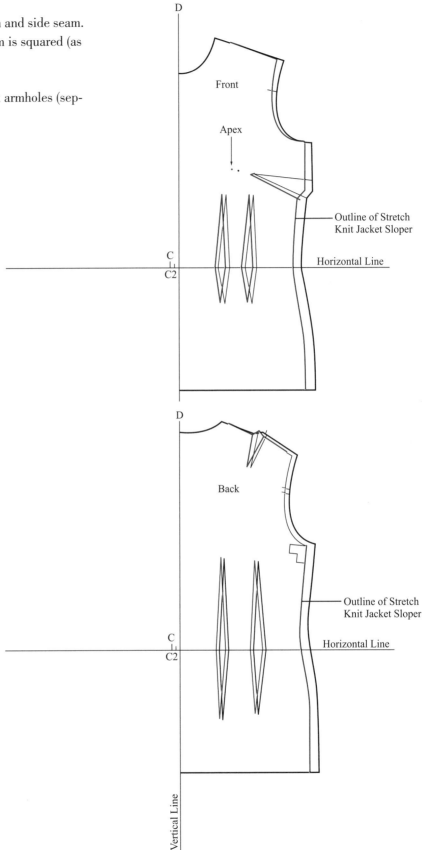

Figure 8.5c Grade the side seam

Prepare the Grading Grid for a Sleeve

Figure 8.6a

1. Draw a line across the bicep (squared at the grainline) of the sleeve sloper. Label HBL.
2. Draw the grading grid (see Figure 3.15 on p. 35). Align the grainline of the sleeve sloper on the vertical line and HBL on the horizontal line. Then trace the sloper onto the grid and mark notches.
3. A-B = Mark ⅛" on either side of the grainline on the sleeve cap and wrist.
4. C-D = Mark ¼" on the horizontal line within the underarm.

Grade the Sleeve

Figure 8.6b

1. As you grade, align the HBL on the horizontal line.
2. Place the sleeve grainline on (A). Trace the *front* capline to the notches, and mark the wrist.
3. Place the sleeve grainline on (B). Trace the *back* capline and mark the wrist.
4. Place the *back* sleeve HBL on (C) and front sleeve HBL on the horizontal line; then mark the *back* under-sleeve/underarm point. Place the *front* sleeve HBL on (D), and mark the *front* under-sleeve/underarm point. Use the sleeve sloper to connect the under-sleeve curve capline.
5. Move the elbow dart ⅛" in toward the grainline.
6. Mark notches in the original position on the sleeve cap. Measure the front and back sleeve cap (separately). Subtract armhole measurements. The length remaining is the sleeve *ease*, which needs to be ¾" to 1" in total. If there is more ease than this amount, an adjustment is necessary. Refer to the "Incorrect Capline/Armhole Ratio" section in Chapter 6 (see Figure 6.9 on p. 102).

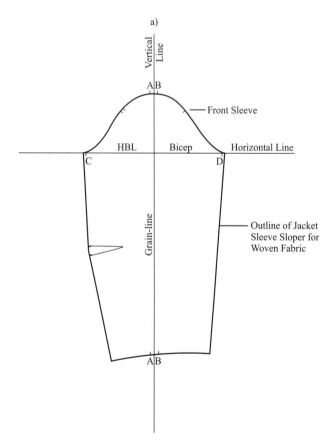

Figure 8.6a Prepare the grading grid

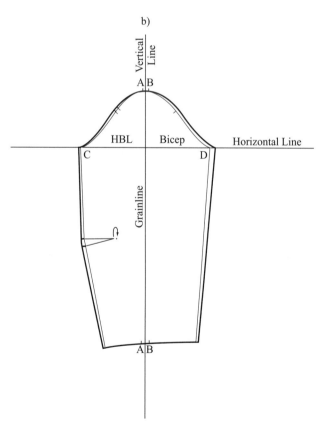

Figure 8.6b Grade the sleeve

Slopers for Cardigans, Sweaters, and Sweater-Jackets

To draft the patterns for cardigans, sweaters, and sweater-jackets, you develop fitted, loose-fit, and over-size slopers from the two-way minimal stretch top slopers with sleeves that were drafted in Chapter 6. (Refer also to Table 2.1 on p. 16.) Wearing ease is incorporated to provide you with a selection of sloper dimensions. The front, back, and sleeve widths are increased and the underarm depth is lowered to create additional room in the body and armscye. These modifications allow these garments to comfortably fit over other garments.

The Grading Measurement Chart in Table 8.1 sets out a range of measurements for grading fitted, loose-fit, and oversized slopers. In Figure 8.7, the grading measurements are marked on the grading grid in a positive direction and are more expansive than the measurements set out on the grading grid in Figure 3.16 on p. 36.

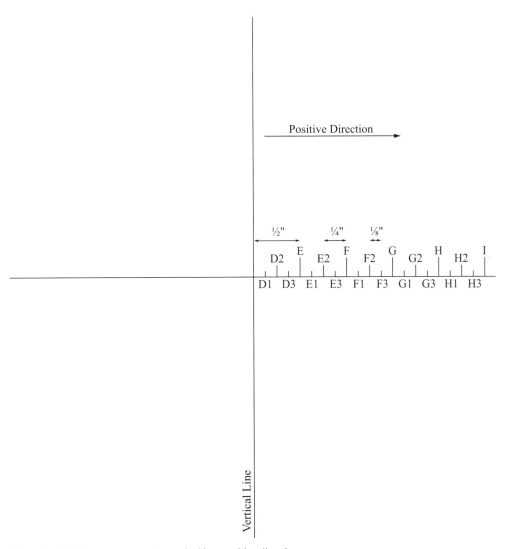

Figure 8.7 Grading measurements marked in a positive direction

Fitted

To create the fitted slopers, you enlarge the minimal stretch top 2" for the total body increase. Table 8.1 charts the grading measurements for increasing the slopers.

Grade the Front and Back

Figure 8.8a

Make sure (X) and codes (C and C3) are recorded on the top slopers (see Figure 6.6 on p. 99). Draw HBL on the underarm of the slopers. Use the same grading method for the front and back.

1. Draw the grading grid and label (D) (see Figure 8.7). Draw the guideline parallel to the horizontal line.

2. Mark grading increments on the horizontal line and guideline in a positive direction from (D):

   - Shoulder Increase = ¼" (D2).
   - Quarter Body Increase = ½" (E).

3. Align sloper (X) on the vertical and horizontal lines. Trace the sloper onto the grid. (Refer to Figure 3.18 on p. 38.)

4. Align HBL on the *horizontal line*. Move sloper (X) on (D2). Mark the shoulder/armhole tip and trace to (C and C3). Cross-mark the apex.

5. Align HBL on the *horizontal line*. Move sloper (X) on (E) and draw the waist to the hip.

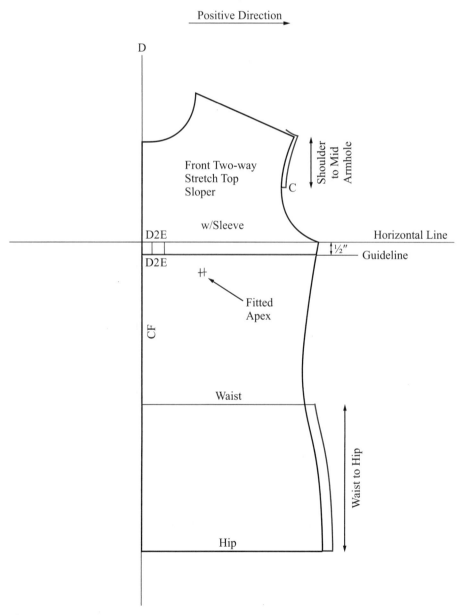

Figure 8.8a Grade the shoulder to the mid armhole and waist to hip

Grade the Underarm and the Underarm to Waist
Figure 8.8b

1. Align the sloper on the *guideline*. Move sloper (X) on (D2). Draw from the mid armhole to the underarm.

2. Align the sloper on the *guideline*. Move sloper (X) on (E). Then draw the underarm curve and underarm to waist.

b)

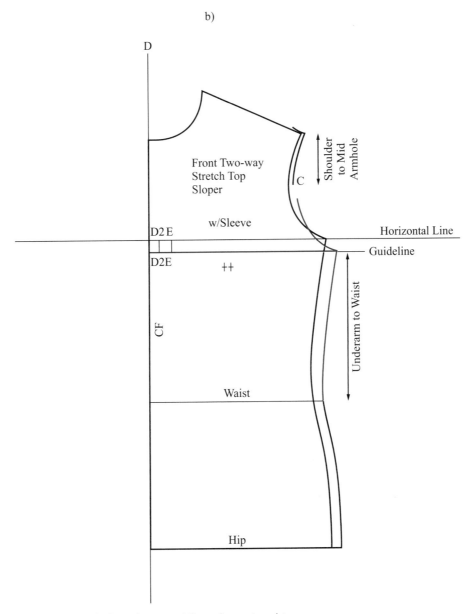

Figure 8.8b Grade the underarm and the underarm to waist

Finish Drawing the Armhole Curve

Figure 8.8c

1. Draw the shoulder line.
2. Draw the armhole curve and equalize at mid armhole.

c)

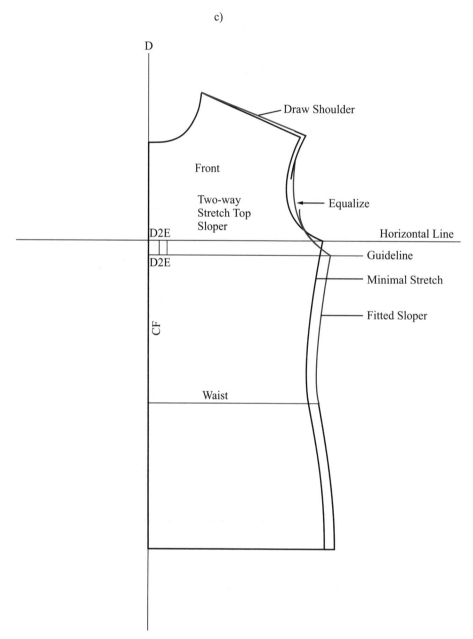

Figure 8.8c Finish drawing the armhole curve

Grade the Sleeve

Figure 8.8d

1. Draw HBL across the bicep (U1) of the sleeve sloper. Draw a guideline halfway between the sleeve cap and HBL. Label (X) (see Figure 6.13a on p. 107).

2. Draw the grading grid and label (D) (see Figure 8.7). Draw the guideline parallel to the horizontal line.

3. Mark grading increments from (D):

   • Sleeve Cap Increase = ⅛" (D1) on horizontal line.

   • Bicep Increase = ¼" (D2) on guideline.

4. Place the sloper on the vertical line and HBL on the horizontal line. Trace the sleeve sloper onto the grid.

5. Place HBL on the *horizontal line* and move (X) on (D1). Draw from the sleeve cap to the halfway point. Also mark the wrist.

6. Place HBL on the *guideline* and move (X) on (D2). Draw the under-sleeve curve from the halfway mark to the underarm and cross-mark.

7. Draw a straight line to connect the underarm to the wrist.

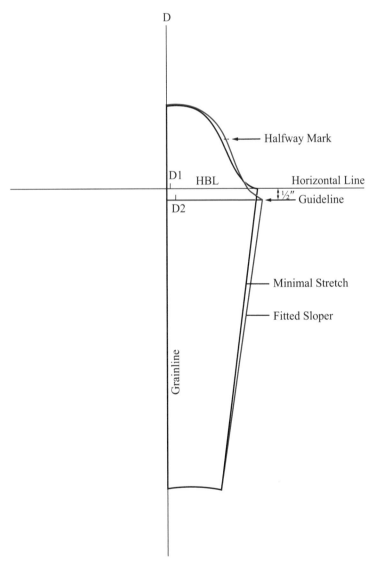

Figure 8.8d Grade the sleeve

Loose-fit

To create the loose-fit slopers, you grade the minimal stretch top slopers in a *positive* direction. The slopers are increased 6" for a total body increase. Table 8.1 charts the grading measurements for increasing the slopers.

Grade the Front and Back

Draw HBL on the underarm of the slopers (see Figure 3.17b on p. 37). Make sure (X) and (C-C3) are recorded (see Figure 6.6 on p. 99).

Prepare the Grading Grid

Figure 8.9a

1. Draw the grading grid and label (D) (see Figure 8.7). Draw the guideline parallel to the horizontal line.
2. Mark the grading increment from (D):

   - Shoulder Increase = ¾" (E2) on the *horizontal line*.
   - Quarter Body Increase = 1½" (G) on the *guideline*.

Trace Sloper, Grade Shoulder and Underarm and Draw Hemline

Figure 8.9a

1. Place the center front sloper on the vertical line and (X) on the horizontal line. Trace the sloper onto the grid.

2. Align the sloper on the *horizontal line*. Move sloper (X) to (E2) and mark the shoulder/armhole and trace to (C and C3). Cross-mark the apex.
3. Align the sloper on the *guideline*. Move sloper (X) to (G). Mark the underarm/side seam and draw the hemline.

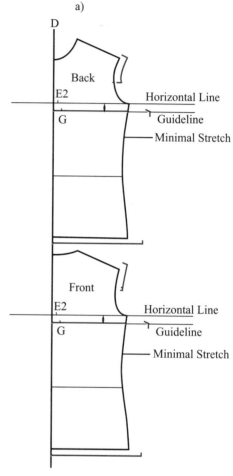

Figure 8.9a Trace the sloper, grade the shoulder and underarm, and draw the hemline

Draw the Shoulder Line, Under-sleeve Curve, and Side Seam

Figure 8.9b

1. Draw a straight shoulder line and side seam.
2. Draw a squared ¼" line at the underarm. Use a French curve to finish drawing the underarm curve. Then measure the front/back armhole length and record.

Grade the Sleeve

Figure 8.9c

1. Draw HBL across the bicep of the sleeve sloper. Draw a guideline halfway between the sleeve cap and HBL. Label (X) (see Figure 6.13a on p. 107). Refer to Table 8.1 for the grading measurements.

2. Draw the grading grid and label (D) (see Figure 8.7). Draw the guideline parallel to the horizontal line.
3. Mark grading increments from (D):
   - Sleeve Cap Increase = ⅜" (D3) on the horizontal line.
   - Bicep Increase = ¾" (E2) on the guideline.
4. Place the sloper on the vertical line and HBL on the horizontal line. Trace the sleeve sloper onto the grid.
5. Place HBL on the *horizontal line* and (X) on (D3). Trace the cap curve to the halfway point.
6. Place HBL on the *guideline* and (X) on (E2). Draw the under-sleeve curve from the halfway point to the underarm. Mark the wrist and draw the sleeve length.

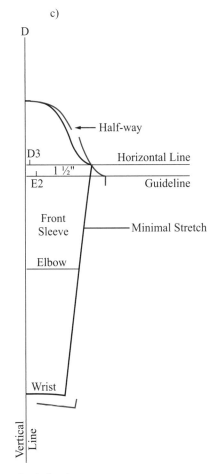

Figure 8.9c Grade the sleeve

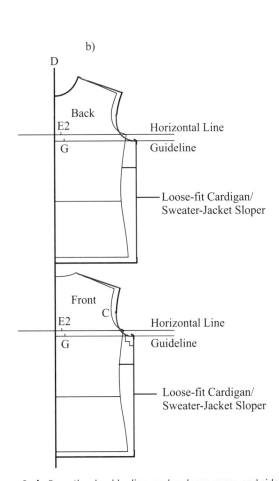

Figure 8.9b Draw the shoulder line, under-sleeve curve, and side seam

Finish Drawing the Sleeve Cap and Underseam
Figure 8.9d

1. Finish drawing the cap curve.
2. Draw a straight line to connect the underseam to the wrist.

3. Lower the elbow half the distance between the horizontal line and guideline.
4. Refer to "Align the Sleeve to the Armhole" section in Chapter 6 to align the sleeve to the armhole. To modify the capline/armhole ratio, refer to Figures 6.10 and 6.11 on p. 103.

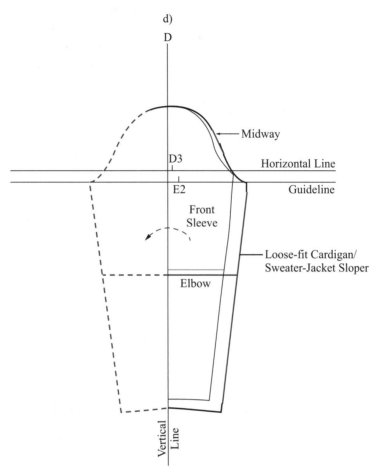

Figure 8.9d Finish drawing the sleeve cap and underseam

Oversized

To draft the oversized slopers, you enlarge the minimal stretch front/back slopers 8" for the total body increase. The underarm and under-sleeve curve are lowered 2" to enlarge the armscye. Table 8.1 charts the grading measurements for increasing the slopers.

Grade the Front and Back

Figure 8.10a

1. Draw HBL on the underarm of the slopers (see Figure 3.17b on p. 37). Use the same grading method for the front and back.
2. Prepare the grading grid (see Figure 8.7). Draw the guideline parallel to the horizontal line.
3. Mark grading increments from (D):
   - Shoulder Increase = 1" (F) on the *horizontal line*.
   - Quarter Body Increase = 2" (H) on the *guideline*.
4. Trace the two-way minimal stretch front/back slopers (with sleeves) on the grading grid.
5. Align HBL on the *horizontal line* and (X) on (F). Draw the shoulder/armhole tip to the armhole (C and C3).
6. Align HBL on the *guideline* and (X) on (H). Cross-mark the underarm/side seam and hem/side seam. Finish drawing the hem.
7. Draw the shoulder line and side seam.
8. Angle the French the curve diagonally from the underarm to mid armhole (C-C3). Trace the underarm curve. Draw a blending line where the two lines adjoin.

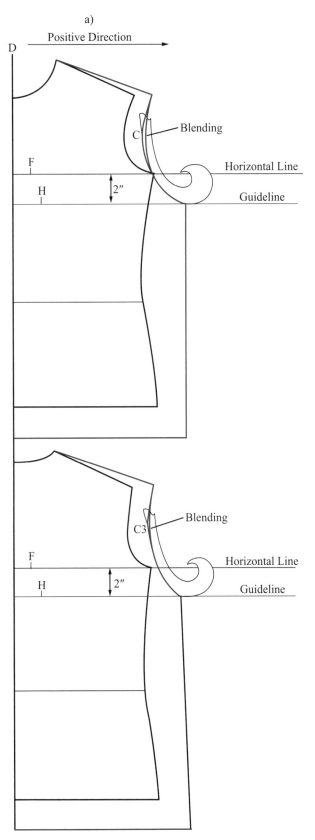

Figure 8.10a Grade the oversized front and back

Draft the Sleeve

Figure 8.10b

As the front/back armhole widens, it changes into a dropped shoulder. For this reason, you draft the oversized sleeve rather than grade it from the minimal stretch sleeve sloper.

1. Measure the total front/back armhole length and record.
2. C-W = Sleeve length minus 1". (Refer to Figure 5.5b on p. 70 to determine the sleeve length.)
3. C-D = ¼" squared.
4. W-B= Half wrist plus 1¼" to 1½" squared out from (W).
5. C-A = 4". Draw a squared lined and label the bicep.
6. U-D = Place a graph ruler on (C), and slant it until half the armhole measurement touches line (U).
7. U-B = Draw the underarm. Square at (B) as shown.
8. Divide the U-C *guideline* into fourths. Draw the shaped capline as shown in the figure. Remeasure the capline. A sleeve for a dropped shoulder *cannot* have any cap ease. Adjust the length if necessary.
9. C-E = Half of C-W. Draw a squared lined and label the elbow.
10. Trace the pattern to the other side to complete the oversized sleeve.

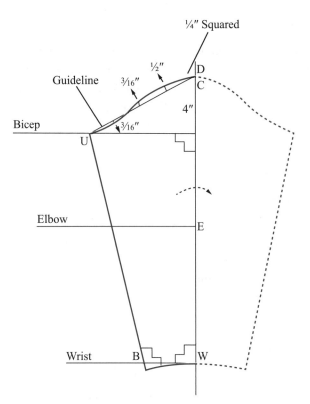

Figure 8.10b Draft the oversized sleeve

PATTERN TIP 8.1: NECKLINE ADJUSTMENT

After drafting the slopers, lower/widen the neckline so that the garment feels comfortable when worn over other clothing. After you adjust the total, the neckline length will be 1" longer.

1. Lower the front neckline ½".
2. Remove ¼" from the shoulder/neckline.
3. Draw a smooth neckline curve. (See Figure 8.11.)

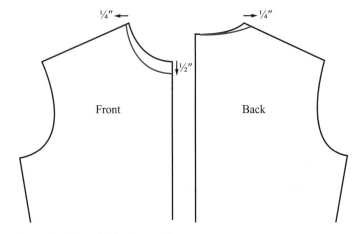

Figure 8.11 Lower/widen the neckline

Cut and Stitch

After the slopers are completed (with the neckline adjusted), cut and stitch the slopers in minimal stretch muslin knit.

1. Cut the back pattern on the fold of the fabric.
2. Cut two fronts. Add a 1" **button extension** for stitching the buttonholes and buttons to the cardigan (look ahead to Figure 8.14). Draw a line on the center front.
3. Add ¼" seam allowances to the shoulder, armholes, and side seams (but not the neckline).
4. To stitch the muslin, refer to the Stitching Order in Table 8.2.

TABLE 8.2: Stitching order for a cardigan

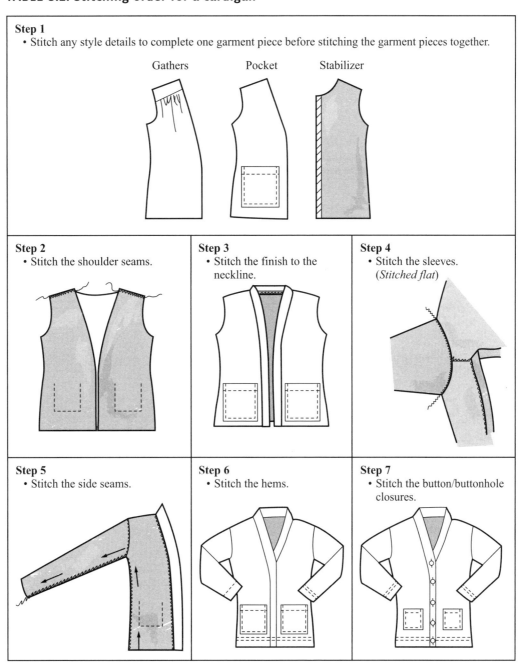

Step 1
- Stitch any style details to complete one garment piece before stitching the garment pieces together.

Gathers   Pocket   Stabilizer

Step 2
- Stitch the shoulder seams.

Step 3
- Stitch the finish to the neckline.

Step 4
- Stitch the sleeves. (*Stitched flat*)

Step 5
- Stitch the side seams.

Step 6
- Stitch the hems.

Step 7
- Stitch the button/buttonhole closures.

Test the Fit

Place the muslins on the form. Pin the center fronts together, and pin any fitting adjustments as needed. Finally, mark these adjustments on the patterns.

What to look for:

✓ Check that there is adequate room in the garment for the fit you envisage.

✓ Check the fit of the armscye. A person may need to wear the muslin for you to judge the fit.

Length Variations

Cardigans and jackets can be various lengths and anywhere in between these lengths (see Figure 8.12).

- *Waist*—Cut on the natural waistline
- *High-hip*—Between the waist and hip
- *Thigh Length*—Between the hip and the knee
- *Knee*—Middle of knee
- *Three-quarter Length*—Mid calf
- *Seven-eighth Length*—Between mid calf and ankle
- *Ankle Length*—A few inches above the floor

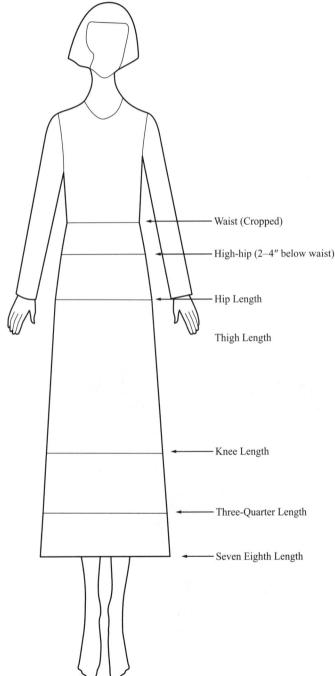

— Waist (Cropped)

— High-hip (2–4″ below waist)

— Hip Length

Thigh Length

— Knee Length

— Three-Quarter Length

— Seven Eighth Length

Figure 8.12 Length variations

Silhouette Variations

Cardigans and jackets can be fitted, loose-fit, boxy, straight-cut, pegged, A-line, or flared, asymmetrical, V or round neck, and with or without a collar or hood (see Figure 8.13). A fitted silhouette hugs the contour of the body. In contrast, a loose-fit silhouette does not follow the contour of the body closely because it has sufficient ease for a roomier fit.

IMPORTANT 8.1: WHICH SLOPERS TO USE

To draft the patterns for cardigans, sweaters, and sweater-jackets, you need to decide whether the garment will be fitted, loose-fit, or oversized. Next, you draft the appropriate slopers in accord with the fit. Another factor to consider is the type, weight, and drape of knit you are using when deciding on the fit. (Refer to the "Fabric Selection" section in Chapter 1.)

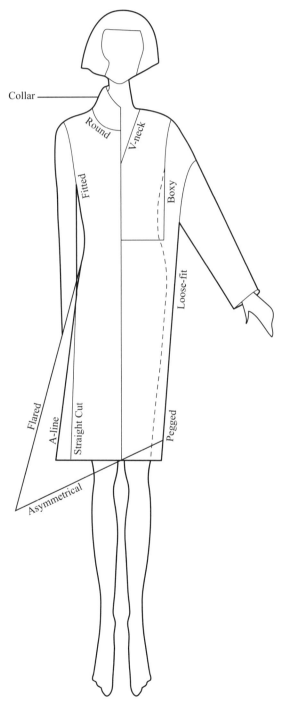

Figure 8.13 Silhouette variations

Pattern Drafting Cardigans

Jackets and cardigans can be constructed from two-way or four-way stretch knits. When designing a cardigan, conduct a stretch test of the knit you plan to use using the stretch gauge in Figure 1.6 on p. 9. Then design your cardigan style to suit the fabric type and weight. Refer to the "Designing for Knits" section in Chapter 1. If pockets are an element of your design, you see how to draft the patterns for three types of pockets in this chapter. Cardigans can be worn open or can be buttoned or have a tie-belt closure. If the cardigan is buttoned, you must add an extension to the center front for the buttons and buttonholes.

Buttonhole/Button Extension

Figure 8.14

1. Add an extension beyond the center front the width of the button diameter. For example, if the button diameter is ¾", then the extension is ¾".
2. The placement of the first buttonhole (down from the neck edge) is half the button diameter plus ¼".
3. Buttonholes can be horizontal or vertical. A buttonhole is ⅛" longer than the button diameter.

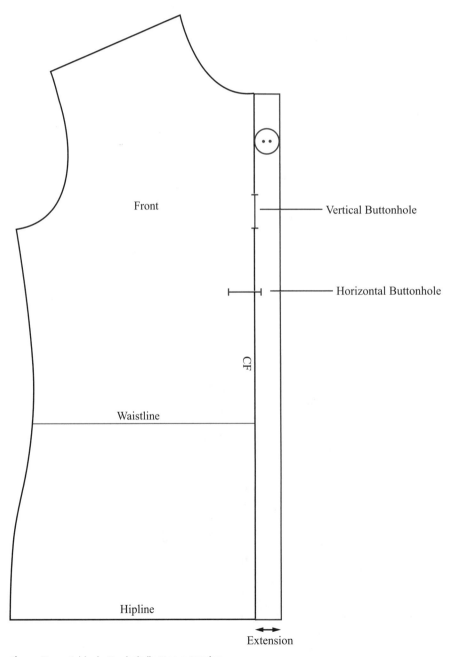

Front

Vertical Buttonhole

Horizontal Buttonhole

CF

Waistline

Hipline

Extension

Figure 8.14: Add a buttonhole/button extension

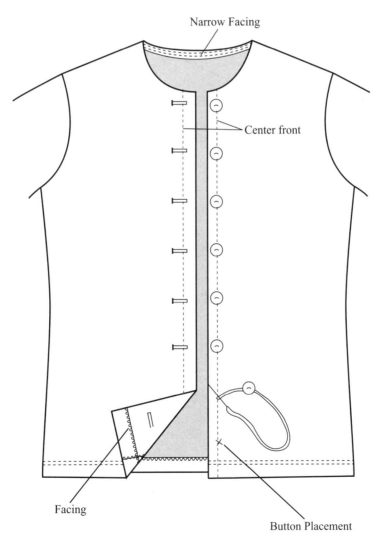

STITCHING TIP 8.1: STITCHING BUTTONS AND BUTTONHOLES

1. The buttonholes are stitched on the right-hand side, and the buttons are stitched to the left-hand side of the garment as indicated in Figure 8.15.
2. When the garment is buttoned, the right front laps over the left front, and the center fronts are aligned.

Pockets for Cardigans

Pockets must be large enough for use and placed at a comfortable height for the hand to enter. Use your hand as a guide when planning pocket size.

Pocket categories are

- *Patch*—A **patch pocket** is stitched to the outside of the garment. The lower edge can be square, rounded, or angled. The top edge can have a facing or band stitched to the edge. (Refer to Figures 8.16 and 8.17 to draft a patch pocket.)
- *Inseam*—An **inseam pocket** is inserted into the seam of the garment, such as a yoke, side seam, or princess line. A pocket bag is attached to the seam allowance and sits within the garment. (Refer to Figure 8.34 to draft an inseam pocket.)
- *Slash*—A **slash pocket** is stitched to a vertical, horizontal, or diagonal slit in the garment. A pocket bag is stitched to the slit and placed within the garment. Welt and zip-up pockets are both slash pockets. (Refer to Figures 8.39 and 8.40 to draft a welt pocket and Figure 8.51 to draft a zip-up pocket.)

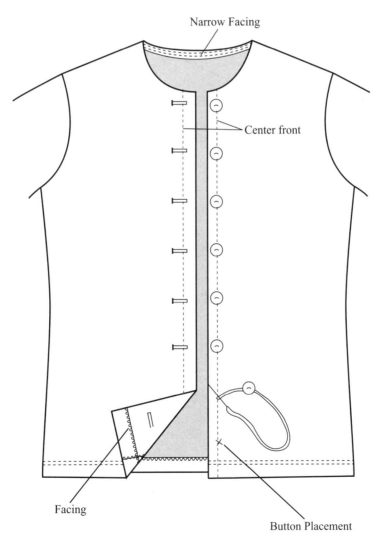

Narrow Facing

Center front

Facing

Button Placement

Figure 8.15 Stitched buttons and buttonholes

Button-front Cardigans

Numerous cardigan designs of different lengths can be buttoned. You learn how to draft two types of button-front cardigans—high-hip and hip length—in the following sections.

 ## Cardigan with V-neck Band and Patch Pockets

Using bands is a popular way to finish the neckline of a cardigan. The band is cut as a straight piece in two sections with a center back seam.

Draft Patterns
Figure 8.16a

1. Trace the front/back slopers onto pattern paper, and determine the length.
2. The band is *twice* the width of the button diameter. For example, if the button diameter is ¾", then the finished band width will be 1½".
3. A-B = Outline the front cardigan edge from the shoulder to half the band width extended beyond the center front.
4. C-D = Draw the width of the front band parallel to the (A-B) edge.
5. C-E = Draw the back band parallel to the neck edge.

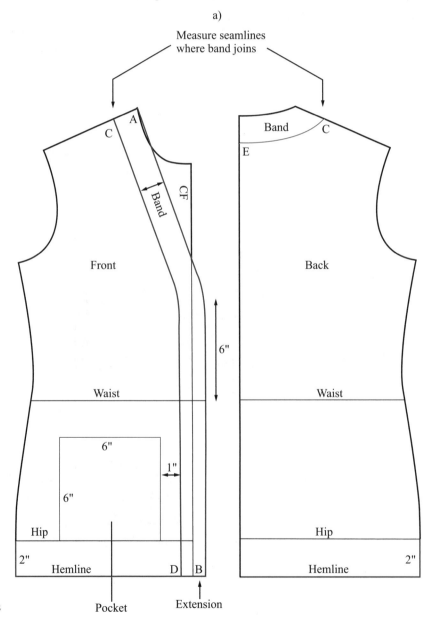

Figure 8.16a: Draft the front and back patterns

Draft the Band
Figure 8.16b

1. Measure front/back seamlines (C-E and C-D) where the band will be joined. Draw a straight line this length on pattern paper.
2. Draft the band pattern twice the finished width. Mark a notch at (C) to correspond with the shoulder seam. In this case, the band is not reduced in length. A shorter band would reduce the front length of the cardigan, and it would not sit correctly.

Draft a Patch Pocket
Figure 8.17

1. Draw the pocket outline on the pattern using your hand as a guide for the size.
2. Trace the pocket from the working pattern.
3. Add a 1" facing to the top edge.
4. Add ½" seam allowance to the remaining pocket edges.

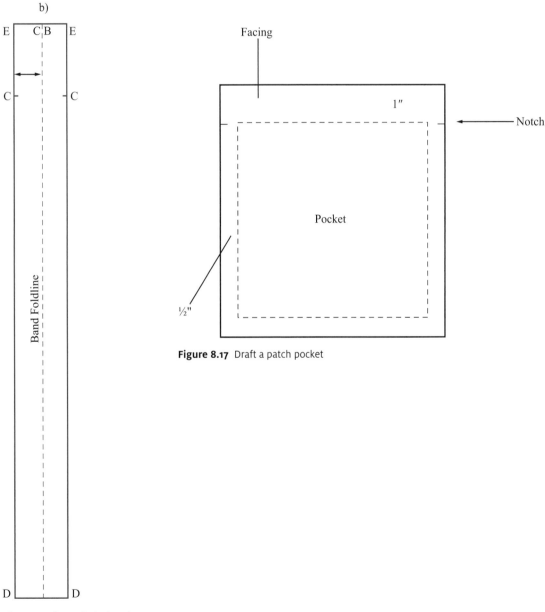

Figure 8.17 Draft a patch pocket

Figure 8.16b Draft the band

Finalize the Patterns

1. Trace the front/back patterns from the working patterns from the seamline where the band is joined. Mark pocket placement.
2. Add a ¼" seam allowance around the edge of the patterns. Add a 1" hem allowance.
3. Label the patterns, draw directional grainlines, and write the number of pieces to be cut.

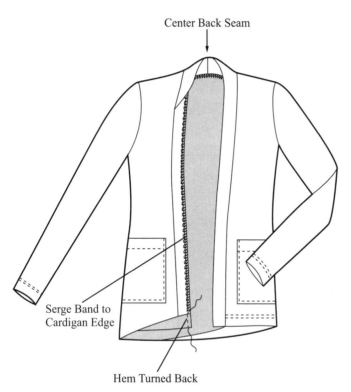

Center Back Seam

Serge Band to Cardigan Edge

Hem Turned Back

Figure 8.18 Stitching a V-neck cardigan

Cardigan with Built-up Neckline and Dolman Sleeves

A cardigan with dolman sleeves can be drafted from the fitted, loose-fit, or over-sized slopers. A feature of the cardigan is the built-up neckline. Facings are applied as a finish to the neckline and front edge of the cardigan.

Draft the Patterns

Figure 8.19

Trace the slopers onto the pattern paper and plot the dolman sleeves. (Refer to Figure 6.45 on p. 132). Label the center front/back neckline (E-F).

Then make the following pattern modifications:

1. Widen the three-quarter sleeves, and raise and curve the underseam to the wider side, as shown in Figure 8.19a.

a)

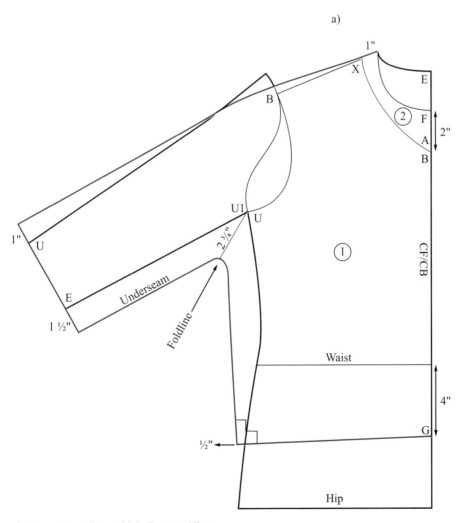

Figure 8.19a cardigan with built-up neckline

2. Draw a slash line from the shoulder to the center front/back and label the sections (1 and 2) (see Figure 8.19a).
3. Trace the pattern from the working pattern, and slash/spread the pattern, as shown in Figure 8.19b.

Draft the Facings

Figure 8.20

1. E-F = Draw a squared line at the front and back neckline.
2. Add a 1" extension parallel to (E-G). Label it "Foldline."

3. Fold the front pattern along the *foldline*, and trace the front neckline and 2" of the shoulder line.
4. Trace the back neckline and 2" of the shoulder line.
5. Outline the edge of the facings.
6. Reduce the height of the facing at the shoulder edge by ⅛".

Figure 8.19b Slash/Spread the Pattern

Draft Interfacing Patterns

Figure 8.20

1. Trace the front facing from the foldline to the facing edge and label.

2. Indicate that interfacing must also be cut for the back facing (see Figure 8.20).

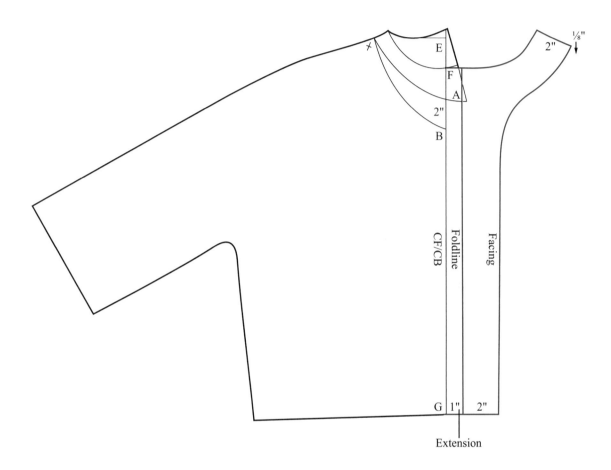

Figure 8.20 Draft the front and back facings

Finalize Patterns

Figure 8.21

1. Add ¼" seam allowances (including the facing edge).
2. Add a 2" hem allowance.
3. Draw directional grainlines.
4. Label the patterns and number of pattern pieces to cut.

STITCHING TIP 8.3: STITCHING THE DOLMAN SLEEVE CARDIGAN

1. Interface the facings.
2. Stitch the shoulder seams of the cardigan and facings. Serge a finish to the facing edge.
3. Stitch the facing to the neckline, understitch, turn, press, and topstitch 2" from the edge (see Figure 8.1b).
4. Stitch the side seams and hem.
5. Stitch vertical buttonholes.

Open-front Cardigans

The following cardigan patterns that you will draft are designed to hang open at the front. These cardigans can have comfortable pockets added if you choose to add this detail.

Flared Cardigan with Collar

This cardigan is knee length with the lower section flaring at the side seams while the top section remains fitted. The collar is also flared and drapes on the front.

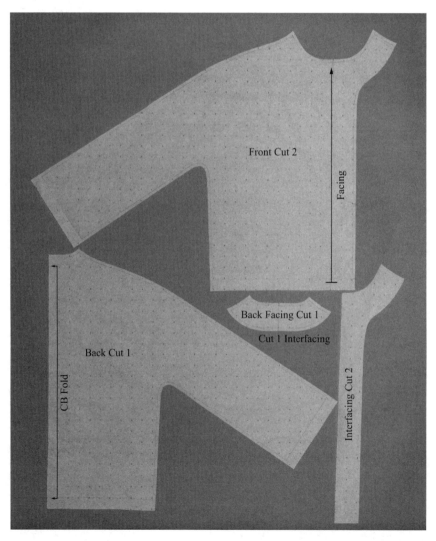

Figure 8.21 Final patterns for the button-front cardigan with built-up neckline and dolman sleeves

Draft the Patterns

Figure 8.22a

1. Trace the fitted front/back and sleeve slopers drafted in Figure 8.8. Draw the (U) line and waistline.
2. F = Extend the center front/back length 6".
3. G = Extend the front/back side seam length 12". Draw a 2" line squared out at side seams. Draw A-line side seams.
4. F-G = Draw a diagonal *front* hemline, mark midway, and draw the grainline (parallel to the center front).
5. K =1" in from the center back on the waistline.
6. H = 1" out from the center back at the hemline.
7. K-H-F = Draw a right angle.
8. F-G = Draw a guideline on the *back* hemline. Mark the midpoint, and draw the grainline (parallel to center back).
9. H-G = Draw a curved back hemline.

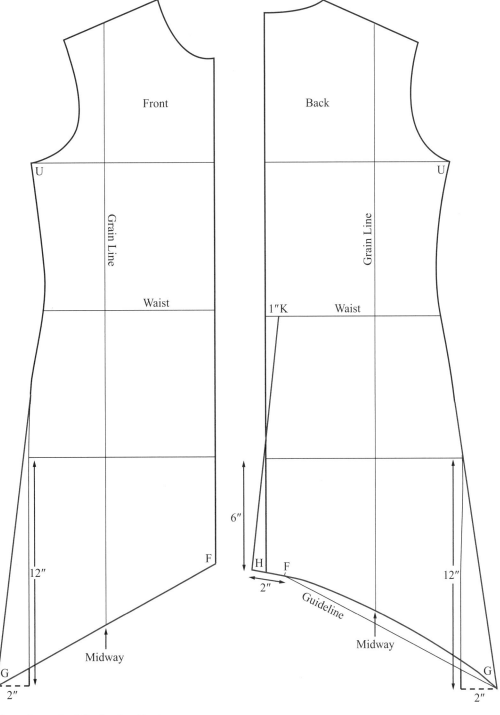

Figure 8.22a Draft the front and back

Draw the Neckline, Yoke, and Slash Lines
Figure 8.22b

1. C-X-F = Draw the front seamline where the collar will be joined (X is 2" above the waist).
2. C-D = Draw the back neckline.
3. Y-E = Draw a diagonal front yoke line.
4. U-Y = Measure the length of the *front* underarm curve. Transfer this measurement to the back.

5. Y-I = Draw a back yoke.
6. I-X-K = Draw the shaped center back seamline.
7. J = Place an L-square on the J-X line, and draw a squared yoke line.
8. X-A-B = Draw front/back slash lines as shown. Label panels (1, 2, and 3).

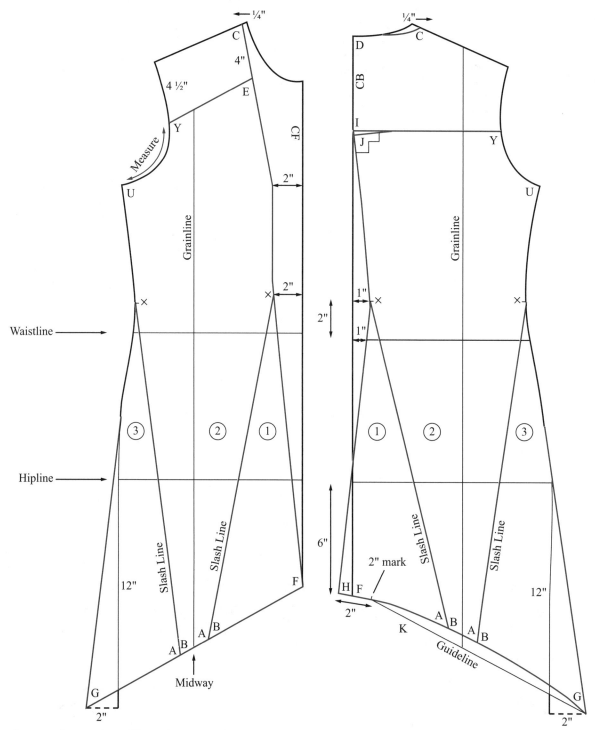

Figure 8.22b Draw the neckline, yoke, and slash lines

Slash/Spread the Pattern

Figure 8.23

1. Trace the front and back from working patterns. Draw slash lines and label sections (1, 2 and 3).
2. Draw a vertical line on pattern paper. Place the front/back grainline of panel (2) on the vertical line and trace.
3. Slash/spread panels (1 and 3), allow a space of 3", and trace each panel.
4. F-G = Draw the *front* diagonal hemline.
5. H-G = Draw the *back* curved hemline.
6. X = Drawing blending seamlines.

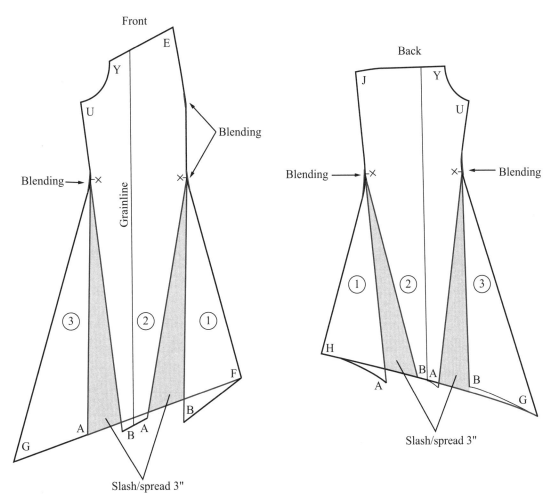

Figure 8.23 Slash/spread the patterns

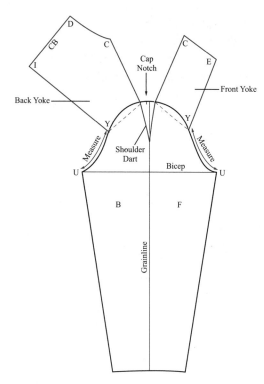

Figure 8.24 Draft the sleeve

Draft the Sleeve
Figure 8.24

1. Trace the sleeve sloper, draw the bicep, and label the front (F) and back (B) sleeves.
2. Transfer the (U-Y) underarm measurement shown in Figure 8.23, and mark this length on the front/back under-sleeve curve.
3. Place the front/back yokes on (Y) and shoulder/armhole on the sleeve cap. Trace the yokes.
4. Draw a curved dart from the shoulder to 3" below the cap notch. You need a space of ¾" to 1" for the dart. (If you don't have space for the dart, see Figure 8.25b.)
5. Align shoulder seams together at (C), and draw a blending neckline.

Sleeve Without Space for the Dart
Figures 8.25a and b

After adding the yokes, if there is no room for the dart on the sleeve cap, slash/spread the pattern and insert the dart as shown.

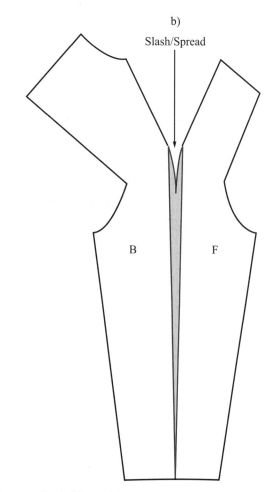

Figure 8.25a Sleeve without space for the dart

Figure 8.25b Slash/spread the pattern to add space for the dart

Draft the Collar

Figure 8.26

1. Measure the front/back seamlines where the collar will be joined.
2. Draw a right angle on pattern paper. On the vertical line, mark the following:
   - D-C = Back neckline.
   - C-E = Shoulder to yoke.
   - E-F = Yoke to collar length (5" up from cardigan hemline).
3. D-H = Draw a squared 2¼" line.
4. On the horizontal line, mark the collar width and square up 6".
5. F-G = Draw a diagonal guideline, mark the midpoint, square down ½", and draw the collar foldline and curved collar line.
6. Fold the pattern along the foldline, and trace the other side of the collar.

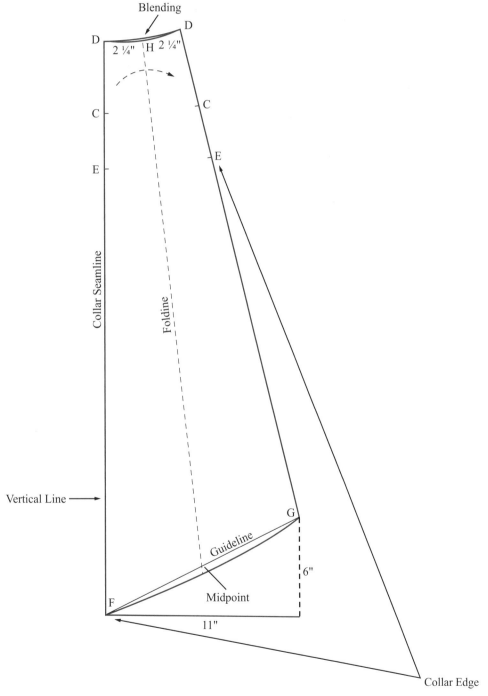

Figure 8.26 Draft the collar

Finalize the Pattern

Figure 8.27

1. Add ¼" seam allowance to both sides of the collar from D-E because both collar edges are stitched to the cardigan (look ahead to Figure 8.28).
2. Add an edge allowance from point (E) around the collar edge and hemline (from where the collar joins) to stitch a turned and topstitched edge finish. (Refer to Pattern Tip 8.2 and Figure 6.63 on p. 144 and Figure 8.26.)

3. Add seam allowances to the remaining pattern edges.
4. Label the patterns, draw directional grainlines, and write the number of pieces to be cut.

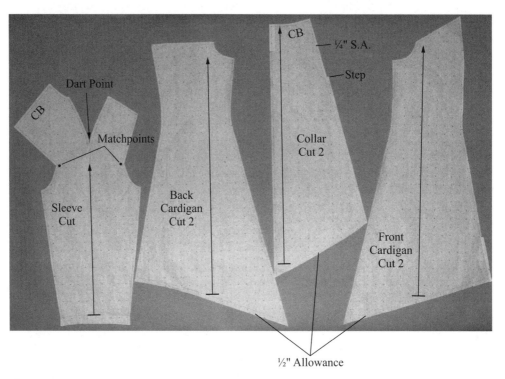

Figure 8.27 Final patterns for the flared cardigan with collar

Stitch the Collar

Figure 8.28

1. At (E), clip the collar to the seamline. Then stitch a
   turned and topstitched edge around the collar edge.
2. Fold the collar with wrong sides together. Stitch the
   collar edges (E-D) to the cardigan.
3. Stitch the remaining collar to the edge of the front
   cardigan.

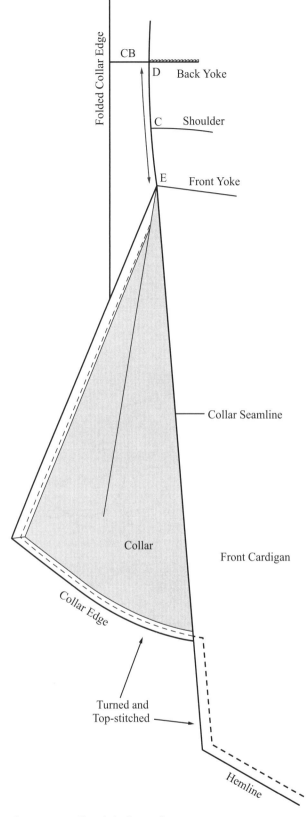

Figure 8.28 Collar stitched to cardigan

Draped Cardigan

This cardigan has a cascading drape that forms when the cardigan edge is aligned on the center front of the torso. To draft the patterns, use the fitted cardigan slopers. In this case, the front and back patterns are joined together, and the side seams are eliminated.

Trace the Slopers

Figure 8.29a

1. Trace both sides of the front slopers onto pattern paper. Align the back sloper underarm (U) and waist (W) to the front sloper. The back sloper overlaps the front at the hip.

2. Trace the back sloper as shown. Then label (H and A-A).

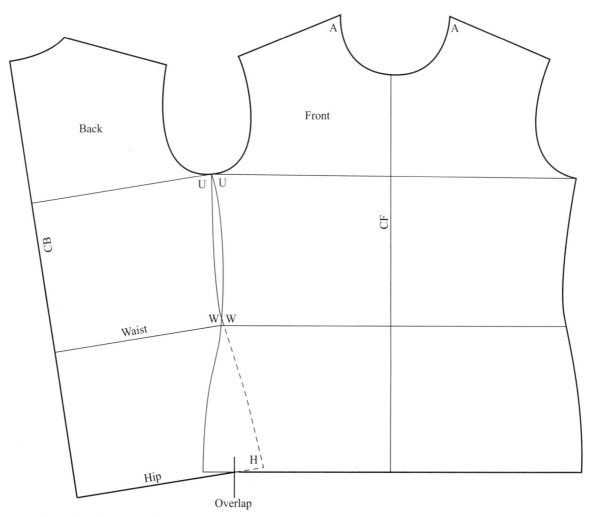

Figure 8.29a Trace the front and back slopers

Draw the Neckline and Hemline

Figure 8.29b

1. Extend the center front to shoulder height.
2. A-B = Draw an 18" guideline (squared at the center front).
3. B-C = Draw a 2" squared line.
4. C-H = Draw a diagonal guideline, mark midway, draw a squared 6" line, and label (D).
5. F = Extend the center back hemline 3" (or to your own length).
6. C-D-E-F = Draw a curved hemline.

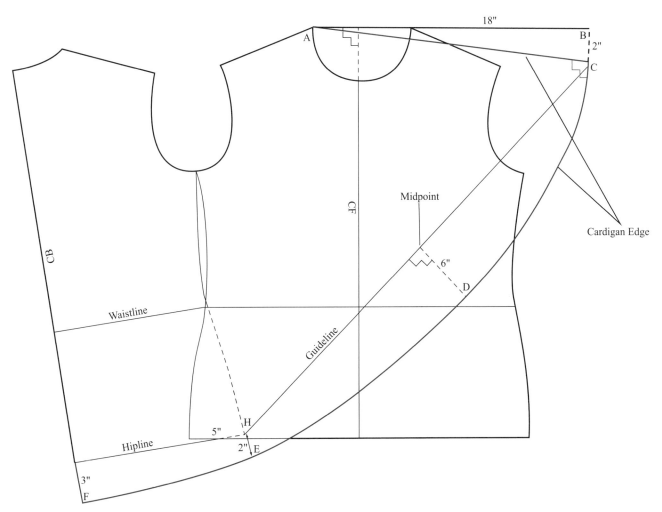

Figure 8.29b: Draw the neckline and hemline

Finalize the Patterns

Figure 8.30

1. Add a ½" allowance to the cardigan edge for a turned and topstitched finish.
2. Draw a directional seamline and mark the matchpoint at (A).
3. Add a ¼" seam allowance to the back neckline and shoulder seams.
4. Draw directional grainlines.
5. Label the patterns and number of pattern pieces to cut.
6. After cutting the cardigan, if the pattern does not fit in the layout when you place it on the fold of the fabric, cut the cardigan with a center back seam.

STITCHING TIP 8.4: STITCHING THE DRAPED CARDIGAN

Stitch a turned and topstitched edge around the front neckline, and the hem edge of the cardigan. Stitch a narrow facing as the back neckline finish (see Figure 6.51c on p. 137).

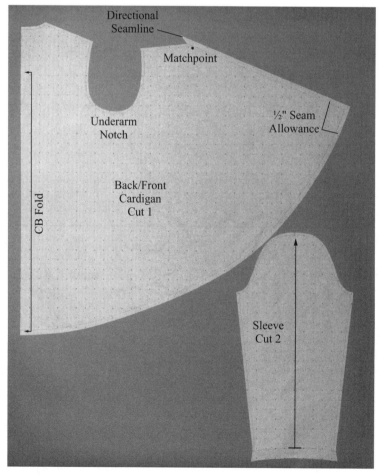

Figure 8.30 Final patterns for the draped cardigan

Wrapped Cardigan with Tie Belt

A wrapped cardigan has an extended wrap-over front and can be designed with a fitted or loose-fit silhouette. The cardigan can be worn open or wrapped and secured with a tie belt. The neck edge of this cardigan folds over into a front collar. For this reason, you must construct the cardigan from a double-sided knit that looks the same on both sides.

Draft the Patterns

Figure 8.31

1. Use the loose-fit or oversized slopers to draft the patterns for this design. Determine the length and outline the side seams.
2. Extend the center front to the shoulder height and hemline.
3. Add the wrap extension (squared at the center front).
4. B-C = Draw a parallel line to CF.

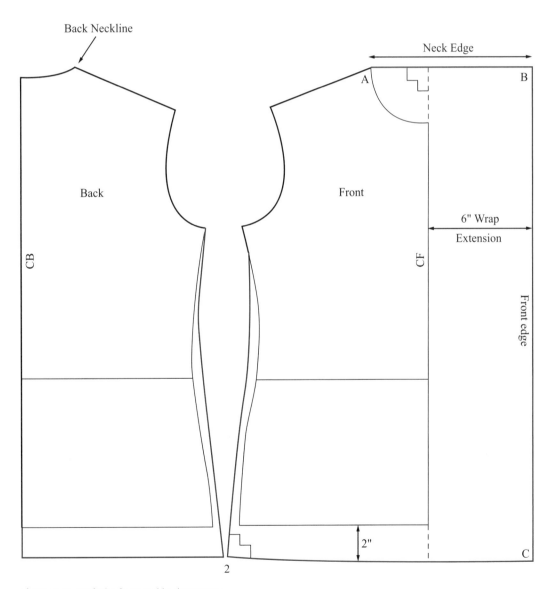

Figure 8.31 Draft the front and back patterns

Tie Belt

Figure 8.32

1. Draft the tie-belt pattern half the total length with a center back seam.
2. Add a ¼" seam allowance to the pattern edge.

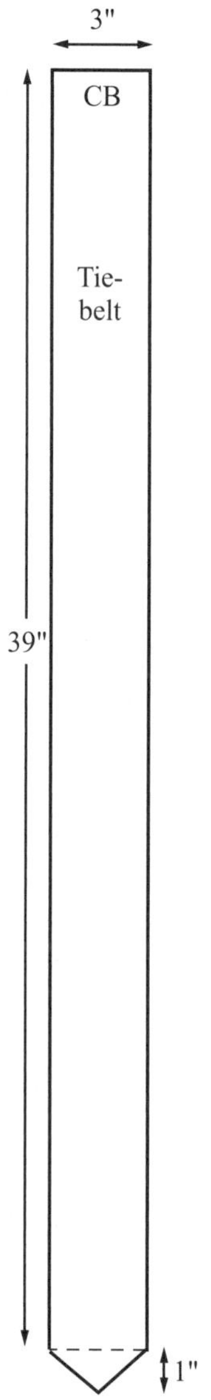

Finalize the Patterns

Figure 8.33

1. Add ¾" seam allowances to the front neck edge, front edge, and hemline. These edges are turned under ¼" and then turned and topstitched.
2. Draw a directional seamline and matchpoint at (A).
3. Add ¼" seam allowances to the remaining seams.
4. Draw directional grainlines and label the patterns.

STITCHING TIP 8.5: STITCHING THE WRAPPED CARDIGAN

Follow the Stitching Order in Table 8.2 to stitch the cardigan. Stitch a turned and topstitched edge finish to the front and hem edges. Stitch a narrow facing to the back neckline of the wrapped cardigan (see Figure 6.51c on p. 137).

Figure 8.32 Draft the tie belt

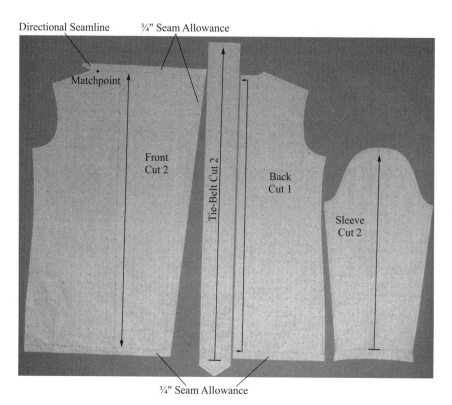

Figure 8.33 Final patterns for the wrapped cardigan with tie belt

Loose-fit Cardigan with Shawl Collar and In-seam Pockets

To draft a pattern for the loose-fit cardigan with shawl collar and in-seam pockets, follow the wrapped cardigan pattern in Figure 8.31. The length is extended, and a shawl collar is added to the wrap extension. Comfortable inseam pockets and wide sleeves are elements that complement a loose-fit style. The optimum fabric choice for this style is a double-sided knit that looks the same on both sides.

Draft the Patterns

Figure 8.34a

1. Trace the front/back *loose-fit* cardigan slopers onto pattern paper, determine the length, and outline the side seams (in this case, the dropped shoulder line directs the position of the side seams). (Refer to Figure 6.47 on p. 134.)

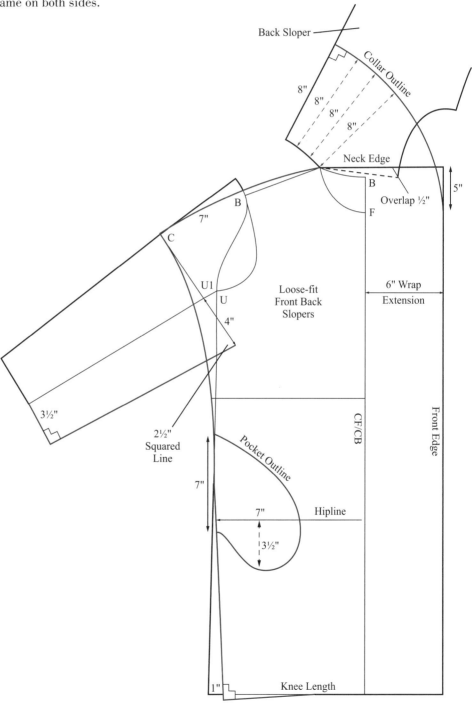

Figure 8.34a Draft the front, back, and sleeve patterns

2. Position the back sloper so the shoulder/armhole overlaps the neck edge ½". Trace the top section of the sloper.
3. Outline the shawl collar from the center back, and blend the collar line to the front pattern edge.
4. Mark a pocket opening on the side seam, and outline the pocket bag.
5. Trace the front, back, and sleeve patterns from the working patterns.

Draft the Pocket Bag

Figure 8.34b

A seam is necessary in the pocket so that the pattern pieces fit efficiently in the pattern layout. The pocket seam will not be visible. If the outer fabric is weighty, you can use a lighter-weight fabric for the pocket bag.

1. Trace the pocket bag to the other side of the seam.
2. Draw a line to indicate the extension. Add the extension to the front/back patterns.
3. Trace the remaining section of the pocket bag. (Refer to Figure 8.35 to see how the final pattern pieces look.)

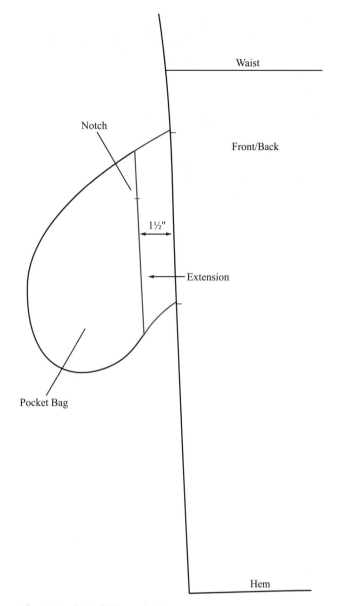

Figure 8.34b Draft the pocket bag

Finalize the Patterns

Figure 8.35

The collar and front edge of the cardigan can be finished with a binding. This type of finish requires no seam allowance added to the pattern edges. (Refer to the "Binding" section in Chapter 6, and see Figure 6.51b on p. 137).

1. Add a pocket bag to the front/back side seams. Add ½" seam allowances to the dropped shoulder/side seam and around the pocket bag.
2. Add a ¼" seam allowance to the other seamlines.
3. Mark matchpoints as shown.
4. Add a 1" hem allowance.
5. Draw directional grainlines and label patterns.

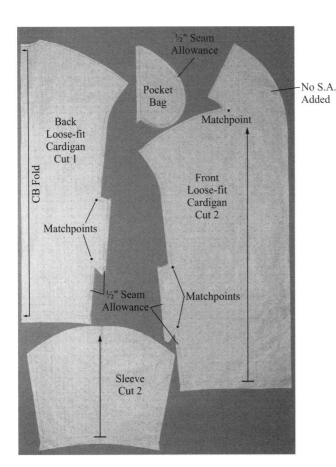

Figure 8.35 Final patterns for the loose-fit cardigan with shawl collar and in-seam pockets

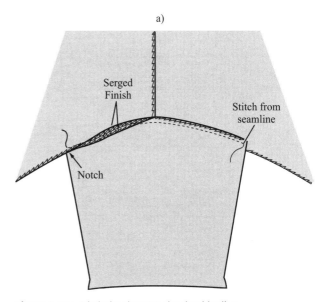

Figure 8.36a Stitch the sleeve to the shoulder line

b)

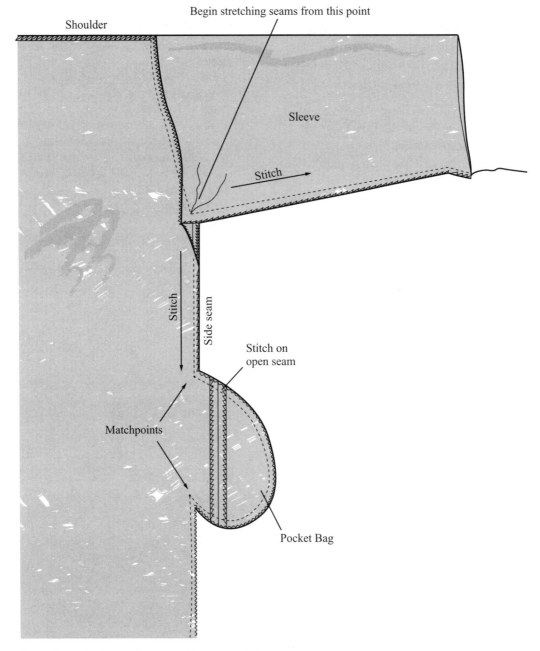

Shoulder

Begin stretching seams from this point

Sleeve

Stitch

Stitch

Side seam

Stitch on
open seam

Matchpoints

Pocket Bag

Figure 8.36b Stitch the side seam and in-seam pocket

Wrap-around-the-body Cardigan

A wrap-around-the-body cardigan must be made from a four-way stretch knit (with length-wise stretch) because it is cut on the length-wise grain of the fabric. The cardigan can be drafted from fitted or loose-fit slopers. The cardigan can be warmly wrapped or worn open with a lovely drape on the front. Figure 8.37 shows how the sleeves are stitched into a circular armhole.

Draft Pattern

Figure 8.38a

1. Draw a right angle on pattern paper.
2. A-B = Front/back sloper hip length.
3. B-X = Front/back sloper hip to underarm length.
4. X-Y = At (X), align the front/back underarm to the vertical line and shoulder/armhole tip on the vertical line. Trace front and back armholes.

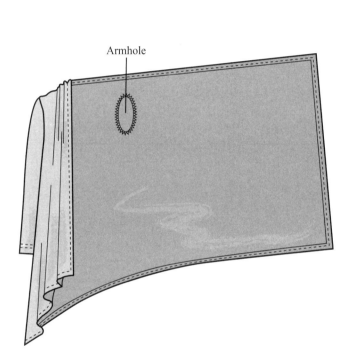

Figure 8.37 Wrap-around-the-body cardigan with the sleeve stitched into a circular armhole

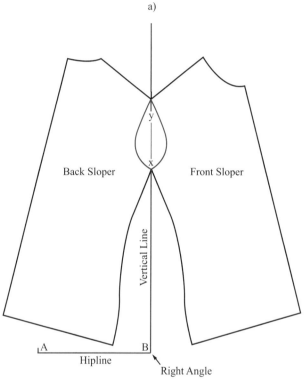

Figure 8.38a Draft the armhole opening

Add the Wrap Section

Figure 8.38b

1. Y-E = Shoulder/neckline height.
2. A-D-E = Draw a right angle.
3. E-F and B-C = Add the wrap length.
4. C-F = Draw a straight line.

5. Draw blending lines at (X-Y). Notch the armhole to correspond with the under-sleeve seam and cap notch.
6. To add an allowance to the pattern edges for a turned and topstitched finish, refer to Pattern Tip 8.2.

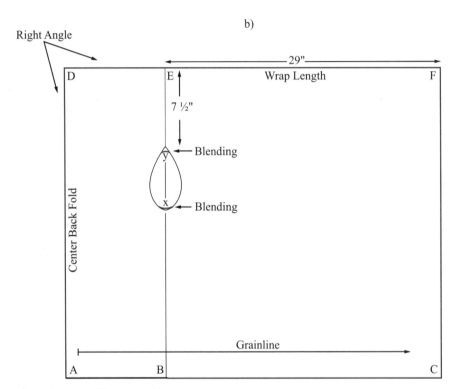

Figure 8.38b Add the wrap section

Pattern Drafting Sweater-Jackets

Sweater-jackets are usually designed with a zipper closure, comfortable pockets, and a collar or a hood. In the following sections, you learn how to draft the patterns for a fitted and loose-fit sweater-jacket. See Table 8.3 to review the Stitching Order for a sweater-jacket.

Pockets for Sweater-Jackets

Sweater-jackets generally have small pockets to fit proportionally a short jacket length. A minimal size pocket will fit a cell phone or carry cash. Sweater-jackets can have patch, inseam, or slash pockets as part of the design. (Refer to the "Pockets for Cardigans" section for a definition of each pocket.) In the following sections, you draft and stitch welt and zip-up pockets. Both are slash pockets.

TABLE 8.3: Stitching order for a sweater-jacket

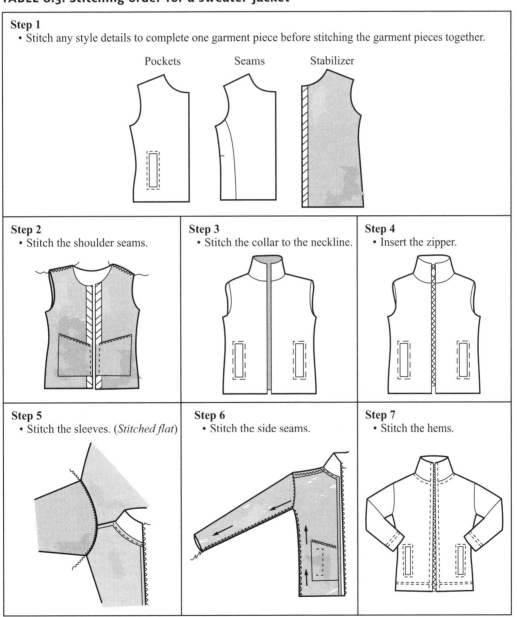

Step 1
• Stitch any style details to complete one garment piece before stitching the garment pieces together.

Pockets　Seams　Stabilizer

Step 2
• Stitch the shoulder seams.

Step 3
• Stitch the collar to the neckline.

Step 4
• Insert the zipper.

Step 5
• Stitch the sleeves. (*Stitched flat*)

Step 6
• Stitch the side seams.

Step 7
• Stitch the hems.

Zip-up Sweater-Jacket with Welt Pockets and Hood

For a zip-up sweater-jacket with welt pockets and hood, like the one shown in Figure 8.2a, calculate the zipper length you require early in the pattern drafting process because you may need to order the zipper online.

Draft Patterns

Figure 8.39a

1. Trace the front/back slopers and determine the length.
2. Plot the front princess line; then transfer the same princess line to the back pattern.
3. Draw a rectangle 5" × ¾" to represent the welt pocket. Label it "Box."
4. Outline the pocket bag.

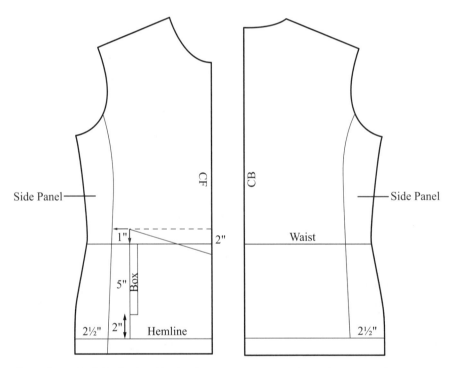

Figure 8.39a Draft the front and back patterns

Draft the Side Panel

Figure 8.39b

1. Draw a vertical line on pattern paper. Trace the side panel on each side of the line (both panels are the same shape).

2. Measure the excess from the waist side seam to the vertical line. Remove this amount from the princess line at the waist.

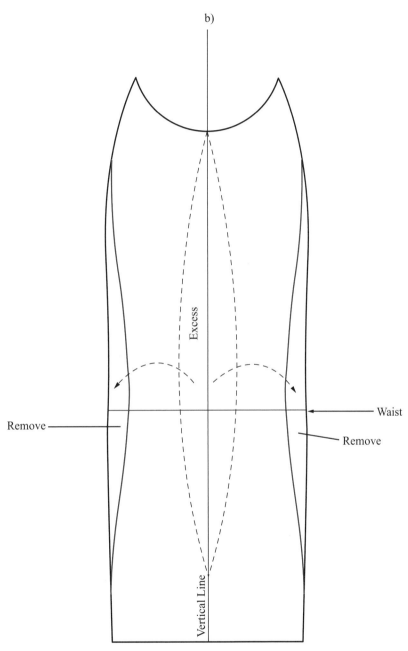

b)

Excess

Vertical Line

Remove

Remove

Waist

Figure 8.39b Draft the side panel

Draft the Welt Pocket

Figure 8.40a

The welt pocket is a slash pocket that can be horizontal, vertical, or diagonal. One piece of fabric forms the welt pocket and the pocket bag. Here, the finished width of the welt is ¾" and is indicated by the rectangle box. The box and welt are identical.

1. Trace the box onto a piece of pattern paper large enough to draft the entire pocket pattern.
2. To the right, draw the welt. Label (A-B). Draw the pocket bag next to the welt.
3. To the left of the box, add 1" and label it "Foldline."

Fold and Cut the Pocket

Figure 8.40b

1. Crease line (A-B), and fold the pattern so the welt is placed under the box.
2. Crease the foldline so you have two layers of paper.
3. Add a ⅜" seam allowance to the center front only and top pocket edge. The lower edge of the pocket bag will align on the jacket hemline.

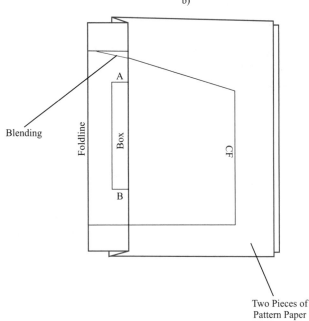

Figure 8.40b Fold and cut the pocket

Hood

A hood can be constructed as one fabric layer (with a visible seam), or it can be lined (in which case the seam is hidden). Consider the weight of the fabric when deciding whether or not to line the hood. Use twill tape to finish the neckline. A hood also can include a drawstring (inserted through the facing) to tighten the edge. One option for the drawstring is to use a braided 45" to 49" shoelace string. (See http://www.laceheaven.com for options.)

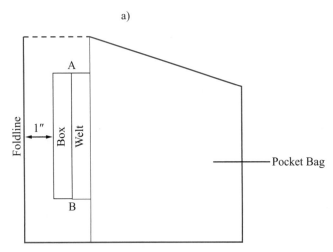

Figure 8.40a Draft the welt pocket

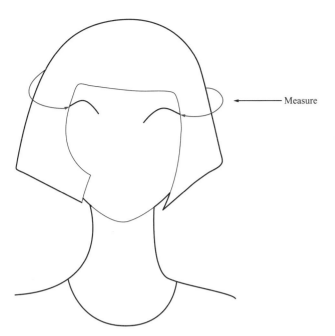

Figure 8.41 Measure around the head from eyebrow to eyebrow

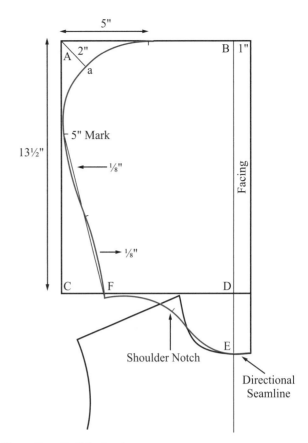

Figure 8.42 Draft the hood

Measure the Head

Figure 8.41

Prior to drafting the hood pattern, measure the head from one eyebrow to the other eyebrow.

Draft the Hood

Figure 8.42

Measure the pattern neckline from the center front to center back. Then double the measurement to determine the total neckline length of the hood.

1. Draw a rectangle on pattern paper:
   - A-B = Half eyebrow to eyebrow measurement.
   - A-C = 13½".
   - C-D = Equal to A-B.
   - B-D = Equal to A-C.
2. Extend the line below (D). Place the center front pattern on line (B-D) and shoulder/neckline tip on line (C-D). Trace the neckline and shoulders. Label (E).
3. D-F = Mark half the total neckline length.
4. E-F = Draw the shaped neckline as shown. Measure the neckline, and adjust the length to the original neckline length. Mark a notch on the shoulder.
5. Mark 5" on each side of (A).
6. G = Draw a 2" line at 45°.
7. Draw a diagonal line from the 5" mark to (F).
8. B-G-F = Draw a shaped hood seam. Draw a squared back neckline at (F).
9. Add a 1" facing to line (B-D) for a serged finish. Add a 1¼" facing for a turned and topstitched finish.

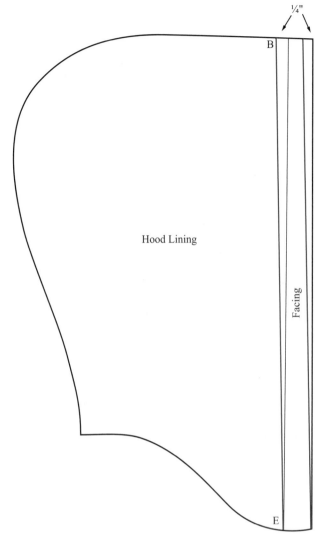

Figure 8.43 Draft the hood lining

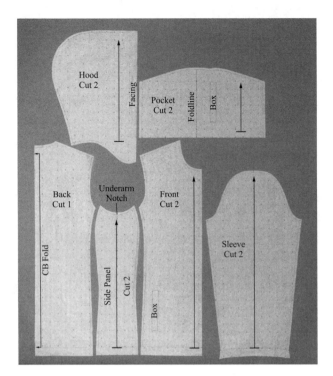

Figure 8.44 Final patterns for the zip-up sweater-jacket with welt pockets and hood

Draft the Hood Lining
Figure 8.43

1. Trace the hood pattern from Figure 8.42.
2. Remove ¼" from the top edge at (B). Draw a straight line from this point to (E). Label the pattern.

Finalize the Patterns
Figure 8.44

1. Add a ⅜" seam allowance to the center front pattern where the zipper will be applied.
2. Add ¼" seam allowances to the remaining pattern edges.
3. Add a 1" hem allowance.
4. Notch the hemline and side panel underarm.
5. Draw directional grainlines; then label the patterns and number of pieces to cut. (See Figure 8.44.)

Stitch the Box
Figures 8.45b through d

1. Place the correct side of the pocket bag and garment together. Align each interfaced pocket box together and pin in place.

a)

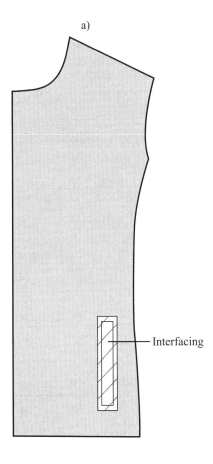

Interfacing

Figure 8.45a Press the interfacing to the garment

b)

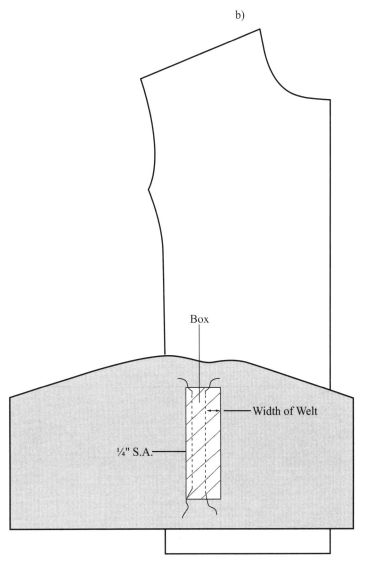

Box

Width of Welt

¼" S.A.

Figure 8.45b Stitch the box

2. Stitch two parallel rows, beginning and ending with backstitches (see Figure 8.45b).
3. Cut a slit between the two rows of stitching to within ¼" of each end. Clip diagonally into the corners up to the stitching (see Figure 8.45c).

c)

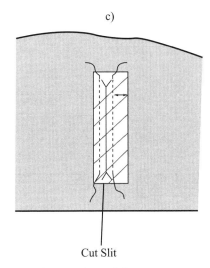

Cut Slit

Figure 8.45c Slit the pocket and clip

4. Turn the pocket through the opening to the wrong side and press. Turn the seam allowance (closest to the side seam) toward the side seam and understitch (see Figure 8.45d).

Form the Welt
Figures 8.45e and f

1. Turn the seam allowance of the pocket (closest to the garment) toward the front. From the correct side, fold the welt to fill the empty box. (The welt folded edge is butted next to the understitched pocket seam.) Press the welt; then pin and edgestitch one side of the pocket (see Figure 8.45e).
2. Fold the pocket edges together, and press the

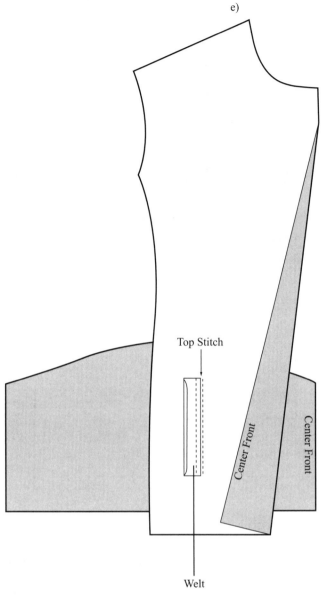

Figure 8.45e Form the welt and edgestitch

folded edge (next to the side seam) (see Figure 8.45f).
3. Lift the garment back to expose the triangles at each side of the welt. Stitch the triangles to the pocket bag (see Figure 8.45f).
4. Edgestitch the remaining three sides of the welt. The welt topstitching will show on the wrong side of the pocket bag (look ahead to Figure 8.47). Begin stitching from the previous row of edgestitching. When completed, pull the threads behind the pocket, tie a knot, and bury threads under the seam.
5. Serge the pocket edge.

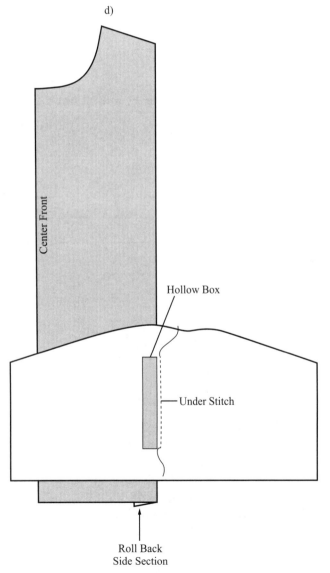

Figure 8.45d Understitch the pocket seam

f)

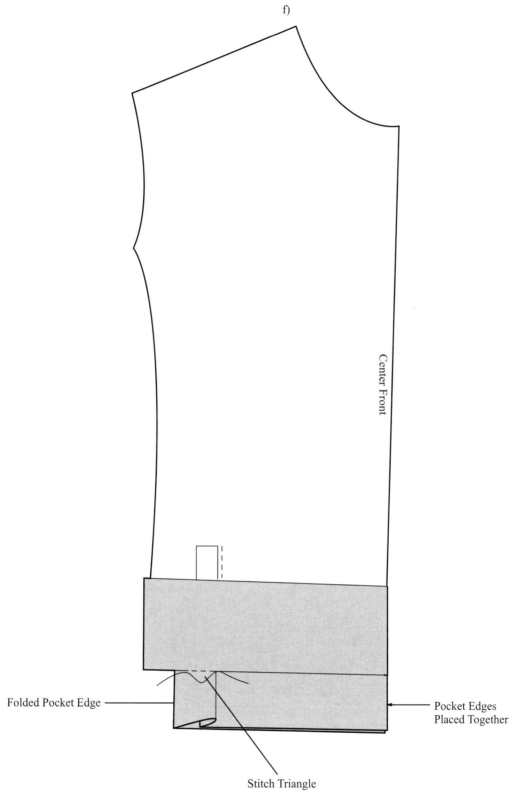

Center Front

Folded Pocket Edge ————

Pocket Edges
Placed Together

Stitch Triangle

Figure 8.45f Stitch triangles to the pocket bag

Stitching the Hood
Figures 8.46a and b; Figure 8.47

1. If the hood has a drawstring, press a small square of interfacing on the facing in the position where the buttonholes will be stitched. Then stitch two buttonholes.
2. Stitch the hood seam.
3. Topstitch the facing (see Figure 8.46a).
4. After the hood is stitched to the sweater-jacket, stitch twill tape to the seam to finish the neck edge (see Figure 8.46b).
5. The inside view of the sweater-jacket in Figure 8.47 shows how all the jacket components are stitched.

a)

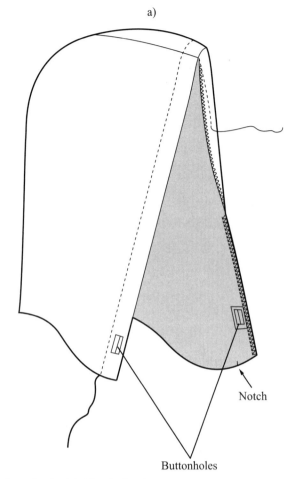

Figure 8.46a Stitching the hood

b)

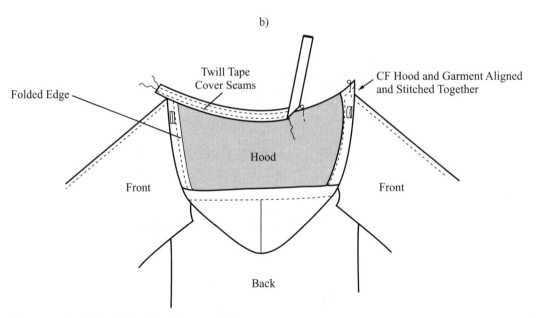

Figure 8.46b Stitching the hood to the sweater-jacket

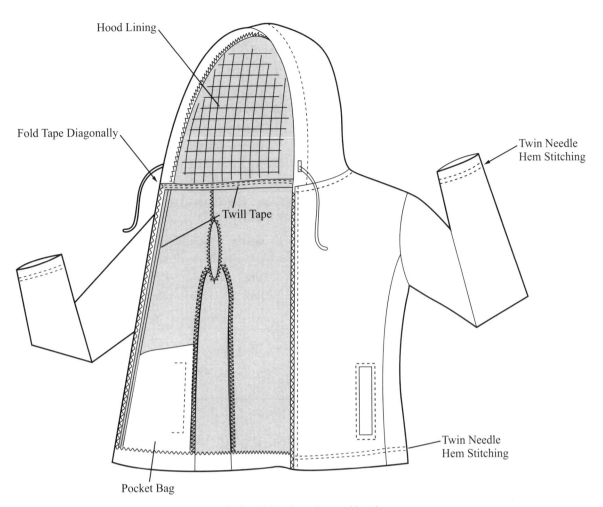

Hood Lining

Fold Tape Diagonally

Twill Tape

Twin Needle
Hem Stitching

Twin Needle
Hem Stitching

Pocket Bag

Figure 8.47 Inside view of the zip-up sweater-jacket with welt pockets and hood

Zip-up Sweater-Jacket with Zip-up Pockets and Collar

To create a zip-up sweater-jacket with zip-up pockets and collar, purchase a plastic auto-lock separating zipper. To determine the length, place the collar, front top, and band pattern seamlines together. Then measure the length from the collar foldline to the lower edge of the band. Add ¼" to this length. Finally, determine the zipper length of the pocket. In this case, it is designed to fit a cell phone. The bands can be cut from a rib knit or self fabric.

Draft the Patterns

Figure 8.48

1. Trace the front/back and sleeve slopers onto pattern paper. Determine the jacket length.
2. Lower the front/back neckline as shown.
3. Draft the bands 3" wide (or to your own specifications).
   - A–B–C–D = Draw the front band (the front and back are the same size).
   - E–F–G–H = Draw the back band.
   - I–J–K–L = Draw the sleeve band.
4. On the front, draw a line 2" in from and parallel to CF. This line will help set up the pocket placement. Draw a line the length of the pocket opening. Draw a line ¼" on each side of the 4" line. Label it "Box."

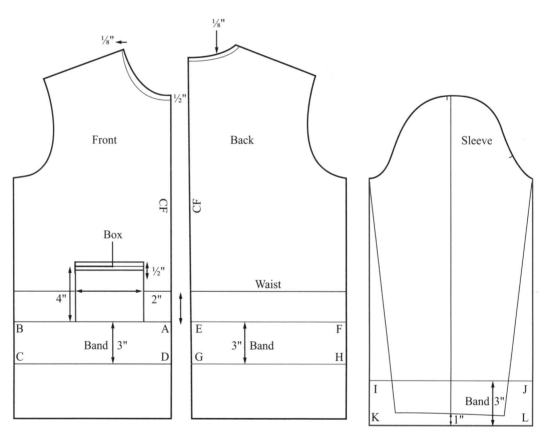

Figure 8.48 Draft the front, back, and sleeve patterns

Draft the Bands

Figure 8.49

1. Draw a horizontal line on pattern paper the total length of the seamline where the band will be joined.
2. Reduce the length by 1/7. (Refer to Figure 6.53 on p. 138.)
3. Double the band width.
4. Mark notches on the hem band.

Draft the Collar

Figure 8.50

1. Measure the pattern neckline from the center front to center back, and double this measurement to determine the total length.
2. Draw a horizontal line on pattern paper the total length of the neckline. Mark notches to correspond with the center back and shoulder seam of the garment patterns.
3. Outline the collar width. Remove ¼" from the foldline of the collar edge. Notch this point.
4. Trace the collar to the other side of the foldline to complete the collar pattern.

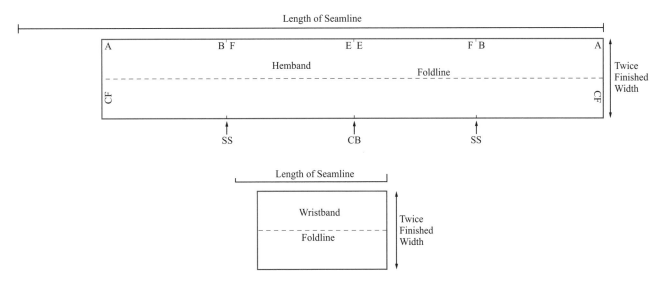

Figure 8.49 Draft the bands

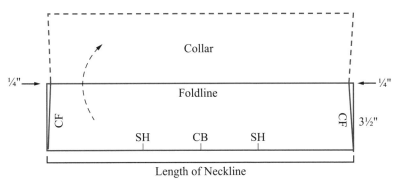

Figure 8.50 Draft the collar

Draft the Zip-up Pocket

Figure 8.51

1. Trace the box on the front pattern shown in Figure 8.48.
2. Draft the pocket bag:
   - Add 1" above the box. Label it "foldline."
   - Add the total width of the pocket bag and box above the foldline.
   - Trace the pocket bag to the lower edge of the box.
3. Add seam allowances: ¾" to the sides and ½" to the top and bottom pocket edges.

Finalize the Patterns

Figure 8.52

1. Add $^3/_8$" seam allowances to the center front top, collar, and band patterns where the zipper will be stitched.
2. Outline "box" on the front pattern and pocket.
3. Notch the lower edge of the front pattern where the pocket bag will be aligned when stitched.
4. Notch the collar foldline.
5. Add ¼" seam allowances to the remaining pattern edges.
6. Draw directional grainlines and label the patterns.

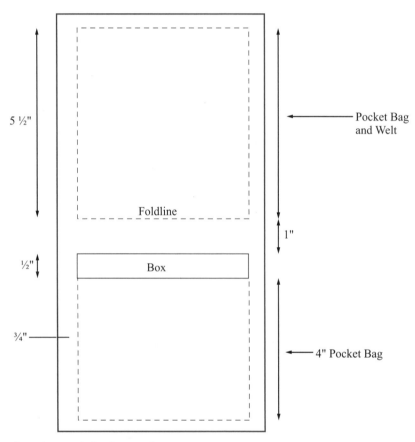

Figure 8.51 Draft the zip-up pocket

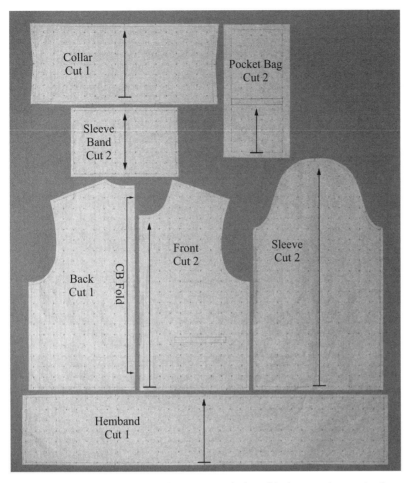

Figure 8.52 Final patterns for the zip-up sweater-jacket with zip-up pockets and collar

STITCHING TIP 8.8: STITCHING THE ZIP-UP POCKET

1. Mark each corner of the box on the wrong side of the garment and pocket.
2. Cut four interfacing pieces in a stable direction 1¼" wide and ½" longer than the box. Outline the box on each piece of interfacing (see Figure 8.53a).
3. Align the interfacing-outlined box on the garment and pocket markings and then press.
4. Place the correct side of the pocket bag and garment together with boxes aligned; then pin.
5. Stitch the four sides of the box (see Figure 8.53b).
6. Cut a slit between the two rows of stitching to within ¼" of each end, and clip diagonally into the corners up to the stitching.
7. Turn the pocket bag inside the garment and press. (The box is now empty awaiting the zipper.)
8. Place the zipper in the empty box, pin, and edgestitch (see Figure 8.53c).
9. Fold the pocket edges together, stitch, and serge the edge. Trim the bottom edge of the pocket if there is excess fabric (see Figure 8.53d).

a)

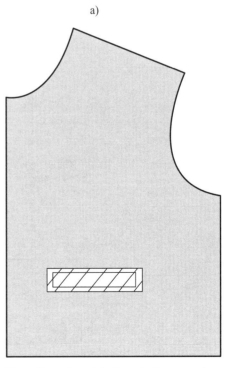

Figure 8.53a Press interfacing to the garment

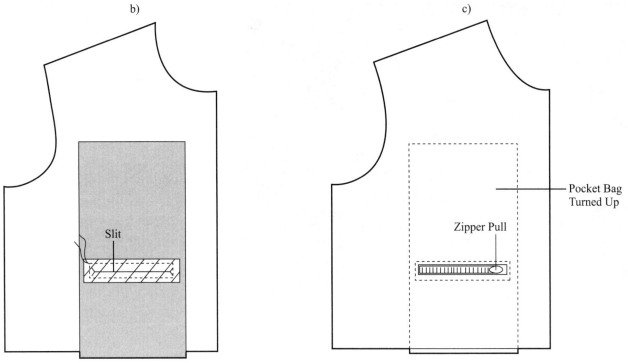

b)

Slit

Figure 8.53b Stitch the box

c)

Pocket Bag
Turned Up

Zipper Pull

Figure 8.53c Stitch the zipper in the pocket

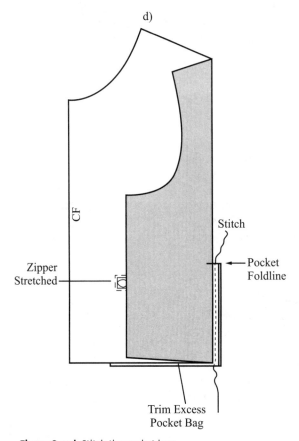

d)

CF

Zipper
Stretched

Stitch

Pocket
Foldline

Trim Excess
Pocket Bag

Figure 8.53d Stitch the pocket bag

Knit It Together

This checklist summarizes what you have learned about drafting slopers and patterns for cardigans and sweater-jackets in this chapter.

- ✓ Slopers for jackets made from knits with minimal stretch are drafted from jacket slopers made for woven fabrics.
- ✓ Slopers for cardigans and sweater-jackets must be larger than top slopers because these garments are worn over other clothing and must feel comfortable.
- ✓ Cardigans, sweaters, and sweater-jackets can be fitted, loose-fit, or oversized.
- ✓ Cardigans and sweater-jackets can have a collar, a hood, and pockets.

Stop: What Do I Do If . . .

. . . my fitted button-front cardigan looks too tight on the form? I used the top slopers to draft the patterns.

To draft patterns for a fitted cardigan, you must enlarge the top slopers 2" to 3" larger. The extra room will generate a comfortably fitted cardigan. (Refer to the "Fitted," "Loose-fit," and "Oversized" sections.)

. . . I want to draft the patterns for the cardigan in Figure 8.1c. However, I would like to incorporate inseam pockets (in the side seams) and a neck band (not buttoned). How do I do this?

The pattern making techniques in this textbook are flexible in use. For this reason, you can use parts of one pattern for other designs. Here's what you do: First, draft the cardigan patterns shown in Figure 8.1c. Next, draft the pocket pattern shown in Figure 8.34b. Last, draft the band pattern to fit the required length of the neckline seam (see Figure 8.16b).

Self-Critique

1. Two different sized slopers can be used to draft the patterns for cardigans. What are they?
2. What sections of the slopers are increased/enlarged to draft loose-fit slopers? (Refer to Table 8.1.)
3. How would you determine the width to add to the pattern for a buttonhole/button extension for the cardigan in Figure 8.1b?
4. What are the three pocket categories? Write a brief description of each.
5. For the cardigan in Figure 8.1f, what would you need to be attentive to when drafting the pocket opening and pocket bag to make sure they are functional?
6. The cardigan in Figure 8.1a has a neckband. The neckband pattern is drafted as a straight pattern piece according to the total length of the seam. The V-neck sweater in Figure 6.1b on p. 96 also has a neckband that is reduced in length. Why does the cardigan band pattern differ from the neckband pattern for the T-shirt? (Refer to the "Neckline Finishes" and "Reduce the Length" section in Chapter 6 and Figure 6.57 on p. 140.)
7. A hood can be constructed in two different ways. What are they? How is each hood pattern drafted?

Key Terms	
Button Extension	Oversized Slopers
Fitted Slopers	Patch Pocket
Inseam Pocket	Slash Pocket
Loose-fit Slopers	Sweater-Jackets

9 Skirt Slopers and Patterns

Skirts made from stretch knit fabrics are versatile pieces that can be paired with a variety of tops. This chapter teaches you how to develop skirt slopers and how to transform them into your own pattern design. By introducing a new silhouette or length modification, skirt styles can be full and flirty, short and curve-flattering, knee length and pencil slim, or beach-loving maxi length.

Skirts made in woven fabrics usually have a structured, interfaced waistband (or waist facing) with a zipper opening. Stretch knit skirts do not need structured waistbands (although they can be made this way). As the chapter progresses, you also learn a number of stitching techniques.

Figure 9.1 a) Skirt with invisible waistband; **b)** skirt with semi-fitted waistband and patch pockets; **c)** flared skirt with fitted separate waistband and side pockets; **d)** gored skirt with separate gathered waistband; **e)** loose-fit maxi-length skirt with topstitched waistband and ruffle; **f)** ankle-length skirt with yoke, fold-over waistband, and split-hem; **g)** tiered skirt; **h)** pegged skirt with yoke; **i)** A-line bandless skirt

Converting Two-way Stretch Hip Foundations into Skirt Slopers

In this chapter, you create a set of skirt slopers from the two-way stretch hip foundations that were drafted in Chapter 5. Refer to Table 2.1 on p. 16 to see how the hip foundation transforms into a skirt sloper. The "Skirt Sloper" is part of the knit family of slopers in Table 2.2 on p. 17.

Skirts can be constructed from two-way and four-way stretch knits. They do not need lengthwise stretch; however, having it does not affect the fit. Here, you make a set of skirt slopers with a curve-hugging fit to match each stretch category: *minimal stretch*, *moderate stretch*, *very stretchy*, and *super stretchy*.

Minimal Stretch

Figure 9.2

You draft a minimal stretch skirt from the two-way stretch hip foundations from Chapter 5 and the dress-piece from Chapter 7.

1. Draw intersecting lines on oak-tag. The *horizontal line* represents the *hipline*. The *vertical line* represents the CF/CB.
2. Place CF/CB (W-H) hip foundation on the vertical line and hipline (H-H1) on the horizontal line. Then trace the hip foundation.
3. Place the CF/CB (H-H1) minimal stretch dress-piece on the horizontal line and (H-L) on the vertical line (see Figure 7.3 on p. 149). Trace the dress-piece.
4. Trace the hip foundation and dress-piece on the other side of the vertical line.

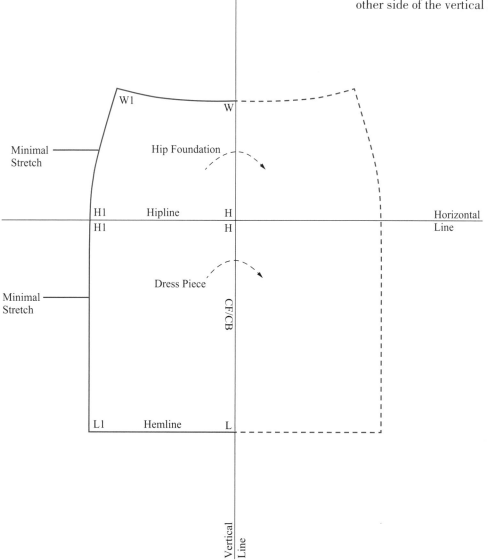

Figure 9.2 Trace the minimal stretch hip foundation and dress-piece onto the grid

Alternatively, draw the dress-piece directly onto the grid:

1. Draw a squared hemline parallel to (H-H1). (Refer to Figure 7.2 on p. 148 for skirt lengths.)
2. L- L1 = Equal length to (H-H1).
3. H1-L1= Draw a straight line.

Moderate Stretch, Very Stretchy, and Super Stretchy

1. Draw a horizontal guideline across the tip of the waist/side seams.

2. Trace the hip foundations in each stretch category onto the grid just as you did for minimal stretch. Each waist/side seam must touch the guideline in each stretch category.
3. Trace the dress-piece in each stretch category onto the grid just as you did for minimal stretch. (See Figure 9.3.)

If the dress-piece has not been graded:

1. Draw the side seams in ½" increments (parallel to the minimal stretch side seam) for each stretch category.

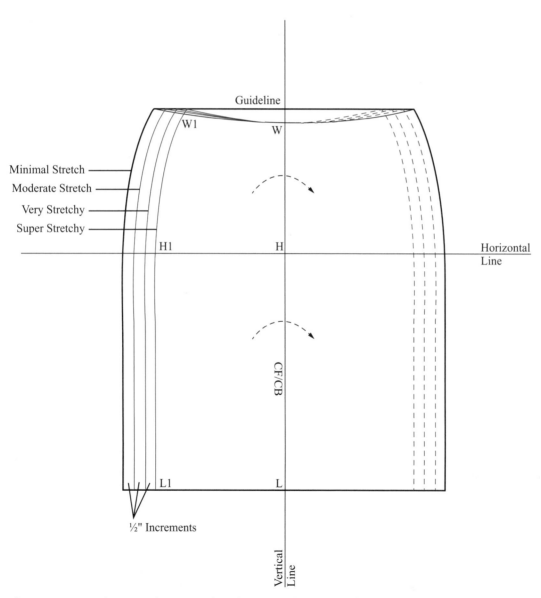

Figure 9.3 Trace moderate stretch, very stretch, and super stretchy onto the grid

Front and Back Skirt Slopers

Figure 9.4

At this point, both sides of the skirt slopers are exactly the same. Follow on to differentiate front and back skirt slopers:

1. Label "Front and Back" skirt slopers.
2. Draw a new vertical line ½" toward the *back* and parallel to the original vertical line. This change makes the front skirt (1" in total) larger than the back skirt sloper. The total hip measurement remains the same.
3. Cut along the *new* vertical line to separate the slopers.

Cut the Waist/Side Seams

1. Cut the front/back minimal stretch waistline from the center front/back toward the side seam only for the distance it is drawn as the same line.
2. Cut the waist/side seams at (W1) in steps for each stretch category, as illustrated in Figure 5.16 on p. 77.
3. Trace and cut the minimal stretch slopers onto oak-tag, and transfer the waistline, as shown in Figure 5.17 on p. 78.
4. Trace and cut the moderate stretch, very stretchy, and super stretchy skirt slopers onto oak-tag as you did for the minimal stretch slopers.
5. Align the side seams together to check that they are equal lengths.

Fabric You'll Need

To stitch a muslin skirt, purchase ¾ yard of two-way minimal stretch double knit. (A perfect fabric is Ponte, which is a medium weight.)

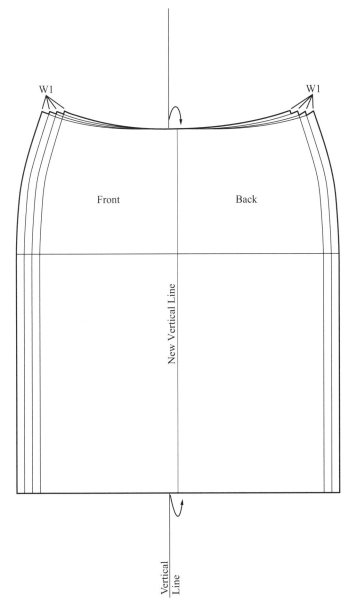

Figure 9.4 Draft the front and back slopers

TABLE 9.1 Stitching order for skirts

Step 1	Step 2
• Stitch any style details to complete a garment piece before stitching the garment pieces together. **Tucks/gathers** **Seams**	• Stitch the side seams. • Stitch the side seams of lining (if the skirt is lined).
Step 3 • Stitch the waist finish. If the skirt is lined: • Attach the skirt and lining waistlines together. • Stitch the waist finish. Other lining methods are outlined in the "Lined Skirts" section.	**Step 4** • Stitch the skirt hem. • Stitch the lining hem (if lined).

Cut and Stitch

1. To cut the skirt, refer to Figure 4.13 on p. 50.
2. Add a ½" seam allowance to the side seams.
3. Stitch the skirt following the stitching order in Table 9.1. Stitch the side seams with a crooked straight stitch, and press seams open so that they are bulk free (see Figure 5.9 on p. 74). (The waist finish does not need to be stitched at this stage.)

Test the Fit

Figure 9.5

Place the skirt on the dress form. Pin any fitting adjustments as needed, and mark these adjustments on the slopers.

What to look for:

✓ Evaluate the hang of the skirt. Also, check that the side seams are aligned to the form.

✓ Check that the skirt length is level (and parallel to the floor).

Finalize the Slopers

1. Write the sloper name "Front/Back Two-way Stretch Skirt Slopers," and document the stretch category on each sloper.
2. Write "CF/CB" on the slopers.
3. Record (W-W1) on each sloper.
4. Draw the waistline and hipline on all slopers. (See Figure 9.6.)

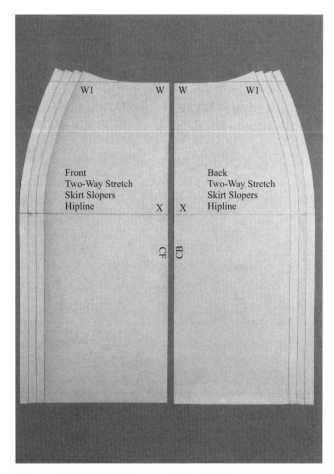

Figure 9.6 Front/back two-way stretch skirt slopers

Choosing the Slopers

Before choosing the stretch category of sloper to use, conduct a stretch test (using the stretch gauge in Figure 1.4 on p. 7) to determine the "stretchiness" of a particular knit. Next, choose the appropriate slopers. There are two ways the slopers can be chosen. Refer to "How to Choose Slopers" in Chapter 2 to learn how to choose the slopers according to the stretch capacity of your knit or for the fit of the garment. For example, a minimal stretch skirt sloper will create a "loose-fit" if the skirt is constructed from a knit with more stretch. Furthermore, the slopers can be enlarged into an "extra loose-fit."

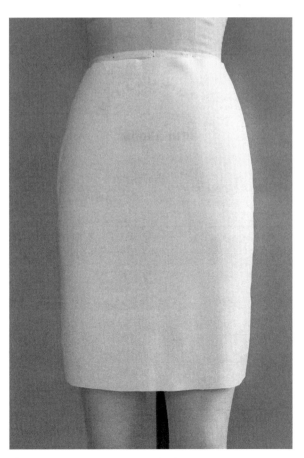

Figure 9.5 Muslin skirt fitted on the form

Extra Loose-fit: Waist and Hip Enlarged

Figure 9.7

1. For a more generous fit, grade the minimal stretch skirt slopers in a positive direction to add 2" extra. The horizontal balance line (HBL) is the hipline of the skirt slopers. For grading, mark (X) on the skirt slopers, as shown in Figure 9.6. Draw the grading grid on oak-tag (see Figure 3.15 on p. 35). Label "D."

2. Mark (E) ½" from (D) on the horizontal line (see Figure 3.16 on p. 36).
3. Place sloper (X) on (D) with HBL on the horizontal line. Trace the minimal stretch slopers on the grading grid.
4. Move (X) on (E) with HBL on the horizontal line. Then trace the front and back skirt slopers.
5. Cut the slopers and label.

Extra Loose-fit: Hip Enlarged

Figure 9.8

If you would like the original waistline but require more room only in the hips, then reshape the hip curve to make the appropriate adjustment.

1. Draw the grading grid and trace the minimal stretch slopers on the grid.
2. Move sloper (X) on (E) with HBL on the horizontal line. Trace the slopers from the hipline to hemline only.
3. Place the minimal stretch sloper over the graded sloper, anchor the hip at the side seam with an awl, and then shift the sloper side/waist until it touches the original waistline. Draw new hip curve.

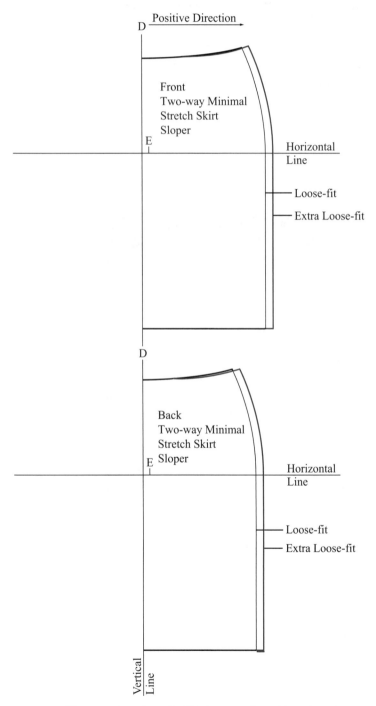

Figure 9.7 Extra loose-fit skirt slopers: waist and hip enlarged

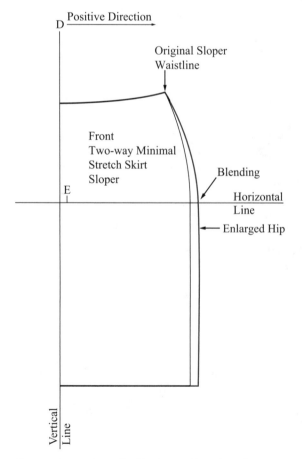

Figure 9.8 Extra loose-fit skirt slopers: hip enlarged

Pattern Drafting Skirts

When you want to draft patterns for skirts, be sure to have the correct patternmaking tools at hand (see Figure 3.1 on p. 20). Refer to Chapter 3 for important pattern drafting principles that, when followed, will create excellent skirt patterns. This chapter outlines how to draft a variety of skirt patterns with a variety of silhouettes, including straight, flared, pegged, circular, draped, and tiered skirts. This chapter also covers patterns for skirts at different lengths, symmetrical and asymmetrical patterns, and lining patterns.

Each skirt requires a waist finish. The "Waist Finishes" section, later in the chapter, outlines how to draft three types of waist finishes for your skirt.

Symmetrical and Asymmetrical Designs

A *symmetrical* skirt looks identical on both sides of the garment (see skirts in Figure 9.1a through e). To draft the patterns for a symmetrical design, trace one side of the slopers onto pattern paper for a quarter of the skirt.

An *asymmetrical* skirt looks different on both sides of the garment (see the skirts in Figures 9.15 and 9.23). The skirt in Figure 9.1f is also asymmetrical because it has a split-hem on one side. To draft the patterns for an asymmetrical skirt, trace both sides of the slopers onto pattern paper. Asymmetrical patterns are labeled right side up (R.S.U.) to indicate how the patterns are to be placed on the fabric according to the asymmetrical design (see Figure 9.24).

Length Variations

Skirts are worn on the lower part of the body and can be varying lengths (see Figure 9.9):

- *Mini*—Thigh length.
- *Short*—Anywhere between mini and knee length.
- *Knee*—Middle of the knee.
- *Midi*—Mid calf length.
- *Maxi*—Anywhere between mid calf and ankle length.
- *Ankle*—A few inches above the floor.
- *Split-hem*—The hemline is divided.
- *Asymmetrical hem*—The hemline is longer on one side than the other.

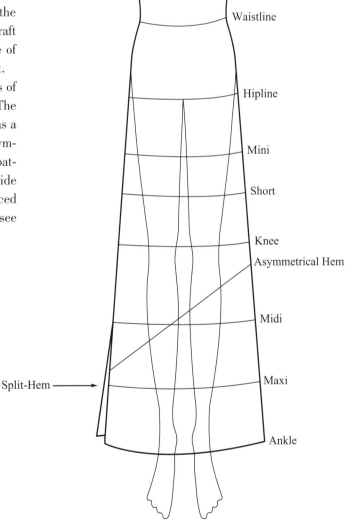

Figure 9.9 Length variations

Silhouette Variations with Design Lines

Figure 9.10

- *Straight*—Slim-fit following the body contour.
- *A-line*—Side seam gradually points out from the hip to the hem.
- *Pegged*—Side seam gradually narrows from the hip to the hemline.
- *Flared*—Fullness is added to create a fluted hemline.
- *Circular*—Fullness is added to create a circular shaped hem.

- *Yoke*—Separate fitted section anywhere between the waist and hip.
- *Extended Waist*—Waist extends above the natural waistline.
- *Gored*—Vertical seamlines from the waistline to hemline create flared panels.
- *Balloon*—Hemline is gathered into a band or elasticized.

Pockets for Skirts

Pockets can be part of a skirt design. For example, the skirt in Figure 9.1b has patch pockets, and the skirt in Figure 9.1c has side-front pockets. To draft the inseam, zip-up pockets, and welt pockets, refer to the "Pockets for Cardigans" section in Chapter 8. To draft patch and side-front pockets, refer to the "Pockets for Pants" section in Chapter 10.

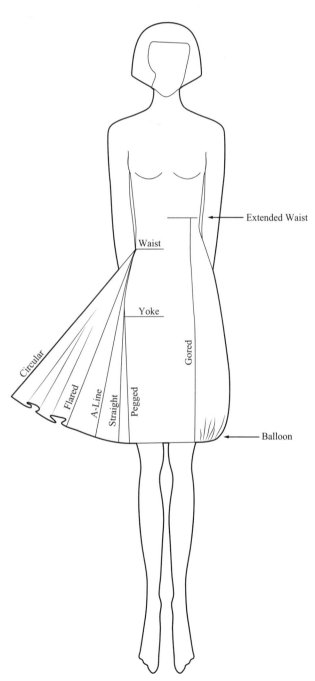

Figure 9.10 Silhouette variations and design lines

A-line and Pegged

Figure 9.11

To draft an A-line skirt, you add width to the side seam/hemline to create an A-shaped silhouette.

1. Trace the front/back skirt slopers onto pattern paper as shown. Label side/waist (A).
2. B = A-line skirt. Mark 1½" out from the hemline and draw a squared-off angle.
3. C = Pegged skirt. Mark 1" in from the hemline and draw a squared-off angle.
4. Trace the front and back skirt slopers onto pattern paper.

Flared

To draft a flared skirt that has an A-line silhouette and a fluted hemline, you add fullness to the hemline. A flared skirt hangs beautifully when constructed from a knit with excellent drape.

Draft the Pattern

Figure 9.12a

Draft the *front* skirt pattern first. Next, draft the back skirt pattern from the front skirt pattern.

a)

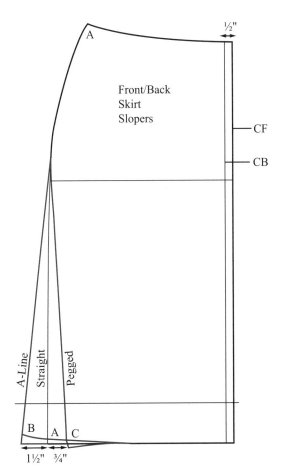

Figure 9.11 Draft an A-line and pegged skirt

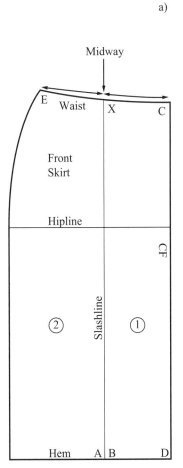

Figure 9.12a Draft a flared skirt

1. Trace the front skirt sloper onto pattern paper. Label (E-C-D).
2. X = Mark midway on the waistline between (E-C).
3. X-A-B = Draw a slash line parallel to the center front.

Draft the Back Pattern

Figure 9.13

To draft the back skirt, remove ½" from the center front, as shown in Figure 9.13.

Slash/Spread the Pattern

Figure 9.12b

1. Cut a slash line to the pivot point (X), *not* through (X).
2. Draw a vertical line on pattern paper. Place CF (C) on the vertical line and hemline (D) 1½" out from the vertical line. Then trace panel (1).
3. Slash/spread the pattern as shown.
4. Draw a straight side seam from the waist to the extended hemline. (A hip curve is not necessary because fullness has been added to the hipline.)
5. Draw a smooth blending waistline and hemline.

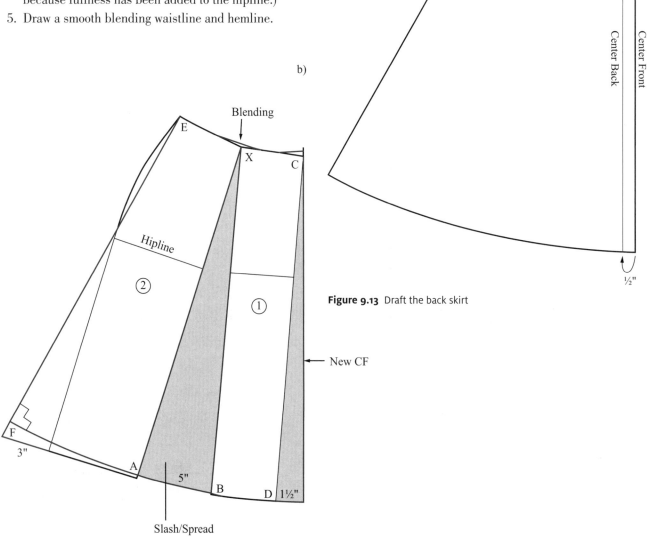

b)

Blending

E

X

C

Hipline

②

①

New CF

Figure 9.13 Draft the back skirt

Remove ½"

Center Back

Center Front

½"

F

3"

A

5"

B

D | 1½"

Slash/Spread

Figure 9.12b Slash/spread the pattern

Finalize the Patterns

Figure 9.14

1. Add a ¼" seam allowance to the waist and side seam. Then add a ½" hem allowance. (A 1" hemline will look bulky when the hemline is flared.)

2. Label the patterns, draw directional grainlines, and record the number of pieces to cut.

Asymmetrical Flared

The design for an asymmetrical flared skirt flares on one side while the other side remains straight (or it can be pegged). This skirt pattern is cut in one piece with one side seam. The skirt in a stripe knit works effectively because the front side seam has vertical stripes and the back side seam has horizontal stripes. You can construct the skirt from two-way or four-way stretch. However, two-way stretch has limited stretchability because only the front skirt will stretch.

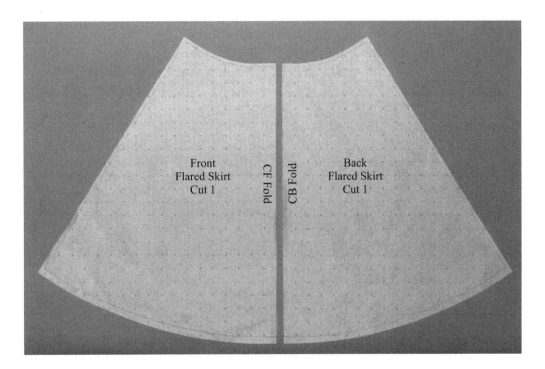

Figure 9.14 Final patterns for the flared skirt

Draft the Pattern

Figure 9.15

1. Draw a right angle on pattern paper. Label (A).
2. Place the front/back slopers on each side of the right angle with the center front/back parallel to the angle. Align (W1) waist on (A). Trace the slopers.
3. A-B = Determine the skirt length.
4. B-C = Draw a hemline to create the flare at the side seam.
5. Draw a blending waistline at side seam (A) and notch.

Finalize the Pattern

1. Add a ¼" seam allowance to the waist and side seam. Add the appropriate hem allowance according to the stitching method (see Stitching Tip 9.1).
2. Label the patterns and draw the center front grainline.

STITCHING TIP 9.1: STITCHING THE HEMLINE

You can stitch a flared, circular, or handkerchief hemline with straight stitches ¼" back from the raw edge. Knits do not fray, so the stitches will secure the edge. Alternatively, serge the hem edge, turn ¼" to the wrong side, and edgestitch the hem.

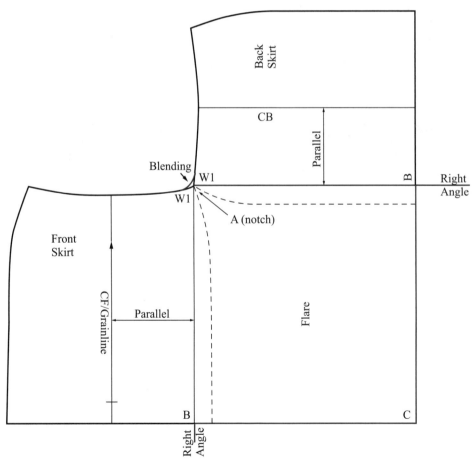

Figure 9.15 Draft an asymmetrical flared skirt

Circular

Figures 9.16a and b

A circle skirt creates fullness at the hemline. A flounce is drafted using the same pattern drafting technique; only the length differs. The pattern has two circles: the inner circle is the seamline, and the outer circle is the hemline. With a simple pattern modification, you can draft a hand-kerchief hemline from the circle skirt pattern.

Draft the Pattern

Figure 9.17

You draft a quarter of the circle pattern first and then draft the full circle pattern from the quarter circle.

1. A radius measurement is required to draw a quarter of a circle. To calculate the radius, measure the total pattern waistline (or seamline) and reduce by ½". (This measurement allows for the seam allowance.) Divide this measurement by 6.30. For example: waist measurement = 27" − ½" = 26½" divided by

6 3/10 (on a fraction calculator) (or 6.30 on a decimal calculator) = 4.20 radius (rounded up to 4¼").

2. Cut a large piece of pattern paper 50" × 50". Fold the paper in half as shown.

3. Draw a horizontal line squared at the foldline. Label (A).

4. A-B = To draw the radius, use an old tape measure. Anchor the tape on (A) with an awl. Punch a hole in the tape measure at the radius. Place a pencil in the hole. Hold the tape measure taut, begin drawing at the side seam, and continue drawing the quarter circle.[1] Measure the quarter circle and multiply by 4 to check you have the correct waist measurement. If it is not correct, adjust the radius.

5. B-C = Draw the skirt (or flounce) length using the tape measure as you did to draw the radius.

---

1   Helen Joseph-Armstrong, *Patternmaking for Fashion Design*, 5th ed. (Upper Saddle River, NJ: Pearson Education, Inc., publishing as Prentice Hall, 2010), 291, 292.

a)

Figure 9.16a Circle skirt

b)

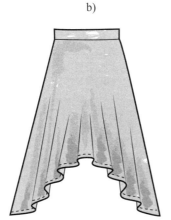

Figure 9.16b Circle skirt with handkerchief hemline

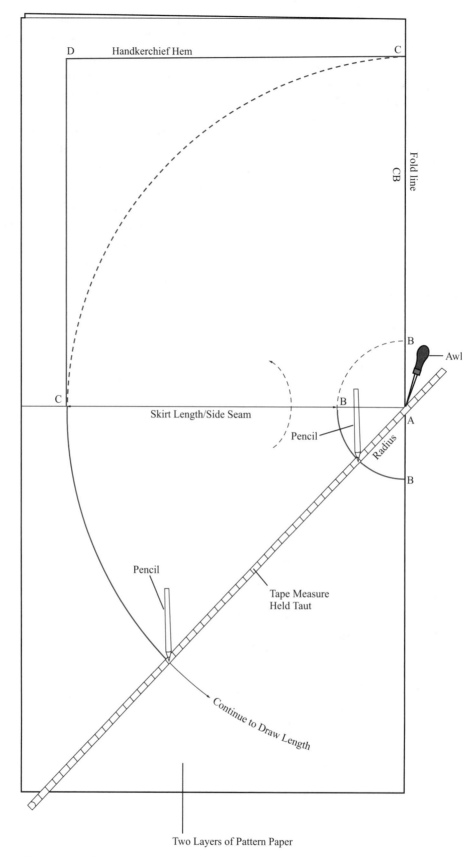

Figure 9.17 Draft a circle skirt

6. Trace the quarter circles on the other side of the pattern to create a full circle. Then cut the pattern.
7. C-D = Draw the handkerchief hemline squared, as shown in Figure 9.17.

Finalize the Pattern

Figure 9.18

1. Add a ¼" seam and hem allowance.
2. Label the pattern, draw the grainline, and record the number of pieces to be cut.

Gathered

Fullness for gathering can be added to the waistline, side seam, or any other skirt seam. Before manipulating the pattern, mark where the gathering will begin and end on the seam. Next, slash/spread or slash/separate the pattern by adding from 50 percent up to double the total length allocated for gathering (or tucks).

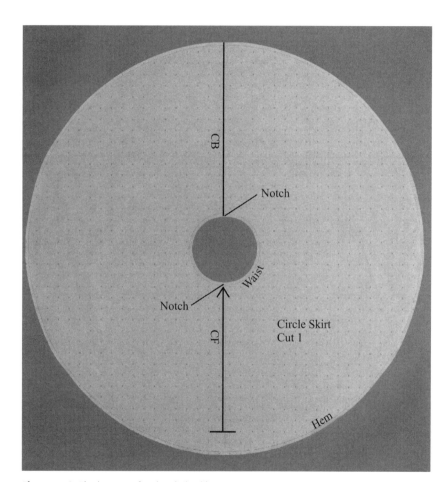

Figure 9.18 Final pattern for the circle skirt

Waist of Pegged, Straight, and Flared Skirts

Figures 9.19, 9.20, and 9.21

When drafting the waist of pegged, straight, and flared skirts, first draft the *front* skirt pattern. Next, draft the back pattern by removing ½" from the center front pattern, as shown in Figure 9.11.

1. Draft a pegged or straight skirt following the pattern shown in Figure 9.11.
2. Draft a flared skirt following the pattern shown in Figure 9.12.
3. For the *pegged* and *straight* skirts, draw a slash line (parallel to center front) to divide the skirt into two sections (see Figure 9.12a). Label (X-A-B).
4. For the *flared* skirt, draw the slash line midway on the waist and hem (see Figure 9.19).
5. Slash/spread or slash/separate the pattern to add fullness for gathering, as shown.
6. Draw blending lines between (A-B).
7. To add extra width for gathering, draw a straight line from the hip to the waist (see Figures 9.19 and 9.21).

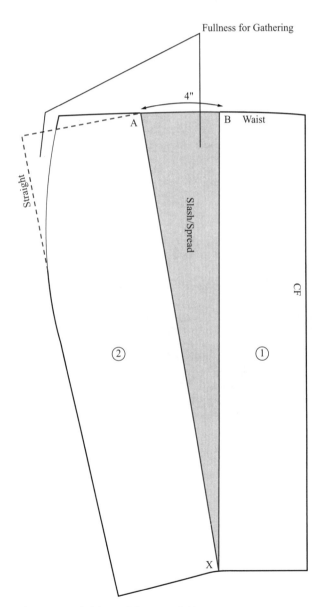

Figure 9.19 Slash/spread the pegged skirt pattern

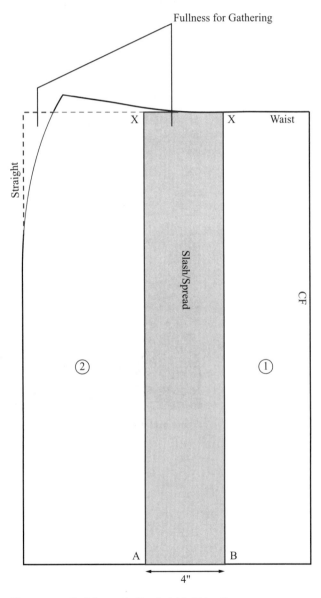

Figure 9.20 Slash/separate the straight skirt pattern

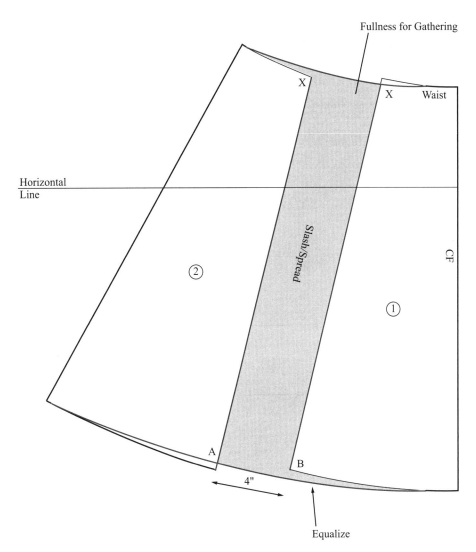

Figure 9.21 Slash/separate the flared skirt pattern

Side Seam

You can gather skirts on one or both side seams to create a symmetrical or asymmetrical skirt.

For gathering to be successful, choose a lightweight knit. The amount you add for gathering can be from 50 percent up to double the length. The skirt can also be lined to hold the silhouette in shape. Trace a copy of the front/back skirt patterns before adding fullness for the lining patterns.

PATTERN TIP 9.1: SKIRT WITH LINING

1. For a *cut-in-one self lining*, join the lining and outer skirt pattern hemlines together to make one pattern piece (see Figure 9.67).
2. For a separate lining, reduce the length of the skirt patterns by ¾" (see Figure 9.69a).

Both Side Seams Gathered

Figures 9.22a and b

To gather both side seams, find the total length to add for gathering and divide by 3.

1. Trace the front sloper, draw slash lines, and label the pattern (see Figure 9.22a).
2. Draw a vertical line on pattern paper. Trace each panel on the vertical line.

3. Spread the pattern ⅓ of the total length between panels (1 and 2). Align panel (2) on the vertical line and trace.
4. Spread the pattern ⅔ of the total length between panels (2 and 3). Trace panel (3).
5. Draw a blending hip curve between panels (1 and 2). Draw a straight side seam between panels (2 and 3).
6. Remove ½" from the center front pattern to draft the back pattern (see Figure 9.11).
7. Add a ¼" seam allowance and 1" hem allowance and draw the grainlines.

a)

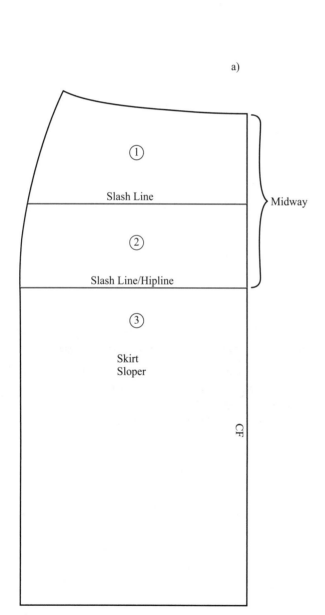

Figure 9.22a Draw slash lines

b)

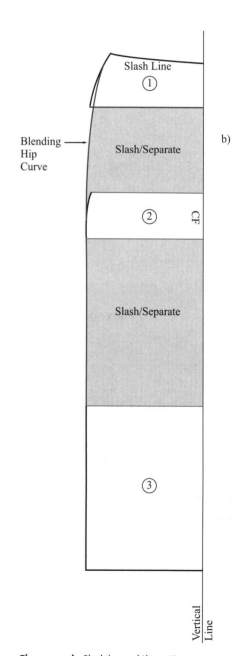

Figure 9.22b Slash/spread the pattern

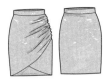

One Side Seam Gathered

Figures 9.23a and b

Here, you gather the front skirt on only one side seam. The back skirt pattern is not gathered, as indicated in Figure 9.26. First, determine the total length to add for gathering and divide by 4.

1. Trace both sides of the front skirt sloper.
2. Draw the curved hemline on both sides of the pattern.

3. Draw slash lines (evenly spaced) and label (see Figure 9.23a).
4. Trace two copies of the skirt pattern (at this stage, both sides of the pattern are the same).
5. On one pattern, draw slash lines and label (see Figure 9.23a).
6. Cut slash lines to (X).

a)

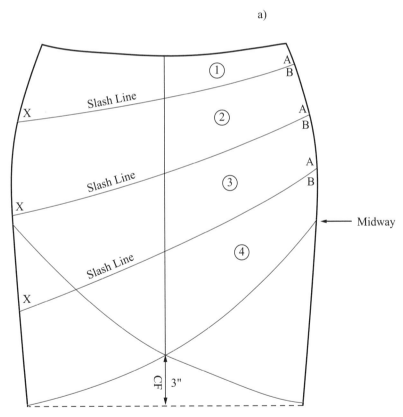

Figure 9.23a Draft the skirt pattern and draw slash lines

7. Draw a vertical line on pattern paper. Place the panel (4) center front/grainline on the vertical line and trace (see Figure 9.23b).
8. Spread the pattern between panels (⅓ of the total length to be added).
9. Draw blending side seams to round angular lines.
10. The other pattern is for the opposite front skirt (which is underneath and not gathered). It is also the lining pattern. Notch this pattern where the lower edge of the gathering aligns on the side seam (see Figure 9.24).

Finalize the Patterns
Figure 9.24

1. On the front patterns, add a ¼" seam allowance to all seams.
2. On the back pattern, add a ¼" seam allowance to the side and waist seams and a 1" hem allowance.
3. Draw the grainlines and label patterns.

STITCHING TIP 9.2: STITCHING THE GATHERED SIDE SEAM

1. After the side seam is gathered, stitch the lining and outer skirt hemlines together, turn the lining to the wrong side, and then press.
2. Align the gathered side seam to the notch of the opposite front. Pin the side seams and waistlines together.
3. The front skirt is now ready to be stitched to the back skirt. (See Figure 9.25.)

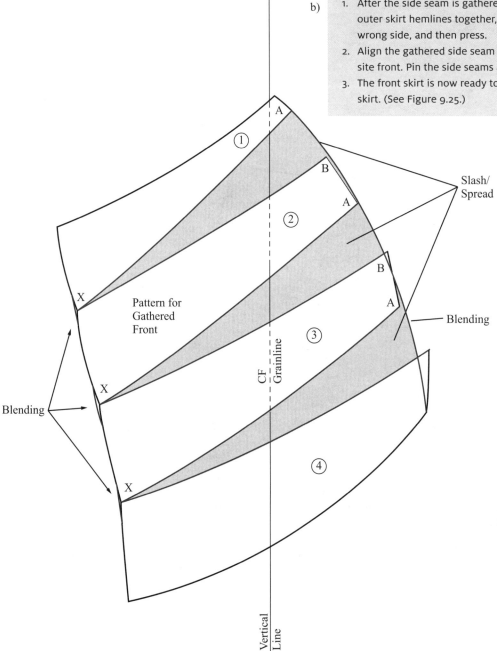

Figure 9.23b Slash/spread the pattern

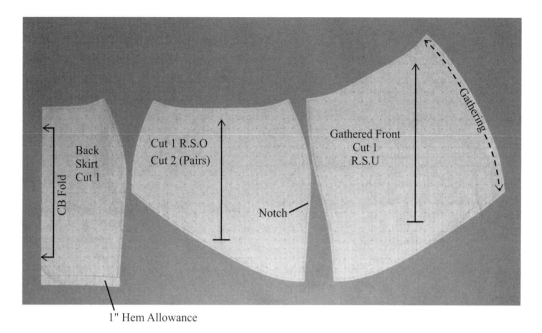

Figure 9.24 Final patterns for the skirt with gathered side seam

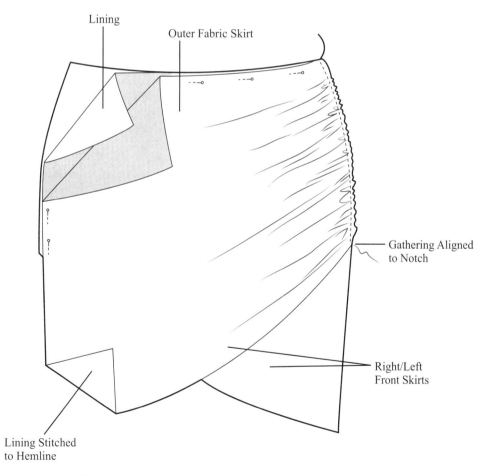

Figure 9.25 Stitching the skirt

Draped

To create draping, you add fullness into the pattern for a cowl, gathering, or tucks.

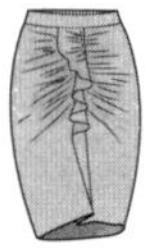

Skirt with Gathering

Figure 9.26a

In this design, you gather the front skirt to create a flounce and draping across the hipline of the front skirt. The front and back skirt patterns are drafted as one pattern piece.

1. Align the sloper front/back side seams together and trace. Label (A-B-C-E).
2. D = Matchpoint for depth of gathering 12" down from (C).
3. Extend the center front beyond C-E and label the new CF.
4. Draw two slash lines evenly spaced between the waist and hip.
5. Trace the front/back as one pattern piece from the working pattern.
6. Cut (A-B and X-Y) hipline and slash lines.

a)

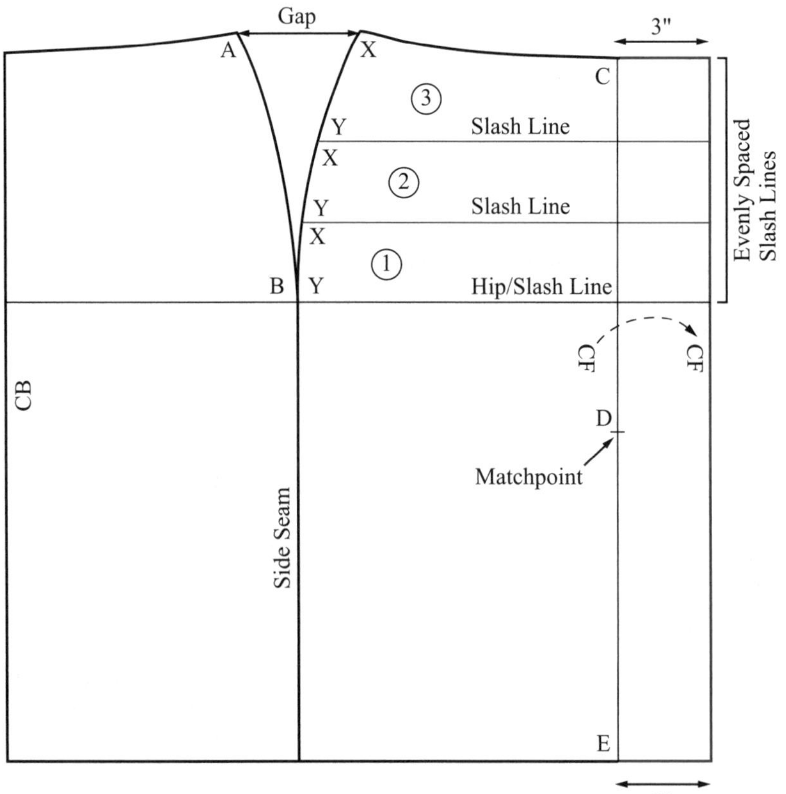

Figure 9.26a Draft draped skirt with gathering

Slash/Spread the Pattern

Figure 9.26b

1. Align the front hip curve (X-Y) of panels (1, 2, and 3) to the back hip curve (A-B) to close the gap. Closing the gap adds fullness for gathering on the center front.

2. On the center, draw a blending line between panels.

3. C-D = Draw a stitching line parallel to the center front. (See Figure 9.26b.)

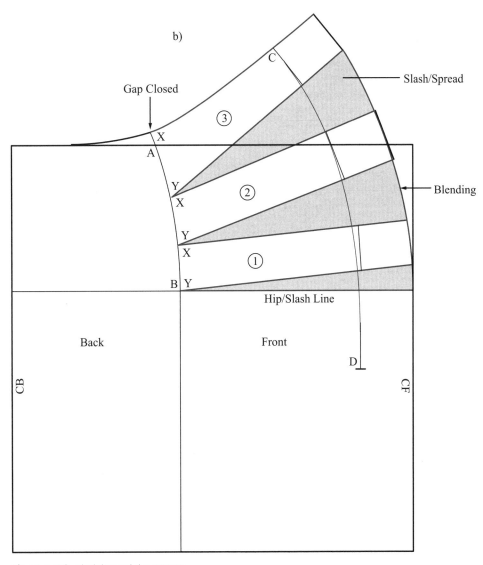

Figure 9.26b Slash/spread the pattern

Finalize the Pattern

Figure 9.27

1. Trace a pattern from the working pattern, and draw a stitching line to the matchpoint.
2. Add a ¼" seam allowance to the waistline and center front seams. Add a 1" hem allowance.
3. Draw the grainline and label the pattern.

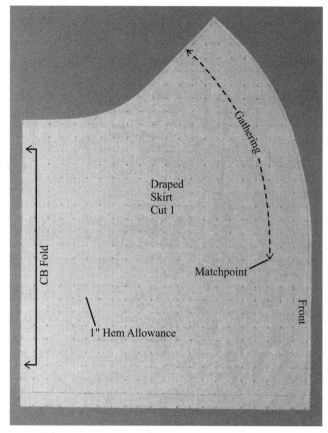

Figure 9.27 Final pattern for the draped skirt with gathering

STITCHING TIP 9.3: STITCHING THE GATHERED FRONT SEAM

1. Place wrong sides of the skirt together, stitch the center front seam, turn, and press.
2. On the correct side, stitch two rows of gathering stitches from the waistline to the matchpoint.
3. Pull the threads to create gathering to the finished length. (In this pattern, it is 8".)
4. Stitch clear elastic on the underside with zigzag stitches over the gathering. Then remove the gathering stitches. (See Figure 9.28.)

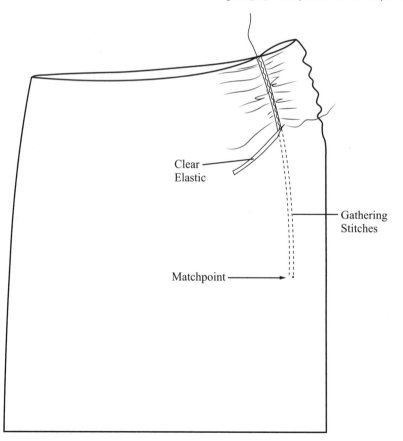

Figure 9.28 Stitching the skirt

Skirt with Cowl and Tucks

Now, you're ready to draft a skirt that has panel seaming. The draped side panel combines a cowl and tucks, which creates the draping.

Draft the Pattern

Figure 9.29

1. Align the front/back side seams together and trace slopers. Label (X) on the hemline.
2. A-C and B-D = Draw panels midway on the hemline to the waist and parallel to the CF/CB.
3. A-E = 3" down from waist.

4. E-F = Draw a pocket line parallel to the hipline. Extend the side seam to line (E-F).
5. Remove ¼" from the waist at (A-B) and curve the panel line to (E-F). Transfer ¼" to the side seam as shown.
6. Mark placement of three tucks 3" down from (E) on the front panel line.

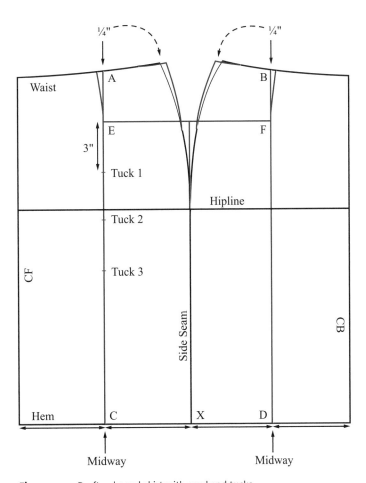

Figure 9.29 Draft a draped skirt with cowl and tucks

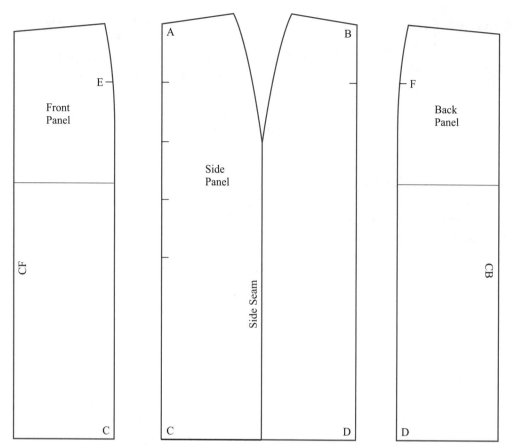

Figure 9.30 Trace the center front/back and side panels

Trace the Patterns

Figure 9.30

1. Trace the center front and center back panels.
2. A-B-C-D = Side panel cut as one pattern piece with tuck markings.
3. Notch the pattern at (E-F) on the front/back panels and side panel.

Slash/Spread the Pattern

Figure 9.31

You use the slash/spread pattern drafting technique to add the cowl and tucks. This is done in two sets of steps.

1. C-D-E-F = Trace the side panel, transfer tuck marks, draw a side seam, and label (X).
2. Cut the slash line (which is the side seam) to (X).
3. Slash/spread the pattern as shown.
4. E-F = Draw a straight line.
5. Draw a blending hemline at (X).

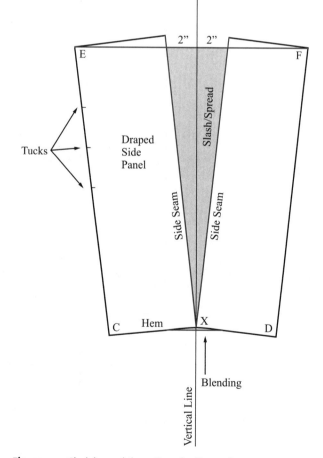

Figure 9.31 Slash/spread the pattern for the cowl

Slash/Spread the Pattern for Tucks

Figures 9.32a through c

1. Trace the pattern shown in Figure 9.31 onto pattern paper.
2. Draw slash lines at each tuck marking parallel to the (E-F) and label. Draw the grainline on panel (4) (see Figure 9.32a).
3. Draw a vertical line on pattern paper. Place the panel (4) grainline on the vertical line and trace. Slash/spread the pattern, as shown in Figure 9.32b.
4. Add a facing above (E-F).
5. Draw a blending side seam between (D-F) only.
6. Fold the tucks between (C-E), as shown in Figure 9.32c. Crease a foldline along (E-F), turn the facing behind the first tuck, and cut the seamline.

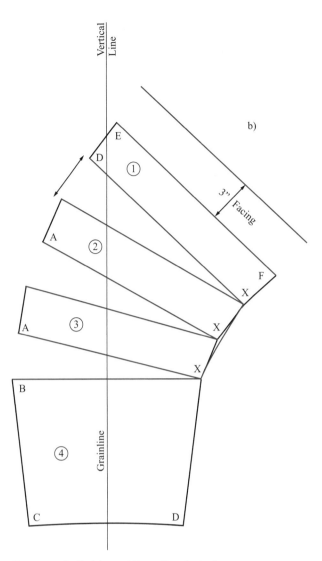

Figure 9.32b Slash/spread the pattern for tucks

a)

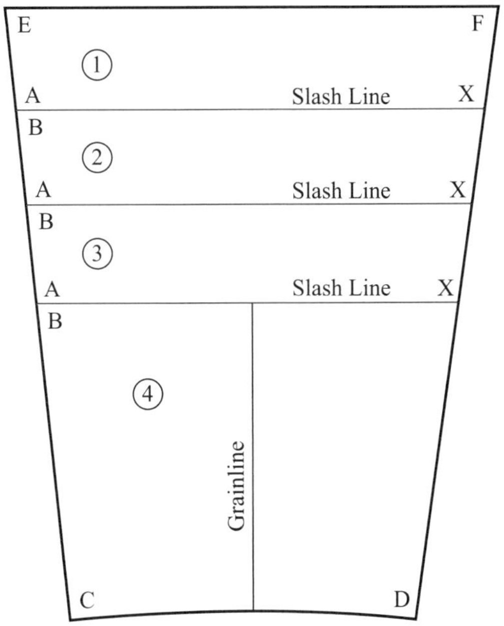

Figure 9.32a Draw slash lines and label the pattern

c)

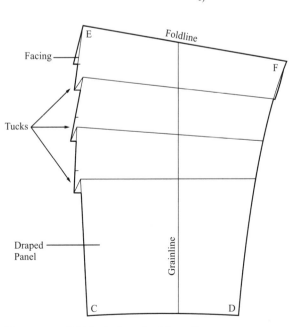

Figure 9.32c Fold the tucks and cut the pattern

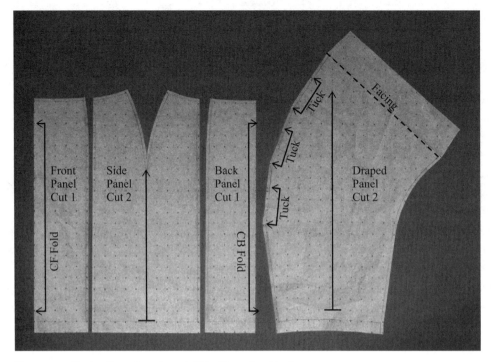

Figure 9.33 Final patterns for a draped skirt with cowl and tucks

Finalize the Patterns

Figure 9.33

1. Add a ¼" seam allowance to all seams.
2. Add a 1" hem allowance.
3. Notch the side panel, draw grainlines, and label the patterns as shown.

STITCHING TIP 9.4: STITCHING THE DRAPED PANEL

1. Stitch side seam darts.
2. Pin tucks, fold the facing to the wrong side, and then pin.
3. Place the draped panel over the side panel and machine baste together.
4. Stitch the side panels to the front/back panels. (See Figure 9.34.)

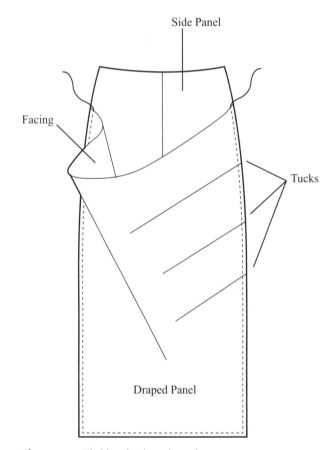

Figure 9.34 Stitching the draped panel

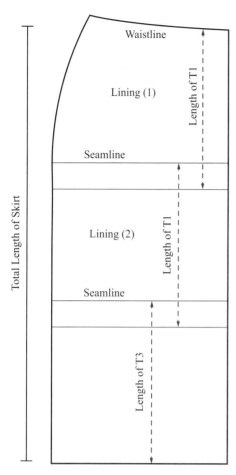

Figure 9.35 Plan placement for the front lining and tiers

(Diagram labels, top to bottom along the skirt)
Waistline
Lining (1)
Length of T1
Seamline
Lining (2)
Length of T1
Seamline
Length of T3
Total Length of Skirt

Tiered

The tiered skirt in Figure 9.1g has flared fabric pieces (tiers) stitched to the waistline, hipline, and hem edge of a base lining. You can construct the lining and tiers from the same fabric if the fabric weight is suitable.

Draft the Patterns

Figure 9.35

First, draft the front patterns. Next, draft the back patterns from the front patterns.

1. Determine the finished length of the skirt (lower edge of tier 3).
2. Draw seamlines for tiers.

Lining and Tier Patterns

Figures 9.36a through c

1. From the working pattern, trace lining patterns (1 and 2) (see Figure 9.36a).
2. Trace tiers (1 and 2), draw slash lines, and label the pattern (see Figure 9.36b).
3. Slash/spread tiers (1 and 2), as shown in Figure 9.36c. Tiers 2 and 3 will use the same pattern piece.

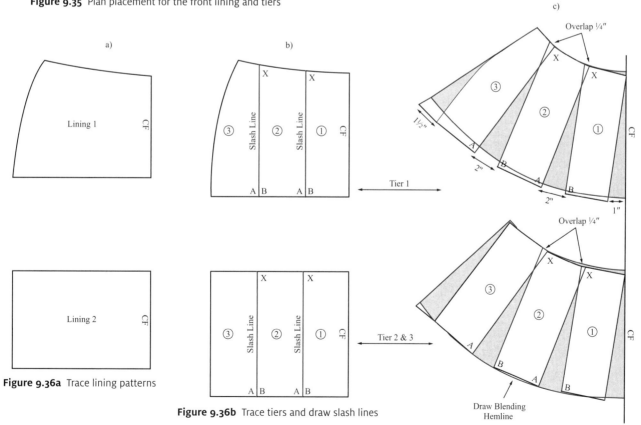

Figure 9.36a Trace lining patterns

Figure 9.36b Trace tiers and draw slash lines

Figure 9.36c Slash/spread the tiers

4. There is a slight change to the slash/spread method:
   - Cut *through* the slash lines to separate the panels.
   - At waist and hipline (X), overlap the pattern ¼" because the curved seamlines create additional stretch. (In total, 1" is removed from the back/front.)
5. Draw the hemline of each tier parallel to the seamline.

Finalize the Patterns

To draft the back patterns, remove ½" from the center front patterns. Draw directional grainlines. Then add a

¼" seam allowance. Finally, add hem allowances. (Refer to Stitching Tip 9.1 for the hem allowance.)

IMPORTANT 9.1: LAYERING THE TIERS

Figure 9.37 shows how the tiers are layered rather than how they are stitched.

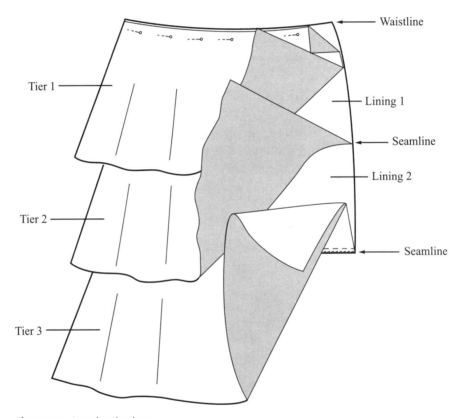

Figure 9.37 Layering the tiers

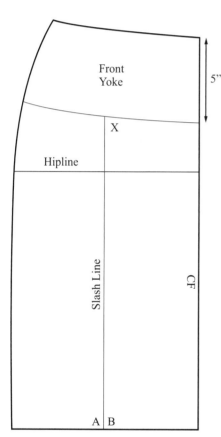

Yoke

The yoke seamline can be placed anywhere between the waist and hip (see Figure 9.10). This seamline can be a V-shape or contoured to your own design. The skirt in Figure 9.1h has a yoke depth of 5".

Draft the Yoke

Figures 9.38 and 9.39

1. Draw the front sloper onto pattern paper. Then determine the skirt length.

2. Plan the depth of the yoke and draw the yoke seamline (see Figure 9.38).
3. Trace both sides of the front yoke pattern.
4. Draft the back yoke by removing ½" from the center front. (See Figure 9.11.)
5. Label patterns "Cut 2."
6. Add a seam allowance, draw the grainlines, and label the patterns. (See Figure 9.39.)

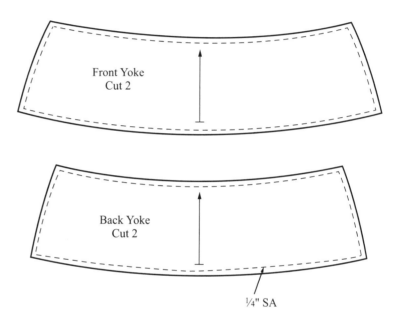

Figure 9.39 Final yoke patterns

Figure 9.38 Draft the yoke pattern

STITCHING TIP 9.5: STITCHING THE YOKE

You can cut both the front and back yokes from the same fabric if the two layers together are not bulky. Alternatively, use a lighter-weight knit for the *under* yoke. After stitching the yoke, apply a waist finish (see Figure 9.40). The skirt can be bandless or have a **separate waistband** stitched to the waist opening (see Table 9.2).

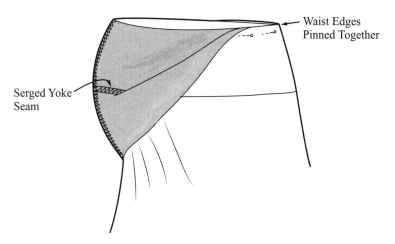

Figure 9.40 Stitching the yoke

 Gored

A gored skirt has six or more shaped panels to create an alternative flared skirt. This is an ideal style to construct from a double knit.

Draft the Pattern

Figure 9.41

The gored skirt you draft in this section is fitted over the hipline and flared to the hemline (see Figure 9.1d).

1. Trace the front and back slopers, draw the hipline, and determine the skirt length.
2. A-B = Draw a guideline parallel to CF from the hemline to the waistline. Label C-A.
3. Remove ¼" from the waist and curve the guideline to (E). Add ¼" to the side seam as shown.
4. Add 2" to 3" on each side of (A) and out from (B) to flare the hemline. Draw a squared line at the hemline (perpendicular) to the seamline.
5. Draw the grainline parallel to the CF.
6. Draft the back gored skirt following the same pattern drafting instructions as you used for the front.

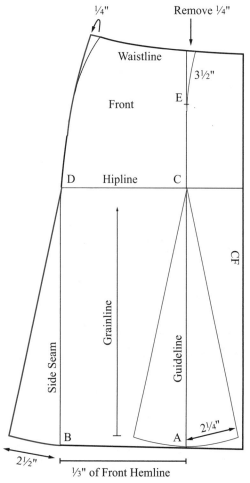

Figure 9.41 Draft the gored skirt

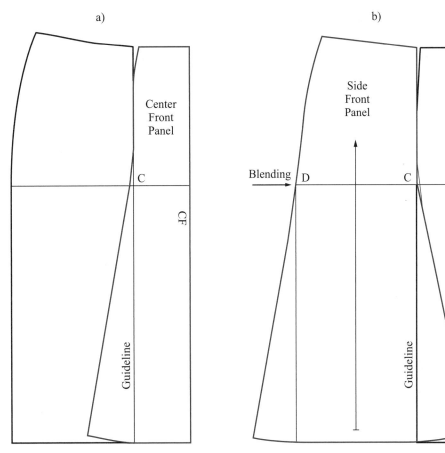

a)

Center
Front
Panel

C

CF

Guideline

Figure 9.42a Trace the center front panel

b)

Side
Front
Panel

Blending → D   C

Guideline

Figure 9.42b Trace the side front panel

Trace the Panels

Figures 9.42a through c

1. Trace the center front (and back) panel from the working pattern (see Figure 9.42a).
2. Trace the side front panel from the working pattern (see Figure 9.42b).
3. Align the panel seamlines together. Then draw a smooth continuous hemline (see Figure 9.42c).

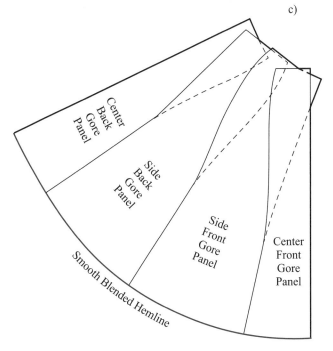

c)

Center
Back
Gore
Panel

Side
Back
Gore
Panel

Side
Front
Gore
Panel

Center
Front
Gore
Panel

Smooth Blended Hemline

Figure 9.42c Align the panels and draw a smooth continuous hemline

Finalize the Patterns

Figure 9.43

1. Label the patterns, draw grainlines, and notch patterns as shown.
2. Add a seam allowance: If the skirt is constructed from a double knit, add a ½" seam allowance to the panel seamlines and stitch open the seams. Add a 1" hem allowance and handstitch.
3. If the knit is lightweight, add a ¼" seam allowance and serge closed the seams. Add a ½" hem allowance and stitch a turned and topstitched hem.

Split-hem

A long slender skirt such as the one in Figure 9.1f would benefit from a split to allow more freedom of movement. A split divides the hem. You can place the split-hem on any seam—side, center back/front, or any other vertical seamline.

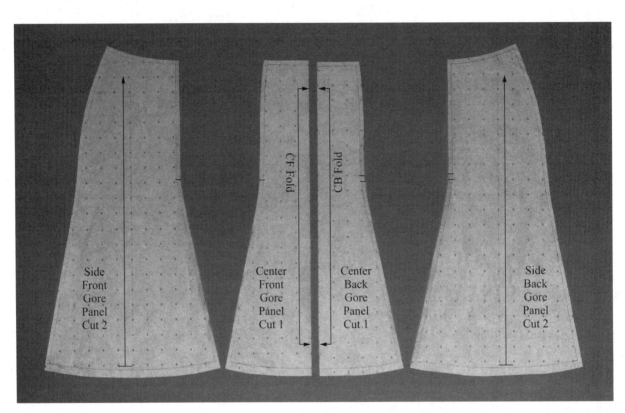

Figure 9.43 Final patterns for the gored skirt

Draft the Pattern

Figure 9.44a

When a split-hem is on *one* side of the garment, it is an asymmetrical design; therefore, you need to draft a full set of patterns. A *longer* split is needed for a long skirt and a *shorter* split for a short skirt, as shown in Figure 9.44a.

1. Mark the length of the split with a matchpoint.
2. Add a 1" facing the same width as the hem allowance.
3. Add a ¼" seam allowance to all seams and a 1" hem allowance.
4. Curve the edge of the facing because this makes serging easier (see Figure 9.44b).

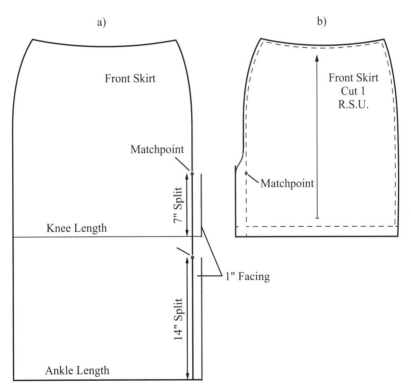

a)   b)

Figure 9.44a Draft a skirt with a split-hem

Figure 9.44b Draft the facing; then add a seam and hem allowance

a)

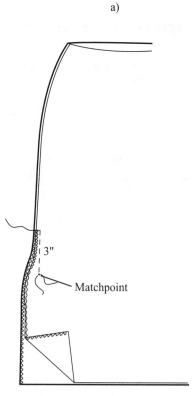

3"

Matchpoint

Figure 9.45a Serge the facings

b)

Press S.A.

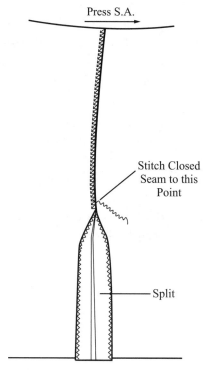

Stitch Closed
Seam to this
Point

Split

Figure 9.45b Stitching the split

Flounce and Ruffle

A flounce and ruffle can be stitched to the hem edge or inserted into the seam of a skirt (or top, cardigan, or dress; see Figure 9.47). A flounce is a circular shape with inner and outer circles. When the inner circle of the fabric is straightened, the outer circle flutes. A ruffle is a straight piece of fabric that is gathered and stitched to a seam or hem edge.

Draft the Skirt

Figure 9.46

1. Trace the front/back skirt slopers onto pattern paper. Then determine the skirt length.
2. Determine the width of the ruffle/flounce.
3. Draw the seamline where the flounce/ruffle will be stitched. Measure the *total seam length*.

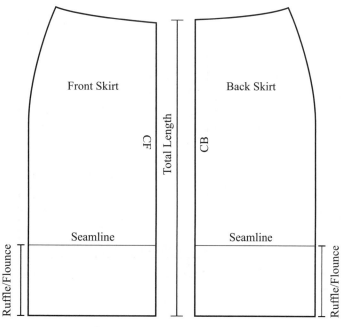

Figure 9.46 Draft the skirt pattern

Draft the Flounce
Figure 9.47

You draft a flounce pattern following the same pattern drafting instructions used in the "Circular" skirt section earlier in this chapter (see Figure 9.17). Only the proportion of the pattern differs.

Asymmetrical Flounce
Figure 9.48

The skirt in this design has a flounce that dips down in the back.

Draw a graduating circle for the asymmetrical hemline. (The hemline can also be drawn to your own design.)

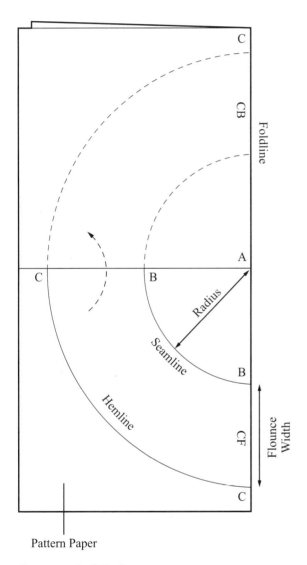

Figure 9.47 Draft the flounce

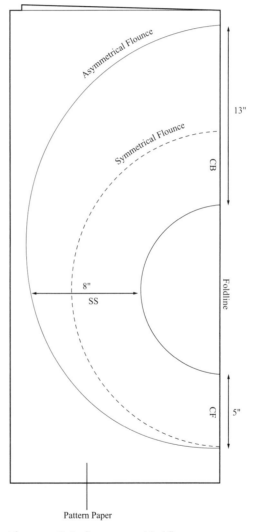

Figure 9.48 Draft an asymmetrical flounce

Gathered Flounce

Figure 9.49

In this skirt design, the flounce is gathered. The flounce also dips down in the back in the same way the skirt dips in Figure 9.48. Two flounce patterns are required for a gathered flounce. The inner circle is gathered and stitched to the hem edge.

1. Draft the flounce inner circle as shown.
2. The flounce side seams must be equal length.

STITCHING TIP 9.7: STITCHING THE GATHERED FLOUNCES

After you cut the circles, slit the side seams, join the flounces together, gather the inner circle, and stitch the flounce to the skirt.

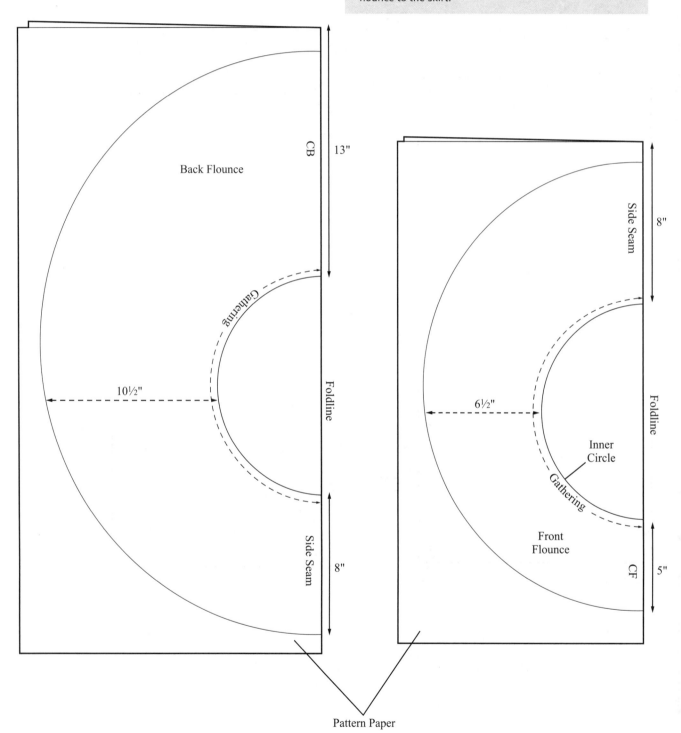

Figure 9.49 Draft the gathered flounces

Finalize the Flounce Patterns

1. Add ¼" seam and hem allowances.
2. Draw the grainline and label the pattern.
3. Draw the grainline, notch the center front/back flounce, and label the pattern, as shown in Figure 9.18.

Draft the Ruffle

A ruffle is a straight pattern piece with extra length incorporated for gathering. You can stitch a ruffle to the hemline or seamline of a skirt, top, dress, or cardigan.

1. For the length of the ruffle pattern, add from 50 percent up to twice the total seam length where the ruffle will be stitched, as shown in Figure 9.50a. Add twice the seam length for a ruffle constructed from a lightweight knit.
2. Add a ½" seam allowance to the seam that will be gathered. (After you stitch the seam, you can serge it back to ¼".) Add ¼" hem allowance (see Figure 9.50b).
3. Draw the grainline and label the pattern.

a)

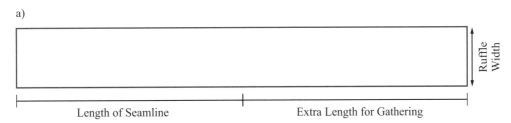

Length of Seamline   Extra Length for Gathering

Ruffle Width

Figure 9.50a Draft the ruffle

b)

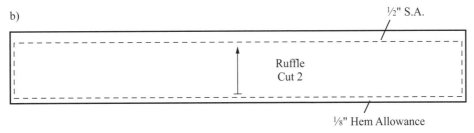

½" S.A.

Ruffle
Cut 2

⅛" Hem Allowance

Figure 9.50b Final ruffle pattern

Waist Finishes

The examples in this chapter are all **pull-on skirts** with an elasticized waist. (The waist finishes can also be used with pants.) The elastic controls the stretchability of the waist opening and *must* expand to fit over the hip yet feel snug and comfortable on the waist after it contracts.

Types of Waist Finishes

Three types of elasticized waist finishes can be applied to the waist opening of skirts or pants. Refer to Table 9.2 to see each style of waist finish.

TABLE 9.2 Waist finishes

Type of Finish	Fit of Waist Finish	Style of Waist Finish
Cut-all-in-one Waistband: The waistband is incorporated into the skirt/pant pattern. For A-line, straight, and pegged skirts and pants.		
Invisible Waistband (Not Topstitched)	Fitted	
Topstitched Waistband	Semi-fitted Loose-fit	
Separate Waistband: A separate straight piece of fabric is prepared and stitched to the waist opening. It can be used on any skirt or pant style.		
	Fitted	
	Semi-fitted Loose-fit	
Bandless: The waist finishes on the natural waistline. This type of waist finish requires a lining. The elastic is stitched to the waistline of the lining.		
	Fitted	

Fit of Waist Finish

Some waist finishes are smooth and *fitted*, other waist-bands are *semi-fitted*, and still others are *loose-fit* (see Figure 9.51). Refer to Table 9.2 to see each style of waist finish.

- **Fitted Waist Finish**—The waist fits closely to the natural sloper waistline and lies flat after completion. The waist finish can be a waistband cut-all-in-one, a separate waistband, or bandless.
- **Semi-fitted Waist Finish** and **Loose-fit Waist Finish**—This type of waist finish has *ease* added to the patterns to allow size flexibility and comfort around the waistline. The total amount added for a semi-fit is approximately 4". The total amount added for a loose-fit is 6" to 16". The waist finish can be a waistband cut-all-in-one or a separate waistband.

Length and Width of Elastic

Figures 9.52a and b

Refer to Table 9.3 for the type and width of elastic to use and how to determine the length.

Width of elastic:

Decide the width of elastic at the pattern drafting stage because it directs the width of the waistband.

Length of elastic can be determined in one of two ways:

1. Measure the front and back patterns along the waistline (do not include the seam allowance). Double this measurement for the total length. Reduce length 1" for the elastic length (see Figure 9.52a).
2. Stretch the elastic around the waistline of the form or body and pin. Slip the elastic over the hip to check that it stretches adequately for a pull-on skirt or pant (see Figure 9.52b).

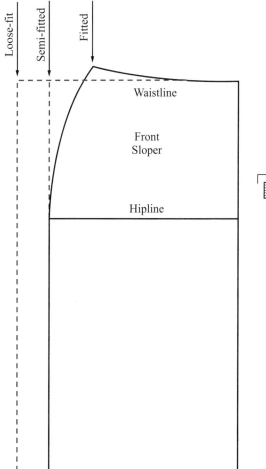

Figure 9.51 Draft the skirt pattern for fitted, semi-fitted, and loose-fit waist finishes

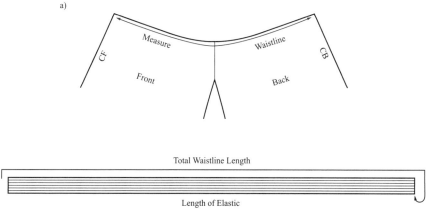

Figure 9.52a Measure the pattern waistline

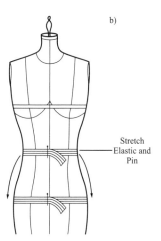

Figure 9.52b Stretch elastic around the waistline of the form

Cut-in-one Waistband

Refer to Table 9.2 for information about the **Cut-in-one Waistband**. In this style, the waistband is incorporated into the skirt/pant. Refer to Table 9.3 and choose a suitable type of elastic because the width of elastic directs the width of the waistband.

TABLE 9.3 Elastic type, width, and length

Type of Waist Finish	Type of Elastic				Width of Elastic	Length of Elastic	
	Woven Elastic	**Braided Elastic**	**Knitted Elastic**	**Nonroll Elastic**	(Wider elastic feels tighter than narrow elastic)	Measure *pattern* waistline and reduce length 1"	Stretch elastic around waistline of *dress form* or *body*
Cut-in-one Waistband							
Invisible Waistband: *Fitted* — Elastic stitched to waist opening, turned and secured at the side seams	X	X	X		Skirts ¾"–1" Pants ¾"–2"	X	
Topstitched Waistband: *Semi-fitted/Loose-fit* — Elastic stitched to waist opening or threaded through a casing	X		X		½"–2"		X
Separate Waistband							
Fitted — Elastic threaded through a casing; use nonroll elastic	X		X	X	¾"–1½"	X	
Semi-fitted/Loose-fit — Elastic threaded through a casing; use nonroll elastic	X		X		¾"–2½"	X	X
Bandless (Without Waistband)							
Fitted — Elastic stitched to waistline (Use ⅜"–½" wide for short skirts in lightweight knits. Use ¾" wide to support longer skirts.)	X	X			⅜"–¾"	X	

Invisible Waistband: Fitted

The fitted waistband looks invisible and has a flat, smooth appearance, as you can see in Figure 9.1a. It does not have a seam or top-stitching to indicate there is a waistband. You first draft the front waistband pattern. Then you draft the back waistband from the front waistband.

The skirt can also be lined. To draft the lining patterns, refer to the "Separate Lining" section later in the chapter.

Draft the Pattern

Figures 9.53a through c

1. Draft the front and back patterns using the same pattern drafting instructions. Trace the skirt slopers on pattern paper.
2. A-B = Label "Waistline" (see Figure 9.53a).
3. A-C = Add a waist extension (width of the elastic plus ⅛") and draw parallel to the waistline. Label it "Foldline."

4. C-D = Add facing equal to (A-C).
5. Measure the length of the front waist (A-B).
6. C-E = Mark an equal length to (A-B) (see Figure 9.53b).
7. B-E = Draw a straight guideline, followed by a blending line.
8. D-F = Length of waistline from blending line (B) on the side seam to (A).
9. E-F = Draw a straight line. (When the facing folds back along the foldline, it will fit comfortably behind the waist extension.)
10. Cut the front skirt pattern. Place the front pattern over the back pattern with side seams at the waistline and hipline aligned. Trace the front waist extension/facing to the back skirt.
11. Place the side front/back facing (E-F) together and draw a blending line across the top edge (see Figure 9.53c).
12. Add a ¼" seam allowance to the edge of the facing and side seams.

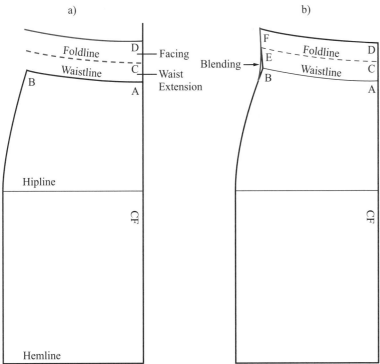

Figure 9.53a Draft the waist extension and facing

Figure 9.53b Draw side seams of the waist extension and facing

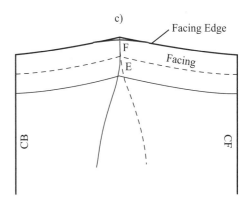

Figure 9.53c Draw a smooth blending line on the facing edge

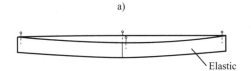
a)

STITCHING TIP 9.8: JOINING THE ELASTIC AND STITCHING THE INVISIBLE WAISTBAND

The beauty of this invisible waistband is that it has a sleek, smooth appearance on completion. Refer to the Stitching Order in Table 9.1 to stitch the skirt.

1. Join the elastic so it is circular.
   - Edge-to-edge: for joining heavier-weight elastics—nonroll, woven, and knitted (see Figure 9.54a).
   - Overlapped: for joining lightweight braided elastic (see Figure 9.54b).
2. Quarter-mark the waist opening and the elastic (see Figure 9.55a).
3. Place the elastic on top of the skirt around the wrong side of waist opening. Align the elastic join on the center back, and pin the waist and elastic quarter-marks together (see Figure 9.55b).
4. With the elastic facing up, stitch the elastic to the edge. Use *wide* serging or zigzag stitches, as shown in Table 4.2 on p. 60. Stretch the elastic between quarter-marks as you stitch so that the elastic tension is evenly distributed (see Figure 9.55b).
5. Fold the elastic/facing to the wrong side of the garment.
6. Stitch in the ditch of the side seam from the correct side to secure the waistband in place.

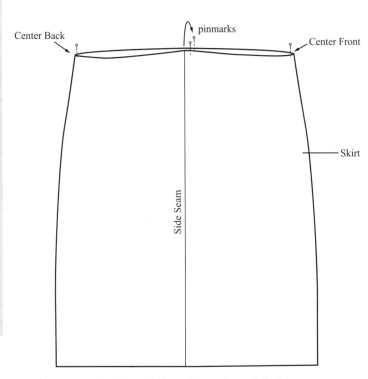

Figure 9.55a Quarter-mark the waist opening and elastic

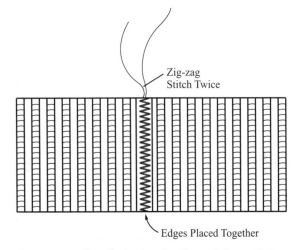

a)

Figure 9.54a Align elastic edges together and zigzag stitch

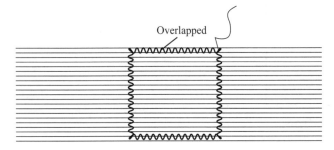

b)

Figure 9.54b Overlap the elastic and zigzag stitch

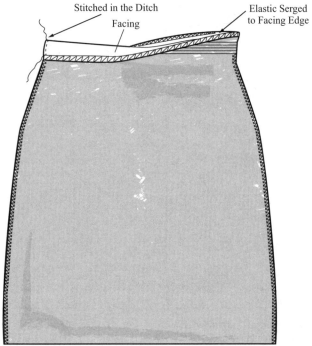

b)

Figure 9.55b Stitch elastic to the facing

Topstitched Waistband: Semi-fitted and Loose-fit

Refer to Table 9.3 to choose the appropriate type of elastic for a topstitched waistband that is semi-fitted or loose-fit (see Figure 9.1b and e). The elastic can be as narrow as ½" or as wide as 2". Use only narrow elastic for a short skirt in a lightweight knit.

Draft the Pattern

1. Draw a squared line across the waistline for the required fit. Label it "Waistline."
2. A-B = Add the waistband extension twice the width of the elastic plus ½".
3. Draw a waistband parallel to the waistline. (See Figure 9.56.)

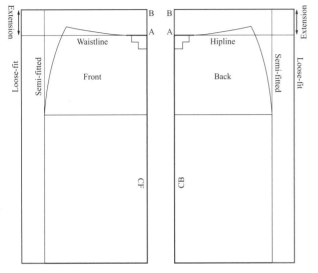

Figure 9.56 Draft the topstitched waistband

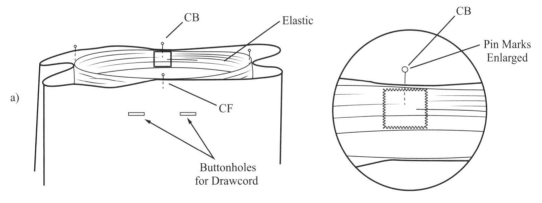

Figure 9.57a Pin elastic and the waist opening quarter-marks together

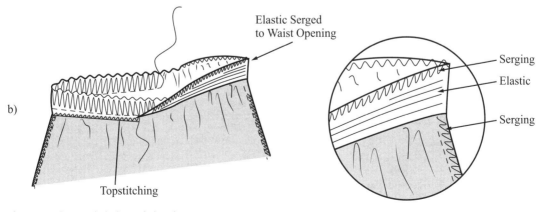

Figure 9.57b Topstitch the waistband

Separate Waistband

The waistband can be fitted, semi-fitted, loose-fit, or
gathered prior to joining it to the waist opening (see
Figures 9.1c, d, g, and h). Use nonroll elastic because
the elastic is threaded through a casing. (Refer also to
Table 9.3.)

Fitted

Figures 9.58a and b

1. Determine the total waistline length by measuring
   the pattern waistline (see Figure 9.52a).
2. Draw a line the total waistline length (see Figure
   9.58a).
3. Reduce length 1".
4. The waistband *width* is double the elastic width
   plus ⅜".
5. Add a ¼" seam allowance around the waistband
   (see Figure 9.58b).
6. Draw the grainline in the direction that gives the
   greatest stretch and label pattern.

a)

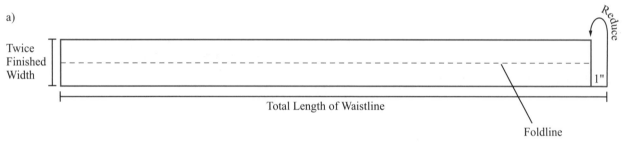

Figure 9.58a Draft a fitted waistband

b)

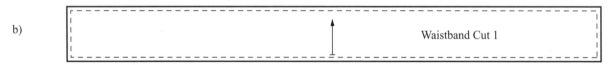

Figure 9.58b Final waistband pattern

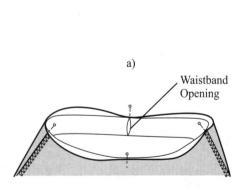

Figure 9.59a Quarter-mark the waist opening and elastic

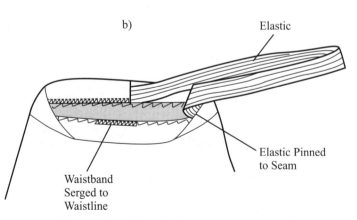

Figure 9.59b Stitching the fitted separate waistband

Semi-fitted and Loose-fit

Figures 9.60 and 9.61

1. Measure the pattern waistline for semi-fitted or loose-fit, as shown in Figure 9.60. Double this measurement for the total length.
2. Draw a line on pattern paper the total waistline length (see Figure 9.61).
3. The waistband *width* is double the elastic width plus ⅜".
4. Add a ¼" seam allowance around the waistband pattern (see Figure 9.58b).
5. Draw the grainline in the direction that gives the greatest stretch in the length of the waistband and label pattern.

a)

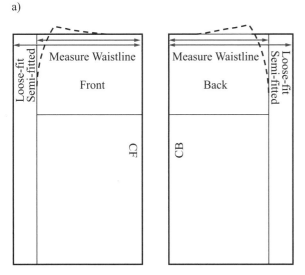

Figure 9.60 Draft semi-fitted and loose-fit skirt patterns

b)

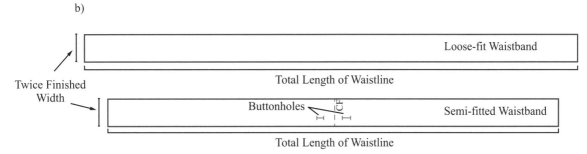

Figure 9.61 Draft semi-fitted and loose-fit waistbands

Fold-over Waistband

Figures 9.62 and 9.63

You can add a fold-over waistband above the waistline of the skirt or pant pattern. When the waist opening folds over, it stretches to grip the hip and sits securely without requiring any elastic. (Refer to the skirt in Figure 9.1f.) In this pattern, the fold-over waistband is added to the yoke pattern drafted in Figure 9.38 and 9.39.

1. Draw intersecting lines on a large piece of pattern paper.
2. Place the center front yoke on the vertical line with the side/waist touching the horizontal line. Trace the pattern (see Figure 9.62).

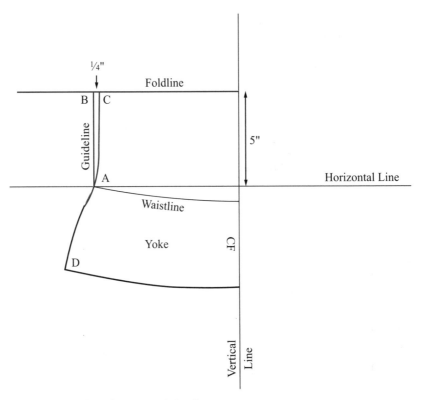

Figure 9.62 Draft the fold-over waistband

3. Draw the foldline parallel to the horizontal line.
4. A-B = Draw the guideline squared at the horizontal line.
5. B-C = Mark ¼" inside the guideline.
6. C-D = Draw a smooth curved side seam.
7. Fold the pattern along the "foldline" so that you have a double layer of pattern paper. Trace the pattern to the other side to form a double-sided pattern (see Figure 9.63).
8. Trace the fold-over waistband to the back yoke pattern.
9. Add ¼" seam allowances to all pattern edges.
10. Label the patterns, draw the grainlines, and document the number of patterns to cut.

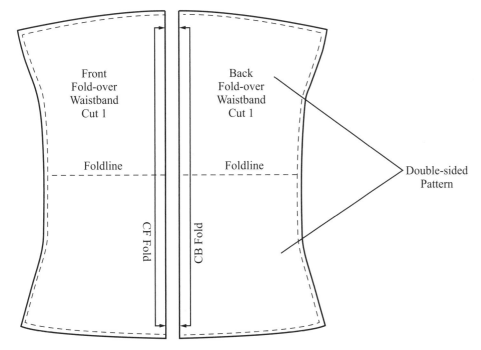

Figure 9.63 Final fold-over waistband patterns

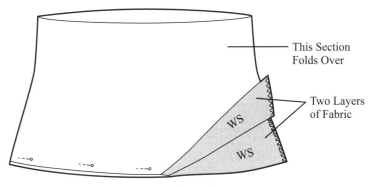

Figure 9.64 Stitching the fold-over waistband

Bandless

A **bandless** skirt does not have a waist-band. (Refer to the skirt in Figure 9.1i.) When you draft the patterns, follow the natural waistline of the slopers for a fitted waist (see Figure 9.51). This type of skirt must have a lining. Refer to Table 9.2 to determine the elastic type, width, and length of elastic.

(Refer to the skirt in Figure 9.1i.)

a)

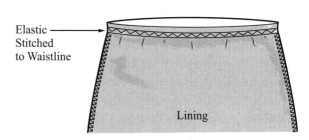

Elastic Stitched to Waistline

Lining

Figure 9.65 Stitch elastic to the lining

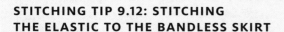

STITCHING TIP 9.12: STITCHING THE ELASTIC TO THE BANDLESS SKIRT

The elastic is zigzag stitched to the lining waistline, as indicated in Figure 9.65. The stitches function as the understitching and keep the waist seam rolled inside the skirt.

1. Join the elastic (see Figure 9.54b).
2. Quarter-mark the lining and outer fabric waist openings and the elastic.
3. Place the elastic on the *wrong side* of the lining ⅜" from the waist edge. Pin the elastic join to the center back skirt and align the markings (see Figure 9.65).
4. For ⅜" wide elastic, stitch one row of zigzag stitches (or twin needle stitching) on the center of the elastic (see Figure 9.65). For wider elastic, stitch two rows of zigzag stitches to apply the elastic. (Stitch the elastic edge closest to the waistline first and then stitch the other side.)
5. Place the lining inside the outer skirt with correct sides placed together. Align side seams, center fronts, and center backs. Stitch the waist seam.
6. Turn the lining inside the garment; then align side seams, pin, and stitch-in-the-ditch of the side seam to secure the lining and outer fabrics together (see Figure 9.66).

b)

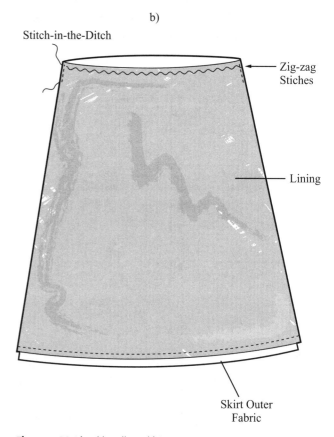

Stitch-in-the-Ditch

Zig-zag Stiches

Lining

Skirt Outer Fabric

Figure 9.66 Lined bandless skirt

Lined Skirts

A lining can be cut-in-one self lining or a separate lining. Refer to the "Choosing Lining" section in Chapter 1 for some helpful lining suggestions.

Cut-in-one Self Lining

The cut-in-one self lining method produces clean lines with no topstitching on the hemline. The outer skirt and lining patterns are drafted as one pattern piece. The same fabric is used for the outer skirt and the lining; plus, the hemline is a folded edge. When choosing the fabric, place two layers of the fabric together and test the "hand." For more information, refer to the "Fabric Selection" section in Chapter 1. This skirt with cut-in-one self lining must have a straight or pegged silhouette (see Figure 9.11).

Draft the Patterns

Figure 9.67

1. Draft one *full* set of front and back skirt patterns. Then trace another set of patterns.
2. Join the two patterns together at the hemline as shown to create a double-sided pattern. The hemline is the *foldline*.

3. Add ¼" seam allowances to the side seams and waistline.
4. Draw directional grainlines, notch the hemline, and label the patterns. (Refer to Figure 7.34 on p. 178 to see the cut-in-one self-lined completed dress pattern.)

STITCHING TIP 9.13: STITCHING A SKIRT WITH CUT-IN-ONE SELF LINING

For this skirt, you do not need to finish the seams because they will not be visible. To produce smooth flat seams, stitch ¼" pressed open side seams. Serging the seams will create bulk.

1. Place correct sides of the front and back skirts together, match notches, and pin.
2. Stitch side seams from one waist opening to the other waist opening.
3. Fold the skirt by placing the *wrong* sides together and aligning waist edges. (The hemline is now a foldline.)
4. Stitch the waist finish. (See Figure 9.68.)

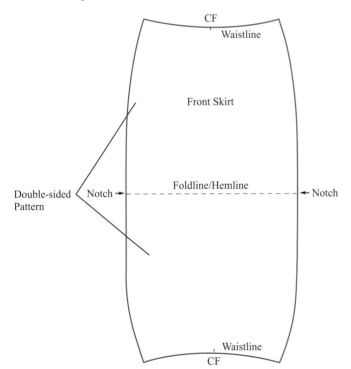

Figure 9.67 Draft the cut-in-one self lining pattern

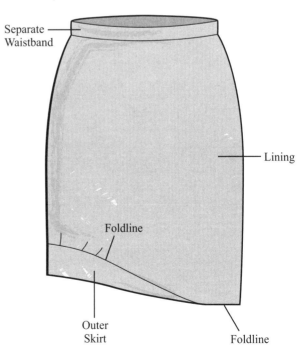

Figure 9.68 Skirt with cut-in-one self lining

Separate Lining

A separate lining can be the lining for a skirt with a separate waistband or a skirt with an invisible waistband. Draft the lining patterns from the outer skirt patterns.

Draft the Lining Patterns
Figures 9.69a and b

1. Trace another copy of the front/back patterns onto pattern paper.
2. Reduce the length of the lining patterns ¾" in length.
3. Label the patterns, draw the grainlines, and document the number of pattern pieces to cut.

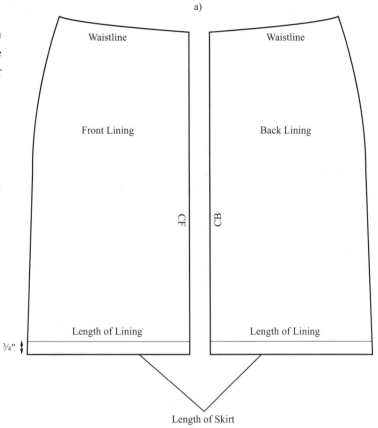

Figure 9.69a Draft the lining patterns

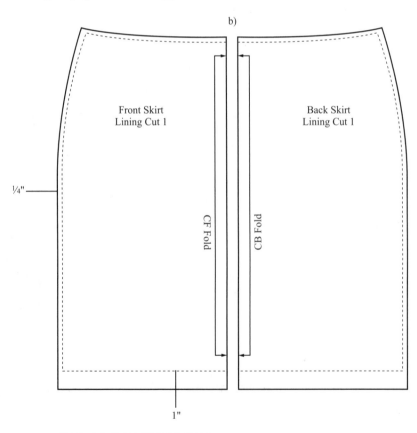

Figure 9.69b Final lining patterns

Draft the Pattern

Figure 9.71

A shorter/narrower lining pattern determines the shape of the balloon-hem.

1. The outer skirt patterns need fullness added to the hemline. Draft the flared skirt pattern shown in Figure 9.12 so that the hemline is half or double the length of the lining hemline.
2. Make sure the waistline of the lining patterns and outer skirt patterns are the same length.
3. The outer skirt length should be approximately 4" longer than the lining pattern.

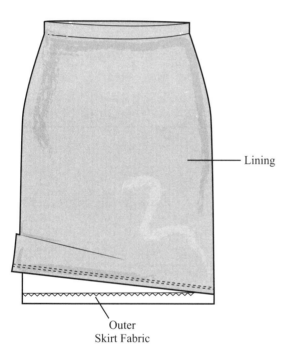

Figure 9.70 Skirt with separate lining

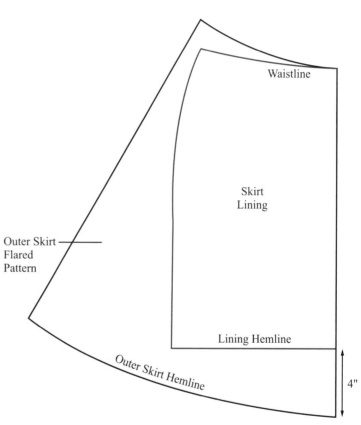

Figure 9.71 Draft a balloon-hem skirt

Skirt with Balloon-hem

The success of a skirt with a balloon-hem depends on the weight and draping qualities of the fabric. If the fabric is lightweight, then use the same fabric for the outer skirt and the lining. The seam that joins the outer skirt and lining together must be approximately 2" above the finished hemline.

1. Stitch the side seams of the skirt and lining.

2. Quarter-mark both hemlines separately.

3. Place the outer skirt inside the lining with correct sides facing. Match hem edges and markings together (see Figure 9.72a).

4. With lining facing up, stitch the hem edges together, stretching the lining to fit between markings. As the lining is stretched, the skirt hem will gather.

5. Stitch *clear elastic* to the seam allowance to stabilize the hem and to prevent it from stretching out of shape. Align waist edges together and stitch the waist finish. The finished balloon-hem is illustrated in Figure 9.72b.

b)

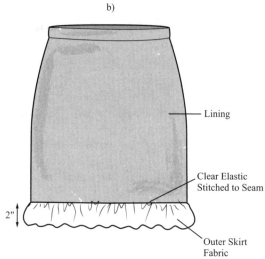

Figure 9.72b Stitched skirt with balloon-hem

a)

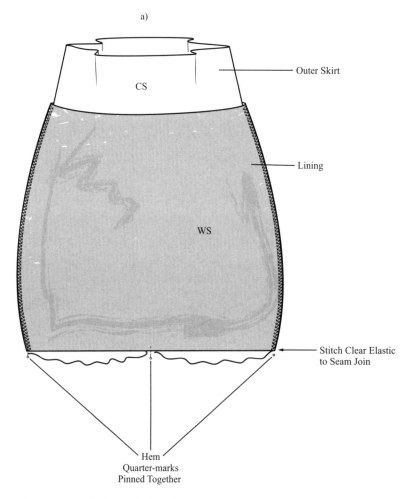

Figure 9.72a Stitching the balloon-hem

Knit It Together

This checklist summarizes what you have learned about drafting the skirt slopers and patterns in this chapter.

- ✓ The skirt slopers are drafted from the hip foundation.
- ✓ Skirts can be made from minimal stretch, moderate stretch, very stretchy, and super stretchy two- and four-way stretch knits.
- ✓ Skirts can be any length, a variety of silhouettes, and symmetrical and asymmetrical designs.
- ✓ Skirts constructed in stretch knits can have an elasticized waist finish. Therefore, they are "pull-on" skirts.
- ✓ A skirt can have a waistband, or it can be bandless.
- ✓ The waist finish can be fitted, semi-fit, or loose-fit.
- ✓ Skirts can be lined.

Stop: What Do I Do If . . .

. . . my waist opening is too tight to pull up over the hips?

Add extra width to the front/back patterns out from the side seams at the waistline to lengthen the waist opening. (Refer to Figure 9.60.)

. . . I want to draft the patterns for the skirt in Figure 9.1h and I can't find the pattern drafting instructions in this textbook?

Transfer your learning by using the pattern drafting techniques in this textbook to create other pattern designs. Here's what you can do:

1. Draft the pegged skirt patterns in Figure 9.11.
2. Draw the yoke line (see Figure 9.38).
3. Slash/spread the pattern to add fullness (for gathering) into the skirt seamline that joins to the yoke line (see Figure 9.19).

Self-Critique

1. What would influence your patternmaking decisions to make certain a pull-on straight long skirt would be functional when walking, sitting, or dancing?
2. Refer to Table 9.3. What are the criteria for choosing elastic for the long skirt in Figure 9.1e?
3. How would you determine the elastic length for the waistline of the bandless skirt in Figure 9.1i? (Refer to Table 9.3.) What type and width of elastic would you use?
4. Could the flared skirt in Figure 9.1c have an invisible waistband like the skirt has in Figure 9.1a? If not, why?
5. Sketch the skirt in Figure 9.1a with an asymmetrical hem flounce added. How would you draft and label the flounce patterns? (Also refer to the "Pattern Labeling" section in Chapter 3.)
6. What pattern changes would be required to incorporate gathering along the top edge of each tier of the skirt in Figure 9.1g?
7. Define these waist finishes: waistband cut-all-in-one, separate waistband, and bandless. For each waist finish, what silhouette does the skirt need to have to be successful?
8. At what stage of the stitching order would the waistband of the skirt in Figure 9.1h need to be stitched? (Refer to Table 9.1.)

Key Terms
Bandless
Fitted Waist Finish
Loose-fit Waist Finish
Pull-on Skirts
Semi-fitted Waist Finish
Separate Waistband
Waistband Cut-all-in-one

10

Pant Slopers
and Patterns

Women with an active lifestyle will appreciate a touch of stretch in their pants as well as an elasticized waist finish. Stretch pants can be worn as multipurpose clothing. The stretchability of the fabric and elastic make them ideal for dressy occasions, casual everyday activities, or sporting pursuits. The fabric and design unite performance, comfort, versatility, and style. These features make stretchable pants foundational to a woman's wardrobe.

By following the instructions in this chapter, you will learn to create patterns from the two-way and four-way stretch pant slopers for your own pant designs. Figure-flattering leggings, bike shorts, a loose-fit jumpsuit, contoured boot-leg pants, a body-hugging unitard, and flared palazzo pants are just a few styles outlined in this chapter.

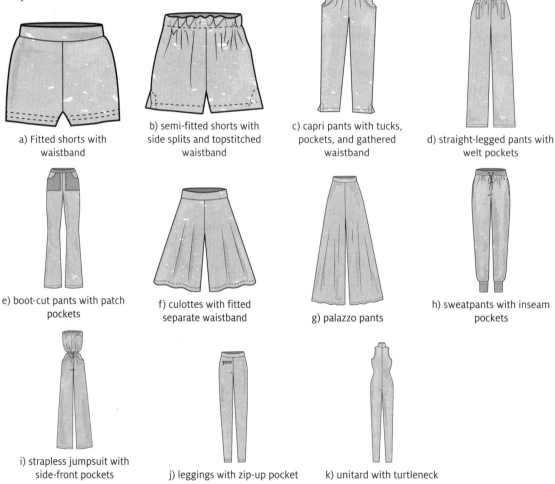

a) Fitted shorts with waistband

b) semi-fitted shorts with side splits and topstitched waistband

c) capri pants with tucks, pockets, and gathered waistband

d) straight-legged pants with welt pockets

e) boot-cut pants with patch pockets

f) culottes with fitted separate waistband

g) palazzo pants

h) sweatpants with inseam pockets

i) strapless jumpsuit with side-front pockets

j) leggings with zip-up pocket

k) unitard with turtleneck

Figure 10.1 a) Fitted shorts with waistband; **b)** semi-fitted shorts with side splits and topstitched waistband; **c)** capri pants with tucks, pockets, and gathered waistband; **d)** straight-legged pants with welt pockets; **e)** boot-cut pants with patch pockets; **f)** culottes with fitted separate waistband; **g)** palazzo pants; **h)** sweatpants with inseam pockets; **i)** strapless jumpsuit with side-front pockets; **j)** leggings with zip-up pocket; **k)** unitard with turtleneck

Converting Two-way Stretch Hip Foundation into Pant Slopers

In this chapter, you learn how to draft a set of pant slopers in each stretch category (*minimal stretch*, *moderate stretch*, *very stretchy*, and *super stretchy*). You create the pant slopers from the hip foundation that was drafted in Chapter 5. Look back at the Knit Family in Table 2.1 on p. 16 to see how the slopers for pants evolve. In addition, Table 2.2 lists other pant variations that you can draft from the pant slopers.

Later in this chapter, you learn how to reduce the length of the two-way stretch pant slopers to create four-way stretch pant slopers. You can use these slopers to draft patterns for **activewear shorts**, leggings and catsuits, or **unitards**. The activewear shorts you design are for sport and fitness. The unitard/catsuit is a one-piece garment that covers the body from the neck to the knees or ankles.

Minimal Stretch

First, you draft the master pant slopers for a two-way minimal stretch knit. They enable you to grade the pant slopers into stretch categories. These slopers have a curve-hugging fit.

Crotch Depth
Figure 10.2
A measurement for the crotch depth is required to draft pant slopers.[1] To draft pant slopers for a customer, measure from the waist to hip as shown. An average measurement is also specified in the following section.

---

1   Helen Joseph-Armstrong, *Patternmaking for Fashion Design*, 5th ed. (Upper Saddle River, NJ: Pearson Education, Inc., publishing as Prentice Hall, 2010), 570.

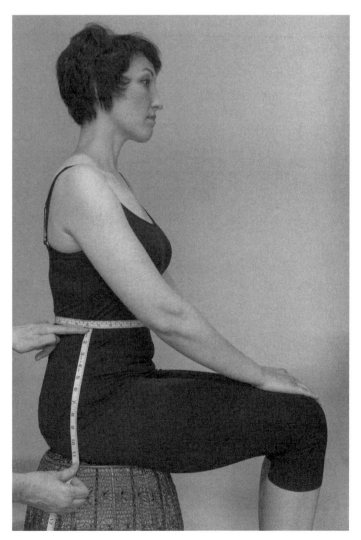

Figure 10.2 Measure the crotch depth

Draft the Front Pant

Figure 10.3a

1. Draw a right angle on pattern paper.
2. Place (W-H) of the hip foundation on the vertical line and (H-H1) on the horizontal line. Trace and label (W-W1-H-H1).
3. W-C = Mark the crotch depth (Size 8 = 9¾", Size 10 = 10", Size 12 = 10¼"). Draw the crotch parallel to H-H1 and squared at (C).
4. B-C = Equal length to (H-H1).
5. H1-B = Draw a straight line.
6. C-C1 = ¼ of (H-H1). (Cut a piece of paper this length and fold into four sections to calculate the measurement.)
7. C-A = Half of (C-C1) marked on a 45° angle.
8. G = Halfway between (B-C1).
9. G-G1 = Draw the grainline parallel to (W-C) and mark the pant length. An average length for a 5'9" height is 38". Draw a horizontal squared line at (G1) for the ankle.
10. A-A1 = Mark half the total ankle measurement equally on each side of the grainline. Average total ankle length (Size 8 = 9½", Size 10 = 10", Size 12 = 10½").
11. Mark halfway between (D-G1).
12. K-K1 = Draw a line parallel to (B-C) 1" above the halfway mark. Mark half the total knee measurement equally on each side of the grainline. Knee measurement (Size 8 = 13½", Size 10 = 14", Size 12 = 14½").
13. Square the knee and ankle horizontal balance lines at the grainline as shown.

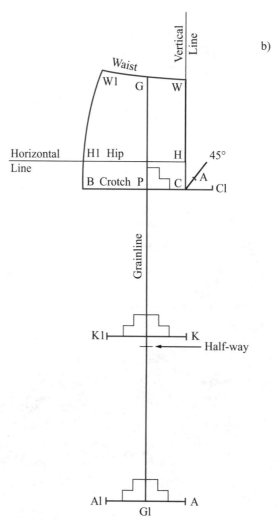

Figure 10.3a Draft the front pant

Draw the Crotch Curve, Inseam, and Side Seam

Figure 10.3b

1. H-X = 1".
2. X-A-C1 = Draw the crotch curve.
3. B-K1, K1-A1, C1-K, K-A = Draw straight lines.

Draw the Curved Inseam and Side Seam

Figure 10.3c

1. I = Mark the halfway point on (C1-K) and ¼"
   squared line inside the inseam.
2. C1-I-K = Place a hip curve on each point, and draw
   a curved inseam.
3. Mark ⅛" inside (B). Place a hip curve on (H1) and
   ⅛" mark, and draw a blended side seam.
4. Draw blending lines at (K and K1) as shown.

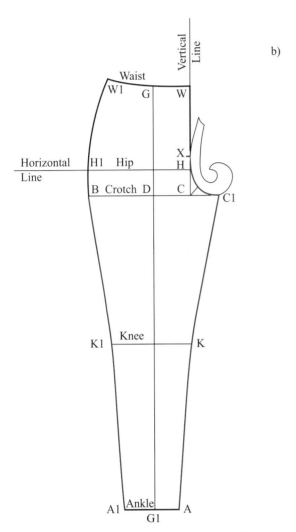

Figure 10.3b Draw the crotch curve, inseam, and side seam

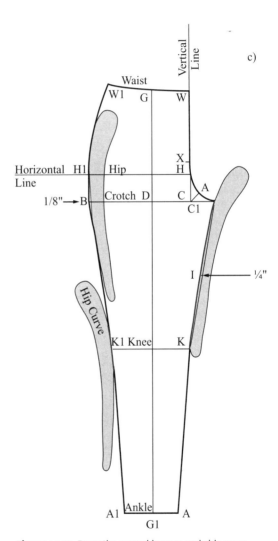

Figure 10.3c Draw the curved inseam and side seam

Draft the Back Pant

Figures 10.4a and b

Next, you draft the back pant sloper from the front pant sloper. Use another color to outline the back sloper.

1. Extend the crotch line past (C1) (see Figure 10.4a).
2. C-C2 = ⅓ of (H-H1).
3. Trace the front inseam (C1-K1) onto pattern paper (see Figure 10.4b).
4. Align the tracing at (K1) to the working pattern outline at (K1) and anchor. Then align C1 to C2. With a tracing wheel, transfer the shape of the front inseam and crotch depth to the back sloper. The back

inseam will be slightly lower than the (C2) crotch depth, as shown in Figure 10.4a.

5. C1-C2 = Connect the points and draw a squared corner at (C2).
6. E = Place an L-square ruler on the hip line (H and W1). Draw the center back seam and waist.

a)

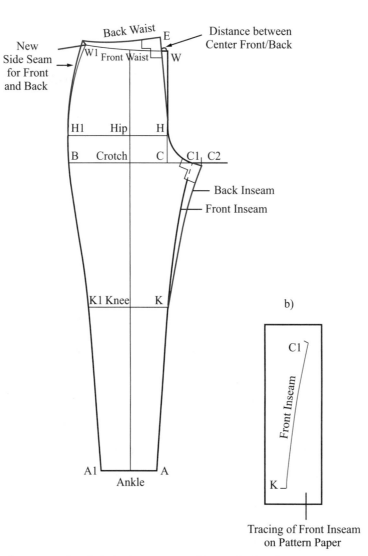

b)

Tracing of Front Inseam on Pattern Paper

Figure 10.4 a) Draft the back pant pattern; **b)** Trace the front inseam

Side Seam Adjustment

1. Extend the back waistline out from W1. Measure the distance between the center front and center back waist along the front waistline at (W). (It will be between ⅜" and ¾").
2. Add half this measurement to the side seam out from (W1).
3. Place (H1) of the hip foundation on the pant draft at (H1), and anchor with an awl. Align foundation (W1) to the new waist position, and redraw the hip curve to the waist. (This is the new front/back side seam.) The new waist/side seam is now approximately ⅛" above the back waist at (W1). Blend this point to the front and back waistline.
4. Trace the front and back pant slopers onto pattern paper and label.
5. Transfer the balance lines (hip, crotch, and knee) and grainlines. The crotch level on the back inseam is slightly above the front crotch level at (C1). The crotch level of front/back will align at the side seams.

Align the Slopers

Figure 10.5

The "Pattern Drafting Principles" section in Chapter 3 discusses the importance of trueing the patterns. This procedure involves blending, equalizing, and squaring and checking that the seamlines are equal length. To check this, **walk the pattern**. Place one pattern on top of the other pattern with the waist (or crotch) edges together. The pattern underneath should remain stationary while you move the top pattern every couple of inches (anchoring it with an awl) to check how the seam lengths compare.

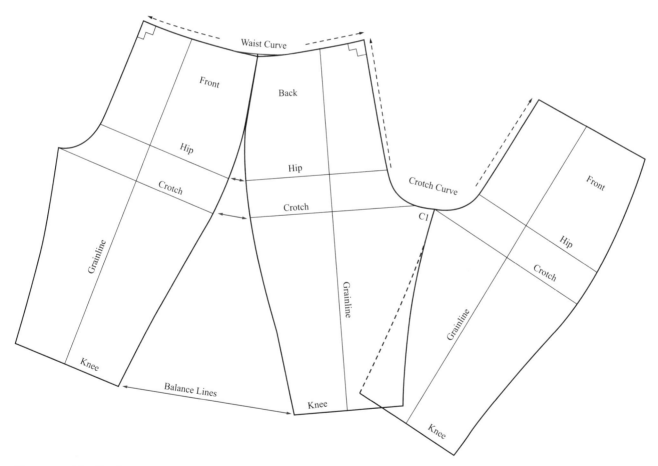

Figure 10.5 Align the slopers

- ✓ Check that the center front and back at the waist are squared (see Figure 10.5).
- ✓ Check that the seams are the same length and that the hip, crotch, and knee balance lines are perfectly aligned.
- ✓ Check that the grainlines are squared at the balance lines (see Figure 10.12).

Fabric You'll Need

To stitch a muslin pant to check the fit, purchase 1⅓ yards minimal stretch knit. Do a stretch test using the stretch gauge in Figure 1.6 on p. 9 to make sure the stretch of the knit is correct because the amount of stretch affects the fitting. (A perfect muslin knit is medium-weight Ponte.)

Cut and Stitch

1. Before layout, cut the fabric on grain. (See Figure 4.3 on p. 42.)
2. Cut the pant from double folded fabric following the layout in Figure 4.4 on p. 44.
3. Add ¼" seam allowances (waist and hem allowances are not necessary). A waist finish is not stitched at this point.
4. Stitch the pant following the Stitching Order in Table 10.1.

TABLE 10.1 Stitching order for pants

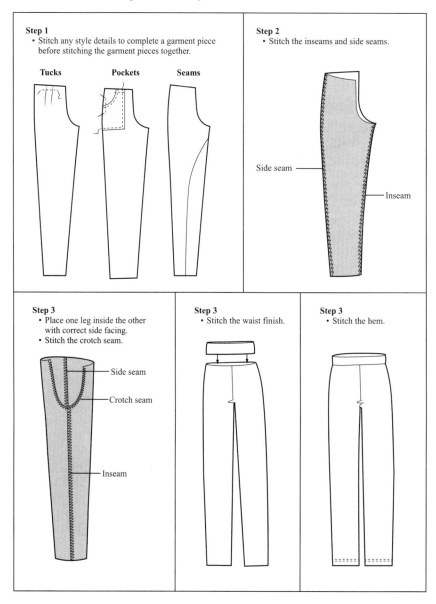

Test the Fit

Figure 10.6

Place the pants on the pant form. Also ask someone to wear the pants. Pin any fitting adjustments as needed. Then mark these adjustments on the slopers. (See Figures 10.6a and b.)

What to look for:

- ✓ Evaluate the hang of the pants; check that the side seams are aligned to the form.
- ✓ Check the fit around the waist and hip; do not tighten the waist because it needs to stretch to fit over the hips.
- ✓ Check that the pants feel comfortable during all movement (walking, crouching, and bending).
- ✓ Check that the length is accurate.

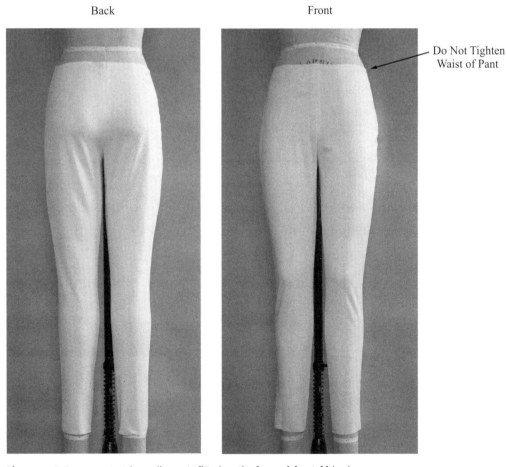

Back   Front

Do Not Tighten Waist of Pant

Figure 10.6 Two-way stretch muslin pants fitted on the form; **a)** front; **b)** back

Finalize the Slopers

Figure 10.7

1. Transfer the paper patterns onto oak-tag.
2. Write the sloper name "Front/Back Two-way Stretch Pant Slopers," and document the stretch category.
3. Transfer the balance lines (hip, crotch, and knee) and draw the grainlines.
4. Label (X) on the front sloper for grading purposes. The back sloper (X) is not labeled at this point.

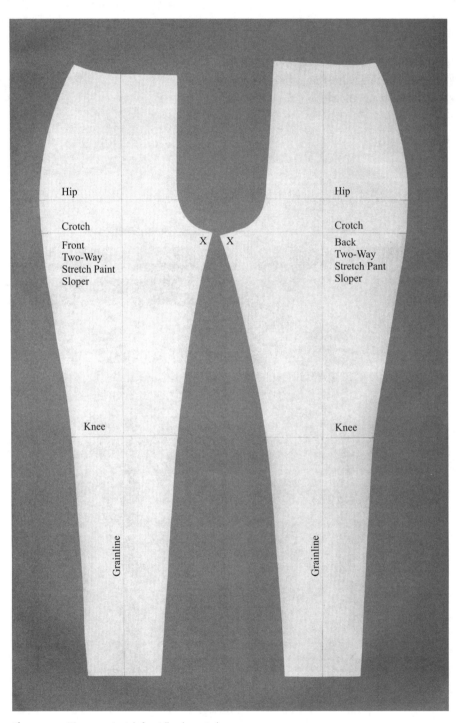

Figure 10.7 Two-way stretch front/back pant slopers

Grading Two-way Stretch into Stretch Categories

The next step is to grade slopers for moderate stretch, very stretchy, and super stretchy knits from the minimal stretch master pant slopers that you just drafted. Since these knits have more stretch, you need to decrease the slopers. Use the same grading method to grade the front and back slopers.

Prepare the Grading Grid

Figure 10.8

1. Draw the grading grid on oak-tag. Label (D).
2. From (D), mark grading increments (C2, C1, C, B2, B, A3, and A) in a negative direction. (Refer to Figure 3.16 on p. 36.)

Horizontal Balance Line (HBL)

Figure 10.9

The HBL on the front pant sloper is the crotch line. On the back pant sloper, the crotch line *is not* the HBL. For grading purposes only (this is not permanent), draw HBL (parallel to the crotch depth) across the inseam/crotch as shown. Label (X).

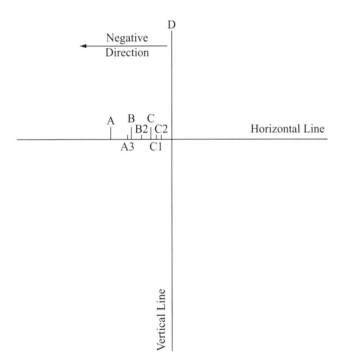

Figure 10.8 Prepare the grading grid

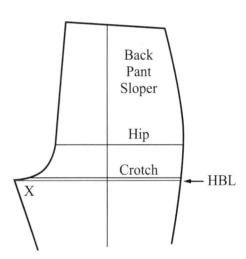

Figure 10.9 Draw (HBL) on the back pant sloper

Trace Minimal Stretch Slopers onto the Grading Grid

Figure 10.10

1. Place sloper HBL (X) on (D) and the horizontal line as shown. The grainline must be parallel to the vertical line. Trace the sloper onto the grid.
2. Draw a horizontal guideline squared at the center front to the side seam.
3. Transfer the hip and knee balance lines and the grainline. Take time to do this, as each line must be squared at the grainline.

Grade Moderate Stretch, Very Stretchy, and Super Stretchy

Use the same grading increments and grading method to grade the back pant slopers. As you grade each sloper, you must align HBL on the horizontal line at the appropriate grading increment.

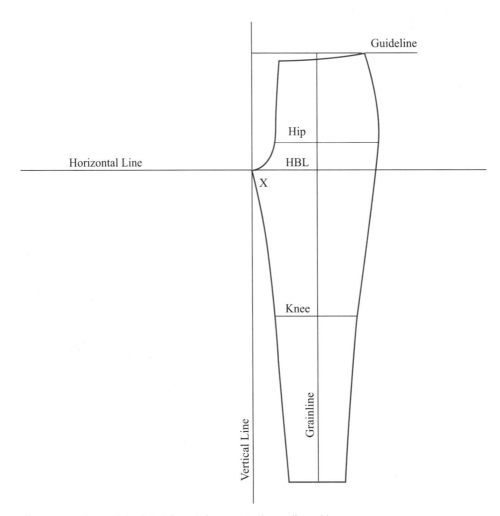

Figure 10.10 Trace minimal stretch pant slopers onto the grading grid

Waist/Side Seam (½" Grade)

Figure 10.11a

The tip of the waist/side seam should touch the guideline when the side seams are graded. Draw the waist to the hip for each stretch category.

1. *Moderate Stretch*—Move (X) on (C).
2. *Very Stretchy*—Move (X) on (B).
3. *Super Stretchy*—Move (X) on (A).

Ankle (¼" Grade)

Figure 10.11a

Draw a 1" line at the ankle for each stretch category.

1. *Moderate Stretch*—Move (X) to (C2).
2. *Very Stretchy*—Move (X) to (C).
3. *Super Stretchy*—Move (X) to (B2).

Knee (3/8" Grade)

Figure 10.11a

Draw a 2" line at knee level for each stretch category.

1. *Moderate Stretchy*—Move (X) to (C1).
2. *Very Stretchy*—Move (X) to (B2).
3. *Super Stretchy*—Move (X) to (A3).

a)

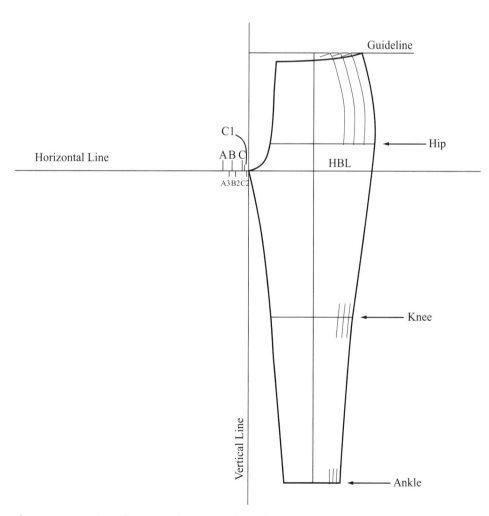

Figure 10.11a Grade moderate stretch, very stretchy, and super stretchy

Finish Drawing the Slopers

Figure 10.11b and c

Place the minimal stretch sloper on each graded outline and finish drawing the waistline. Also use the sloper to connect the side seams between the hip, knee, and ankle in each stretch category.

b)

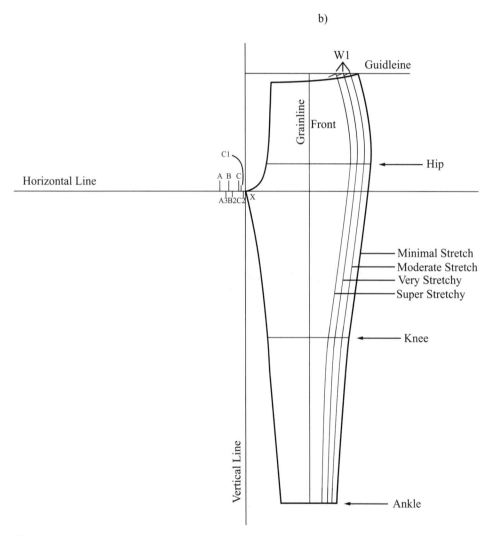

Figure 10.11b Finish drawing the front waist and side seams in all stretch categories

c)

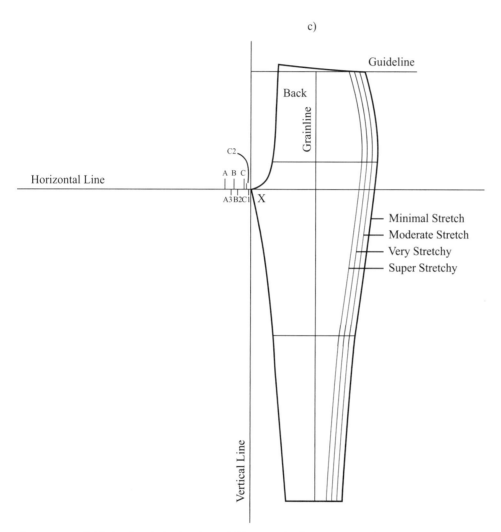

Guideline

Back

Grainline

C2

Horizontal Line

A B C

A3 B2C1 X

Minimal Stretch
Moderate Stretch
Very Stretchy
Super Stretchy

Vertical Line

Figure 10.11c Finish drawing the back waist and side seams in all stretch categories

Cut the Slopers and Redraw the Grainlines
Figure 10.12

1. Cut the front and back moderate stretch slopers. (Minimal stretch slopers were drawn onto the grid for grading purposes only. They do not need to be cut again.)
2. Cut the waist/side seams at (W1) in steps for each stretch category, as illustrated in Figure 5.16 on p. 77.
3. Place the minimal stretch sloper on top of each graded sloper. Align the sloper waist/side seam to each newly graded sloper in each stretch category. Use a tracing wheel to transfer the original waistline, as shown in Figure 5.17 on p. 78.
4. Align the side seams of the front and back slopers together to check they are equal lengths.
5. Redraw new grainlines parallel to the minimal stretch grainline. Place the grainline halfway between the inseam and side seam of the ankle.

Align the Slopers

✓ Check that the center front/back at the waist are squared (see Figure 10.5).
✓ Check that the front/back side seams and inseams are equal lengths and that the hip, crotch, and knee balance lines are perfectly aligned (see Figure 10.5).
✓ Check that the grainlines are squared at the balance lines (see Figure 10.12).

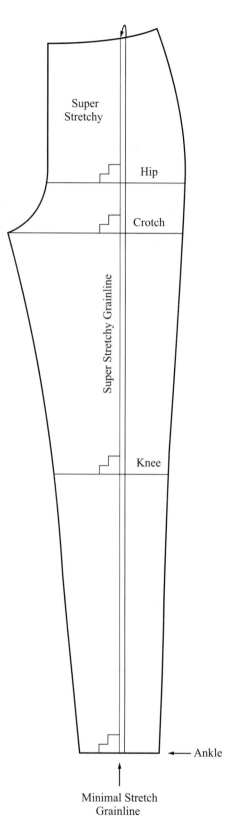

Figure 10.12 Cut the slopers and redraw the grainlines

Finalize the Slopers

Label the slopers "Front/Back Two-way Stretch Pant Slopers" in each stretch category. When the slopers are stacked, the hip, crotch, and knee balance lines should be in alignment. The position of the grainlines for each stretch category will differ. (See Figure 10.13.)

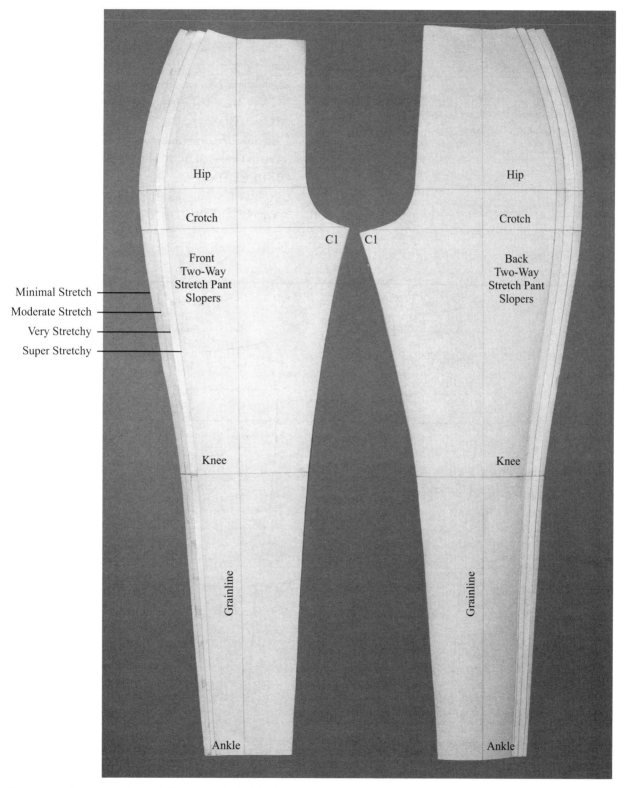

Figure 10.13 Two-way stretch pant slopers in each stretch category

Reducing Two-way Stretch Slopers into Four-way Stretch

Leggings, activewear shorts, cycling shorts, unitards, or catsuits must be constructed from four-way knits with spandex/Lycra. These styles require four-way stretch pant slopers to draft the patterns. (Refer to the "Four-way Stretch" section in Chapter 1 for more information.)

Very Stretchy

To offset the lengthwise stretch of four-way knits, you reduce the length of the two-way very stretchy and/or super stretchy pant slopers.

Mark the Reduction

Figure 10.14a

In this case, you reduce the length 3" between the waist and knee of the front/back slopers. You can fine-tune the overall length when individual patterns are drafted. Mark the reduction in the same position on the front and back slopers.

1. Trace the two-way very stretchy pant slopers onto pattern paper.
2. Guideline 1 = Draw halfway between the waist and hip. Mark 1" below guideline 1. Label "REDUCTION."
3. Guideline 2 = Draw halfway between the crotch level and knee. Mark 1" above guideline 2. Label it "REDUCTION."
4. Guideline 3 = Knee level. Mark 1" below guideline 3. Label it "REDUCTION."

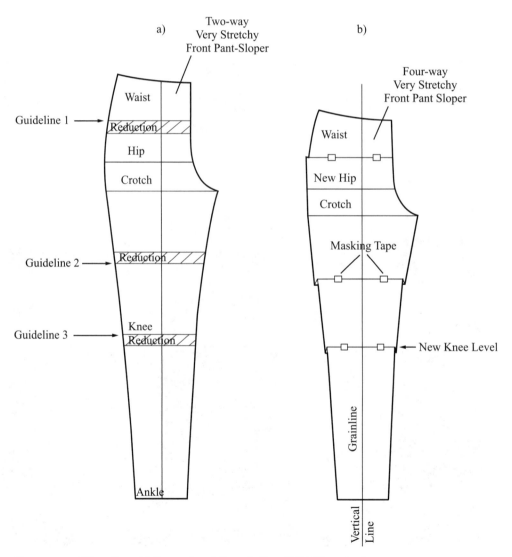

Figure 10.14 a) Draw the guidelines and mark the reduction; **b)** Fold the reduction

Fold the Reduction
Figures 10.14b and c

1. Fold the "REDUCTION" section by placing the parallel lines together to shorten the length of the sloper. Secure with masking tape (see Figure 10.14b).
2. Draw a vertical line on pattern paper. Align the sloper grainline on the vertical line and trace the reduced pant sloper.
3. At the hip level, remove ⅛" from the side seam. Use a hip curve to equalize the inseam and side seam to eliminate irregular line lengths (see Figure 10.14c).
4. Check that the front/back inseams and side seams are the same length (see Figure 10.5).
5. Check that the grainlines are squared at the balance lines (see Figure 10.12).

Fabric You'll Need

Purchase 1⅛ yard minimal stretch knit. Do a stretch test using the stretch gauge in Figure 1.6 on p. 9 to make sure the knit is four-way stretch because the amount of stretch affects the fitting.

Cut, Stitch, and Fit
Figure 10.15

Next, cut, stitch, and fit the four-way stretch pant on the form as you did for two-way stretch. In this case, the pants will be a tight fit.

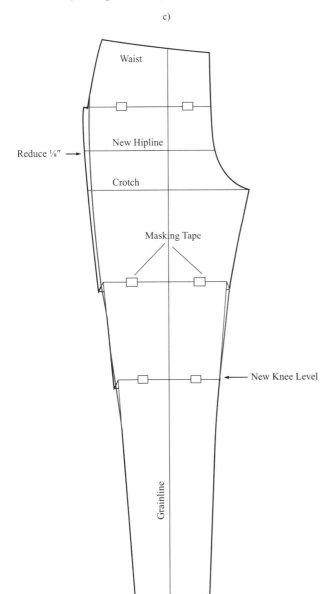

Figure 10.14c Draw the blending side seam and inseam

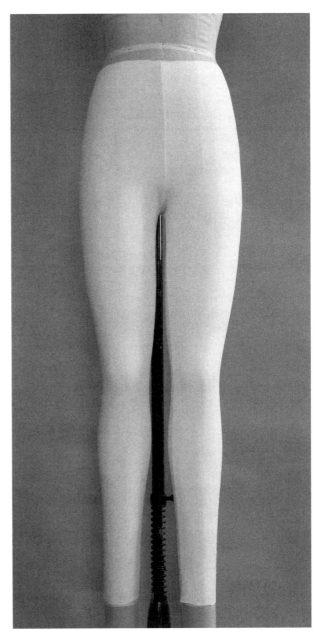

Figure 10.15 Muslin four-way stretch pants fitted on the form

Finalize the Slopers

Figure 10.16

1. Transfer the slopers onto oak-tag.
2. Write the sloper name "Front/Back Four-way Stretch Pant Slopers" and document the stretch category.

Grading Four-way Stretch

To grade the four-way very stretchy pant slopers into super stretchy pant slopers, refer to the following figures:

- Figure 10.8—Draw the grading grid and mark grading increments C, C1, and C2.

- Figure 10.10—Trace the very stretchy slopers onto the grading grid.
- Figure 10.11— Follow the grading method for moderate stretch.

Pant Slopers for Stable Knits

Pants constructed from a stable knit (such as double knit with minimal stretch) can have waist darts, a structured waist band, and a zipper closure. To draft the pant patterns, use the pant slopers for woven fabric and grade them 2" smaller to remove ease from the patterns.

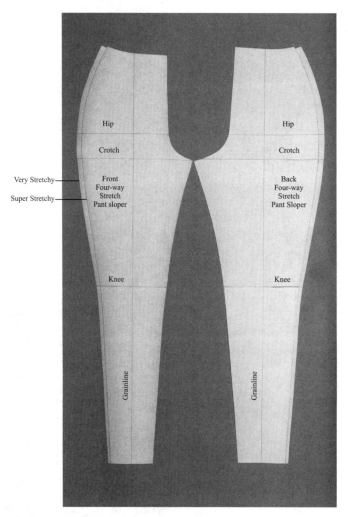

Figure 10.16 Four-way stretch pant slopers

Choosing the Slopers

To choose the appropriate slopers for your pant design, begin by conducting a stretch test (using the stretch gauge in Figure 1.6). Next, choose the appropriate slopers. Refer to "How to Choose Slopers" in Chapter 2 to learn how you can choose slopers according to the stretch capacity of your knit or for the fit of the garment. If you choose the sloper for the fit of the garment, the minimal stretch pant slopers will create a "loose-fit" if the pants are constructed from a knit with more stretch. Furthermore, the slopers can be enlarged into an "extra loose-fit."

Extra Loose-fit

Figures 10.17a and b
If you desire even more room in the pants, then grade the minimal stretch pant slopers in a positive direction and add 2" to the waist and hip. You also can lower the crotch depth to allow more room.

Make sure "X" is marked on the front pant sloper, as shown in Figure 10.7, and on the back pant sloper, as indicated in Figure 10.9.

1. Draw the grading grid onto oak-tag. On the horizontal line (in a positive direction) from (D), mark (E) ½", (D3) ⅜", and (D2) ¼" (see Figure 10.17a).
2. Draw a guideline ½" below and parallel to the horizontal line (see Figure 10.17a).
3. Trace the minimal stretch pant slopers onto the grading grid (see Figure 10.17b).
4. Align HBL on the *horizontal line.* Move (X) on (E) and draw the waist to the hip. Next, move (X) on (D3) and mark the knee level. Last, move (X) on (D2) and mark the ankle.
5. Align HBL on the *guideline.* Place (X) on (D), and draw a lowered crotch depth.
6. Use the master sloper to finish drawing the side seam (see Figure 10.11b).
7. Cut the slopers and label "Extra-Loose Fit."

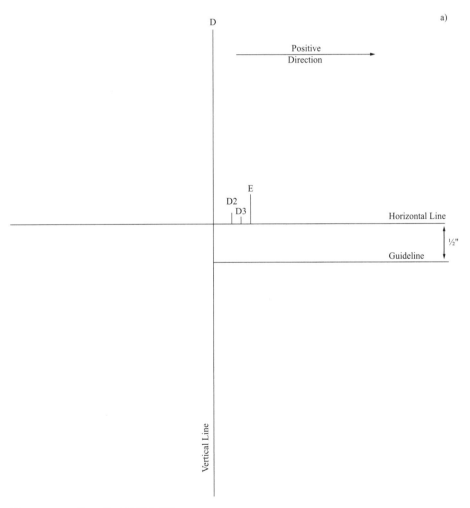

Figure 10.17a Draw the grading grid

Pattern Drafting Pants

When you want to draft patterns for pants, be sure to have the correct patternmaking tools at hand (see Figure 3.1 on p. 20). Chapter 3 outlines important pattern drafting principles that, when followed, will create excellent pant patterns. From the basic pant slopers, the silhouette can be changed as well as the length to create different pant styles, as shown in Figures 10.1a through k.

Pants can be constructed from two-way and four-way stretch knits. Many pant styles do not need the length-wise stretch; however, having it will not affect the fit of the pant. Other styles such as activewear shorts, leggings, and unitards/catsuits *must* be constructed from four-way stretch knits.

**IMPORTANT 10.1:
WAIST FINISHES**

Pants require a waist finish. The "Waist Finishes" section in Chapter 9 outlines how to draft a cut-in-one invisible waistband, separate waistband, and bandless waist finish for skirts (see Table 9.2 on p. 284). If you look at Figures 9.1a through i, you will observe that many of the same waist finishes on the skirts are used for the pants in Figures 10.1a through h.

Before you draft the pant patterns, you must choose the type, width, and length of elastic. The elastic chart in Table 9.3 on p. 285 will guide you when selecting the elastic. Refer also to Table 3.2 on p. 28 to see each type of elastic.

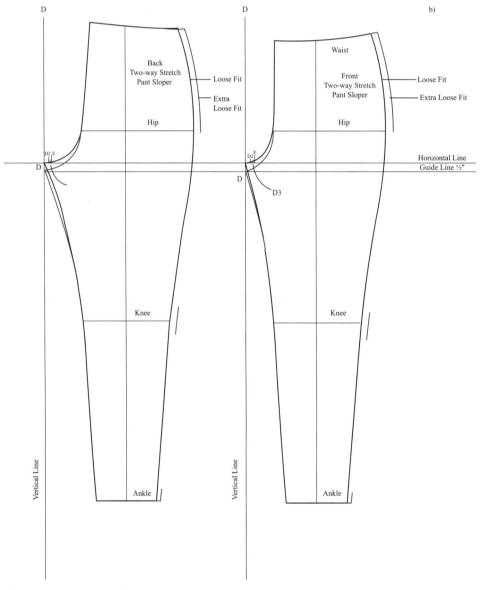

Figure 10.17b Extra-loose fit pant slopers waist and hip enlarged

Pockets for Pants

In the "Pockets for Cardigans" section in Chapter 8, pockets are categorized as patch, inseam, and slash pockets. Chapter 8 also outlines the pattern and stitching instructions for patch, inseam, welt, and zip-up pockets. The same styles of pockets can be a part of pants. What differs is the proportion and placement of the pockets.

This chapter explains how to draft the patterns for side-front pockets, inseam pockets, and another style of patch pocket. You also learn how to modify the welt and zip-up pockets for pants.

> **IMPORTANT 10.2:**
> **PLANNING THE POCKET SIZE**
>
> Pockets can be placed horizontally, vertically, or diagonally on pants. The **pocket bag** is a pouch stitched inside the garment for the hand to rest in or to use as a compartment for keys, cash, or a cell phone. Use your hand to determine the length of the pocket opening and depth of the pocket bag. (See Figure 10.18.)

Patch Pocket

Figures 10.19a, b, and c
Here, you stitch a patch pocket to the outside of the boot-cut pants shown in Figure 10.1e.

1. A-E = Draw the pocket opening with a French curve, as shown in Figure 10.19a. Add ⅛" out from (E) so that the opening is not tight.

2. B-C-D = Outline the pocket shape (see Figure 10.19a).

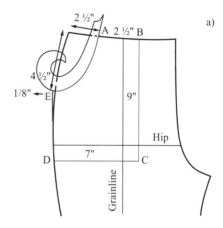

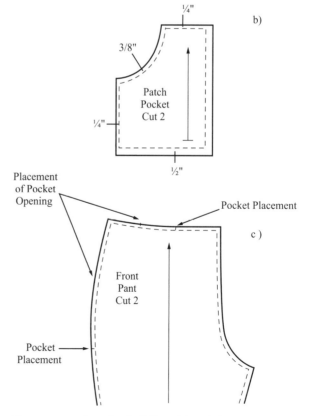

Figures 10.19a, b, and c Draft the patch pocket

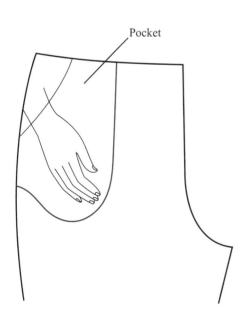

Figure 10.18 Plan the pocket size

3. Trace the pocket pattern (A-B-C-D-E) from the working pattern, and add the seam allowance. Label the pocket pattern, and draw the grainline (see Figure 10.19b).
4. Notch the pocket placement (A-E) on the front pant pattern (see Figure 10.19c).

a)

b)

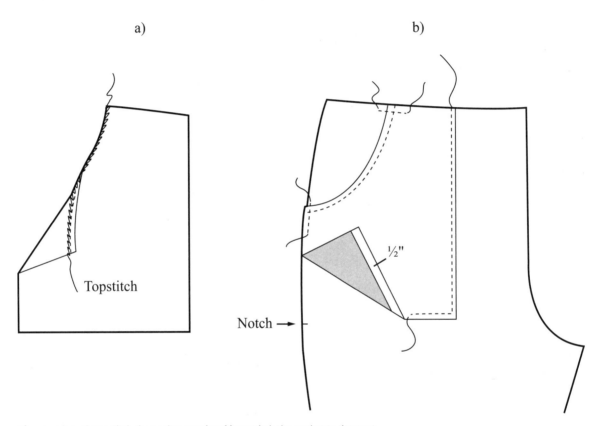

Figure 10.20 a) Topstitch the pocket opening; **b)** topstitch the pocket to the pant

Side-front Pocket

Figures 10.21a through d

A **side-front pocket** has a slanted opening from the high-hip to the waist. This style of pocket is part of the pants in Figure 10.1c and the jumpsuit shown in Figure 10.1i.

1. A–D = Mark a pocket opening on the waist and side seam. Add ⅛" out from (D) so that the opening will not be tight. Draw a diagonal line. Then draw a curved pocket opening to the ¼" mark (see Figure 10.21a).
2. B–C = Outline the shape of the pocket bag.
3. A–B–C–D = Trace the pocket bag pattern (see Figure 10.21b).
4. X–B–C–D = Trace the side-front/pocket bag pattern and notch pocket placement (A–D), as shown in Figure 10.21c.
5. Trace the pant pattern from the (A–D) pocket opening (see Figure 10.21d).
6. Add a ¼" seam allowance to the pocket opening side, waist, and other seams. Add a ½" seam allowance around the pocket bag.

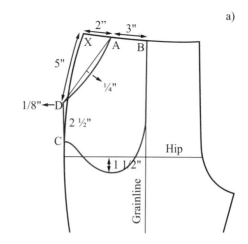

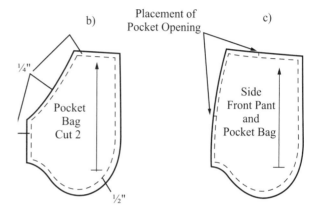

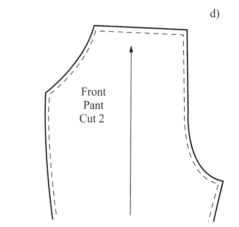

Figures 10.21 a–d Draft the side-front pocket

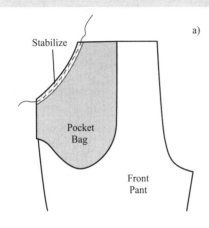

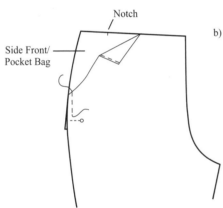

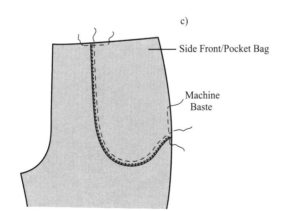

Figure 10.22 a) Stitch the pocket bag to the pocket opening; **b)** Align the pocket opening to the side front/pocket bag; **c)** Stitch the pocket bag

Inseam Pocket

Figures 10.23a and b

The sweatpants shown in Figure 10.1h have inseam pockets and a topstitched waistband. The topstitching secures the upper edge of the pockets in place. Here, the inseam pockets have been planned on the pant pattern that is drafted in Figure 10.33.

1. X-Y = Mark the pocket opening on the side seam.
2. A-B-C = Outline the shape of the pocket bag (see Figure 10.23a).
3. A-B-C = Trace the pocket bag pattern, add a seam allowance, and notch the pocket opening. Label the pattern and draw the grainline (see Figure 10.23b).
4. Trace the front pant pattern. Add a ⅜" seam allowance to the front/back side seam of the pant patterns, and notch the pocket opening (X-Y).

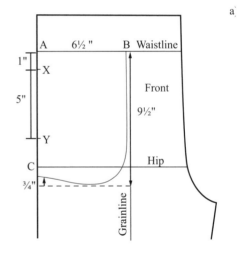

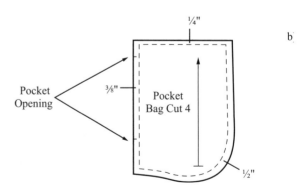

Figures 10.23a and b Draft the inseam pocket

STITCHING TIP 10.4: STITCHING THE INSEAM POCKET

1. Serge the edges of the four pocket bags.
2. Stitch a pocket bag to each front/back side seam (see Figure 10.24a).
3. Align side seams together, and stitch either side of the pocket opening (see Figure 10.24a).
4. Topstitch the front pocket opening only (see Figure 10.24b).
5. Serge the side seams.
6. Stitch the edges of the pocket bag together.
7. When the elastic waistband is stitched, the top edge of the pockets will be hidden under the waistband, as shown in Figure 10.24c.

a)

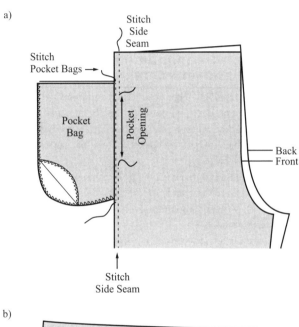

b)

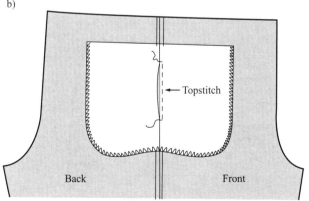

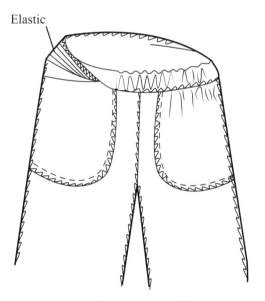

Figure 10.24c Inside view of pants with inseam pockets

Figure 10.24 a) Stitch the pocket bag to the pants; **b)** topstitch the front pocket opening

Welt Pocket

Figures 10.25a through c

The pants shown in Figure 10.1d have welt pockets and a topstitched waistband. The topstitching secures the upper edge of the pockets in place (see Figure 10.25c). To draft the pocket pattern, refer to the "Pockets for Sweater-Jackets" section in Chapter 8. The pocket needs a slight modification for pants, however.

1. Draw the placement of the welt 5" to 6" long on the front pattern, as shown in Figure 10.25a.
2. Follow the instructions in Figures 8.40a and b on p. 252 to draft the pocket pattern. Only the pocket shape differs (see Figure 10.25b).

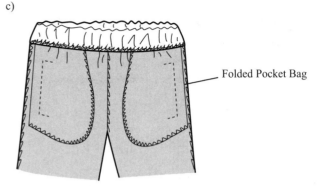

Figure 10.25c Inside view of pants with welt pockets

3. Fold the pattern like shown in Figure 8.40b on p. 230 to form the welt, and finish drafting the pocket pattern.
4. To stitch the welt pockets, refer to Figures 8.45a through f on pp. 255–257.

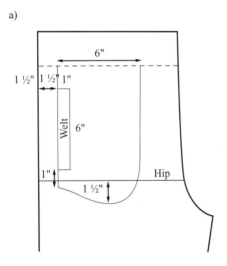

a)

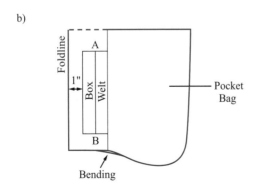

b)

Figure 10.25 a) Plan the pocket placement; **b)** Draft the pocket pattern

---

PATTERN TIP 10.1: DRAFTING THE ZIP-UP POCKET PATTERN

The sleek legging in Figure 10.1j has a zip-up pocket. In Figure 8.2a on p. 181, the same zip-up pocket is part of a sweater-jacket. You can now use the same pattern drafting principles to draft the pocket pattern for your pants. (See Figure 10.26.)

1. Draw a line centered on the front pant pattern (squared to the grainline) for the zipper placement. Mark with matchpoints. Label the pattern "L.S.O." (for left side only).
2. To draft the pocket pattern, refer to Figures 8.48 and 8.51 on p. 238 and on p. 240.
3. To stitch the zip-up pocket, refer to Figure 8.45 on p. 233.

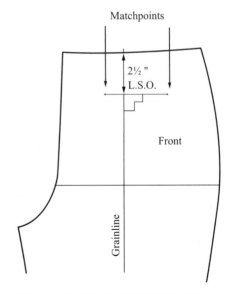

Figure 10.26 Plan the pocket placement

Length Variations

Pants can be varying lengths, as indicated on the body in Figure 10.27. In Figure 10.28, each length is indicated on the front sloper. Narrow-legged tapered pants must finish at the ankle or higher. Pants with wider leg openings are cut longer. For example, boot-cut pants finish below the ankle and rest on the shoes or boots. Palazzo pants are extremely wide legged and floor length.

- *Shorts*—Between crotch and thigh
- *Activewear shorts*—Between shorts and Bermuda shorts
- *Bermuda shorts*—Just above the knee
- *Capri*—Calf length (approximately halfway between the knee and ankle)
- *Seven-eighths*—Between Capri and Cropped
- *Cropped*—Above the ankle
- *Ankle*—Ankle length
- *Floor length*—To the floor

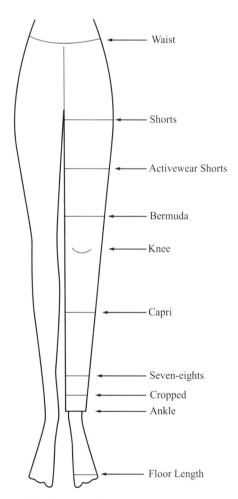

Figure 10.27 Length variations

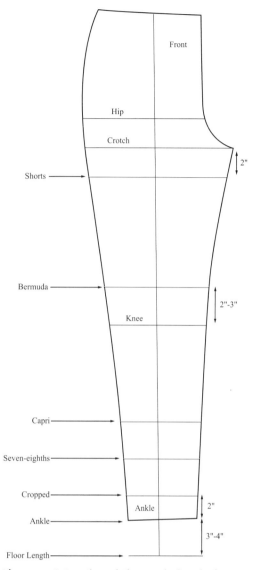

Figure 10.28 Lengths variations marked on the front sloper

Shorts

Fitted and semi-fitted shorts are featured in Figures 10.11a and b. Now you're ready to draft these patterns. (To draft patterns for short-shorts, refer to the "Boy-cut Panty" section in Chapter 11.)

PATTERN TIP 10.2: DETERMINING THE SHORTS LENGTH

To determine the shorts length, measure down from the front inseam (C). Do not measure down from the back crotch line because the back crotch line is slightly above (C). When the back sloper in Figure 10.4 was drafted, the crotch/inseam became slightly higher than the front crotch line in order for the inseams to match perfectly in the length.

Fitted

Figures 10.29a and b

The fitted shorts have tapered side seams and inseams to create a slim-fit (see Figure 10.1a).

1. Trace the front/back two-way stretch pant slopers to the knee. Transfer the hip, crotch, and grainline. Label (A and C).

2. Mark the shorts length down from inseam (C). Draw the hemline parallel to the crotch line. Label it "Hemline."

3. B and D = Mark ¼" inside and below the hemline of the inseam and side seam, as shown in Figure 10.29a.

4. A-B = Reshape the side seam (you may need to remove a small amount from the hip, as in Figure 10.29a).

5. C-D = Draw straight inseams.

6. B-D = Draw a curved hemline.

7. Place the side seams of the front and back patterns together. If there is a length inconsistency, equalize by drawing a new hemline to make the seams the same length (see Figure 10.29b).

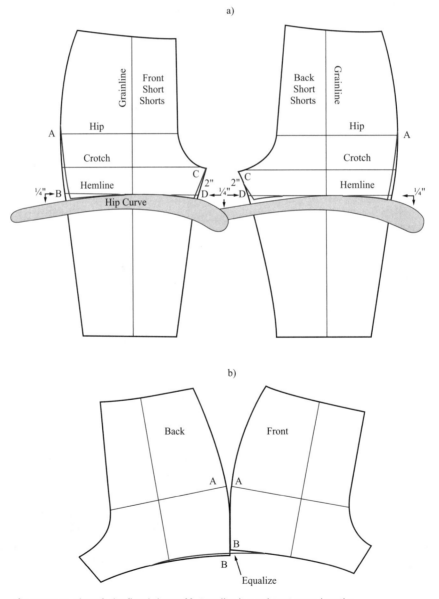

Figure 10.29 **a)** Draft the fitted shorts; **b)** Equalize inconsistent seam lengths

Add a Hem Allowance

The hem allowance must have directional seamlines when the seams are shaped. This ensures that the hem allowance is not tight when turned back. Use this method to add a hem allowance to any length pant.

1. B-D = Mark 1" up from the hemline. Draw a guideline.
2. Add a shaped 1" hem allowance below the hemline.
3. E-F = Position a graph ruler on the guideline of the side seam and inseam (as shown on the back). Draw a line to the hem edge.
4. B-E and D-F = Draw straight lines from the hemline to the hem edge. (See Figure 10.30a.)

Align the Patterns

1. Align the front/back side seams and inseams together to check they are the same length. Adjust if necessary.
2. Place the hem allowance inseams and side seams together. Then draw a smooth blending hem edge. (See Figure 10.30b.)

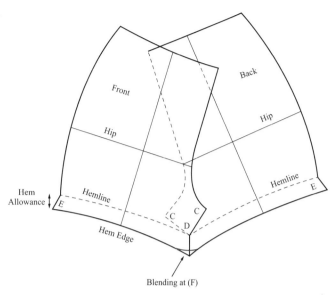

Figure 10.30b Draw a blending hem edge

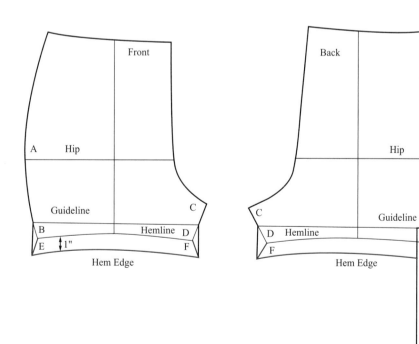

Figure 10.30a Add a hem allowance

Finalize the Patterns

1. Add ¼" seam allowances to the inseam, side, crotch, waist, and waistband.
2. Label the patterns "Front/Back Fitted Shorts."
3. Draw the hipline and grainlines.
4. Document the stretch category and number of pattern pieces to cut. (See Figure 10.31.)
5. A draft of the fitted separate waistband is shown in Figure 9.58a.

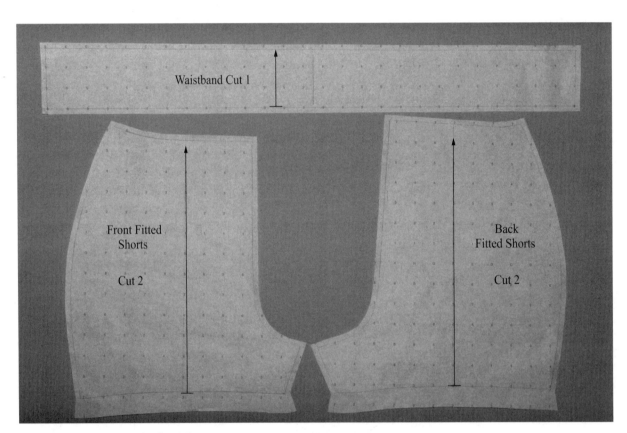

Figure 10.31 Final patterns for fitted shorts

Semi-fitted

Figure 10.32

The semi-fitted shorts have a roomier fit than the fitted shorts (see Figure 10.1b). The patterns are also suitable to use for shorty pajamas. The shorts have a waistband cut all-in-one with the shorts pattern.

1. Trace the front/back two-way stretch pant slopers to the knee. Transfer the hip, crotch, and grainline.

2. Draw a guideline squared to the grainline from the side seam/waist tip to the center front/back. Extend the CF/CB up to the guideline (see Figure 10.32).

3. Mark the shorts length down from inseam (C). Draw the hemline parallel to the crotch. Label it "Hemline."

4. A–B = Add 1" to the side seam.

5. E–F = Draw the side seam. Extend the hemline to the side seam.

6. D = Mark the inseam ¼" out and below the hemline.

7. C–D = Draw a straight inseam. Curve the hemline from the grainline to (D) (see Figure 10.32).

a)

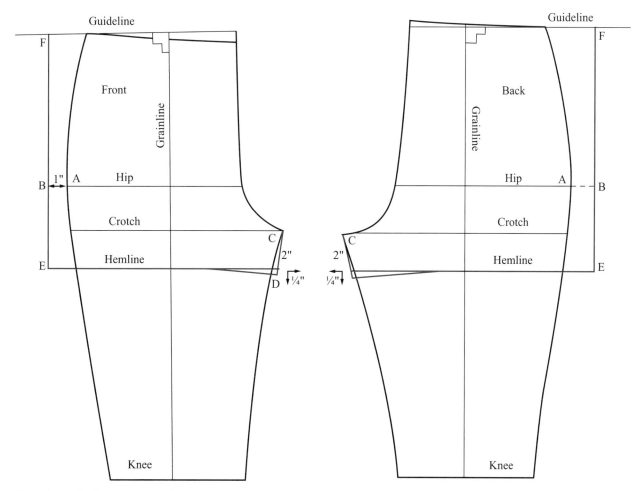

Figure 10.32 Draft semi-fitted shorts

8. F-G = Add a front waist extension (above the guide-line) twice the width of the elastic plus ½" (see Figure 10.33).

9. F-J = On the center back, add the waist extension above the sloper waist, and on G-F, add the exten-sion above the guideline on the side seam.

10. Draw a line centered on the waist extension.

11. H-I = Extend the center back and side seam to the center line.

12. G-J = Equal length to (H-I).

13. Compare the side seam lengths. If necessary, adjust the back length to match the front side seam length.

14. Add a 1" hem allowance. (Refer to Figure 10.30a.)

b)

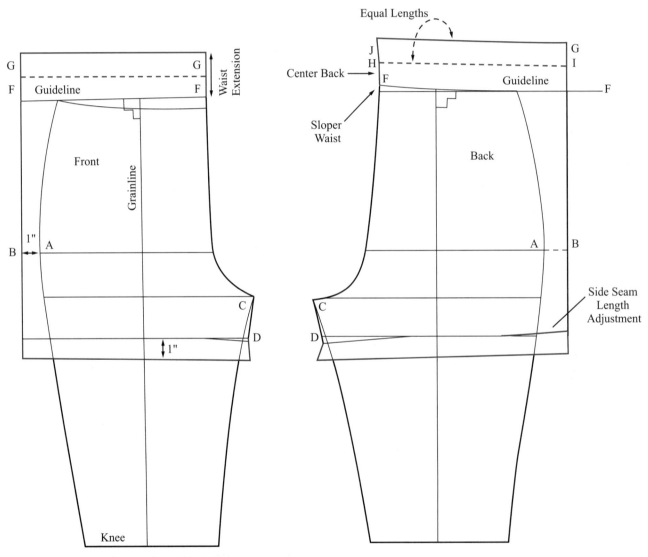

Figure 10.33 Add a waist extension and hem allowance

Finalize the Patterns

Figure 10.34

1. Draw line (F) on the final patterns to indicate the waistline.
2. Add ¼" seam allowances to the inseam, side, and crotch and to the waistband.
3. Label the patterns "Front/Back Semi-fitted Shorts."
4. Draw the grainlines and document the number of pattern pieces.

PATTERN TIP 10.3: ADDING A SPLIT-HEM

Shorts, capri pants, or ankle length pants can have side splits in the hem (see Figure 10.1c). To accommodate the split, follow the same pattern drafting technique for adding a split-hem to the skirt pattern in Figures 9.44a and b on p. 279. Mark a matchpoint for the split 2" up from the hem on the side seam. To stitch the split-hem, refer to Figures 9.45a and b on p. 279.

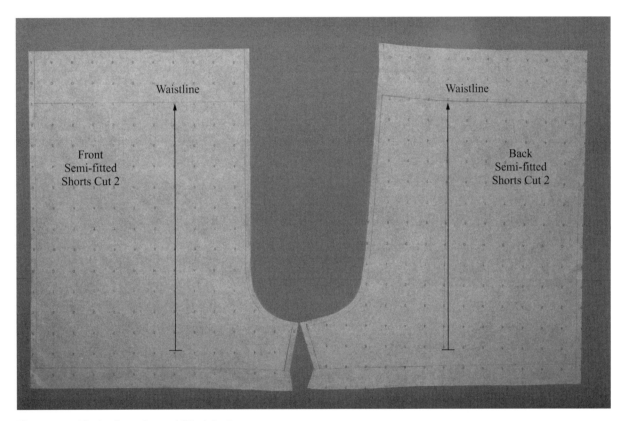

Figure 10.34 Final patterns for semi-fitted shorts

Bermuda Shorts, Capri, Seven-eighths, and Cropped Pants

Figure 10.35

The front sloper in Figure 10.28 indicates the length to cut Bermuda shorts, capris, seven-eighths, and cropped pants. If the shorts and pants are slim-fit and tapered from the hip to ankle, use the same pattern drafting method in Figure 10.29 to add the hem allowance. The only difference is the length.

Silhouette Variations

You can draft a variety of silhouettes by modifying the tapered pant slopers (see Figure 10.36). Refer also to Figures 10.1a through k to see each silhouette.

- *Tight-fit*— Follow the contour of the legs (for styles such as leggings; see Figure 10.1j).
- *Tapered*—Narrows from hip to ankle (see Figure 10.1c).
- *Straight*—Leg is straight from hip to hem length (see Figure 10.1d).
- *A-line*—Side seam is shaped outward from hip to hem (see Figure 10.1f).
- *Wide-leg*— Leg is flared from hip to hem (see palazzo pants in Figure 10.1g)).
- *Boot-cut*—Legs are tapered to the knee and flare out to the hem (see Figure 10.1e).

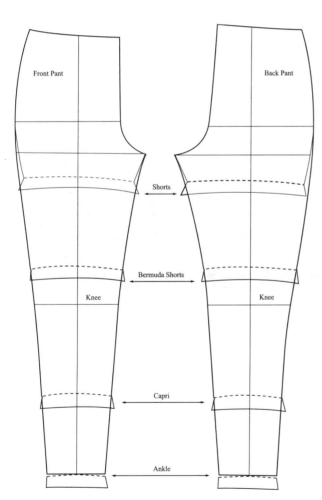

Figure 10.35 Adding the hem allowance to slim-fit tapered pants

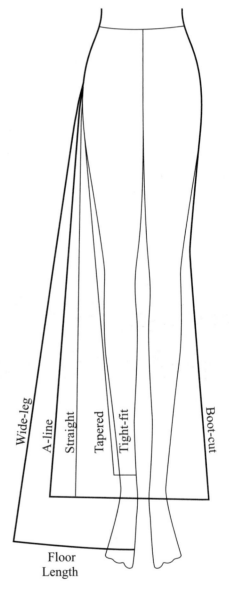

Figure 10.36 Silhouette variations

Tapered and Straight

The pattern for long tapered or straight pants can also be used for pajama pant patterns. The pants can be cut at any length (see Figure 10.27).

Draft the Patterns
Figure 10.37

1. Trace two-way stretch front/back full-length slopers onto the working pattern.
2. Draft the semi-fitted shorts pattern and waist extension in Figures 10.32 and 10.33.

3. C-D = Reshape the inseam for tapered or straight-legged pants.
4. H-B = Draw the front/back tapered side seams.
5. H-I = Draw the front/back straight side seams.
6. Add 1" to 1½" extra length for straight-legged pants.

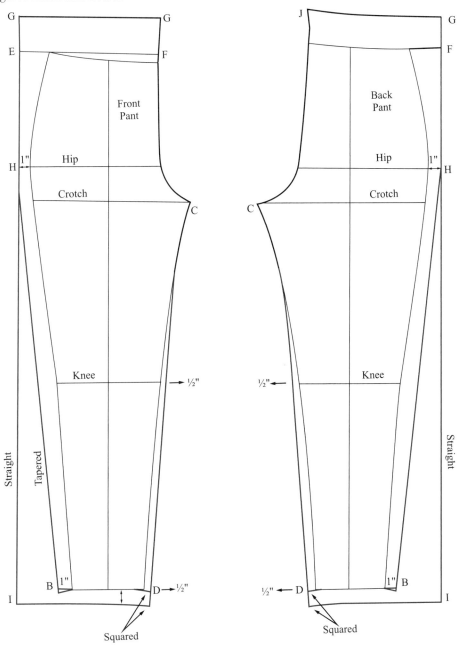

Figure 10.37 Draft tapered and straight semi-fitted pants

A-line

A-line pants are flared outward on the side seam from the hip to the hem. Extra width is also added to the inseam.

Draft the Patterns

Figure 10.38

1. Trace the front/back two-way stretch pant slopers onto pattern paper.
2. Extend the hemline beyond the inseam and side seam.
3. C-D = Draw the front/back inseams.

4. H-B = Draw the front/back side seams.
5. Add 1" to 1½" extra length.
6. Square the hemline at the side seams.

Flared

In this section, you draft boot-cut pants, culottes, and palazzo pants. All these styles in Figure 10.1 are flared to create wider leg openings.

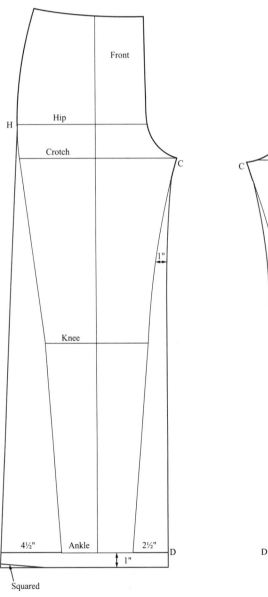
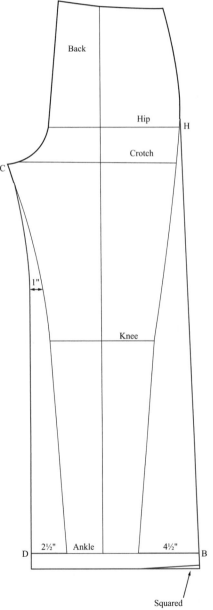

Figure 10.38 Draft A-line pants

Boot-cut

Boot-cut pants are tapered to the knee and flare out to the hem. Traditionally, they are cut to accommodate boots.

Draft the Patterns

Figure 10.39

1. Trace the front/back two-way stretch pant slopers onto pattern paper.
2. C-E-B = Draw the tapered/flared side seams.
3. A-D = Draw the flared inseams from the knee to hem.
4. Add 1" to 1½" length, squared at the inseam/side seam.
5. Draw a blending line at the knee.

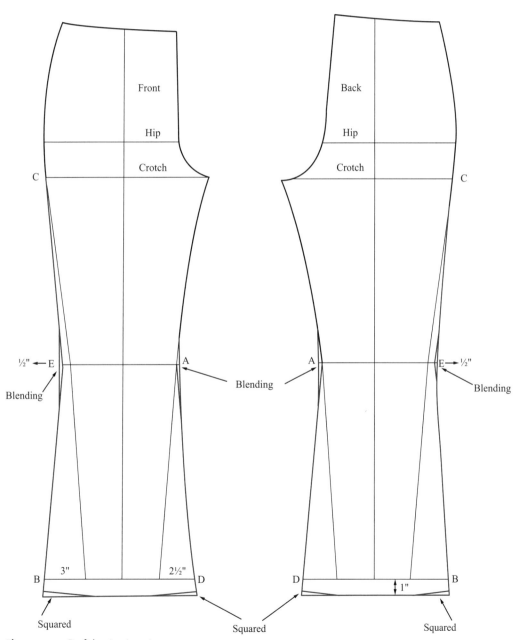

Figure 10.39 Draft boot-cut pants

Culottes

Culottes are a flared, split-divided skirt that is commonly knee length or calf length. You draft patterns for culottes from the two-way stretch *skirt* slopers.

Draft the Front Pattern

Figure 10.40a

Draft the flared skirt patterns outlined in Figures 9.12a, 9.12b, and 9.13 on p. 254. Then follow on to draft the front culottes pattern.

1. A-B = Crotch depth plus ¾" (Size 8 = 9¾", Size 10 = 10", Size 12 = 10¼").
2. B-C = half hip foundation measurement (H-H1) minus ¾".
3. D-E = Equal to B-C squared out from (D).
4. C-E = Draw a straight line.
5. X = 1" below halfway mark between (A-B).
6. B-Y = 1½" marked on a 45° angle.
7. X-Y-C = Draw a curved crotch line.

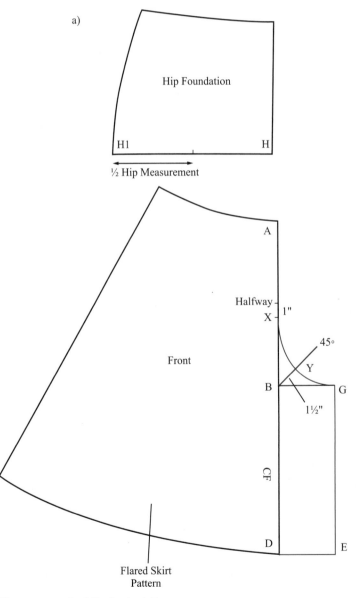

Figure 10.40a Draft the front culottes

Draft the Back Pattern

Figure 10.40b

1. A-B-D = Draft as per front pattern.
2. B-F = Half hip foundation measurement (H-H1).
3. D-G = Equal to B-F.
4. F-G = Draw a straight line.
5. X = Halfway between (A-B).
6. B-Y = 1¾" marked on a 45° angle.
7. X-Y-F = Draw a curved crotch line.

Align the Patterns

✓ Check that the pattern inseams and side seams are equal lengths.
✓ Check that points (C-E-F-G) are all squared.

b)

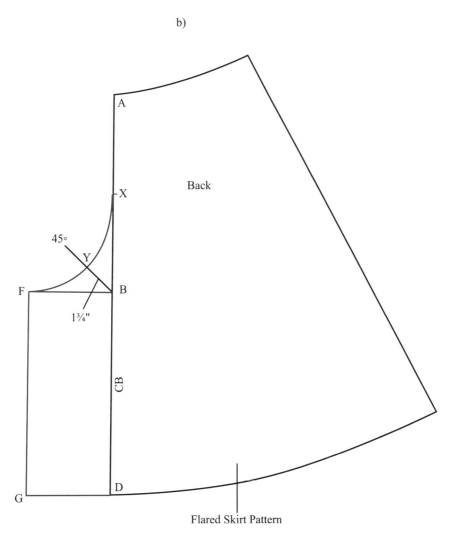

Figure 10.40b Draft the back culottes

Cut, Stitch, and Fit

Figure 10.41

Cut, stitch, and fit the culottes. (Follow the Stitching Order in Table 10.1.) Notice how the culottes drape beautifully when they are constructed from a medium-weight knit with excellent drape. Make any necessary pattern adjustments.

1. To finalize the pattern, add ¼" seam allowances.
2. Add a ½" hem allowance and label the patterns. (To stitch the hem, refer to Stitching Tip 10.1.)

Palazzo

Palazzo pants are wide floor-length pants. You add fullness to the hemline by using the slash/spread pattern drafting technique.

Figure 10.41 Muslin culottes fitted on the form

Draft the Patterns

Figures 10.42

Only the front pattern is shown. Draft the back flared pants pattern in the identical way.

1. Draft the front/back A-line pants in Figure 10.38.
2. Lengthen the pattern to floor length. Mark midway on the hemline.
3. Draw a slash line parallel to the grainline from the midway point to the waist and then label.

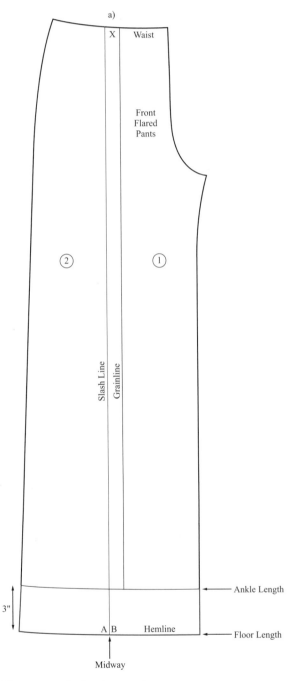

Figure 10.42 Draft palazzo pants

Slash/Spread the Patterns

Figure 10.43a and b

1. Slash/spread the pattern as shown in Figures 10.43a and b.
2. Draw a smooth blending hemline.

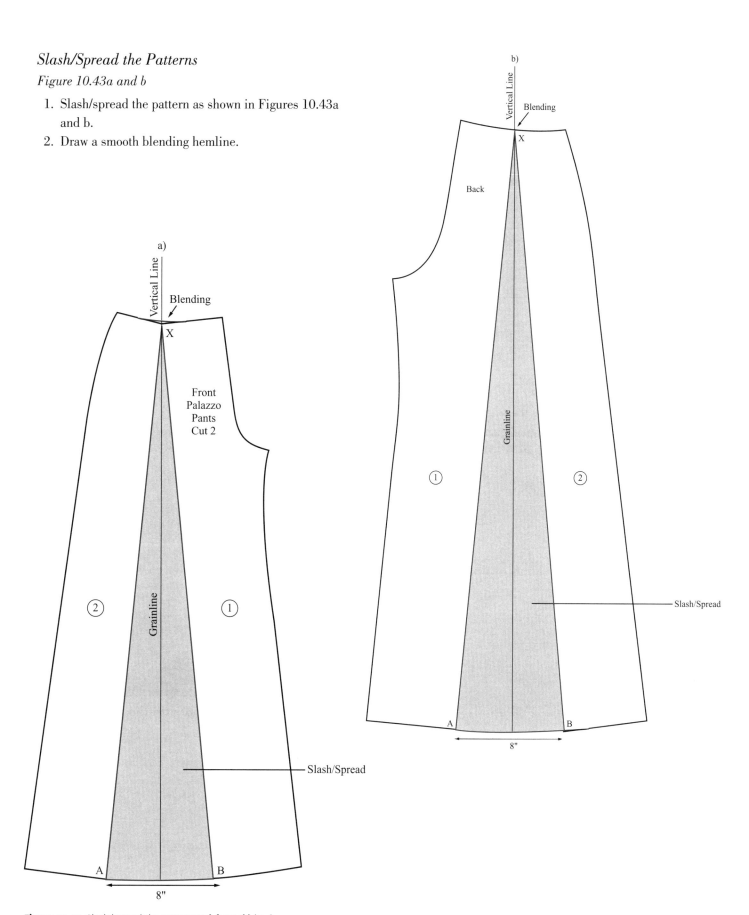

Figure 10.43 Slash/spread the patterns; **a)** front; **b)** back

Cut, Stitch, and Fit

Figure 10.44

Cut, stitch, and fit the palazzo pants. (Follow the Stitching Order in Table 10.1.) Notice how the palazzo pants drape beautifully when they are constructed from a light- to medium-weight knit.

1. To finalize the patterns, add ¼" seam allowances to the inseams, side, crotch, and waist seams.
2. Add a ½" hem allowance and label the patterns. (To stitch the hem, refer to Stitching Tip 10.1.)

Gathered

The sweatpants you draft in this section are gathered on the front waist with a fitted waistband and ankle bands (see Figure 10.1h). To create a slender fit, do not gather the back waist. You add fullness by using the slash/spread pattern drafting technique. The sweatpants can also have a slouchy loose-fit. Refer to Figure 10.17 to draft the slopers.

Figure 10.44 Muslin palazzo fitted on the form

Draft the Patterns

Figure 10.45a

1. Trace the appropriate two-way stretch front/back slopers onto pattern paper and draw the grainlines (which are also the slash lines).
2. Add 1" length. (Extra length is required for a slight pouch after the bands are joined.)
3. G-H = Draw the ankle bands.
4. D-E = Draw straight side seams. Extend the inseam to the (E-F) hem.
5. Label (A-B-X) front slash line and panels 1 and 2.

a)

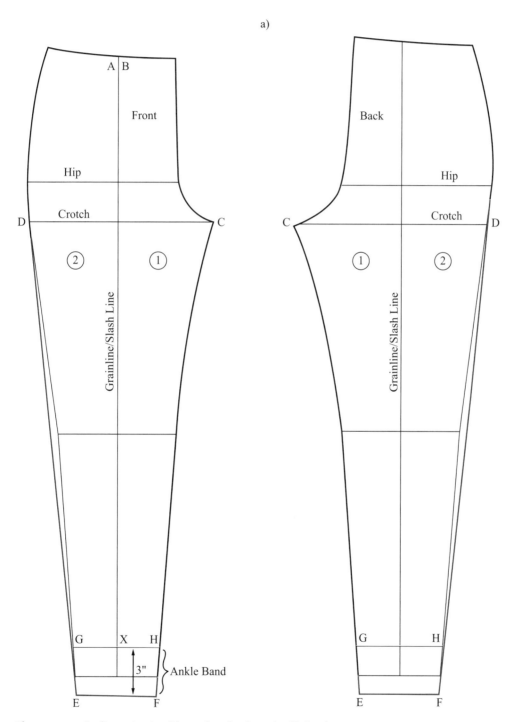

Figure 10.45a Draft sweatpants with a gathered waist and ankle bands

Slash/Spread the Pattern

Figure 10.45b

1. Slash/spread the waistline as shown.
2. Draw a blending waistline. Notch the position of gathering on the waistline. (If the sweatpants have side-front pockets, start the gathering ½" back from the pocket opening.)

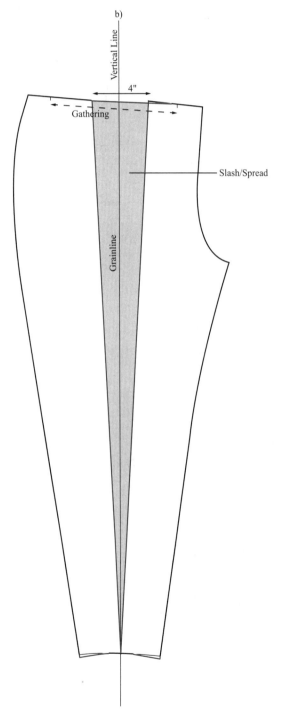

Figure 10.45b Slash/spread the pattern

Draft the Ankle Band

Figure 10.45c

1. G-H = Measure the combined front/back ankle length.
2. Draw a line this length on pattern paper.
3. Reduce the length by 1/7.
4. Draft the ankle band twice the finished width as shown.
5. To finalize the sweatpants patterns, add ¼" seam allowances to the inseams, side, crotch, ankle, and waist seams.
6. Add a ¼" seam allowance to the perimeter of the ankle band pattern.

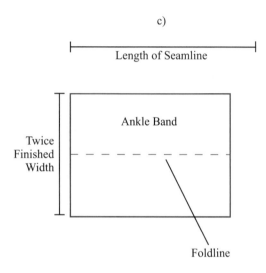

Figure 10.45c Draft the ankle band

Tucked

The pants in Figure 10.1c have waist **tucks** that are formed when a piece of folded fabric is sewn in place. In the "Gathered" section, you added fullness to the waist for gathering. Follow the same pattern drafting technique here to add fullness to the pattern to create tucks.

1. Divide the 4" added for gathering into two evenly sized tucks centered on the waist (see Figure 10.46).
2. After the seam allowance is added, fold the tucks, and then cut the pattern waistline and notch the tucks (see Figure 10.47).
3. Refer to the Stitching Order in Table 10.1 to stitch the tucks.

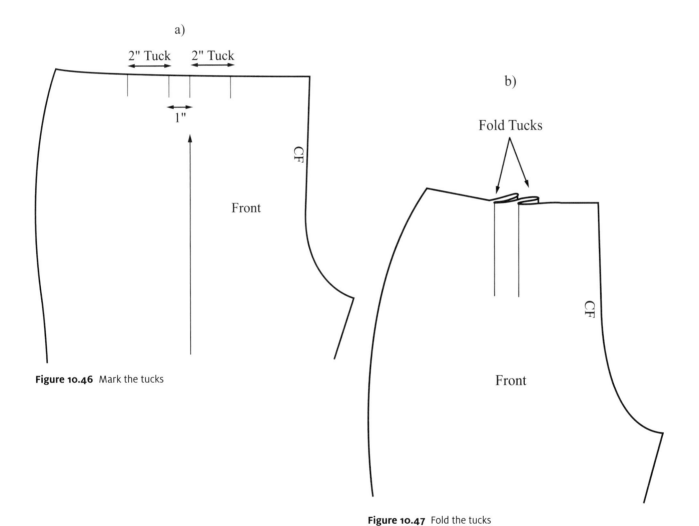

Figure 10.46 Mark the tucks

Figure 10.47 Fold the tucks

Pants Variations

The pant slopers provide a base for drafting other pant-related clothing such as leggings, jumpsuits, and unitards or catsuits. In Table 2.2 on p. 17, these garments are listed as part of the Pant Family.

Jumpsuit

Jumpsuits can have sleeves, or they can be sleeveless or strapless. They can be worn at any length (short, capri, or ankle length). A jumpsuit with a low neck will slip easily onto the body without needing a zipper opening. This section illustrates how to combine the top foundations with pant patterns to create a jumpsuit pattern.

Draft the Patterns

Figures 10.48a and b

To draft a basic jumpsuit pattern, you combine the two-way stretch front/back top foundations with the two-way stretch front/back pant slopers. Jumpsuits do not need to be tightly fitted.

1. Draw a right angle on pattern paper.
2. Place the center front/back top foundations on the vertical line with the waistline (W-W1) placed on the horizontal line. Trace the foundations. (You do not need to draw the waist section below the horizontal line.)

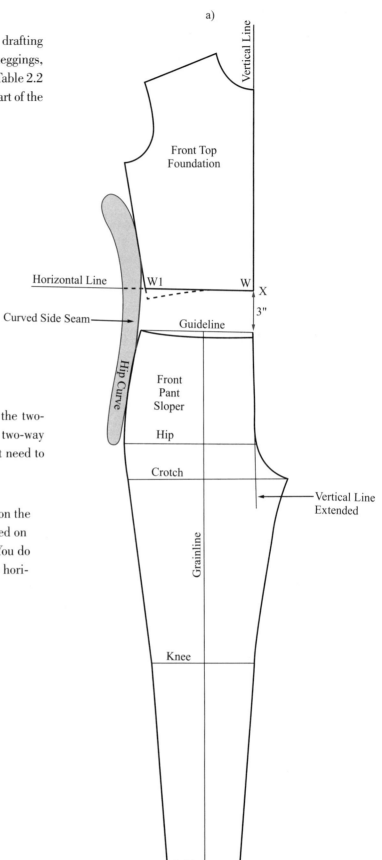

a)

Figure 10.48a Draft a basic front/back jumpsuit: curved side seam

3. Extend the vertical line beyond the hip.
4. Draw a guideline 3" below and parallel to (W-W1) (or longer for a more slouchy fit). The extra length will accommodate an elasticized waist casing.
5. Align the side seam/waist of the front/back pant slopers on the guideline. Trace the slopers. (You don't need to trace the back section above the guideline.)
6. Transfer the grainline and the hip and knee balance lines.
7. Draw a curved or straight side seam to connect the top foundation and pant slopers into one pattern piece. If curved, draw the front side seam first. Then transfer the shape to the back side seam.
8. Align the underarm, waist, and hipline together and make sure the front/back lengths match.

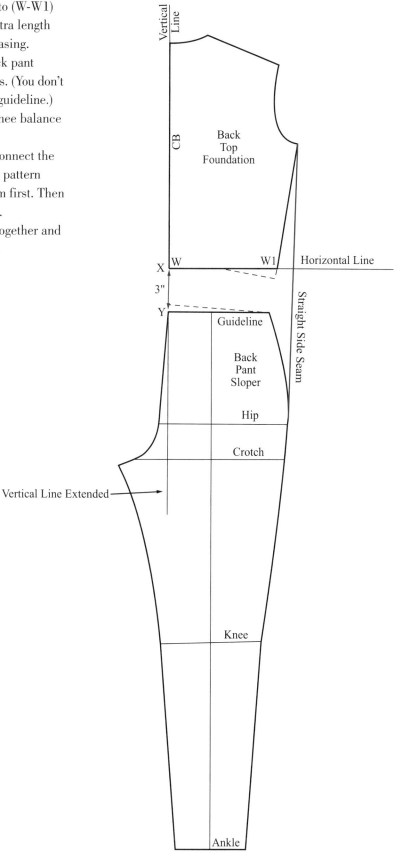

Figure 10.48b Draft a basic front/back jumpsuit: straight side seam

Finalize the Patterns

Figure 10.49

In the same way, finalize the front/back jumpsuit patterns.

1. Draw the waistline in the center of (X-Y).
2. Extend the grainline to the shoulder.
3. The seams of the jumpsuit are extra long, so notches are required as shown.

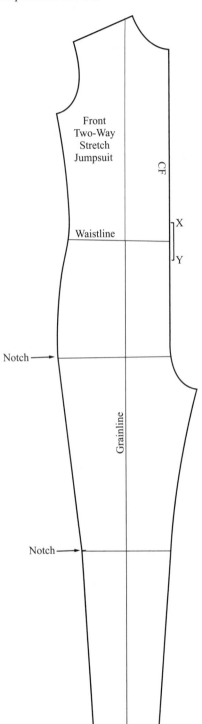

Figure 10.49 Finalize the basic jumpsuit patterns

Sleeveless Round Neck Jumpsuit

Figures 10.50a and b

For the sleeveless round neck jumpsuit, the waist seam allows you to cut the top section on the fold. Draft the front/back jumpsuit patterns in the same way.

a)

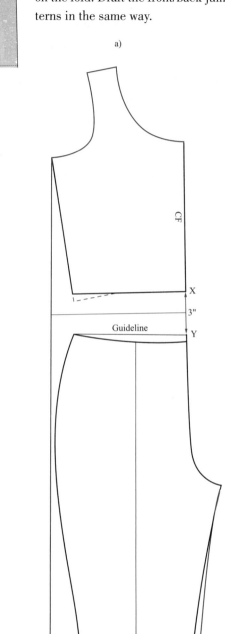

Figure 10.50a Draft the sleeveless round neck jumpsuit

1. Refer to Figure 6.24 on p. 117 to draft the scoop neck.
2. Refer to Figure 6.18 on p. 112 to alter the top pattern with sleeves into a sleeveless pattern.
3. Refer to Figure 10.28 to draft capri length pants.
4. Refer to Figure 10.37 to draft straight-legged pants.
5. Add length between (X-Y).
6. Draw the side seam to combine the top and pants into a jumpsuit pattern (see Figure 10.50a).
7. Draw the waistline between (X-Y).
8. Trace the patterns and add a seam and hem allowance (see Figure 10.50b).
9. Add an extension above the pant waistline (width of the elastic plus ¼") for the casing (see Figure 10.50b).

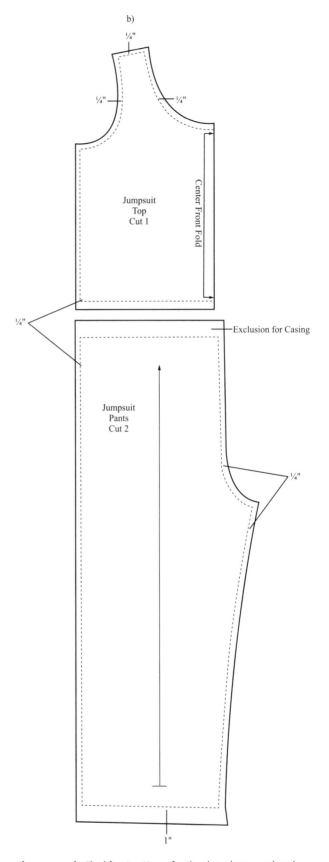

b)

Jumpsuit
Top
Cut 1

Center Front Fold

Exclusion for Casing

Jumpsuit
Pants
Cut 2

¼"

¼"

¼"

¼"

¼"

1"

Figure 10.50b Final front patterns for the sleeveless round neck jumpsuit

STITCHING TIP 10.5: STITCHING THE JUMPSUIT

If the jumpsuit has a casing, you must stitch muslin to check the jumpsuit has adequate length. You can stitch the casing or place a tie around the waist (to imitate a casing).

Stitch the jumpsuit in the following order:
1. Stitch the *top* shoulder and side seams.
2. Stitch the *pant* inseams, side seams, and crotch seam.
3. Stitch the top and pant waist seam.
4. Stitch the casing.

Leggings

Leggings are skinny pants made from four-way stretch knits that fit like a second- skin. Lycra-blend fabric moves with the body when walking, running, or exercising and is a good fabric for this type of pants.

Draft the Pattern

Figures 10.51a and b

You use the front and back four-way stretch pant slopers to draft the leggings. The slopers are joined together to eliminate the side seam and make one legging pattern.

1. Draw a vertical line onto pattern paper.
2. On the sloper front/back hips, mark 1" in from the side seam and label it "X" (see Figure 10.51a).

3. Align the front/back (X) on the vertical line and side seam at the ankle on the vertical line. Trace the slopers (see Figure 10.51b).
4. Draw a new waistline and label (A-B).

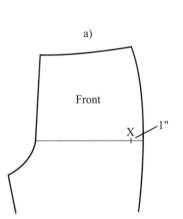

a)

Figure 10.51a Mark "X" on the hipline

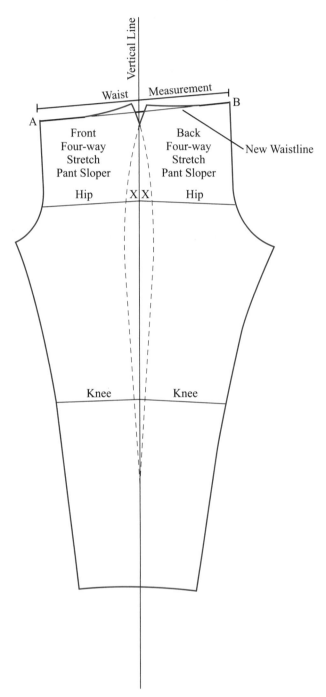

Figure 10.51b Draft the leggings

Remove Excess Waist Length

Figures 10.51c and d

There is now excess length at the waistline that you must remove.

1. Measure the waistline (A-B) (see Figure 10.51b). Double this length for the total waist measurement. Subtract the form (or body) waist measurement from this length. Divide by 4. For example, the pattern waistline measures 15" × 2 = 30". Form waistline = 28". The difference between the pattern and form waistlines = 2", divided by 4 = ½" excess.

2. A-C and B-D = Remove "excess" (½" in this draft).
3. C-D = Place an L-square ruler on the hipline (C-D) and raised ¼" above the waistline. Draw a new center front/back seamline and short squared line to mark the waist. Then draw a blending waistline.
4. Check that the inseams are equal lengths. If they don't match perfectly, equalize the inseam lengths (see Figure 10.51d).

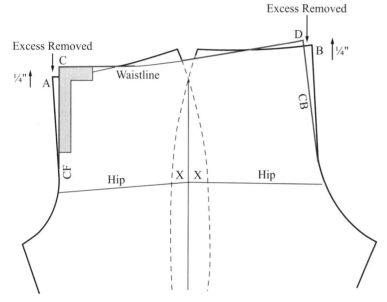

Figure 10.51c Remove excess waist length

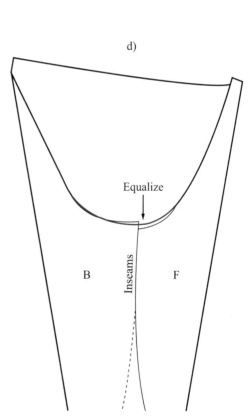

Figure 10.51d Equalize the inseams

Waist Finish for Leggings

Figure 10.52

To fit the leggings accurately, you must stitch a waist finish. In this pattern, you add a waist extension above the waistline for the topstitched waist finish. A separate waistband and waistband cut-all-in-one are other alternative waist finishes that present a sleek, flat look on leggings.

1. Add an extension above the waistline (C-D) the width of the elastic plus ¼". Extend the line beyond the center front/back.
2. E-F = Mark the width of the waist extension below the waistline on the center front/back. Draw a straight guideline.
3. G-H = Position a graph ruler on the guideline at (E-F), and draw a vertical line.
4. G-C-E and H-D-F = Draw straight lines to connect each point to create directional seamlines.

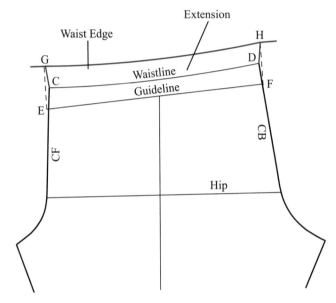

Figure 10.52 Add a waist extension to the leggings

Cut, Stitch, and Fit

Cut two leggings pieces from a four-way stretch knit to make one pair of leggings. (Refer to the layout in Figure 4.14 on p. 51.) Stitch the leggings following the Stitching Order in Table 10.1 (omit stitching the side seam). Also stitch the waist finish. Place the leggings on the pant form or on a person (see Figure 10.15). Pin any fitting adjustments and make the necessary pattern changes.

What to look for:

✓ Check that the length is correct.
✓ Check that the leggings have a snug fit.
✓ Check that the waist finish is comfortable.

Finalize the Pattern

To finalize the pattern, refer to Figure 4.14 on p. 51.

1. Draw straight hip and crotch balance lines.
2. Label the patterns "Four-way Stretch Leggings."
3. Record the stretch capacity and number of pieces to cut.
4. Indicate the length for shorts, activewear shorts, and capri leggings on the pattern.

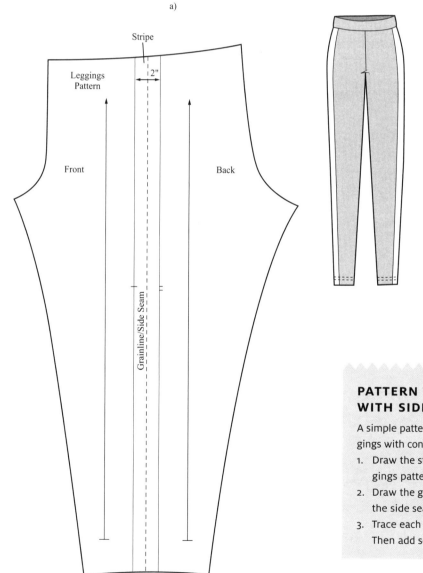

a)

PATTERN TIP 10.4: LEGGINGS WITH SIDE SEAM STRIPES

A simple pattern modification creates eye-catching leggings with contrasting side seam stripes. (See Figure 10.53.)
1. Draw the stripe centered on the side seam of the leggings pattern. Notch the seamlines.
2. Draw the grainlines on each pattern piece (parallel to the side seam grainline).
3. Trace each pattern piece from the working pattern. Then add seam and hem allowances.

Figure 10.53 Leggings with side seam stripes

Activewear Shorts

Activewear shorts have a tight fit and are constructed from a four-way stretch spandex blend. Athletic clothing is fashionable to wear outside the gym because the stretchiness of the fabric feels comfortable. Activewear shorts for cycling must be stitched with gripper elastic to keep the hem in place when cycling (see Figure 10.56).

Draft the Patterns
Figure 10.54

You draft activewear shorts from the leggings pattern. The only adjustment is the length.

1. Mark the shorts length, as shown in Figure 4.14 on p. 51.
2. Draw a straight hemline squared at the grainline.
3. Reduce the hem length and redraw the shaped inseams and hemline. This removes 1" from the leg opening for a tight fit.
4. The hem allowance must have directional seamlines that reflect the same inseam shape above the hemline. Follow the method of adding the hem allowance to the shorts, as shown in Figure 10.30.

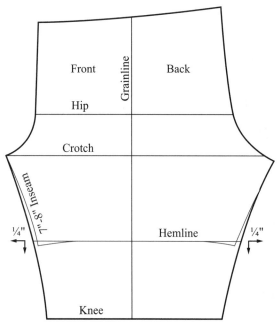

Figure 10.54 Draft activewear shorts

a)

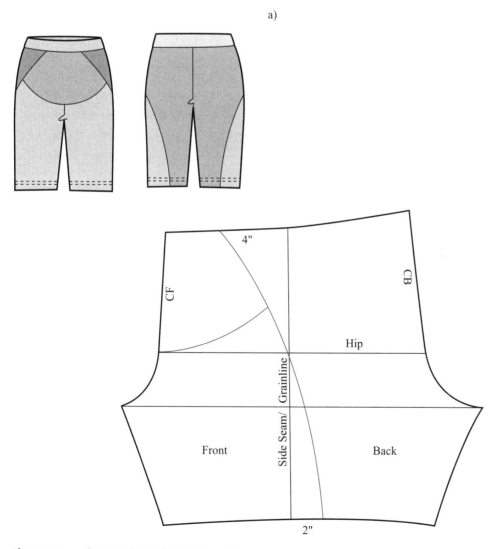

Figure 10.55 Activewear shorts with curved seams

Unitard

A unitard can have a low scooped neckline or a turtleneck, as indicated in Figure 10.1k, with an opening down the center front/back. To achieve a super tight fit, a unitard must be constructed from a four-way stretch knit so that trapeze artists, gymnasts, and athletes can move with ease when performing. If the unitard has sleeves, refer to "Reducing a Two-way Stretch Sleeve into Four-way Stretch" section in Chapter 6.

Draft the Pattern

Figure 10.57

A unitard pattern is a one-piece pattern that combines the front and back four-way stretch top foundations with the four-way stretch pant patterns.

1. Draw a right angle on pattern paper. Extend a vertical line to accommodate the length of the pant patterns.

2. Place the center front/back top foundations on the vertical line with waistline (W-W1) placed on the horizontal line. Then trace (do not draw the waist section below the horizontal line) and label (U).

3. Make the appropriate armhole adjustment if the unitard is sleeveless (see Figures 6.18a and b on p. 112).

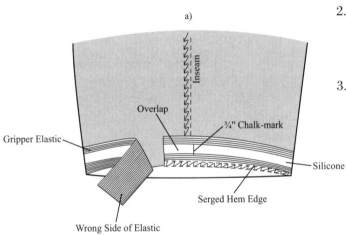

a)

Figure 10.56a Serge elastic to the wrong side of the leg opening

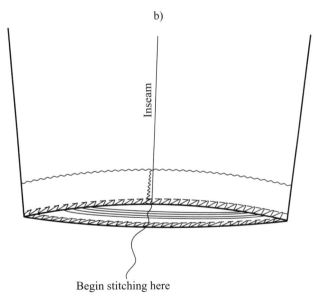

b)

Figure 10.56b Zigzag stitch the top edge of the elastic

4. Place the pant waist/side on the horizontal line and the grainline parallel to the vertical line. Trace the pant slopers; then transfer the hip, crotch, and knee balance lines and the grainline. Label ankle (A).

5. Draw a curved side seam to combine the top foundation and the pant sloper.

6. Place the front pattern to the back pattern, aligning underarms, side seams, waists, and hiplines together. Then trace the front side seam shape to the back.

7. Match the front/back side and inseams together to check that they are of equal length with balance lines aligned.

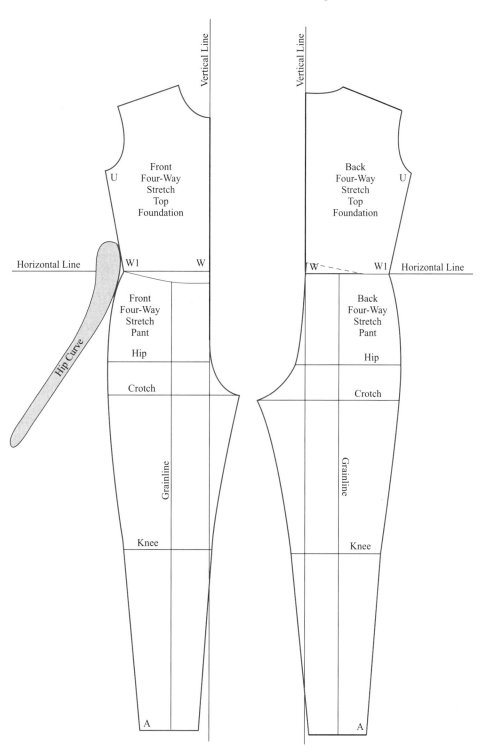

Figure 10.57 Draft the front and back unitard

Eliminate the Side Seam

A unitard is best designed without a side seam for a smooth, sleek fit.

1. Draw a vertical line onto pattern paper.
2. At the hip level on the front/back patterns, mark 1" in from the front/back side seam and label (X) (see Figure 10.51a).
3. Place the front/back side seam (U-X-A) on the vertical line (ankles can also overlap) to eliminate the side seam.
4. Measure the excess along the waistline from each side seam to the vertical line. Remove this amount from the center front/back waist.
5. If there is any excess on the side seam (below the knee on either side of the vertical line), then remove this amount from the inseams. (See Figure 10.58.)

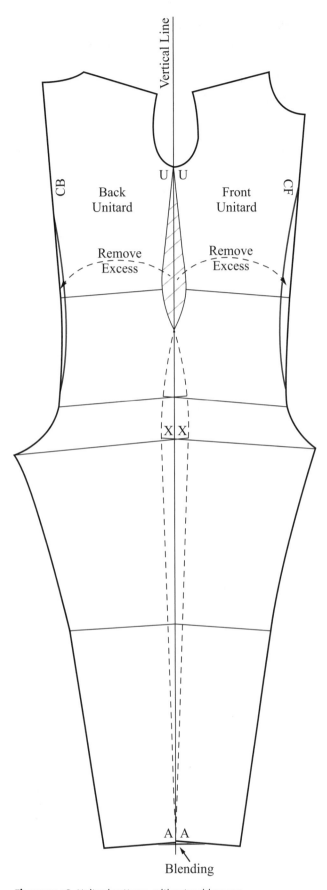

Figure 10.58 Unitard pattern: without a side seam

STITCHING TIP 10.7: STITCHING THE UNITARD

1. Purchase a piece of fabric the length of the pattern.
2. Place the fabric on the lengthwise fold. Cut two unitard pieces following the leggings layout in Figure 4.14 on p. 51.
3. Add ¼" seam allowances to the shoulders, crotch, and inseams.
4. Notch the front/back waist and knee levels so that the seams can be aligned when stitched together.
5. Stitch the inseams and crotch seam as directed in Table 10.1. Leave a 6" center back opening down from the neck edge to allow the unitard to comfortably slip onto the pant form (or body).
6. Join the shoulders.
7. If the unitard has sleeves, stitch the sleeve underarm seams. The sleeves are stitched into a circular armhole (and not flat) because the unitard has no side seam.

Test the Fit

Place the unitard on the form (see Figure 10.59). Pin any fitting adjustments as needed to make the unitard fit properly. Also have a person wear the unitard.

What to look for:

✓ Check how the unitard functions on the body when in motion.

✓ Check how the sleeve fits when the arm is bent and stretched. Add length to the wrist if the sleeve length is too short.

Finalize the Pattern

1. Label the pattern "Front/Back Four-way Stretch Unitard" and document the stretch category.

2. Draw horizontal lines across the waist and hip from the center front to the center back. Both lines should be squared at the vertical line (which is the grainline). (See Figure 10.60.)

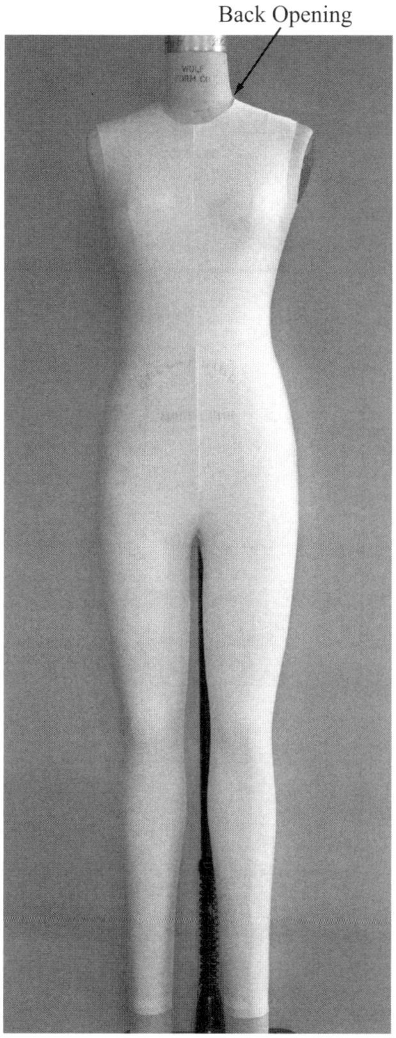

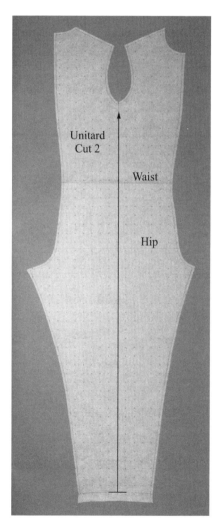

Figure 10.59 Unitard fitted on the form

Figure 10.60 Final unitard pattern

Unitard with Turtleneck

Figure 10.61

In Figure 10.61, the unitard has a center back opening, and the turtleneck collar fastens with Velcro® (a sew-in hook-and-loop tape). One side has tiny hooks (rigid side), and the other side has loops (soft side). When the two are pressed together, they fasten.

Draft the Turtleneck

Figures 10.62a through c

To draft a double turtleneck pattern, refer to the "Turtle-neck" section in Chapter 6.

1. Lower the front neckline ½" (see Figure 10.62a).
2. On the center back, mark the 6" opening with a matchpoint, and add the facing, as shown in Figure 10.62b.
3. Draft a double turtleneck pattern. (A suitable finished width is 2".)
4. Add a 1" extension to one side of the turtleneck and notch, as indicated in Figure 10.62c.
5. Add ¼" seam allowances to the collar.

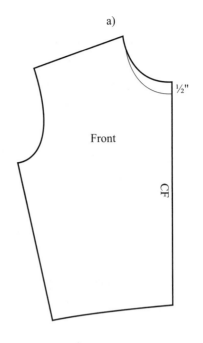

a)

Front

CF

½"

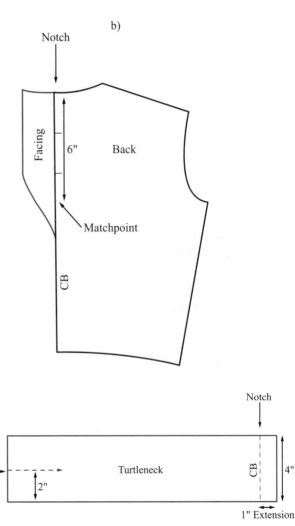

b)

Notch

Facing

6"

Back

Matchpoint

CB

Foldline for Double Turtleneck

2"

Turtleneck

CB

4"

Notch

1" Extension

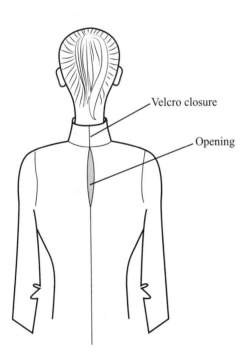

Velcro closure

Opening

Figure 10.61 Unitard with turtleneck collar and center back opening

Figures 10.62a, b, and c Draft the turtleneck collar

a)

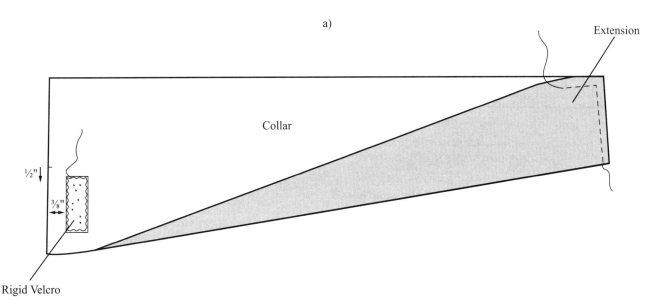

Figure 10.63a Stitch rigid Velcro to the turtleneck

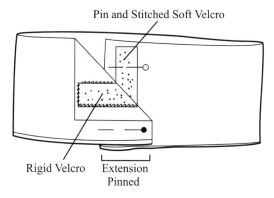

Figure 10.63b Stitch soft Velcro to the extension

Knit It Together

This checklist summarizes what you have learned about drafting the pant slopers and patterns in this chapter.

- ✓ The pant slopers are drafted from the hip foundation.
- ✓ Pants can be constructed from two- and four-way stretch knits.
- ✓ Pants can be any length, a variety of silhouettes, and symmetrical and asymmetrical designs.
- ✓ Pants constructed in stretch knits are "pull-on" pants and require an elasticized waist finish.
- ✓ Pants can have a waistband or can be bandless.
- ✓ The waist finish can be fitted, semi-fit, or loose-fit.
- ✓ Pants can be lined.

Stop: What Do I Do If . . .

. . . my pant muslin (for my own design) is too tight? Can I grade the patterns larger?

Yes, you can. Follow the same pattern grading technique for grading slopers into stretch categories. Grade the patterns in a positive direction to enlarge them. Refer to the "Extra Loose-fit" section and see Figure 10.17.

. . . I eliminate the side seams of the semi-fitted shorts pattern in Figure 10.32? Would it make a suitable shorty pajama pattern?

Yes, join the front and back semi-fitted shorts patterns together to eliminate the side seam. The pattern grainline will be on the side seam. Then cut two fabric pieces to make a pair of shorty pajamas.

Self-Critique

1. List the order (1, 2, 3, 4, etc.) that you must draft the following patterns before drafting the *unitard* pattern.

   _____ Two-way stretch hip foundation

   _____ Four-way stretch pant slopers

   _____ Four-way stretch top foundations

   _____ Legging pattern

   _____ Two-way stretch top foundations

   _____ Two-way stretch pant slopers

   _____ Four-way stretch hip foundations

   _____ Two-way stretch pant slopers

   _____ Draft unitard pattern

2. How are the front/back pant slopers aligned?
3. What are the three main pocket categories?
4. How would you draft functional pockets in pants?
5. How would you change the front palazzo pattern in Figure 10.43a to incorporate four tucks on the waist?
6. If the customer would like pockets incorporated into the palazzo pants like those in Figure 10.1g, what pocket style would you recommend?
7. What are directional seams? Why does the hem allowance of the pattern for the fitted shorts in Figure 10.1a need directional seams? (Refer to the "Key Definitions" section in Chapter 3.)
8. Can you eliminate the side seam of pant patterns? If so, how? Where would you draw the pattern grainline? (Refer to the "Leggings" section.)

Key Terms	Pocket Bag	Tucks	Walk the Pattern
Activewear Shorts	Side-front Pockets	Unitards	

11 Lingerie Slopers and Patterns

Lingerie can be designed with elegance and comfort in mind in luxurious fabrics such as soft-to-the-touch sumptuous silk, Pima cotton, bamboo, and modal. Key items such as panties, a camisole, pajamas, and a teddy complete any well-knit wardrobe (see Figures 11.1a through j).

Adding a touch of lace or a satin trim takes one design from being ordinary to extraordinary. This chapter includes many details about drafting panty and camisole patterns and stitching techniques. One important aspect of designing lingerie is to get the fit right because the comfort and function of these garments are crucial to their success. Choosing the right type of knit and getting the elastic proportions right are also essential to creating panties and camisoles successfully.

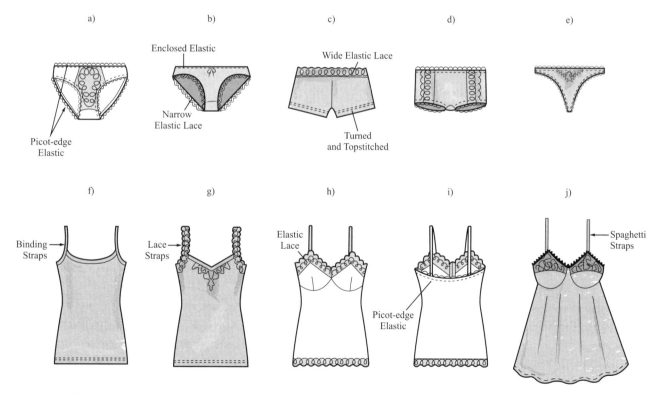

Figure 11.1 a) Lace-trimmed panty with hi-cut leg-line; **b)** low-rise leg-line panty; **c)** boy-cut panty with wide scallop edge lace; **d)** lace-trimmed mid-rise boy-cut panty; **e)** thong with lace appliqué; **f)** round neck camisole with binding; **g)** V-neck camisole with lace appliqué; **h)** front lace-trimmed bra-top camisole; **i)** back bra-top camisole; **j)** flared camisole with two-piece bra-top

Lingerie Supplies

- *Fabric* for lingerie must feel soft against the skin. Panties need to be made from four-way stretch knits so that they mold to the body and feel comfortable when on the move. A **camisole**, on the other hand, can be constructed from two-way or four-way stretch knits. The amount of stretch, weight, hand, drape, sheerness, color, and surface texture of the fabric must be taken into consideration. For example, consider the texture and color of lace. Lace can feel rough next to the skin, and a red cami may not sell as well as a neutral skin color cami. The composition of the fabric must also be considered because lingerie needs to be washed frequently. Any trims you choose must have the same laundering requirements as the lingerie fabric.
- *Elastic* must be soft and lightweight and feel comfortable next to the skin. It must also have good wash-and-wear qualities. Many types of elastic that have attractive edges can be used for lingerie. Picot, ruffle, and scallop edges are just a few choices.
- *Elastic lace* with a scallop edge can also be used as an edge finish for panties, camisoles, or just shoulder straps. A camisole is an underwear/outerwear garment, so the lace complements the style of garment. A camisole is also referred to as a "cami."
- *Bra cups* can be inserted into a shelf bra, which can be part of a cami to give extra support to the bust. Order the bra cups according to your dress size (or form size), and make sure the bra cups are washable.

Choosing the Slopers

Before drafting patterns for lingerie, determine the stretch capacity of the knit you plan to work with using the stretch gauge in Figure 1.6 on p. 9. Then choose the appropriate stretch category of top slopers to draft the patterns. There are two ways the slopers can be selected. The first way is to use the slopers that match the stretchiness of your chosen knit. The second way is to choose a different sloper to create a roomier fit with more ease. (Refer to "How to Choose Slopers" in Chapter 2 to learn more.) Furthermore, the slopers can be enlarged for a more generous fit.

Pattern Drafting Panties

You can draft a variety of panty styles from the panty slopers. Some styles are shown in Figures 11.1a through e. Before you begin to draft the panty slopers, have on hand the patternmaking tools shown in Figure 3.1 on p. 20.

Converting Four-way Stretch Hip Foundation into Panty Slopers

You draft **leg-line panty** and **boy-cut panty** slopers from the four-way stretch hip foundation (see Table 2.1 on p. 16). Both styles are shown in Figure 11.1. A leg-line panty is cut around the top of the leg at different heights (see Figures 11.1a and b). The boy-cut panty is styled similar to men's briefs and has short legs extending below the crotch (see Figures 11.1c and d). Panties must be made from four-way stretch knits so that they mold to the body and feel comfortable when on the move.

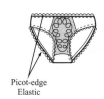

Picot-edge Elastic

Leg-line

You draft the slopers for a leg-line panty in this section. A leg-line panty can be **high-rise, mid-rise,** or **low-rise** (see Figures 11.1a and b). High-rise sits on the waistline and gives full coverage. Mid-rise sits on the high-hip and gives modest coverage. Low-rise is a brief panty that sits on the hips. The panty slopers are drafted from the *four-way stretch* hip foundation. (Keep the working pattern to draft a thong.)

Draft the Patterns

Figure 11.2a

1. Align the four-way super stretchy hip foundation on a vertical line. Trace and label (W-W1-H-H1). Also transfer the horizontal waistline.
2. W-S = 5¾".
3. X-S = Draw guideline (1) parallel to H-H1.
4. X-B = ½". At (B), square up a ½" line.

Draw the Front Legline

Figure 11.2b

1. W1-B = Draw a new hip curve.
2. Divide B-S into four equal sections.
3. F = Square up a ½" line.
4. R = Square up a ⅜" line (the other mark is not used).
5. W-D = Crotch depth (Size 8 = 10", Size 10 = 10¼", Size 12 = 10½").
6. Divide S-D into three equal sections.
7. Square a line at the following points:

   - D-T = 1½" crotch width.
   - M-N = 1⅛".
   - L-O = 1 ⅜".

8. B-F-R-O-N-T = Draw the front legline curve.

a)

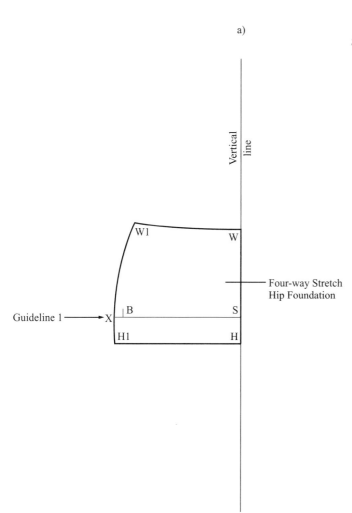

Figure 11.2a Draft a leg-line panty

b)

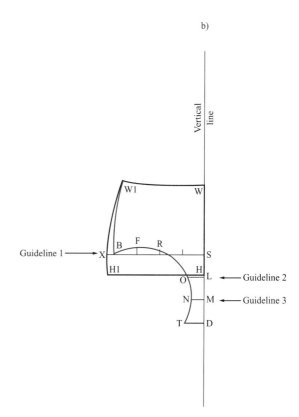

Figure 11.2b Draw the front leg-line

Draw the Back Legline

Figure 11.2c

The back legline is drafted from the front legline.

1. B-T = Draw the guideline as shown.
2. C = Midway on the guideline, draw a ⅝" squared line.
3. B-A and T-K = ¼".
4. B-A-C-K-T = Draw the back legline curve.

Draft the Crotch-piece

Figure 11.3a

The **crotch-piece** is stitched inside the panty to provide protection and comfort. The fabric must be breathable and soft next to the skin. The crotch-piece for the leg-line panty is joined to the front and back panty with *two* seamlines (see Figure 11.4c). (Keep the working patterns because you will use them to create swimsuit slopers.

There is only *one* back crotch seam for a swimsuit in Chapter 12.)

1. W1-W-D-T-B = Trace the front panty onto pattern paper. Label the crotch (T-D). Then extend the CF vertical line down from (D).
2. Align the back panty on the vertical line with the crotch line (T-D) aligned to the front (T-D). Next, trace the back panty. Check that the front/back leg line is a smooth continuous line. Then adjust if necessary.
3. D-Y = 1". At (Y), draw a guideline parallel to (T-D).
4. X-Y = 4½". At X, draw a guideline parallel to (T-D).
5. Z = ¾" toward (T).
6. E = ¼" toward (T).
7. Z-Y and E-X = Draw the curved crotch line.
8. (E-X-Y-Z-) Trace the crotch-piece. Draw the crotch line (T-D).

a)

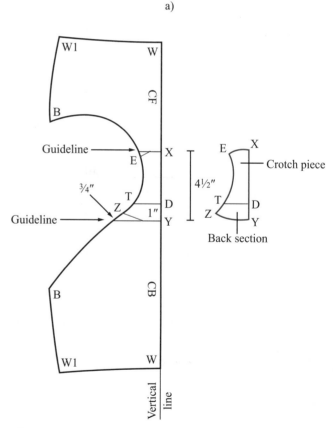

c)

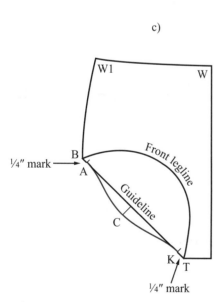

Figure 11.2c Draw the back legline

Figure 11.3a Draft the crotch-piece

Align the Patterns

Figure 11.3b

Place the front/back side seams together as shown. For an alternative shape, outline the **hi-cut** legline on the front/back patterns. Hi-cut panties allow comfort and freedom of movement and elongate the length of the leg.

- ✓ Check that the legline is a continuous blending line. Adjust if necessary.
- ✓ After a fitting, if extra length is required over the buttock, reshape the back legline as shown.

b)

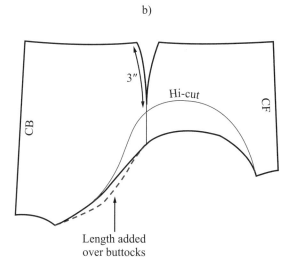

Figure 11.3b Align the patterns

Fabric You'll Need

Purchase ⅜ yard of four-way stretch knit to stitch a test-fit muslin panty. The stretch of the knit must match the stretch category of the sloper to get an accurate fit. Use the stretch gauge in Figure 1.6 on p. 9 to ascertain the stretch of the knit.

Cut and Stitch

1. Cut the panty following the layout in Figure 4.16 on p. 52.
2. Add ¼" seam allowances to the side seams and crotch seams.
3. Stitch the panty following the Stitching Order in Table 11.1.

TABLE 11.1 Stitching order for leg-line panty

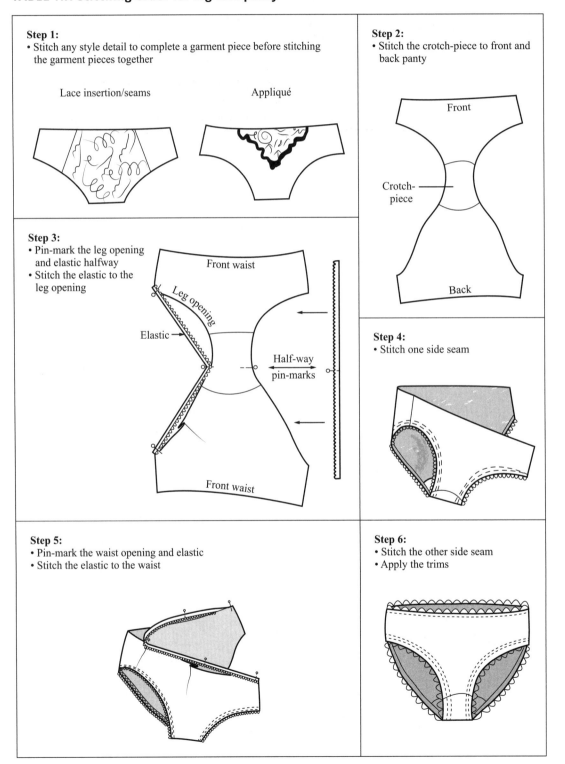

Step 1:
• Stitch any style detail to complete a garment piece before stitching the garment pieces together

Lace insertion/seams

Appliqué

Step 2:
• Stitch the crotch-piece to front and back panty

Front

Crotch-piece

Back

Step 3:
• Pin-mark the leg opening and elastic halfway
• Stitch the elastic to the leg opening

Front waist

Leg opening

Elastic

Half-way pin-marks

Front waist

Step 4:
• Stitch one side seam

Step 5:
• Pin-mark the waist opening and elastic
• Stitch the elastic to the waist

Step 6:
• Stitch the other side seam
• Apply the trims

TABLE 11.2 Stitching order for boy-cut panty

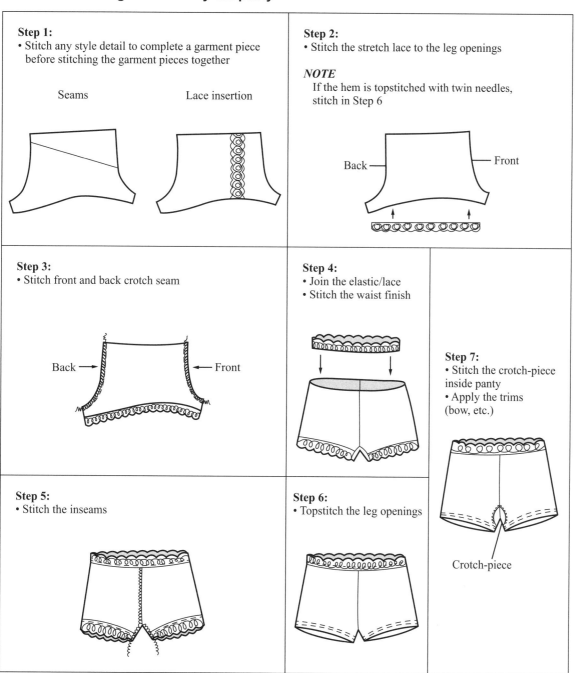

Step 1:
- Stitch any style detail to complete a garment piece before stitching the garment pieces together

Seams   Lace insertion

Step 2:
- Stitch the stretch lace to the leg openings

NOTE
If the hem is topstitched with twin needles, stitch in Step 6

Back   Front

Step 3:
- Stitch front and back crotch seam

Back →   ← Front

Step 4:
- Join the elastic/lace
- Stitch the waist finish

Step 7:
- Stitch the crotch-piece inside panty
- Apply the trims (bow, etc.)

Crotch-piece

Step 5:
- Stitch the inseams

Step 6:
- Topstitch the leg openings

TABLE 11.3 Stitching order for camisoles

Step 1:
• Stitch any style detail to complete a garment piece before stitching the garment pieces together
• Stitch the front neckline finish

Appliqué   Front neckline finish   Stitch seams

Bra-top

Serge

Step 2:
• Stitch the separate straps

Step 3:
• Stitch the side seams

Step 4:
• Stitch the neckline finish and straps (if applicable)

Step 5:
• Stitch the hem

Step 6:
• Stitch the trims

• Attach the separate straps to the neckline

STITCHING TIP 11.2: STITCHING THE CROTCH-PIECE

You stitch the crotch piece to the leg-line panty in *step 2* in the Stitching Order in Table 11.1.

1. Cut the leg-line front/back panty pieces in fabric. Cut two crotch-pieces: one in self fabric and one in lining fabric (see Figure 4.16 on p. 52).
2. Place the correct sides of the *front* panty and the crotch piece together. Place the correct side of the crotch lining underneath the panty facing the wrong side. Then pin and stitch the three-layered *front* crotch seam (see Figure 11.4a).
3. Place the correct sides of the *back* panty and crotch piece together. Place the correct side of the crotch lining to the wrong side of the back panty. Then pin and stitch the three-layered *back* crotch seam to finish stitching the crotch-piece (see Figures 11.4b and c).

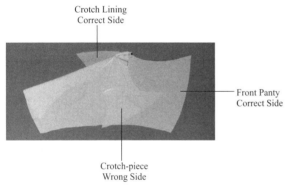

Figure **11.4a** Stitch the crotch-pieces to the front pant

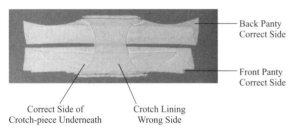

Figure **11.4b** Stitch the back crotch seam

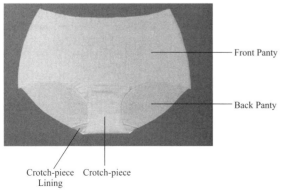

Figure **11.4c** Crotch-pieces stitched to the leg-line panty

Test the Fit

Figure 11.5

Fit the panty on the form. Also ask someone to wear the panty. Pin any fitting adjustments as needed.

What to look for:

✓ Check the fit around the waist and hip.
✓ Check that the panty feels comfortable during all movement (walking, crouching, and bending).
✓ Check that there is adequate coverage over the buttocks.

Finalize the Patterns

1. Trace both sides of the crotch-piece to make one pattern piece. Notch the center of the front and label as shown in Figure 4.16.
2. Indicate *mid-rise* and *low-rise*, which are drawn parallel to the waistline 1½" apart. High-rise is the waistline.
3. Label the slopers "Front/Back Leg-line Panty," as shown in the fabric layout in Figure 4.16 on p. 52.

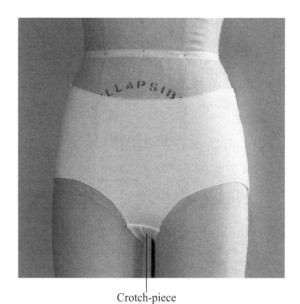

Figure **11.5** Leg-line panty fitted on the form

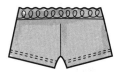

Boy-cut Panty

A boy-cut panty like the one in Figure 11.1c offers full-coverage to the front and back and provides a smooth foundation under tight-fitting clothing.

Draft the Pattern

Figure 11.6a

1. Trace the four-way super stretchy hip foundation onto pattern paper. Label (W-W1-H-H1). Draw the horizontal waistline.
2. W-C = Crotch depth (Size 8 = 10", Size 10 = 10¼", Size 12 = 10½").
3. H1-B = ½". At (B), square up a ½" line.
4. W1-B = Draw the new hip curve.
5. C-D = Draw a line that is an equal length and parallel to (H-B).

6. B-D = Draw a straight line.
7. C-M = ⅓ of (H-H1).
8. C-J = 1¼" length marked on a 45° angle.
9. H1-A = 1".
10. A-J-M = Draw the curved crotch line.

Draw the Back and Front Inseams

Figure 11.6b

1. M-Y = 1⅛". Draw guideline (1) squared down from (M).
2. At (Y), draw guideline (2) parallel to (M-D)
3. Y-G = ⅝".
4. M-G = Draw the back inseam. Place a ruler on the inseam, and draw a ¼" squared line at (G).
5. N-E = Draw a parallel front inseam 1" within the back inseam (M-G). The front inseam is the same length as the back inseam. Square a ¼" line at (E).
6. D-L = 1¾". Draw a ¼" squared line at L.

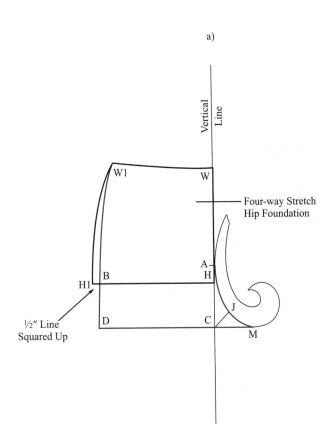

a)

b)

Figure 11.6a Draft a boy-cut panty

Figure 11.6b Draw the front/back inseams

Draw the Front/Back Legline

Figure 11.6c

1. L-E = Draw a guideline from the side seam to the front inseam and *not* from the squared ¼" lines.
2. Mark midway on the guideline and draw an intersecting squared line.
3. O = ⅝" squared *up*.
4. P = ⅜" squared *down*.
5. L-O-E = Draw the front legline from the squared ¼" lines (L-E).
6. L-P-E-G = Draw the back legline from ¼" squared lines (L-G). Angle the hip curve, and draw a curved legline over the buttock.

c)

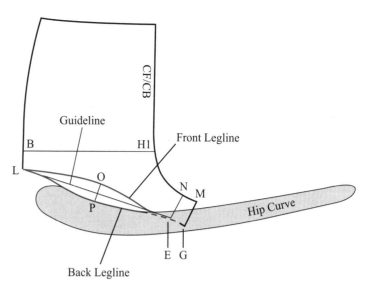

Figure 11.6c Draw the front and back legline

Align the Patterns

Figure 11.7

✓ Check that the front and back inseams are equal lengths when placed together.
✓ Check that the legline has a smooth curve when the side seams are placed together.

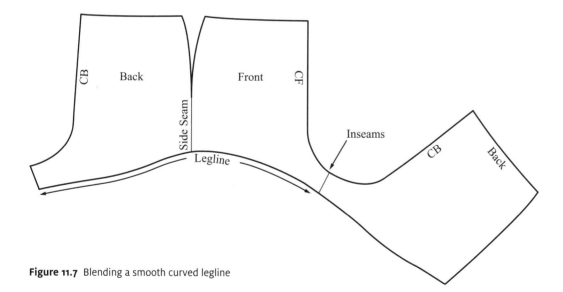

Figure 11.7 Blending a smooth curved legline

Eliminate the Side Seam

Figure 11.8a

1. Draw a horizontal line on pattern paper.
2. Align (W-W1) waistline of the *front* panty on the horizontal line and trace.
3. Align (W-W1) waistline of the *back* panty on the horizontal line. Adjust the pattern so there is an equal amount of *excess* at the waist opening at (W1-W1) and an *overlap* on the hipline. Trace the back panty.

Remove Waist Excess

The waist measurement is now too long because of the *excess* in the waistline.

1. Measure the *excess* between (W1-W1). Mark half this measurement in from the center front/back waistline.
2. F-B = Align an L-square ruler on the CF/CB to the excess mark and ¼" above the waistline. Draw a new center front/back seamline and waist curve to the original waistline.
3. Draw a blending curved legline.
4. Trace the one-piece boy-cut panty pattern onto pattern paper. (See Figure 11.8b.)

a)

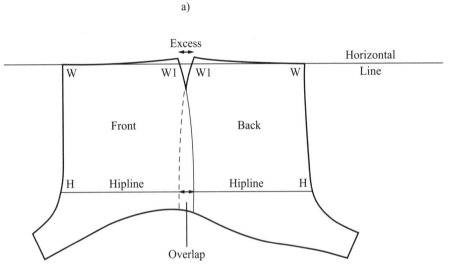

Figure 11.8a Eliminate the side seam

b)

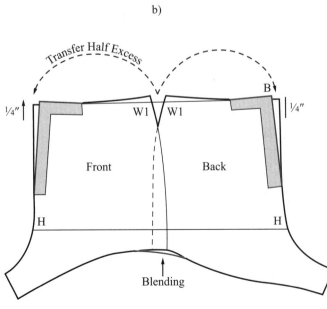

Figure 11.8b Remove the excess waist length

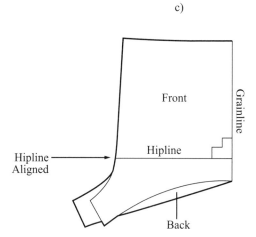

c)

Front

Grainline

Hipline

Hipline →
Aligned

Back

Figure 11.8c Determine the grainline

Determine the Grainline

Figure 11.8c

1. Fold the pattern in half by aligning the CF/CB hiplines together.
2. The creaseline is the grainline that is at a right angle to the hipline.

Draft the Crotch-piece

Figure 11.9

1. Draw intersecting lines on pattern paper.
2. Draft the crotch-piece as shown.

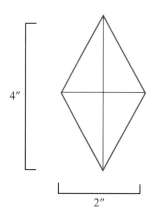

4″

2″

Figure 11.9 Draft the crotch-piece

Fabric You'll Need

Purchase ⅜ yard of four-way stretch knit to match the stretch category of the sloper. Use the stretch gauge in Figure 1.6 on p. 9 to ascertain the stretch of the knit.

Cut and Stitch

1. Lay out and cut the panty following the pattern layout in Figure 4.17 on p. 53.
2. Add ¼″ seam allowances to the center front/back and inseams.
3. Stitch the panty following the Stitching Order in Table 11.2.
4. Stitch the crotch piece to the boy-cut on completion of the panty. (Refer to the Stitching Order in Table 11.2.)

Test the Fit

Figure 11.10

Fit the panty on the form. Also ask someone to wear the pants. Pin any fitting adjustments as needed.

What to look for:

✓ Check the fit around the waist and hip.
✓ Check that the panty feels comfortable during all movement (walking, crouching, and bending).
✓ Check that there is adequate coverage over the buttocks.

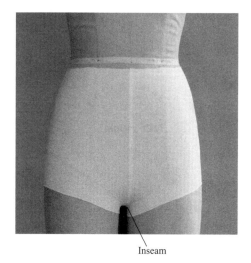

Inseam

Figure 11.10 Muslin boy-cut panty fitted on the form

Finalize the Pattern

Refer to Figure 4.17 on p. 53 to label the slopers.

1. Label the pattern "Boy-cut Panty."
2. Label "Crotch-piece Cut 1."
3. Transfer the grainlines and record the stretch category.
4. Mark *mid-rise* and *low-rise* on the slopers for future panty designs. The spacing is 1½" apart and drawn parallel to the waistline.

Grading Panties

The leg-line panty and boy-cut panty shown here were drafted for a four-way super stretchy knit. Next, you will grade very stretchy and moderate stretch slopers. You will not grade minimal stretch slopers because they are only for drafting patterns constructed from two-way stretch knits. The crotch-piece remains the same size for all stretch categories. Transfer the leg-line and boy-cut panty patterns onto oak-tag.

Leg-line

You grade the patterns in a positive direction to create very stretchy and moderate stretch slopers.

Prepare the Grading Grid

Figure 11.11

Draw the grading grid onto pattern paper. From (D), mark ½" increments (E and F) in a *positive* direction. Refer to Figure 3.16 on p. 36 to see the grading increments.

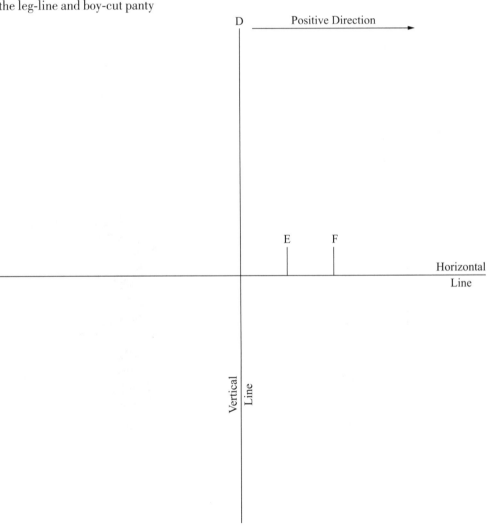

Figure 11.11 Prepare the grading grid

Draw the Horizontal Balance Line (HBL)

Figure 11.12

1. Align an L-squared ruler on sloper CF and touching the side seam/legline. Draw the HBL.
2. Draw the HBL squared at CB to the side seam/ legline.
3. Label (X) on the slopers.

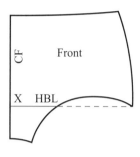

Figure 11.12 Draw the horizontal balance line on the slopers

Very Stretchy

Figure 11.13a

1. Place the center front/back sloper on the vertical line (D) with HBL placed on the horizontal line. Trace the super stretchy front/back slopers onto the grading grid.
2. Move the front/back sloper (X) on (E). Trace the waistline and side seam to the horizontal line. Trace 2" of the front legline and 1" of the back legline as shown.

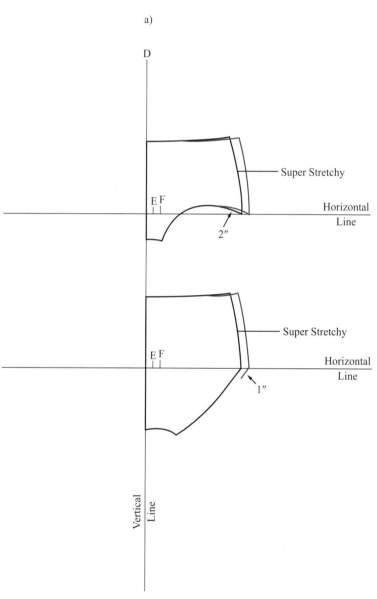

Figure 11.13a Grade very stretchy

Moderate Stretch

Figure 11.13b

Move front/back sloper (X) on (F) with HBL on the horizontal line. Trace the waistline, side seam, and legline as previously drafted.

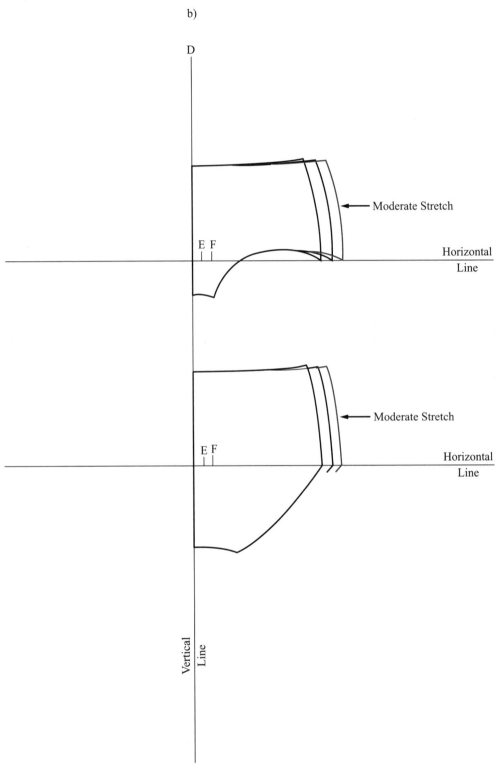

Figure 11.13b Grade moderate stretch

Draw the Front/Back Legline

Figure 11.13c

1. Use the hip curve to connect the *front* legline from the 2" mark to the outlined legline.
2. Use the sloper to draw the remaining back legline. Align the sloper to the 1" mark and crotch line. Draw a blending legline for each stretch category as shown.

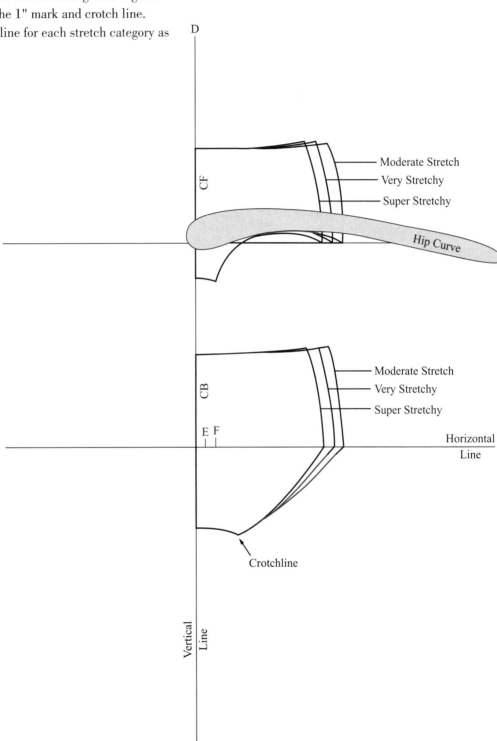

c)

Moderate Stretch
Very Stretchy
Super Stretchy

Hip Curve

Moderate Stretch
Very Stretchy
Super Stretchy

Horizontal Line

Crotchline

Vertical Line

Figure 11.13c Draw the front/back legline

Cut the Slopers
Figures 11.14a and b

1. Cut the side seam/waistline (W1) and side seam/legline (B) in steps for each stretch category, as shown in Figure 11.14a.
2. Trace the front and back moderate stretch slopers onto oak-tag. Use a tracing wheel to transfer the newly graded waistline and legline (see Figure 11.14b). Then cut the slopers.
3. Finally, cut the very stretchy slopers.

b)

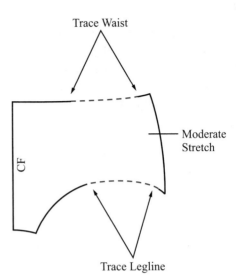

Figure 11.14b Draw the waistline and legline curve

a)

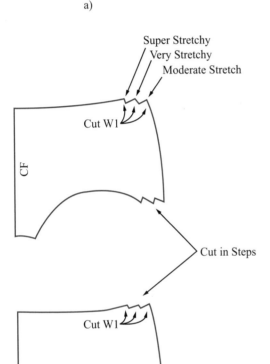

Figure 11.14a Cut the waist/side seam and legline/side seam in steps

Align the Slopers

✓ Check that the front/back legline in each stretch category has a smooth leg curve when the side seams and crotch-piece are placed together (see Figure 11.3b).

Finalize the Slopers
Figure 11.15

To complete the slopers, label them and record the stretch category.

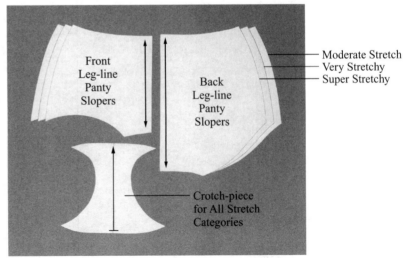

Figure 11.15 Panty-leg slopers graded in each stretch category

Boy-cut

The sloper for the four-way super stretchy boy-cut panty was drafted in Figures 11.6, 11.7, and 11.8. You grade the boy-cut panty in a *positive and negative* direction because it is a one-piece pattern. Label (Y) on the front sloper and (X) on the back sloper, as shown in Figure 11.16a.

Prepare the Grading Grid

Figure 11.16a

The boy-cut sloper is drawn on the grid first. Then you mark the grading increments on the grid. The sloper horizontal balance line is the hipline. Label (X-Y) on the slopers only. With every grading move, you align HBL on the horizontal line.

1. Draw intersecting lines on oak-tag.
2. Align the sloper HBL on the horizontal line and the grainline on the vertical line. Trace the sloper onto the grid.
3. Mark ½" increments (B-C) in a negative direction.
4. Mark ½" increments (E-F) in a positive direction.

a)

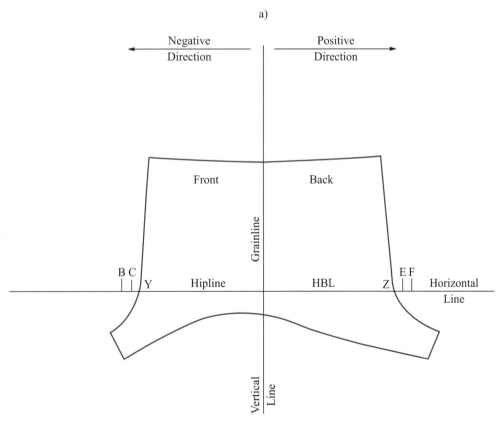

Figure 11.16a Prepare the grading grid

Very Stretchy

Figure 11.16b

1. Move sloper (Y) on (C). From the grainline, trace the waistline, center front/crotch, inseam, and legline to within 2" of the grainline.
2. Move sloper (X) on (E). From the grainline, trace the waistline, center front/crotch, inseam, and ½" of the legline.

Moderate Stretch

Figure 11.16b

1. Move sloper (Y) on (B). From the grainline, trace the waistline, center front/crotch, inseam, and legline to within 2" of the grainline.
2. Move sloper (X) on (F). From the grainline, trace the waistline, center front/crotch, inseam, and ½" of the legline.

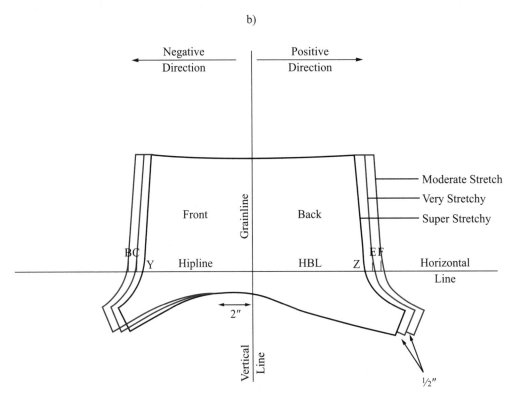

Figure 11.16b Grade very stretchy and moderate stretch

Cut the Slopers

Figure 11.17

1. In steps, cut the moderate stretch sloper with the front/back inseam/legline as shown.
2. Trace the moderate stretch sloper onto oak-tag, tracing around the steps.
3. Use a tracing wheel to transfer the front legline.
4. Place the super stretchy back sloper on the ½" legline mark. Then angle the sloper to the original legline. Draw the moderate stretch legline.
5. Cut the very stretchy sloper, and transfer the legline as it was done previously.
6. Check that the legline has a smooth curve when the inseams are placed together.

Finalize the Slopers

Figure 11.18

Label the slopers "Boy-cut Panty," draw the grainlines, and record the stretch category.

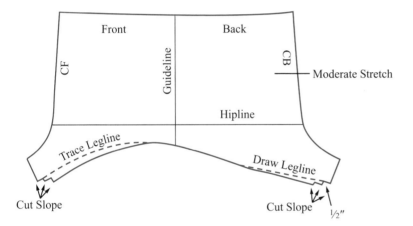

Figure 11.17 Cut the slopers

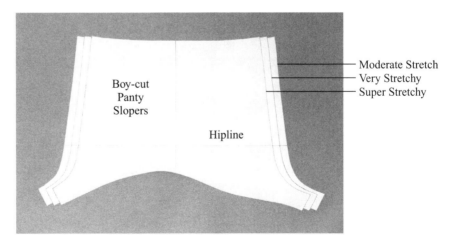

Figure 11.18 Boy-cut panty slopers graded in each stretch category

Panty Variations

By changing the silhouette of the leg-line panty slopers, you can create a thong. You also can modify the boy-cut panty slopers to create a variation of the boy-cut panty by removing the center front/back seams and adding a separate crotch-piece.

 ## Thong

Figure 11.19a

Many women find wearing a thong comfortable and practical because it eliminates panty lines under snug-fitting pants and skirts.

1. Trace the front/back four-way stretch leg-line panty from the working patterns drafted in Figure 11.2c. Modify into low-rise. (Refer to Figure 4.16 on p. 52 to see low-rise marked on the final slopers.)
2. S-D = ⅜" (total crotch width is ¾"). (See Figure 11.19a.)

3. W1-A = Mark a ¾" to 1½" side seam width.
4. A-S = Shape the front legline.
5. D-E = Draw the length of the crotch piece.
6. Cut, stitch, and fit the thong on the pant form. Add ¼" seam allowances. You do not stitch the crotch piece at this stage. You stitch it to the crotch seam and secure it to the leg opening when it is elasticized.
7. Label the patterns and draw the grainlines. Record the stretch category and the number of pieces to cut (see Figure 11.19b).

b)

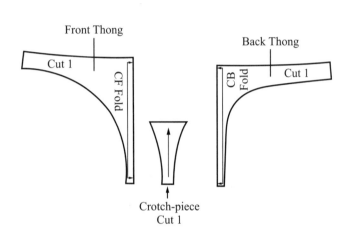

Figure 11.19b Final patterns for the thong

a)

Four-way Stretch Leg-line Panty Slopers

Figure 11.19a Draft a thong

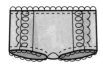

Boy-cut Panty Without Center Front/Back Seams

The panty in Figure 11.1d is another style of boy-cut panty with side seams and no center front/back seams. You draft the patterns from the classic boy-cut panty pattern.

Draft the Patterns

Figures 11.20a and b

1. Trace (or draft) the front/back boy-cut panty patterns (see Figure 11.6c). The panty is mid-rise level.
2. Extend the center front/back to below the crotch.

Front:

1. H-Y = 2" below hipline.
2. Y-A = Squared 1" line.

3. Y-C = ⅝" up from (Y).
4. A-C = Draw the curved crotch line.
5. E = ¼".
6. A-E = Draw the legline, raising it ¼" as the curve is drawn.

Back:

1. H-X = 3¼" below hipline. X-B = Squared 1¼" line.
2. X-D = ¼" up from (D).
3. B-D = Draw the curved crotch line.
4. E = ¼".
5. E-B = Draw the curved legline using a hip curve as shown.
6. Measure lengths (H-C and H-D). Mark this length from (H) around the front/back crotch curve. Measure the total "extra length" that remains to the crotch/inseam.

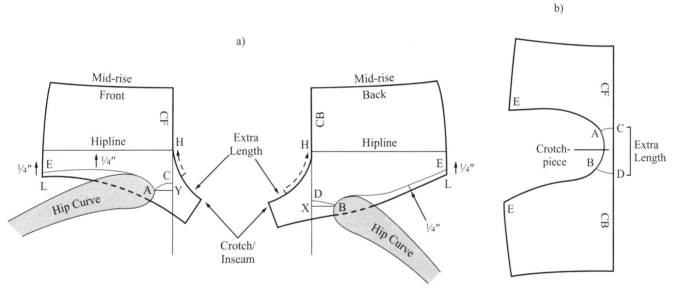

Figure 11.20a and b Draft the boy-cut panty without center front/back seams

Draft the Crotch-piece

1. Draw a vertical line on pattern paper.
2. Align the CF of the panty on a vertical line; then trace and label crotch line (A-C). From (C), mark the total "extra length."
3. Align the back crotch (D) on a vertical line to the "extra length," and trace the back panty.

Finalize the Patterns

Figure 11.21

1. Trace the front/back panty patterns to the crotch line (A-C and B-D).
2. Align side seams together to check that there is a smooth curved legline.
3. A-C-D-B = Trace the crotch-piece onto a folded piece of pattern paper, and cut a full pattern piece.
4. Label the patterns, record the stretch category, and draw the grainlines as shown.

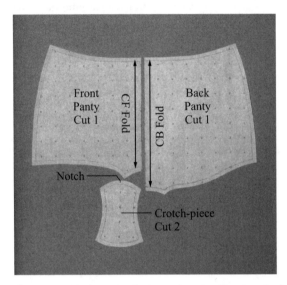

Figure 11.21 Final patterns for boy-cut panty without center front/back seams

Panty Finishes

Leg-line and boy-cut panty waist openings *must* be elasticized. Leg-line panty openings also must be elasticized. Boy-cut leg openings *do not* need to be elasticized; however, they can be elasticized. Narrow ⅜" wide picot and braided elastics are commonly used to elasticize the waist and leg openings. Elastic lace (1" and ⅜" wide) also provides an attractive finish. (Refer to Table 3.2 on p. 28 to see each type of elastic.)

Length of Finish

Figure 11.22a through d

Elastic and elastic lace *must* be cut shorter than the length of the waist or leg opening. Cutting the finish shorter results in the opening lying smooth and flat after the finish is applied.

To calculate the length of the finish:

1. Measure the pattern waistline and double for the total measurement (see Figures 11.22a and b).
2. Measure the pattern leg opening (see Figures 11.22b and c).
3. Reduce the waist length 2" to determine the elastic/lace length (see Figure 11.22d).
4. Reduce the leg opening length 1½" to determine the elastic/lace length (see Figure 11.22d).

a)

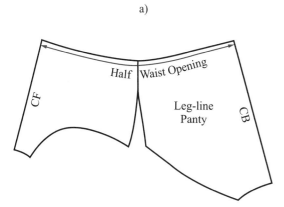

Figure 11.22a Measure the waist opening

b)

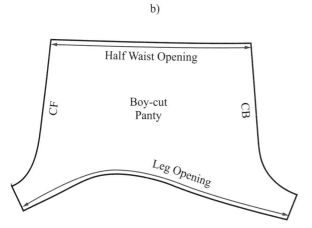

Figure 11.22b Measure the waist and leg opening

c)

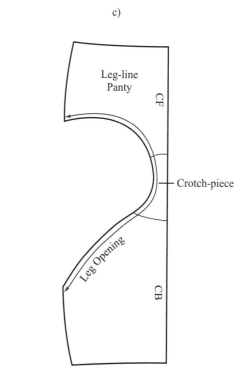

Figure 11.22c Measure the leg opening

d)

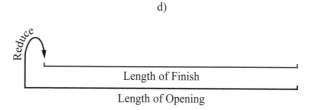

Figure 11.22d Determine the length of the finish.

Stitching the Finish

Before you stitch the finish, you divide and pin-mark the leg and waist openings into equal sections. You also divide the finish into equal sections. Next, you align the pin-marks and stretch the finish so that the fabric lies flat as it is stitched to the opening. (Refer to Tables 11.1 and 11.2.)

Picot Edge

Figure 11.23

A delicate picot edge will show from the correct side of the panties after the elastic is stitched to the waist and leg openings (see Figure 11.1a). The elastic will sit next to the skin, so purchase elastic that feels soft.

1. If the elastic is ⅜" wide, then add this amount to the pattern for turning the folded edge.
2. Place the elastic on the correct side of fabric.
3. Stitch the elastic in place with wide zigzag stitches (or serging).
4. Turn the elastic to the wrong side. From the correct side, topstitch the turned edge with smaller zigzag stitches to enclose the elastic edge underneath.

Enclosed

Figure 11.24

Enclosing the elastic is the perfect method to use when applying elastic (such as braided elastic) that does not match the fabric color. After you stitch the elastic, you enclose and fully cover it (see Figure 11.1b).

1. Add an edge allowance to the panty leg/waist openings the width of the elastic.
2. Place the elastic on the wrong side of the fabric.
3. Zigzag stitch (wide) or serge the elastic to the opening. Enclose the outer edge of the elastic as you stitch because it will prevent the elastic from rolling out.
4. Turn the elastic and fabric to the wrong side. From the correct side, topstitch the turned-back edge with twin needles (or zigzag stitches).

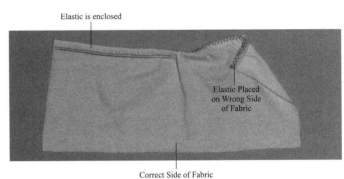

Figure 11.24 Stitching enclosed elastic.

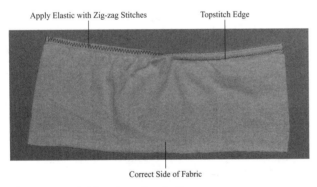

Figure 11.23 Stitching picot edge elastic.

Elastic Lace

Elastic lace is an edging that can be applied to panties and camisoles (see Figures 11.1c, h, and i). Stitch the lace using small zigzag stitches or a three-stitch zigzag because the stitches blend with the texture of lace.

Narrow Lace

Figure 11.25

Refer to Figures 11.1b to see narrow elastic lace applied to the leg-line panty.

1. Add a ¼" edge allowance to the panty leg/waist openings.
2. Place the wrong side of the lace ¼" over the fabric edge as shown.
3. Zigzag stitch the edge of the lace to the panty opening.

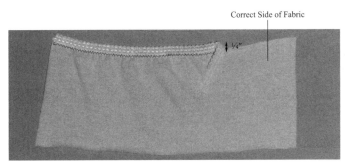

Figure 11.25 Stitching narrow elastic lace   .

Wide Lace

Figures 11.26 and 11.27

1. Place the wrong side of the lace over the correct side of the fabric. Align the lace edge with the fabric edge and pin in place (see Figure 11.26).
2. Zigzag stitch the lower lace edge (see Figure 11.26). (This is how the elastic lace is stitched to the waist of the boy-cut panty in Figure 11.1c.)
3. If the lace has a scallop edge, stitch around the scallop shape (see Figure 11.27). (This is how the elastic lace is stitched to the cami in Figures 11.1h and i.)
4. Cut the fabric away under the lace close to the lace edge (using appliqué scissors) as shown.

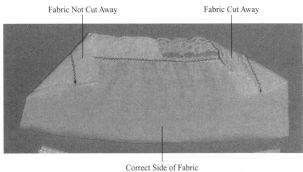

Figure 11.26 Stitching wide elastic lasce

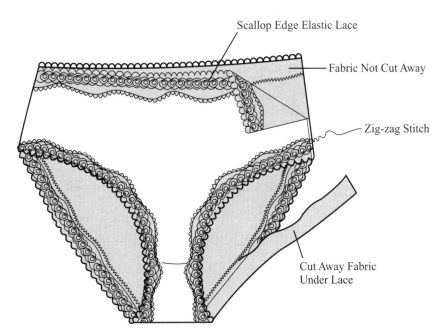

Figure 11.27 Scallop-edge elastic lace stitched to panty

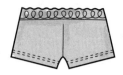

Turned and Topstitched

Figure 11.28

As mentioned previously, the leg openings of boy-cut panties do not need to be elastized. They can be turned and topstitched, as shown in Figure 11.1c. Add a ½" seam allowance to the leg opening.

1. Turn the hem allowance to the wrong side.
2. From the correct side, topstitch the leg opening with twin needles. (See Figure 11.28.)

Twin Needle Topstitching

½" Hem Allowance

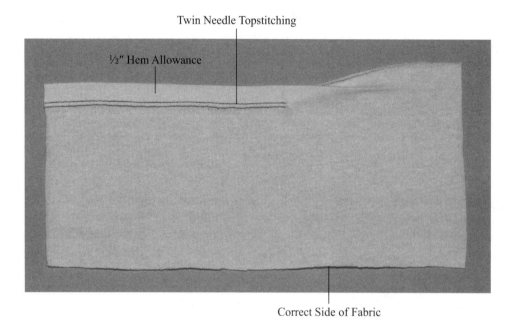

Correct Side of Fabric

Figure 11.28 Turned and topstitched.

Pattern Drafting Camisoles

A camisole is a versatile garment because it can be worn as an underlayer for warmth, worn as a pajama top, or worn peeking out under a business jacket. A cami can have a simple design and shapely fit. It can have a bra-top, round or V-shape neckline, flared silhouette, and lace trim (see Figures 11.1f through i).

Camisoles can be constructed from minimal stretch, moderate stretch, very stretchy, and super stretchy two-way and four-way stretch knits. Camisole patterns are drafted from the top slopers. Refer to Table 2.2 on p. 17 to see the camisole listed under "Top Sloper." You use the sleeveless top slopers to draft the patterns for camisoles. To adjust the slopers, refer to the "Sleeveless Top Slopers" section in Chapter 6.

Round-neck

Figure 11.29

The front and back patterns for the round-neck cami uses the same pattern piece.

1. Trace the *front* two-way stretch sleeveless top sloper onto pattern paper in the appropriate stretch category. Label the (B) underarm.
2. F = ¼" in and down from the (B) side seam/underarm.
3. F-E = Draw a squared guideline.
4. E-A = 1½" up from (E) on center front.
5. S-C = ⅓ of shoulder length.
6. C-D-A = Draw a right angle guideline.
7. N = Midway between (A-E). Draw a squared ¼" line at (N).
8. D-U = 1".
9. F-U-N = Draw the curved neckline and underarm as shown.

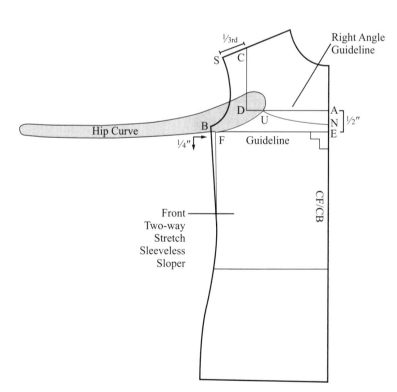

Figure 11.29 Draft a round-neck camisole

Fabric You'll Need

Purchase ⅝ yard of lightweight two-way or four-way stretch jersey knit in the same stretch category that the patterns were drafted for. Use the stretch gauge in Figure 1.6 on p. 9 to ascertain the stretch of the knit.

Cut and Stitch

1. Lay out the cami patterns following Figure 4.15 on p. 52. You don't need to cut and stitch the neckline finish at this point.
2. Add a ¼" seam allowance to the side seams.

Test the Fit

Figure 11.30

Fit the cami on the dress form.

What to look for:

✓ Check that the neckline is the correct depth and shape.
✓ Check that the strap length is measured from front to back and the length is documented.

Finalize the Patterns

Cut a piece of pattern paper large enough for the left and right fronts. Fold the paper and trace the cami pattern. Cut one complete pattern.

1. Label the pattern "Front/Back Round-neck Cami" and "Cut 2."
2. Add a ½" hem allowance and ¼" seam allowance. The amount of allowance you add to the pattern to stitch the neckline finish is determined by the chosen finish.

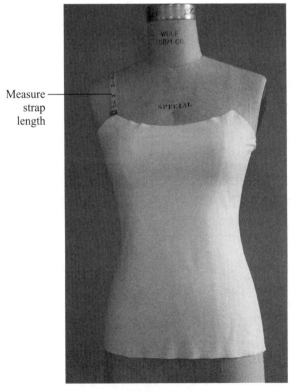

Measure strap length

Figure 11.30 Muslin round-neck camisole fitted on the form

V-neck

Figure 11.31a and b

Trace the *front* two-way stretch sleeveless top sloper onto pattern paper in the appropriate stretch category. Label (B) underarm and draw the waistline. Cross-mark apex (A) if you plan to draft the bra-top camisole further on.

1. F = ¼" in and down from the (B) side seam/underarm (see Figure 11.31a).
2. F-N = Draw squared guideline (1).
3. C-D = Draw guideline (2) 2" above and parallel to guideline (1).

4. U = Midway between (F-N) draw a line squared up to guideline (2).
5. F-U-N = Draw straight lines to connect each point.
6. Midway on F-U and U-N, draw a ⅛" line square down. Draw the shaped neckline to the ⅛" mark.
7. N-E = 2". At (E), square a 2" line. From this point, draw the curved back neckline.
8. Check that the neckline has a smooth shape when the front/back side seams are aligned (see Figure 11.31b).

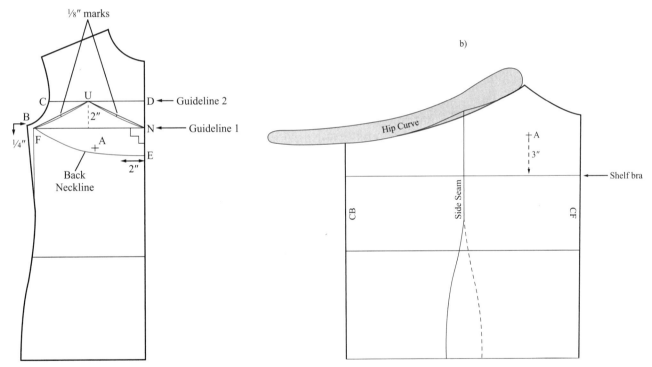

Figure 11.31a Draft a V-neck camisole

Figure 11.31b Align the patterns

Cut, Stitch, and Fit

Figure 11.32

To cut, stitch, and fit the camisole, refer to the "Round-neck Camisole" section earlier in this chapter and follow the same instructions. To determine the strap length, measure from the front V to the back neckline, via the shoulder (see Figures 11.32a and b).

Finalize the Patterns

Figure 11.33

1. Notch the strap position on the back pattern. Cross-mark the apex on the front pattern.
2. Write the pattern name "V-neck Camisole" and the number of pattern pieces to cut.
3. Draw the grainlines and record the stretch category.

a)   b)

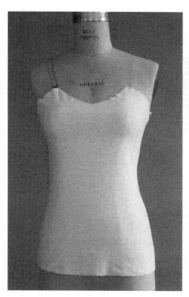

Figure 11.32a Muslin V-neck camisole fitted on the form.

Figure 11.32b Measure the strap length.

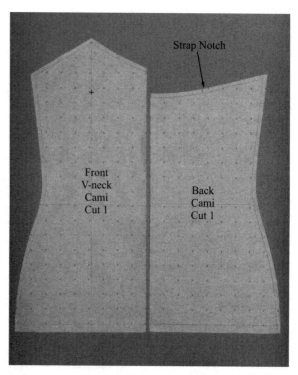

Figure 11.33 Final patterns for V-neck camisole

Bra-top

A bra-top is a separate piece that gives a cami a more defined bust shape (see Figures 11.1h and i). A lace edge finish adds a touch of class to the edge of the bra-top.

Draft the Patterns

Figure 11.34a

1. Draft the front/back V-neck cami patterns shown in Figure 11.31. Draw the waistline and cross-mark the apex (A).
2. Lower the neckline (N).
3. B-D = 3" below apex (A). Square a line at (D).
4. A-H = Draw a line from the apex to the hem parallel to CF. Label (Z) where the lines intersect.

5. Mark ⅝" on each side of (Z). Lower apex (A) ½". Draw dart legs from (K) to the lowered apex.
6. L-M = ¼" on each side of (Z). Draw vertical lines to (H). (This is "excess" to be removed.)
7. F-C = 2" (or to your own design).
8. C-K and K-N = Draw the curved bra-top shape using a hip curve or French curve.

Trace the Pattern Pieces

Figure 11.34b

1. F-U-N-K-C = Trace the bra-top from the working pattern.
2. Fold the dart toward the center front. Cut the bra cup pattern; leave a section of pattern paper at the side as shown.

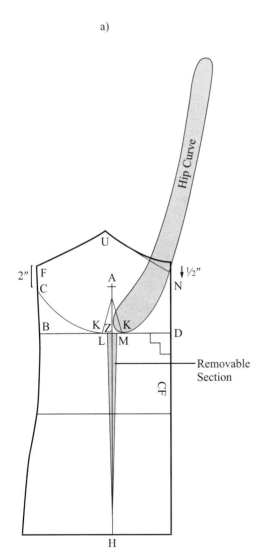

Figure 11.34a Draft the bra-top cami

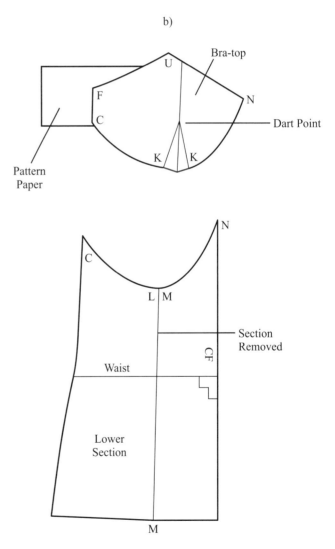

Figure 11.34b Trace the bra top and lower section

3. Trace the lower section of the cami.
4. Cut line (L to H) and place on the L to M line to remove the "excess."
5. Square a line from the side/waist to the center front.
6. The center front hemline dips slightly, which will allow extra length.

Align the Bra-top to the Lower Section
Figure 11.34c

1. Fold the dart closed and pin in place.
2. Walk the bra-top seamline around the lower section seamline to compare the lengths. Begin by placing center fronts together, and then use an awl to anchor the bra-top seamline as you move the pattern in increments toward the side seam.
3. Mark the position of the dart leg on the lower section (this will be a notch).

4. The bra-top side seam will be shorter than the lower section.
5. Place a graph ruler along the side seam of the lower section, and extend a line to add extra width to (F-B).
6. Align the front/back cami patterns, and draw a blending neckline.

Cut, Stitch, and Fit
Figure 11.35

Cut, stitch, and test-fit the cami on the dress form. Add ¼" seam allowances to the side and bra-top seams. Then notch the dart position on the lower section. (To stitch the bra cup to the bottom section of the cami, refer to Table 11.3.) Finally, make any pattern adjustments.

c)

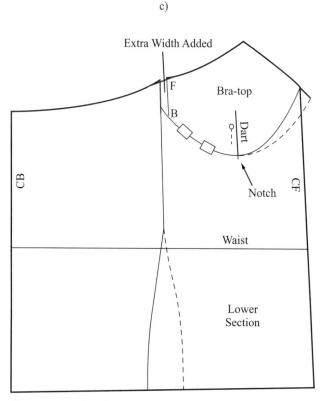

Figure 11.34c Align the bra-top and lower section seamlines together.

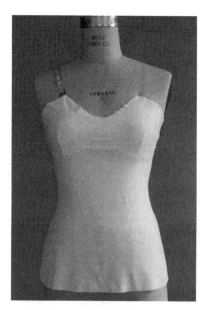

Figure 11.35 Muslin bra-top camisole fitted on the form

Finalize the Patterns

Figure 11.36

1. Label the patterns "Front/Back Bra-top Cami."
2. Draw grainlines. The bra-top grainline is an extension of the center of the dart.
3. Notch the dart legs and mark the dart point on the bra-top pattern.
4. Notch the dart position on the lower section.
5. Record the stretch category and the number of pattern pieces to cut.

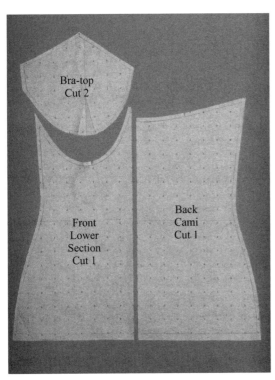

Figure 11.36 Final patterns for bra-top cami patterns

a)

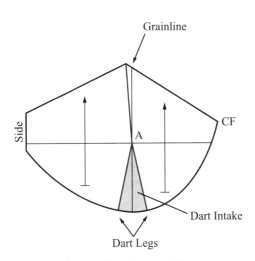

Figure 11.37a Draft a two-piece bra-top pattern

PATTERN TIP 11.1: DRAFTING A TWO-PIECE BRA-TOP

A two-piece bra-top can have a vertical or horizontal seamline that divides it into two sections (see Figure 11.1j).

1. Trace the darted bra cup pattern drafted in Figure 11.34, draw a grainline, and cross-mark the apex (A) (see Figure 11.37a).
2. Draw a *vertical* line from the apex to the strap position. Cut the pattern into two pieces by removing the dart intake (see Figure 11.37b).
3. Square a *horizontal* line at the grainline through apex (A) (see Figure 11.37a). Cut along one dart leg to the apex. Align the dart legs together to close the dart. Draw a blending line across the apex (see Figure 11.37c).
4. Draw grainlines on each pattern piece, and label the patterns as shown.

b)

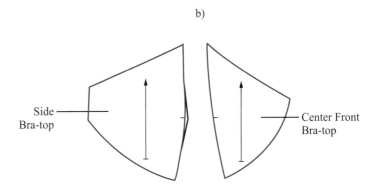

Figure 11.37b Two-piece bra-top with vertical seamline

c)

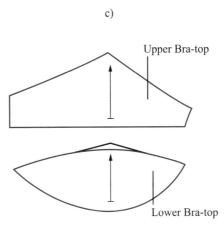

Figure 11.37c Two piece bra-top with horizontal seamline

Shelf bra

Figures 11.38a and b

A **shelf bra** is a lining stitched inside a camisole that fits over the bust area to add additional support. The shelf bra can be constructed from self fabric or a knit lining. Elastic is sewn to the bottom edge of the shelf bra to enable it to cling under the bust. A shelf bra can also have removable bra cups inserted into a pocket opening. Use soft foam cups because they give a nice smooth fit. Cups are available in assorted shapes and sizes.

a)

b)

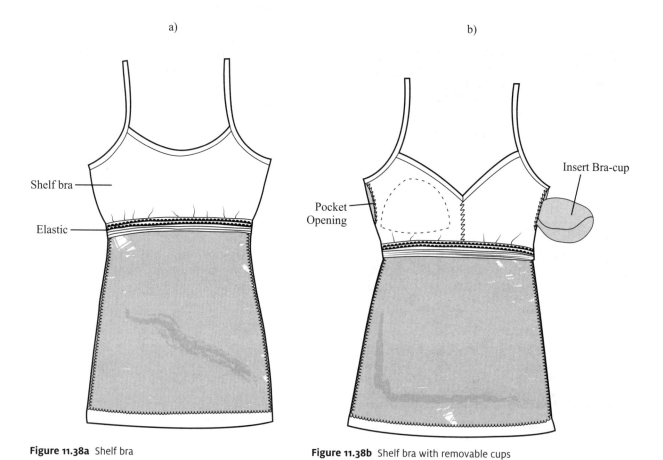

Shelf bra

Elastic

Pocket Opening

Insert Bra-cup

Figure 11.38a Shelf bra

Figure 11.38b Shelf bra with removable cups

Draft the Patterns

Figure 11.39

You can draft the front and back shelf bra patterns from the round or V-neck cami patterns. Refer to Figure 11.31b to see the shelf bra depth marked 3" below the apex.

1. Trace the front/back shelf bra patterns onto pattern paper.
2. Mark a 2½" opening on the *front* side seam for the bra cups to be inserted.
3. Add a ¼" seam allowance to the side seams and hem edge. Add an allowance to the neckline for the chosen neckline finish.
4. Label the patterns, add the grainlines, and document the number of pieces to cut. If the shelf bra has bra cups, then cut *two* front pieces and cut *one* back piece.

STITCHING TIP 11.3: STITCHING THE SHELF BRA WITH A POCKET OPENING FIGURE 11.40

1. Serge the opening (along the side seam), turn a ¼" edge to the wrong side, and topstitch with zigzag stitches.
2. Place wrong sides of the two fronts together and pin the side seams. Zigzag stitch the center fronts together.
3. Fold the opening out of the way. Place the correct side of the front/back together and stitch the side seams.
4. Join the elastic so it is circular (see Figure 9.54 on p. 288).
5. Serge the lower edge of the shelf bra. Pin-mark or chalk-mark the lower edge and the elastic into four equal sections.
6. Place the elastic edge ¼" over the serged edge, align markings, and topstitch with wide zigzag stitches or twin needle topstitching. (See Figure 11.38.)

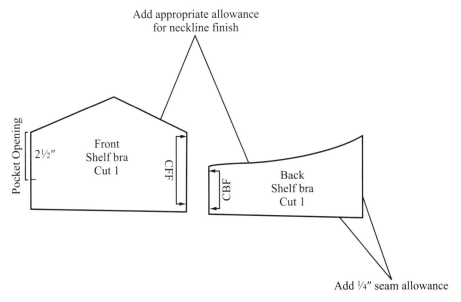

Figure 11.39 Draft of the shelf bra patterns

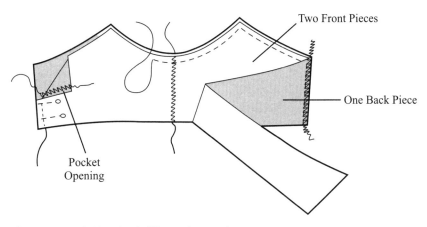

Figure 11.40 Stitching the shelf bra pocket opening

Camisole Variations

A cami can be gathered at the neckline or under the bust seam. The silhouette can be A-line or flared. You can change the bra-top cami patterns drafted in Figure 11.34 to create a new design by using the slash/spread pattern drafting technique.

1. To add gathering to the bra-top under the bust seam, slash/spread the pattern 3" (including the dart intake). (See Figure 11.41.)
2. To create a flared silhouette, slash/spread the lower pattern section (L/M-H) line (in Figure 11.34b) to add fullness to the hemline. (See Figure 11.41.)

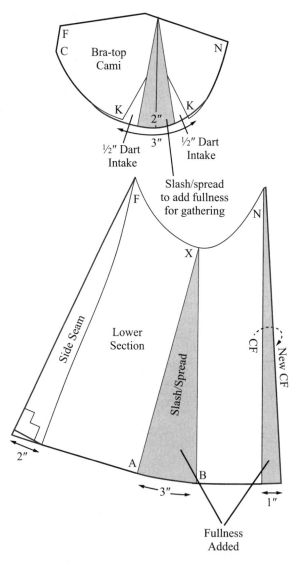

Figure 11.41 Cami variation using the slash/spread pattern drafting technique

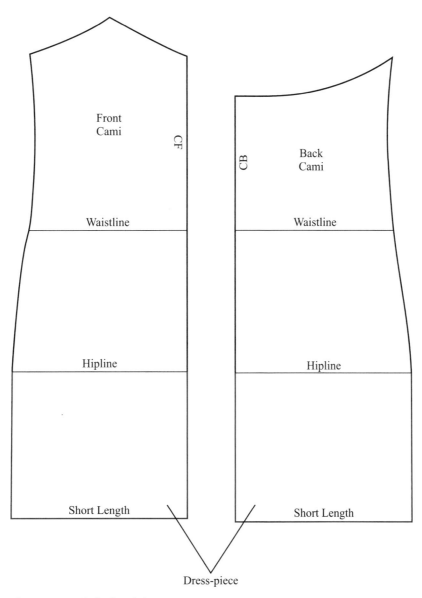

Cami-dress

Figure 11.42

A **cami-dress** is a camisole of dress length. To draft a cami-dress, add the dress-piece drafted in Figure 7.3 on p. 149 to the hipline of the front and back cami patterns. Determine the hem length according to the design.

Front
Cami

CF

CB

Back
Cami

Waistline

Waistline

Hipline

Hipline

Short Length

Short Length

Dress-piece

Figure 11.42 A draft of cami-dress pattern

Teddy

A **teddy** is a loose-fitting garment for sleepwear. It can be fashioned from combining the front/back cami patterns with the front/back shorts patterns. Extra length is added between (X-Y) to accommodate a casing and to make sure the teddy is comfortable when worn. The teddy patterns can also be shorts jumpsuit patterns. The teddy wasitline is drawn midway between (X-Y), as shown in Figure 11.43. The patterns can be separated to create a waist seam. In this case, the center front/back top patterns can be cut on the fold.

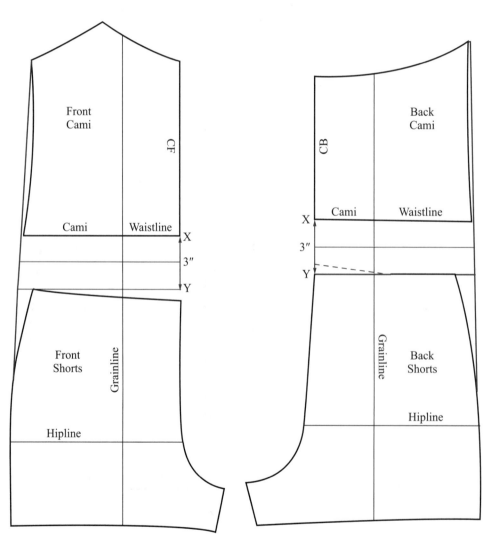

Figure 11.43 A draft of teddy patterns

Neckline Finishes

Elastic lace, picot edge elastic, and enclosed elastic (for elastic that does not color match the fabric) are waist and leg opening finishes that you can use as stretchable neckline finishes. (Refer to the "Panty Finishes" section earlier in this chapter.) The finish you choose must allow a cami to stretch comfortably on the body and not feel tight or constricting. The neckline finish does not need to be fully elasticized. The front neckline can have a nonstretch lace and an elasticized back neckline. This combination will create a functional cami. A binding is also an appropriate neckline finish that is not elasticized and will stretch to fit. Refer to Figures 11.1f through j to see a variety of neckline finishes.

Length of Finish

Figure 11.44

The elastic/lace or binding *must* be cut shorter than the length of the neckline opening. This ensures that the finish will lie flat after it is stitched to the neckline.

1. Place side seams of the front/back patterns together. Then measure the neckline pattern in two sections: the front neckline and then the side/back neckline.
2. Reduce the length to determine the length of the finish. (The reduction will be specified for each finish.)

Stitching the Finish

Pin-mark the center back cami halfway on the finish. Then align and pin together the neckline and finish markings. You cut the finish shorter than the neckline opening and stretch it to fit the neckline between markings as it is stitched.

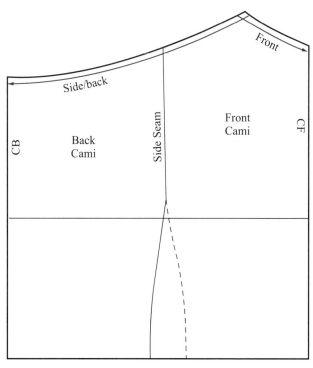

Figure 11.44 Measure the cami neckline

Elastic Lace

Figure 11.45

1. After measuring the pattern neckline, reduce the length by 1½" for the total lace length. Reduce the *front* neckline by ¼" (½" in total) and reduce the *side/back* neckline by ½" (1" in total). For the hemline, reduce the length 1½".
2. Add ½" for joining the lace.
3. Stitch a ¼" seam; then finger press open and zigzag stitch the seam edges to hold them in place.
4. Place the wrong side of the lace over the correct side of the garment with the scallop edge aligned to the neckline edge. Align pin-marks and stitch the lower edge of the lace with small zigzag stitches.
5. Cut the fabric away under the lace, as shown on the panty in Figure 11.27.

Elastic

If the entire cami is elasticized, it will feel too tight. An elasticized back combines well with an elastic lace (or nonelastic lace) front neckline, as shown in the cami in Figure 11.1i. To stitch the elastic, refer to the "Panty Finishes" section, and follow the same stitching techniques to stitch a picot edge or enclosed elastic (see Figures 11.23 and 11.24).

1. Reduce the length of the back neckline by 1" to calculate the elastic length.
2. Add a ½" seam allowance for joining the elastic to the side seams.

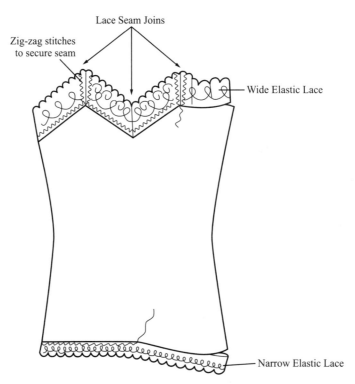

Figure 11.45 Stitching elastic lace to the neckline and hemline

Binding

Figures 11.46 and 11.47a and b

A binding can be used to finish the neckline of tops, cardigans, and camisoles. You *do not* add a seam allowance to any pattern edge where a binding is applied because the binding encases the raw edge.

1. Measure the length of the neckline length (see Figure 11.44). Reduce 2" for the binding length. Reduce the front neckline ¼" (½" in total) and reduce the side/back neckline 1½".
2. Draft the binding pattern to the appropriate length and 1¼" wide. The finished binding width is approximately ¼" (see Figure 11.46).
3. If shoulder straps are a continuation of the neckline finish, add the strap length to the binding pattern and notch where the front neckline joins to the straps (see Figure 11.46).
4. Draw the pattern grainline. You can cut the binding on the crossgrain, lengthwise grain, or bias grain (see Figure 4.15 on p. 52).

5. Stitch the binding to the neckline with a ¼" seam allowance. Stitch the front neckline first, which is *step 1* in the Stitching Order in Table 11.3.
6. Stitch the side/back binding, and leave a ½" opening on the back neckline for the strap to be inserted (see Figure 11.47a).
7. Fold the straps in half with correct sides placed together and press. Turn a ¼" folded edge to the wrong side along each side of the strap (see Figure 11.47b).
8. Fold the strap in half and hand baste (see Figure 11.44a).
9. Topstitch the binding with twin needles or wide zigzag stitches from the correct side. Begin stitching at one strap end. As you approach the ½" opening, insert the strap and continue stitching (see Figure 11.47a).
10. Turn the strap up (toward the shoulder) and topstitch to secure in place (see Figure 11.47a).

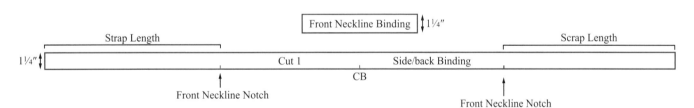

Figure 11.46 Draft the binding patterns

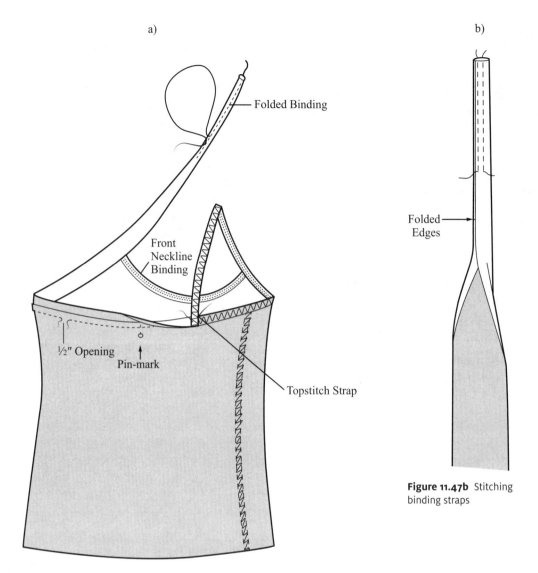

a)

Folded Binding

Front
Neckline
Binding

½" Opening

Pin-mark

Topstitch Strap

Figure 11.47a Stitching the binding to the neckline

b)

Folded
Edges

Figure 11.47b Stitching
binding straps

Straps

You can purchase ready-made shoulder straps or use plush elastic, elastic lace, or ribbon. Binding straps or narrow spaghetti straps can be constructed from fabric. These straps are not elasticized. Straps can be separated and stitched to the front/back neckline. A binding neckline finish can also continue into straps (see Figure 11.47). The strap length is approximately 15" long. (You determine the strap length when fitting the cami on the form, as shown in Figures 11.30, 11.32, and 11.35).

Binding

Figure 11.47b

The previous section explained how to stitch a neckline binding that continues into shoulder straps. Refer to Figure 11.46 to draft the strap pattern. To stitch the straps, refer to Figure 11.47b.

Elastic Lace

Figure 11.48

Lace ½" to 1¼" wide makes excellent straps for a cami-sole. The straps require no stitching other than attaching them to the cami front/back neckline.

1. Stitch the straps using a ¼" seam allowance, and then trim to ⅛".
2. Turn the strap back, and then topstitch with zigzag stitches.

Spaghetti

Figure 11.49

Spaghetti straps are narrow ¼" wide straps that are made from fabric.

1. Cut 1" wide fabric strips on the lengthwise grain of a two-way stretch knit the length required.
2. Fold the width in half with correct sides placed together, and press a folded edge.
3. Serge the strap edges together with *wide* serging. (The serging will pad the straps nicely after they are turned.)
4. Place a loop turner up through the center of the strap, hook it around the top edge, and pull the strap back through the tunnel to the correct side.

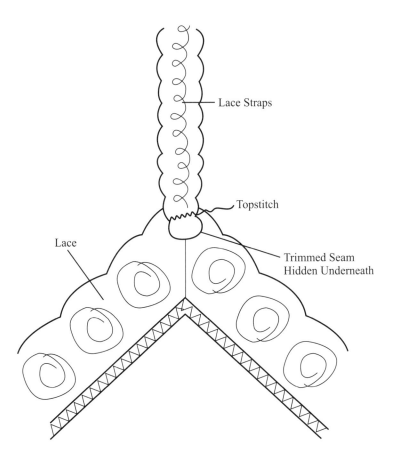

Figure 11.48 Stitching elastic lace straps

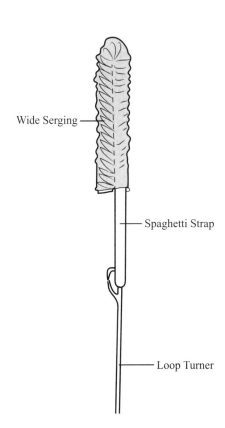

Figure 11.49 Stitching spaghetti straps

Knit It Together

This checklist summarizes what you have learned about drafting patterns for lingerie in this chapter.

- ✓ Panty slopers are drafted from the hip foundation.
- ✓ Panties *must* be constructed from four-way stretch knits.
- ✓ Panties must have elasticized waist and leg openings.
- ✓ Camisole patterns are drafted from the two-way stretch sleeveless top slopers.
- ✓ Camisole straps do not need to be elasticized.
- ✓ Camisoles can be constructed from two-way or four-way stretch knits.
- ✓ Camisole patterns can be converted into a cami-dress or teddy.

Stop: What Do I Do If . . .

. . . I want to draft a flared boy-cut panty in one-pattern piece? Can I stitch lace on the hem edge?

A one-piece pattern can be drafted as follows:

1. Use the moderate stretch boy-cut sloper in Figure 11.18.
2. On the *sloper*, draw two slash lines (in pencil) evenly spaced from waist to hem and squared to the hipline.
3. Slash/spread the pattern and add 1½" of fullness into the hem at each slash line (you will add 3" in total for each leg).
4. Draw a blending hemline and equalize where necessary.
5. You can stitch lightweight nonelastic lace to the hem of each leg opening.

. . . the bra-top cami pattern I drafted is too small for my bust size?

1. Slash/spread the pattern to add an extra dart intake. To do this, draw a slash line from (U-A to Z) (see Figure 11.34a).
2. Cut a slash line to (U), and spread to add an extra ¼" on each side of the slash line at (Z).

Self-Critique

1. What is the criterion for choosing lingerie fabric?
2. What slopers do you use to draft cami patterns?
3. If you choose a nonelastic lace for a cami neckline, how would you need to design the neckline to make sure it is stretchable?
4. Place a check in the box for the fabric type required for each garment.

Garment	Two-way Stretch	Four-way Stretch
Cami		
Legline Panty		
Boy-cut Panty		

5. Why would you use a shelf bra in a cami?
6. Do the straps of a camisole need to be elasticized?
7. What pattern pieces create a teddy pattern? Why is extra length added between the cami and shorts pattern?
8. What is the difference between the stitching orders in Table 11.1 and Table 10.1 when stitching the elastic to the waist of panties and stitching the waist finish to pants?

Key Terms	
Boy-cut Panty	Leg-line Panty
Cami-dress	Low-rise
Camisole	Mid-rise
Crotch-piece	Shelf bra
Hi-cut	Spaghetti Straps
High-rise	Teddy

12 Swimwear Slopers and Patterns

Swimsuits can look stylish when worn on vacation when one is sitting poolside or seaside or engaged in other water-based activities. Depending on the design, a swimsuit can also be worn as a tank top and paired with pants and worn out for lunch or dinner.

Swimsuit designs can reflect current shapes and styling such as a strapless, halter, or draped one-shouldered neckline; ruched seaming; a low back; or skin-exposed cutouts. They can be skimpy or provide full coverage. When a one-piece has too much coverage and a bikini too little, a tankini combined with swim shorts or swim skirt can be the perfect alternative. (See Figures 12.1a–d, 12.2a–e, and 12.3a–e.)

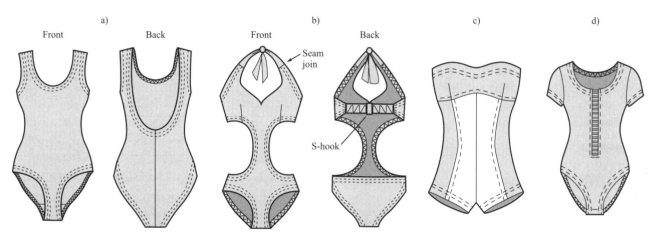

Figure 12.1 a) One-piece tank swimsuit with inbuilt straps; **b)** one-piece cutaway halter swimsuit; **c)** strapless boy-cut swimsuit; **d)** short-sleeve bodysuit

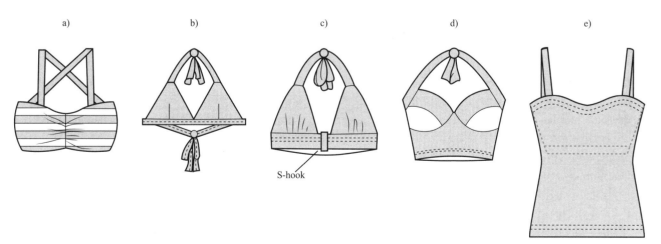

Figure 12.2 a) Bandeau with detachable straps; **b)** darted triangle bikini with binding ties; **c)** gathered triangle bikini with band and S-hook; **d)** bra-top cropkini; **e)** tankini with shelf bra

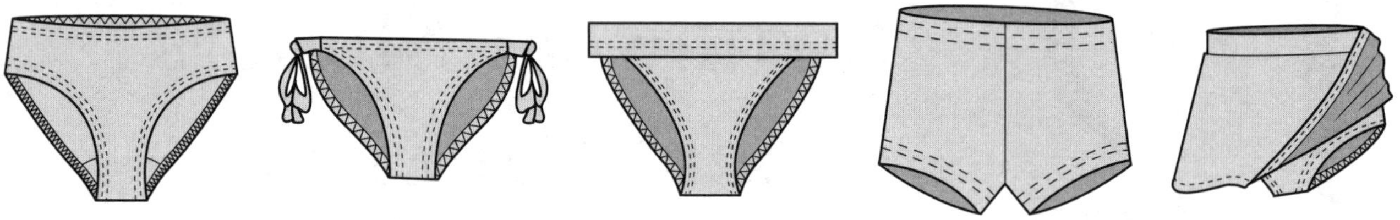

Figure 12.3 a) Basic bikini; **b)** triangle bikini with binding ties; **c)** triangle bikini with waistband; **d)** swim shorts; **e)** swim skirt

For you, as the designer, the key to any successfully designed swimsuit begins by choosing the correct type of fabric, providing an excellent fit, and ensuring quality construction. A focus on wearable, functional swimwear should always be the trademark of good design and will ensure a woman is swim-ready.

Swimwear Supplies

A **swimsuit** is a close-fitting article of clothing used for swimming and sunbathing. It can be one piece or a two-piece bra and panty ensemble. A swimsuit needs to be practical and wearable, and it must stay secure at all times to be swim-ready. To accomplish this, you need to purchase the correct supplies.

- *Fabric* for swimsuits must be a nylon/spandex blend in four-way stretch because it is strong, resilient, and fast-drying and will withstand pool chemicals. These fabrics have 15 to 50 percent spandex. Do not use cotton/spandex knits for swimsuits because the fabric becomes loose and baggy when wet and is not quick drying. (Refer to Table 1.1 on p. 4 in Chapter 1 for more information.)
- *Lining* fabric for knits must stretch at least the same amount (or greater) than the chosen swimsuit fabric.
- *Crotch lining* can be the actual swimwear fabric or the lining fabric. The crotch-piece must have quick-dry and chlorine-resistant qualities (100 percent cotton is not quick drying).
- *Swimwear elastic* must be salt and chlorine resistant. One suitable type is rubber elastic. Another one is *natural swimwear elastic*, which is latex free. (Refer to Table 3.2 and the "Elasticized Edges" section later in this chapter for the appropriate width of elastic to use for different locations on the swimsuit.)

- *Swim cups* are the same types of cups that are used for other garments. They come in a variety of shapes and cup sizes. Purchase cups that reflect the neckline shape of the swimsuit.
- *Fasteners* can be interlocking buckles or S-hooks. A small ½" S-hook fastens detachable straps to the swimsuit. A back closure requires a wider 1" fastener.
- *Boning* is required for a strapless swimsuit to provide support and structure. Purchase covered ¼" wide (6 mm) plastic boning, as it provides flexible support.

Pattern Drafting Swimsuit Slopers

To develop one-piece swimsuit slopers, you combine the four-way super stretchy top foundations and the leg-line panty or boy-cut panty slopers (see Table 2.1 on p. 16). You can use the slopers to draft an assortment of swimsuit styles, some of which are illustrated in Figure 12.1. You also can use the swimwear slopers to draft the patterns for a brief two-piece **bikini, tankini, swim shorts, swim skirt, bodysuit,** and **leotard.** All these styles are part of the knit family in Table 2.2 on p. 17. Refer to Figure 12.2 to see a selection of bikini tops and a tankini. Figure 12.3 illustrates a range of bikini bottoms.

- A tankini is a two-piece bathing suit consisting of a tank top and a bikini bottom.
- Swim shorts are tightly fitted shorts styled similar to a boy-cut panty.
- A swim skirt combines a bikini bottom and a short skirt together.
- A bodysuit is a one-piece tight-fitting garment, with or without sleeves and hooks or snaps under the crotch.
- A leotard is a one-piece tight-fitting garment worn by acrobats, gymnasts, dancers, figure skaters, athletes, and circus performers.

Converting the Four-way Stretch Top Slopers and Four-way Stretch Panty Slopers into Swimwear Slopers

You can use the leg-line or boy-cut panty slopers to develop the swimsuit slopers. Refer to Chapter 11 to draft the slopers. Be sure to have on hand all the patternmaking tools illustrated in Table 3.1 on p. 20.

Draft the Patterns

Figure 12.4

1. Draw a horizontal line on pattern paper. Draw two vertical lines 7" apart and squared at the horizontal line.

2. Place the center front/back four-way super stretchy top foundations on the vertical line with waistlines (W) aligned on the horizontal line. Trace the foundations. Then label (U).

3. Place the panty waistline at (W) on the horizontal line with the center front/back placed on the vertical lines. Trace the panty slopers onto pattern paper. (It is not a concern if the top and panty waistlines are not the same length.) Label (D or L).

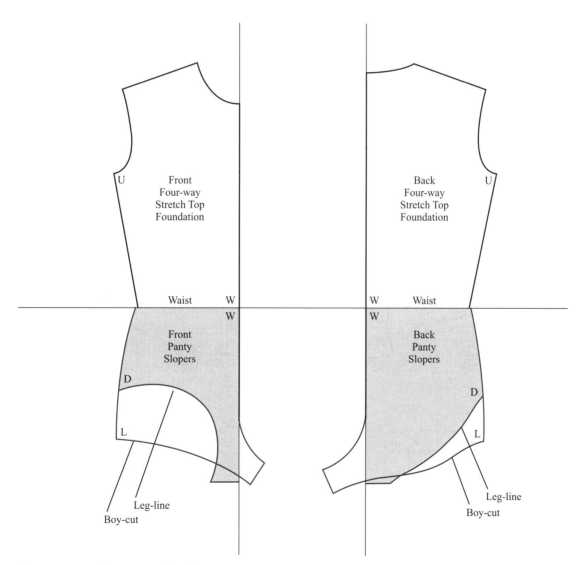

Figure 12.4 Trace four-way stretch top foundations and panty slopers

Change the Top to Make It Sleeveless

Figure 12.5

The four-way stretch top foundations in Chapter 5 were drafted for set-in sleeves. In the "Sleeveless Top Slopers" section in Chapter 6, you changed the slopers into sleeveless top slopers. Follow the same pattern drafting method here to adjust the four-way stretch top foundations into sleeveless foundations. (Refer also to Figures 6.18a and b on p. 112.)

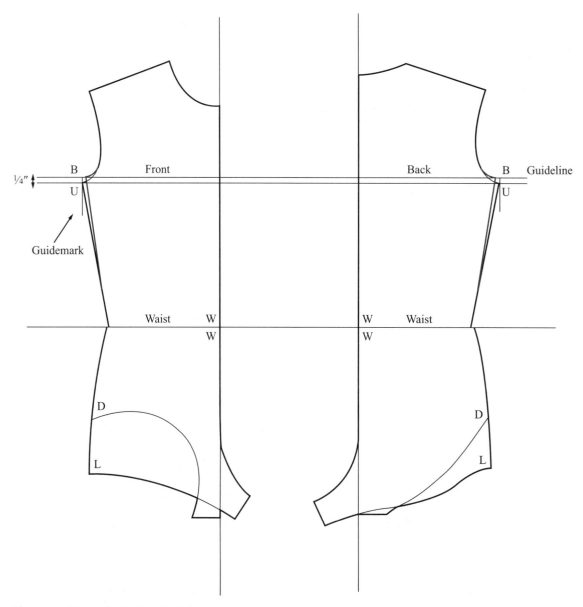

Figure 12.5 Change the top to make it sleeveless

Draw the Side Seam Curve

Figure 12.6

1. On the side seam, mark 3" down from the underarm.
2. Draw a guideline 2" above and parallel to the waistline.
3. I = On the guideline, mark ⅜" inside the side seam.
4. B-I-D = Draw the front side seam only. First, position a hip curve and draw a curved shape at the bust level to the 3" mark. Then reposition the hip curve and draw the side seam from the bustline to (I). Finally, position the hip curve and draw the hip curve.
5. Use the front pattern to shape the back side seam.

Draft the Crotch-piece

Figure 12.7

If the swimsuit is not lined, a crotch-piece is necessary for reinforcement and comfort. You join the crotch-piece with one seam to the back swimsuit only. Then you secure the crotch-piece to the front leg-line when it is elasticized.

1. Draft the crotch-piece following the instructions in Figure 11.3a on p. 366, and make a length adjustment.
2. Transfer the back crotch section (Y-Z-T-D) to the front crotch. Next, trace the final crotch-piece (E-X-Y-Z), and trace the other side as shown.
3. You also can use the crotch-piece for the boy-cut panty for the boy-cut swimsuit (see Figure 11.9 on p. 375).

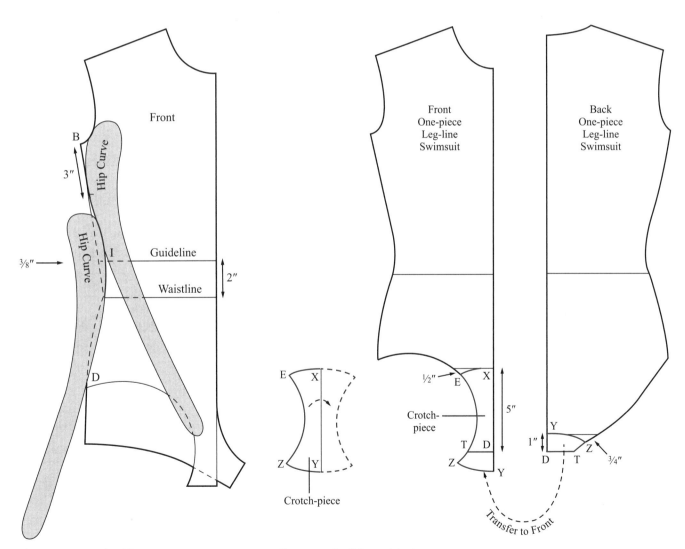

Figure 12.6 Draw the side seam curve

Figure 12.7 Draft the crotch-piece

One-piece Front-darted Swimsuit Sloper

A darted swimsuit allows more room and better coverage for larger-busted women. From the darted swimwear sloper, you can draft other styles requiring bust darts. For example, bust darts shape the triangle bikini top in Figure 12.2b. Furthermore, darts can transform into gathering under the bust.

Draft the Patterns

Figure 12.8a

1. You can develop the darted swimsuit sloper from the leg-line or boy-cut front swimsuit slopers. In this section, you use the front one-piece leg-line swimsuit sloper in Figure 12.7 as a base for developing the darted swimsuit sloper. (The apex was cross-marked on the muslin four-way stretch top foundation in Figure 5.40 on p. 93.) Trace the sloper onto pattern paper and cross-mark the apex.
2. Draw a squared guideline at the center front through the apex to the underarm.
3. B-C = Mark 2" around the armhole.
4. E = 1" below the guideline.
5. C-A-E = Draw a triangle (slash lines).

Create the Bust Dart

Figure 12.8b

1. Cut triangle C-A-E from the working pattern.
2. At (C), overlap ¼" and position the triangle until there is a 1" opening between (E-F) for the dart intake.
3. Add ¼" above the shoulder to replace the ¼" overlap.
4. Draw dart legs from (E-F) to the apex.

Fold the Dart and Draw a Side Seam Curve

Figure 12.8c

1. Mark the dart point ½" back from the apex, and redraw dart legs to the dart point.
2. Fold the bust dart to close as shown. (Leave extra pattern paper at the side seam.)
3. Draw a new side seam, equalize, and draw a blending line to the original side seam. Use a tracing wheel to replicate the same side seam shape on the dart intake.
4. Draw a blending armhole curve.
5. Fold and close the dart, and check that the front/back side seams are equal lengths.

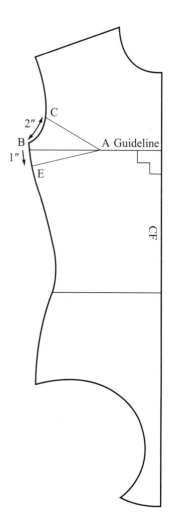

Figure 12.8a Draw guideline and slash lines

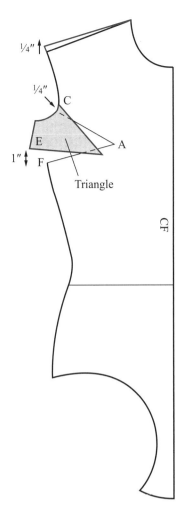

Figure 12.8b Create a dart in the side seam

Figure 12.8c Fold the dart and draw a side seam

Align the Slopers

✓ Check that when the front and back side seams are placed together they are equal lengths with a smooth armhole and leg-line curve.

✓ Check that the waistlines are aligned.

Fabric You'll Need

Purchase 1 yard of 60" wide super stretchy swimwear fabric.

a)

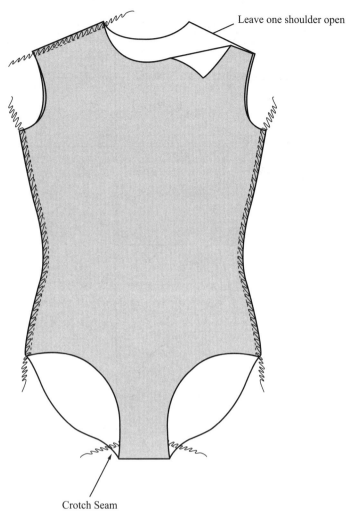

Leave one shoulder open

Crotch Seam

Figure 12.9a Stitching the muslin leg-line swimsuit

b)

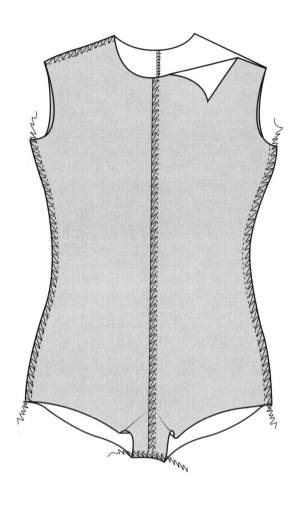

Figure 12.9b Stitching the muslin boy-cut swimsuit

Cut and Stitch

Figures 12.9a and b

1. Cut the muslin swimsuit following the layout in Figure 4.18 on p. 53.
2. Add ¼" seam allowances to the side, shoulder, and crotch seams. (There is no need to stitch the crotch-piece or elasticized openings at this stage.)
3. Stitch the muslin swimsuit. Leave one shoulder open so that you can place the swimsuit on the pant form.

Test the Fit

Figure 12.10a through c

Place each swimsuit on a pant form and pin the shoulder seam. Also ask someone to try on the swimsuit. Then pin any fitting adjustments as needed to make the suit fit tightly. (If the length needs to be shortened or lengthened, refer to the "Length Adjustment" section next.)

What to look for:

✓ Observe how the swimsuit functions when walking, crouching, and bending.
✓ Check that there is adequate length in the swimsuit.
✓ Check that there is adequate coverage over the buttocks.
✓ Check that the apex is positioned correctly.
✓ Check that the bust circle (on the darted muslin swimsuit) covers the bust area. (When the swimsuit is stretched, the circle will enlarge.)

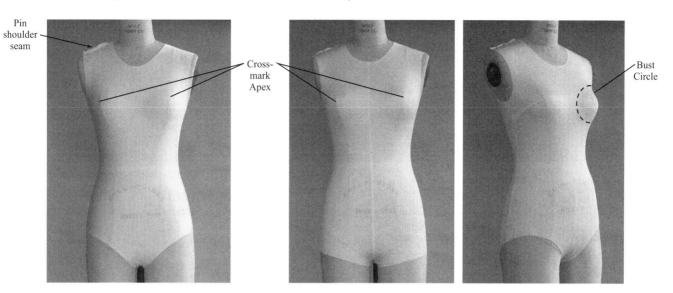

Leg-line Swimsuit   Boy-cut Swimsuit   Front-darted Swimsuit

Pin shoulder seam

Cross-mark Apex

Bust Circle

Figure 12.10 Muslin swimsuits fitted on the form. **a)** Leg-line swimsuit; **b)** boy-cut swimsuit; **c)** front-darted swimsuit

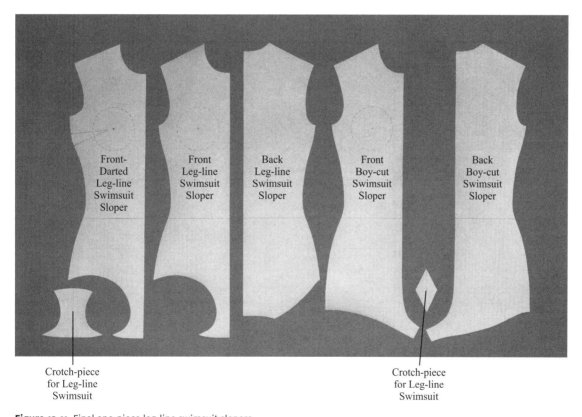

Front-Darted Leg-line Swimsuit Sloper

Front Leg-line Swimsuit Sloper

Back Leg-line Swimsuit Sloper

Front Boy-cut Swimsuit Sloper

Back Boy-cut Swimsuit Sloper

Crotch-piece for Leg-line Swimsuit

Crotch-piece for Leg-line Swimsuit

Figure 12.11 Final one-piece leg-line swimsuit slopers

Finalize the Slopers
Figure 12.11

1. Transfer paper patterns onto oak-tag, draw the waist-line, and indicate the apex by making a hole with an awl.

2. For the boy-cut swimsuit, use the crotch-piece that was drafted in Figure 11.10 on p. 375.

3. Mark the bust circle (2" radius from the apex) to indicate the bust area. This is a useful guide when lowering the neckline or drafting a bikini top or bandeau.

4. Label the slopers and record the stretch category.

Length Adjustment

The swimwear slopers are drafted for an average height. After fitting a muslin swimsuit, if the length is not accurate, you can lengthen or shorten the slopers.

1. Draw two horizontal guidelines squared at the center front/back to expand or reduce the length.
2. Divide the total length to add or reduce.

Lengthen

Figure 12.12a

The total length added to the pattern for lengthening is 2".

1. Slash/spread the patterns to expand the length.
2. Draw a new blending side seam and equalize.

Shorten

Figure 12.12b

The total length reduced on the pattern is 1".

1. Slash/overlap the section designated for reduction.
2. Draw a new blending side seam and equalize.

Swimsuit Variations

The swimsuit slopers can be used to draft a variety of modern swimsuit styles. If a particular style has sleeves (such as a bodysuit or leotard), use the swimwear slopers and the four-way stretch sleeve sloper drafted in Figures 6.16a and b on p. 110.

Some swimsuits have **inbuilt straps** that are incorporated into the swimsuit. These straps can be shoulder or halter-neck straps. Swimsuits can also have separate

a)

b)

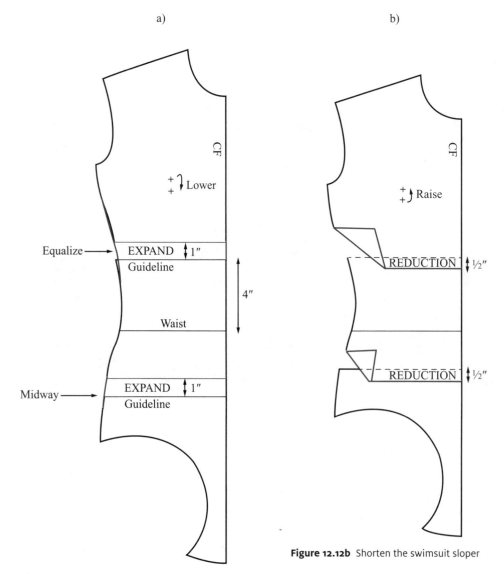

Figure 12.12a Lengthen the swimsuit sloper

Figure 12.12b Shorten the swimsuit sloper

straps that are attached during construction. Strapless swimsuits and a bandeau generally have **detachable straps** that are removable. They can be worn as shoulder straps, crisscrossed, or worn halter style. The straps are elasticized and attached to the swimsuit with S-hooks.

The "Stitching Swimsuits" section later in the chapter explains how to stitch many aspects of a swimsuit, including a lining, detachable straps, boning (for strapless swimsuits), and elasticized edges.

TABLE 12.1 Stitching order for a one-piece swimsuit

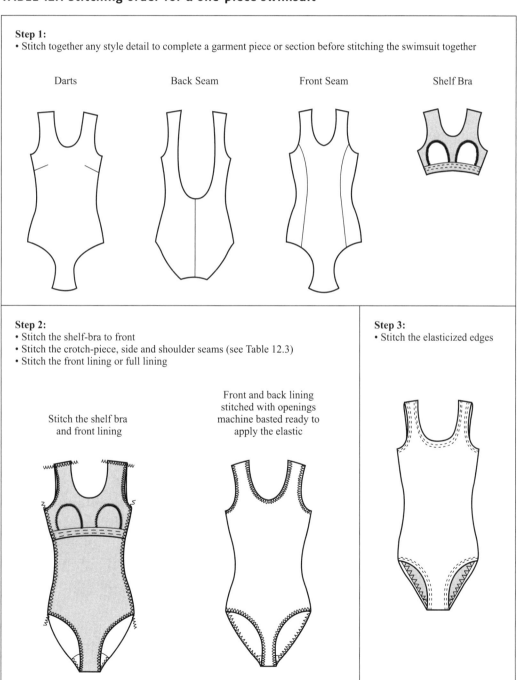

Step 1:
• Stitch together any style detail to complete a garment piece or section before stitching the swimsuit together

Darts   Back Seam   Front Seam   Shelf Bra

Step 2:
• Stitch the shelf-bra to front
• Stitch the crotch-piece, side and shoulder seams (see Table 12.3)
• Stitch the front lining or full lining

Stitch the shelf bra and front lining

Front and back lining stitched with openings machine basted ready to apply the elastic

Step 3:
• Stitch the elasticized edges

One-piece Tank Swimsuit

The tank swimsuit has inbuilt straps and is a classic style. The hi-cut leg-line will elongate the length of the legs, and the shaped center back seam will give a superior fit. All the openings are elasticized.

Draft the Patterns
Figure 12.13a

1. Trace the front and back one-piece swimsuit slopers, draw the bust circle, and label the underarm (B).
2. I = On the shoulder, mark 1¼" in from the front/back neckline and lower ½".

3. I-H = Mark the width of the shoulder straps on the front/back. Then draw a shoulder line.

Front

1. I-E = Draw the neckline shape squared at the center front.
2. B-C = Lower the armhole ½".
3. H-C = Draw the front armhole.
4. D-F = 1½" on the side seam.
5. F-Z = Draw the hi-cut leg-line as shown.

Back

1. Draw a guideline from the center back neckline to 1" within the center back. Label (J).
2. G-J = 2".
3. I-G = Draw the shoulder strap parallel to the center back before curving the low back to the squared line at (G).
4. H-C = Draw the back armhole parallel to the neckline and curve to the underarm.
5. G-J-Y = Draw the shaped center back seam.
6. Draw a grainline on the back pattern parallel to the center back.

Align the Patterns
Figure 12.13b

✓ Check that when the front/back shoulder seams are placed together a smooth armhole and neckline curve are drawn.
✓ Check that when the side seams are placed together the leg-line has a smooth transitioning line drawn from front to back. Adjust if necessary.

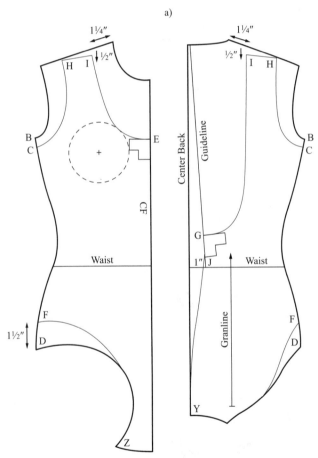

Figure 12.13a Draft a one-piece tank swimsuit

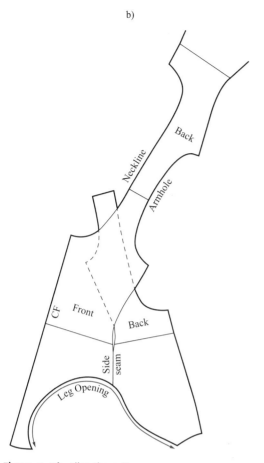

b)

Back

Neckline

Armhole

CF   Front

Back

Side seam

Leg Opening

Figure 12.13b Align the patterns

Cut, Stitch, and Fit
Figures 12.14a and b

Purchase 1 yard of 60" wide super stretchy swimwear fabric.

1. Cut the swimsuit following the layout in Figure 4.19 on p. 54.
2. Add ¼" seam allowances to the side, shoulder, and crotch seams.
3. Stitch the shoulder, crotch, and side seams.
4. Place the swimsuit on the pant form. Pin any fitting adjustments as needed to make the suit fit properly. Mark these adjustments on the pattern before cutting the final swimsuit.

Front   Back

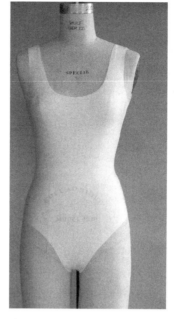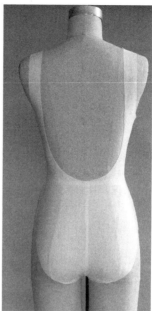

Figures 12.14a and b One-piece tank swimsuit fitted on the form

What to look out for:

✓ Shape/depth of the front and back necklines and armholes—adjust if gaping.
✓ Center back seam—adjust if gaping at the neckline edge.

Finalize the Patterns

Refer to Figure 4.19 on p. 54 to see the final one-piece tank swimsuit patterns.

1. Add ¼" seam allowances.
2. Add an allowance for the elasticized edges ⅛" wider than the elastic width.
3. Label the patterns, draw the grainlines, and record the number of pattern pieces to cut. (See Figure 4.19 on p. 54.)

One-piece Cutaway Halter Swimsuit

The one-piece swimsuit exposes the skin with its cutaway lines. You can outline the cutaway shape and neckline according to your particular design. All the openings of the swimsuit must be elasticized to ensure a close fit.

Draft the Pattern

Figure 12.15a

1. Trace the front leg-line darted swimsuit; then draw dart (A-X-Y), the waistline, and the bust circle.
2. E = Square a line at the center front to the side seam (3" below the apex).
3. A-B = Draw a new dart position moved ¼" toward the center front.
4. Outline the neckline shape to the shoulder tip.
5. H-C = Draw a ¼" section to be removed to contour the neckline.
6. B-G = Outline the cutaway section. (In this draft, [G] is approximately 1¼" below the hipline and squared to the side seam.)
7. X-Y = Draw the armhole and seam join.
8. Draw the shoulder strap from the shoulder tip to the required length/width.
9. Align the side seam of the back swimsuit sloper to the front at (G). Trace to the waist.
10. Outline the hi-cut leg-line.

Dart Manipulation

Figure 12.15b

In this section, you transfer the dart intake to the under bustline (B).

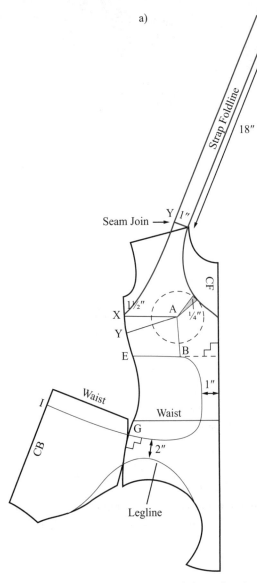

Figure 12.15a Draft a one-piece cutaway halter swimsuit

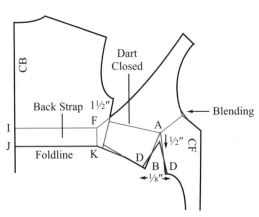

Figure 12.15b Dart manipulation: transfer the side seam dart under the bustline

1. Cut lines (X-A and B-A), but leave 1/16" intact at (A). Next, close the dart intake (X-Y). (Refer to Figure 12.8b.) Now transfer the dart intake to (B).
2. Place lines (H-A and C-A) together to remove the ¼" (see Figure 12.15c). Draw a blending neckline.
3. B-D = Mark ⅛" out from dart legs. Then lower the apex ½".
4. A-D = Draw new dart legs to the dart point.
5. Align the back side seam to the front as shown.
6. Extend the front armhole to (F).
7. F-I-J-K = Outline the back strap.
8. K-B = Fold the dart closed and draw a blending under bustline.

Cut, Stitch, and Fit

Figures 12.16a and b

To cut, stitch, and fit the cutaway halter swimsuit, follow the instructions in the previous "One-piece Tank Swimsuit" section.

Finalize the Pattern

Figure 12.17

1. Trace the front and back from the working patterns. Trace the strap patterns, turn, and trace the other side.
2. Add ¼" seam allowances.
3. Add an allowance for the elasticized edges ⅛" wider than the elastic width.
4. Label the patterns, draw the grainlines, and document the number of pattern pieces to cut. (See Figure 12.17.)

Front   Back

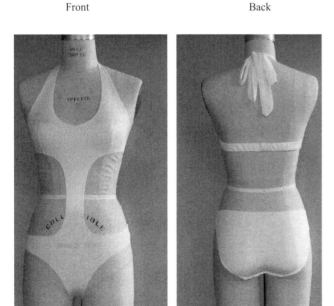

Figure 12.16a and b One-piece cutaway halter swimsuit fitted on the form

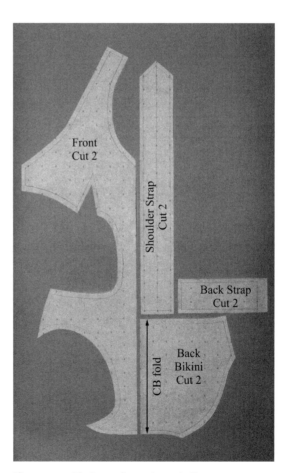

Front
Cut 2

Shoulder Strap
Cut 2

Back Strap
Cut 2

CB fold

Back
Bikini
Cut 2

Figure 12.17 Final one-piece cutaway halter swimsuit patterns

Cropkini

A cropkini is cut midway between the bust and the waist. It is not only for swimming but also for wearing when working out at the gym. You draft the cropkini in this section as a basic shape. The style can be unadorned or designed with a bra-top and/or other design lines. (Refer to Figures 11.34a through c and Figure 11.37 to draft a bra-top.)

Draft the Patterns

Figure 12.18

The front and back patterns are the same; the only difference is the neckline. Draft the front pattern first.

1. Align the front/back shoulders of the swimsuit slopers together. Then trace to the waist as shown.
2. A–X = Mark 4½" below the apex.
3. H–X–B = Draw the *front* under bustline squared at the center front to the side seam.
4. F–E–G = Draw the front/back neckline.
5. C–D = Draw the *front* armhole curve.
6. Fold the pattern across the shoulder, align the center front/back together, and trace the back cropkini.

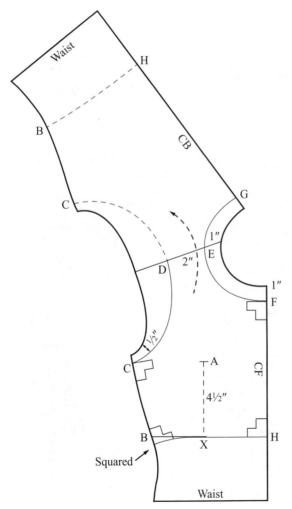

Figure 12.18 Draft the cropkini patterns

PATTERN TIP 12.1: CROPKINI WITH CUTOUT BACK

You can leave the back of the cropkini as a basic shape or designed with a cutout back, as shown in Figure 12.20.

1. Begin by drawing a squared line midway on the center back (G-H) to the armhole (K).
2. Draw the cutout shape, overlapping the lines at the armhole at (L-K).
3. To finalize, trace the upper and lower back patterns. (See Figure 12.19.)

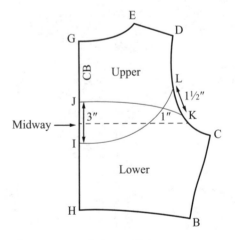

Figure 12.19 Draft the cropkini cutaway back patterns

Cut, Stitch, and Fit

Figure 12.20

Purchase ½ yard of 60" wide super stretchy swimwear fabric.

1. Cut the cropkini following the layout in Figure 4.18 on p. 53.
2. Add ¼" seam allowances to the side and shoulder seams.
3. Staystitch the overlap section on the armholes. Stitch the shoulder and side seams.
4. Place the cropkini on the form. Pin any fitting adjustments as needed. Mark these adjustments on the pattern.

What to look out for:

✓ Shape/depth of the front and back neckline and armhole—Adjust if gaping.
✓ Back cutaway shape—Adjust if gaping.

STITCHING TIP 12.2: STITCHING THE CROPKINI

All the openings of a swimsuit must be elasticized, including the cutout section on the back. Refer to the "Stitching Swimsuits" section to stitch an elasticized finish.

Front   Back

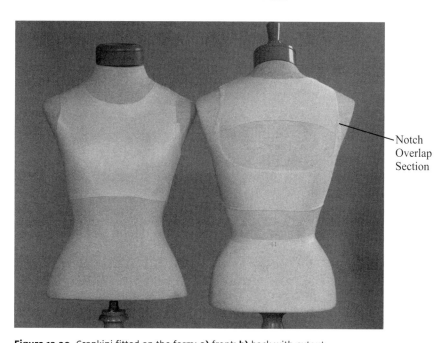

Notch Overlap Section

Figure 12.20 Cropkini fitted on the form; **a)** front; **b)** back with cutout

Tankini

A tankini can be a variety of styles: strapless, fitted, flared, draped, ruched, or tiered. The length finishes on the high-hip. You can draft the tankini patterns from the top patterns in Chapter 6 or the cami patterns in Chapter 11. For example, the camisoles illustrated in Figures 11.1f through j on p. 363 could all be tankinis if they were constructed from swimwear fabric.

Bandeau

There are many design options for a **bandeau**. For example, the front (or side) can be gathered, it can be strapless or have straps, or it can tie in the front like the bandeau ties in Figure 12.25. You learn how to draft the gathered front bandeau pattern using the slash/spread pattern drafting technique after drafting the basic bandeau patterns.

Draft the Patterns

Figures 12.21a and b

You draft the front and back bandeau patterns as one pattern piece and then separate them into front and back patterns. The first patterns you draft here are the lining patterns. You then draft the outer bandeau patterns from the lining patterns.

1. Align the front/back sloper side seams together. Trace the shoulder to the waist, as shown. Then draw the bust circle (Figure 12.21a).
2. A-X = Mark 4" below the apex.
3. H-X = Draw the *front* under bustline squared at the center front to the side seam. Square another line at the side seam and label (B).
4. E-B = Draw a line squared at the center back to (B). Draw a blending line to (H).
5. F-C-D = Draw the front neckline curved around the bust circle to the center back.
6. Trace two copies of the front/back bandeau patterns. Label one set as "Front/Back Bandeau Lining" patterns.
7. To the other set of patterns, add ⅛" to the upper and lower edges of the pattern. This modification makes the lining patterns slightly smaller to ensure that the seamlines stay rolled to the lining side after the bandeau is stitched (see Figure 12.21b).

a)

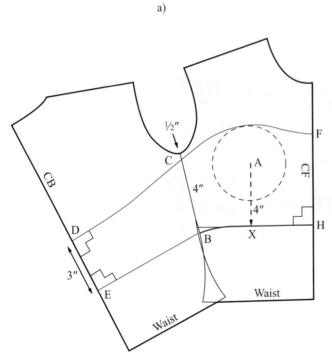

Figure 12.21a Draft the bandeau lining patterns

b)

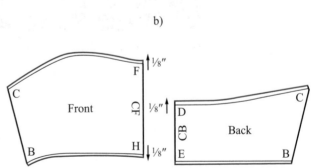

Figure 12.21b Draft the bandeau outer patterns

Cut, Stitch, and Fit
Figures 12.22a and b

Purchase ½ yard of 60" wide super stretchy swimwear fabric. The bandeau and bikini bottom are illustrated as a two-piece swimsuit. At this point, only the bandeau top is discussed. The bikini bottom is discussed in a later section.

1. To cut the bandeau, add ¼" seam allowances to the side seams and stitch.
2. Fit the bandeau on the form, and pin any fitting adjustments as needed to make the top fit snugly. Transfer these adjustments to the patterns.

What to look for:
✓ Check the length/width of the bandeau. It may look generous, but after it is stitched, elasticized, and turned to the correct side, it will narrow.
✓ Mark the placement of the detachable straps following the form princess line, and measure the strap length.

Finalize the Patterns
Figure 12.23

1. Add ¼" seam allowance to the side seams.
2. Add an allowance for the elasticized edges ⅛" wider than the elastic width.
3. Label the front/back patterns, draw the grainlines, and document the number of pieces to cut.

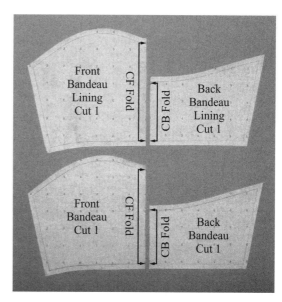

Figure 12.23 Final patterns for the bandeau

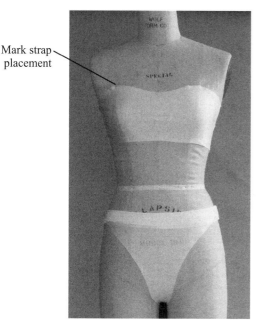
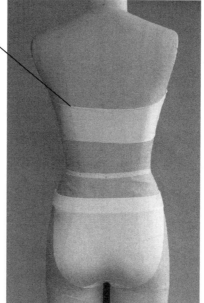

Front   Back

Mark strap placement   Mark strap placement

Figures 12.22a and b Bandeau and bikini with waistband fitted on the form

Bandeau with Gathered Front

You draft the bandeau with front gathering from the lining bandeau pattern shown in Figures 12.23a and b. In this case, you add additional length to the center front pattern for gathering. The gathering can be formed by stitching stretched elastic to the front seam; or the tie, when it is attached, will create gathering. (To stitch the elastic, refer to Figure 4.32 on p. 64.)

Draft the Pattern

Figures 12.24a and b

1. Trace a copy of the front bandeau lining pattern shown in Figure 12.23.
2. Draw the slash lines and label, as shown in Figure 12.24a.

3. Slash/spread the pattern, as shown in Figure 12.24b.
4. Draw a blending center front line.
5. Draw a grainline parallel to panel (2) center front.
6. Trace two copies of the pattern. Label one set as "Front Gathered Bandeau Lining."
7. To the other set of patterns, add ⅛" to the upper and lower edges, as shown in Figure 12.21b. Label this pattern "Front Gathered Bandeau."

Draft the Front Tie

Figure 12.24c

1. Draft half the tie-strap pattern with a curve. (The curve makes the tie easier to serge.)
2. Trace the other side of the strap as shown.

a)

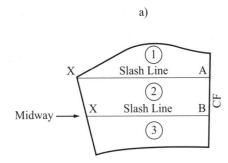

Figure 12.24a Draw the slash lines

c)

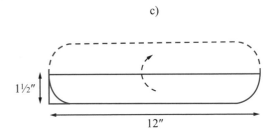

Figure 12.24c Draft the front tie

b)

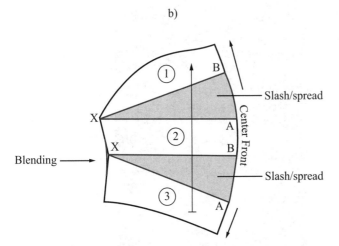

Figure 12.24b Slash/spread the pattern

Cut, Stitch, and Fit

Figure 12.25

The gathered bandeau with tie and swim skirt are illustrated as a two-piece swimsuit. At this point, only the gathered bandeau is fitted. The swim skirt is fitted in a later section.

1. Cut, stitch, and fit the bandeau. When the bandeau is fitted on the form, check that there is sufficient length for gathering. Also check that the tie is the correct length.

2. To finalize the patterns, add ¼" seam allowance to the side seam and tie edges. Add a ⅜" seam allowance for the elasticized edges.

STITCHING TIP 12.3: STITCHING THE BANDEAU

- The front and back top and lower edges of the bandeau must be elasticized.
- A tie-strap does not need to be elasticized.

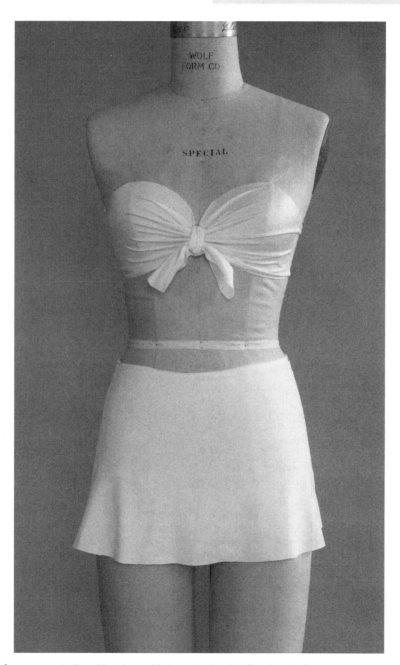

Figure 12.25 Gathered bandeau with tie and swim skirt fitted on the form

Strapless

The strapless swimsuit has boy-cut panty legs and is princess line from the under bust seam to the leg-line. A bust dart is incorporated into the bandeau. (You also can use leg-line slopers.)

Draft the Pattern

Figure 12.26a

1. Trace the front/back slopers and draw the waistline.
2. Draft the front/back bandeau top patterns, mark the apex, and label. (Refer to Figure 12.21a.)
3. T-H = ¾". Draw a curved under bustline.
4. N and M = Midway between T-B under bust and E-B on the back.
5. Draw a guideline parallel to the center front/back from (N and M) to the leg-line.

6. X-A-N-J-K = Draw the front princess seam through the apex.
7. M-J-O = Draw the back princess seam.

Create the Bust Dart

Figure 12.26b

1. Trace the front bandeau pattern (F-T-B-C).
2. Draw and cut line (X-A-N) to separate into two pattern pieces.
3. At (X), overlap the neck edge, and spread the under bust seam at (N) for the dart intake.
4. Mark a lowered dart point below the apex.
5. Draw new dart legs, fold the dart closed, and trace to replicate the same shape as the under bust seam. Draw a blending neckline at (X).
6. Add ¼" beyond (C) at the side seam.

a)

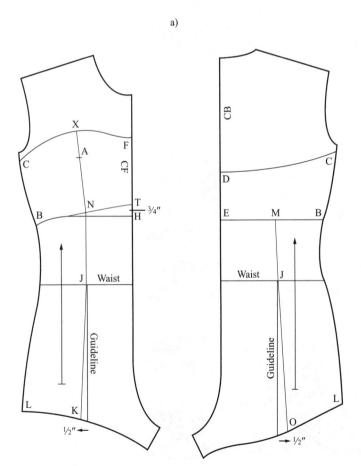

Figure 12.26a Draft a strapless swimsuit

b)

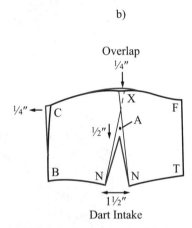

Figure 12.26b Create a bust dart

Finalize the Patterns

Figure 12.27

1. Trace each pattern piece from the working pattern.
2. The front/back bandeau patterns are the lining pattern. Draft the outer bandeau patterns. (Refer to Figure 12.21b.)
3. Label the pattern pieces, draw the grainlines, and add the appropriate seam allowances.
4. Cut two of each pattern piece.

Bikini Tops

There are many varieties of bikini tops to suit everyone's taste. Bikinis can be brief or offer more coverage. A bikini can be darted or gathered to accommodate the bust shape, as shown in Figures 12.2b and c. (Refer to the "Stop: What Do I Do If. . ." section to draft the pattern for the gathered triangle bikini top.)

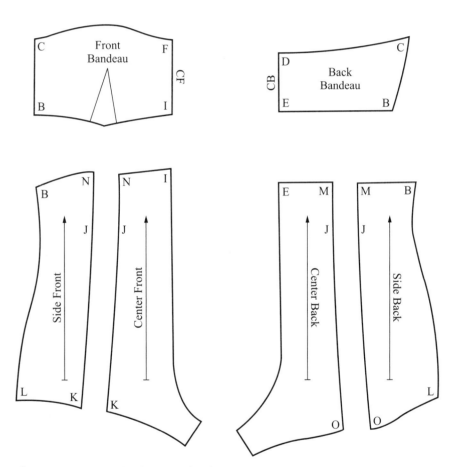

Figure 12.27 Final strapless boy-cut swimsuit patterns

Darted Triangle

The bust darts in the triangle bikini top allow room for the bust and soft molded cups. The halter straps tie at the back neckline. The lower edge of the bikini can be finished with an elasticized binding or elasticized band. You draft this bikini pattern from the front darted swimsuit sloper.

Dart Manipulation

Figure 12.28

1. Transfer the position of the dart from the side seam to the waist.
2. A-B = Draw the new dart position. Slant the line ½" in toward the center front.
3. Place (X-Y) together and close the dart. The dart intake is now located between (B-B).

Draft the Lining Pattern

Figures 12.29a through c

The first pattern you draft is the lining pattern.

1. Draw a guideline through the center of the dart to the shoulder (see Figure 12.29a).
2. Mark ½" below the bust circle on each dart leg. Draw lines squared at the dart leg to the center front (F) and side seam (D).
3. A-B = Draw new dart legs ¼" out from the original dart legs.
4. E = 1" above the bust circle. Square out ¼" on each side of the guideline.
5. D-E and F-E = Draw an outward curved triangle as shown.
6. Fit the triangle on the form. Pin the excess if the neckline is gaping. (In this case, you remove ½" excess by transferring it to the dart intake.) Then draw a new blending neckline from (E-F) (see Figure 12.29b).

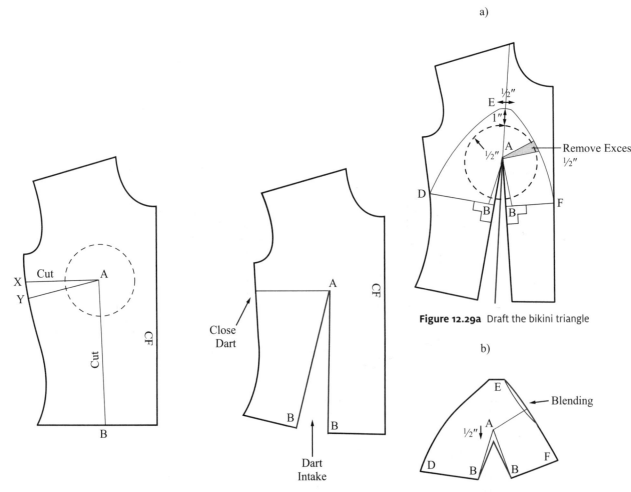

Figure 12.29a Draft the bikini triangle

Figure 12.29b Half-inch excess removed

Figure 12.28 Dart manipulation: transfer the side seam dart to the waistline

7. Mark the dart point ½" below the apex. Draw new dart legs.
8. Fold the dart closed, and draw a straight line across the lower edge (see Figure 12.29c).
9. Draw the grainline from the dart point to the center of (E).

Draft the Outer Triangle

Figure 12.29d

1. Trace the triangle lining pattern.
2. Draw a line from (E) to ⅛" out from (F and D).

c)

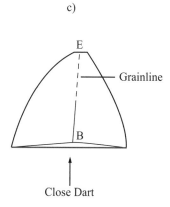

Figure 12.29c Close the dart and reshape the lower edge

d)

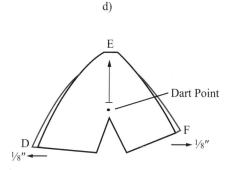

Figure 12.29d Draft the outer triangle bikini

3. Draft the shoulder tie-strap pattern 18" long and 2" wide.

Draft the Binding

Figure 12.30

The bikini triangle has a narrow binding to finish the bottom edge. After drafting the binding/band pattern, notch where the side front joins the binding (or band). You cut both patterns on the lengthwise grain (see Figure 4.20 on p. 55). Refer to Figures 12.32a and b to stitch the binding.

1. For the *under bust* binding, draft the pattern length ¾" shorter than the length of the front bikini (side seam to side seam). To this length, add the tie length approximate to the form or body size. (In this draft, you add 16" for each tie/strap).
2. The width of the *binding* pattern is 1¾". (This width includes the seam allowance.)

Supplies You'll Need

Purchase ⅝ yard of 60" swimwear fabric. Use the actual fabric to achieve an *exact* fit.

Cut and Stitch

1. Cut the bikini top following the layout in Figure 4.20 on p. 55.
2. Add ¼" seam allowances to the pattern edges, including the dart legs.
3. To achieve an accurate fit, stitch the bikini following Stitching Tip 12.4.

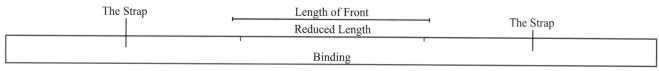

Figure 12.30 Draft the binding pattern

Test the Fit

Figure 12.31

The two-piece bikini is illustrated here. At this point, only the top bikini is discussed. The bikini bottom is discussed in a later section. Place the bikini on the form. Then pin any fitting adjustments to make the bikini top fit snugly.

What to look for:

✓ Dart placement—If not positioned correctly, mark a new dart point.

✓ Neckline and armholes—Pin any gaping.

✓ Length of straps—Adjust if necessary.

Finalize the Patterns

1. Label the patterns and write the number of pattern pieces to cut (see Figure 4.20 on p. 55).

2. Add a ¼" seam allowance to the pattern for the band to be joined. A binding finish does not require a seam allowance added to the pattern.

3. Label the pattern "CF."

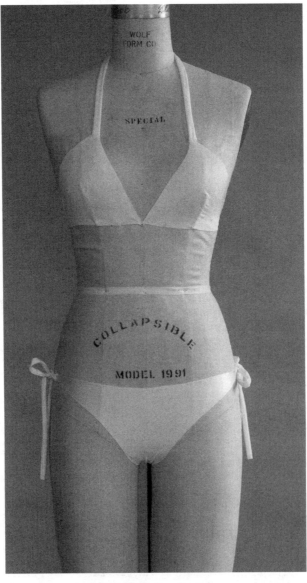

Figure 12.31 Two-piece bikini fitted on the form

STITCHING TIP 12.4: STITCHING THE BIKINI TOP

Refer to the Stitching Order in Table 12.2 to stitch the bikini. A bikini can have soft molded cups inserted between the swim fabric and the lining. Choose a cup shape to reflect the triangle shape of the bikini. The bikini can also be designed without cups. An elasticized binding is applied to the lower edge to ensure a tight fit. You cut the binding and elastic the same length. (To stitch the shoulder straps, look ahead to the "Straps" section.)

1. Stitch and insert shoulder straps to the outer triangle at (E) (see Figure 12.32a).
2. With correct sides together, stitch the outer edges of the bikini and lining pieces together. Stitch clear elastic to the seam allowance (not stretched) as shown.
3. Turn the bikini to the correct side and insert the bra cups (if applicable).
4. Serge the binding to the lower edge (see Figure 12.32b).
5. Place the elastic on the seam allowance, and apply with zigzag stitches. Wrap the binding around the elastic, pin, and topstitch with twin needles.

a)

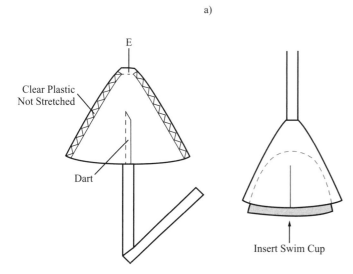

Figure 12.32a Stitch the bikini and insert bra cups

b)

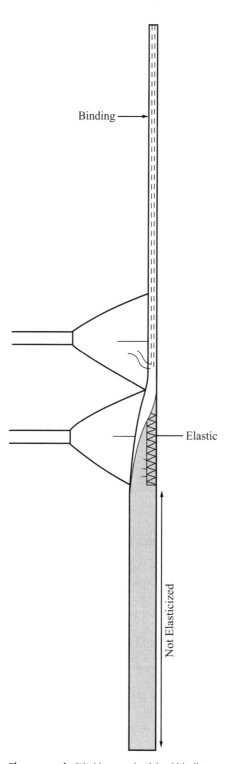

Figure 12.32b Stitching an elasticized binding

TABLE 12.2 Stitching order for a bikini top

Step 1:
• Stitch any style detail to complete garment piece(s) before stitching the bikini together

Darts   Gathers   Seams

Step 2:
• Stitch the separate straps (and elasticize if applicable)
• Attach the straps and stitch lining
> OR
• Stitch the straps as a continuation of the edge finish

Separate straps   Straps and lining attached   Straps as a continuation of the edge finish

Step 3:
• Stitch the elasticized finish to the lower edge of bikini

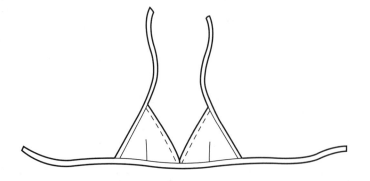

Bikini Bottoms

A bikini bottom can range from full pelvic coverage to a revealing thong (see Figures 12.3a through c). Begin by drafting the pattern for the basic bikini in Figure 12.3a. A bikini bottom can be lined or unlined. If you choose unlined, draft the crotch-piece in Figure 12.7 to fit the bikini shape.

1. To cut the bikini, refer to Figure 4.16 on p. 52.
2. To stitch a bikini bottom, follow the Stitching Order in Table 12.3.
3. To elasticize the waist and leg openings, refer to the "Elasticized Edges" section.

TABLE 12.3 Stitching order for bikini bottom

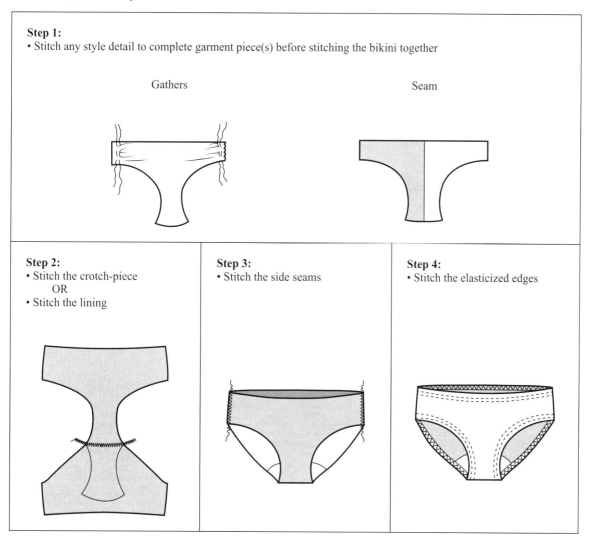

Step 1:
• Stitch any style detail to complete garment piece(s) before stitching the bikini together

Gathers

Seam

Step 2:
• Stitch the crotch-piece
  OR
• Stitch the lining

Step 3:
• Stitch the side seams

Step 4:
• Stitch the elasticized edges

Triangle with Waistband

Figure 12.33

The basic bikini pattern provides an outline that you can use to draft the triangle bikini with waistband shown in Figure 12.3c.

1. Trace the front/back leg-line swimsuit slopers for the low-rise waist (see Figure 12.11).
2. Draw a squared line at the waist/side seam (W1), and blend to the low-rise waist.
3. On the *front*, draw a straight guideline from the 2" waist mark to the leg-line. Next, curve the leg-line as shown.
4. On the *back*, draw a 1" squared line down from the 1" waist mark. Use a hip curve to draw the curved leg-line as shown.
5. Draft the waistband pattern the total length of the front/back waist. Do not reduce the length. The elastic is cut 1" shorter than the finished waistband length.

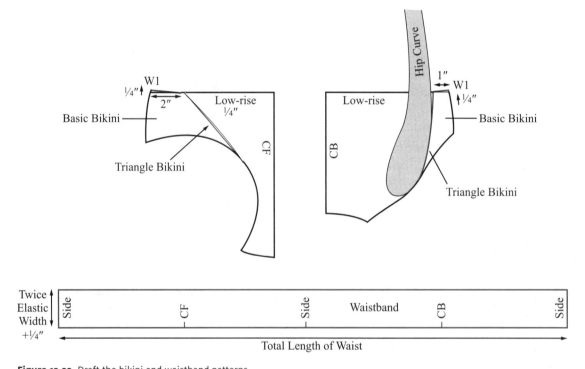

Figure 12.33 Draft the bikini and waistband patterns

Cut, Stitch, and Fit

Stitch the elasticized waistband on the muslin bikini to check the fit around the waistline. (Refer to Figures 9.59a and b on p. 290 to stitch the waistband.). Next, fit the bikini bottom that was previously shown on the pant form in Figure 12.22a.

What to look for:

✓ Check that there is adequate coverage (in length/width) on the front bikini.

✓ Check that there is adequate coverage over the buttocks.

✓ Check that the waistband/elastic is the correct length.

Finalize the Patterns

Figure 12.34

1. Draw the grainlines and add a seam allowance.

2. Label the patterns, and document the number of patterns to cut for a lined bikini.

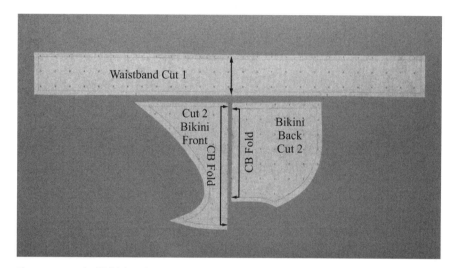

Figure 12.34 Final bikini and waistband patterns

Triangle with Ties

Figures 12.35a through c

The bikini bottom you draft in this section has binding ties, as illustrated in Figure 12.3b. In Figure 12.31, the bikini with binding ties is shown as a two-piece bikini. The ties do not need to be elasticized. The remaining bikini edges must be elasticized, however. To begin, draft the basic front/back bikini patterns shown in Figure 12.32. Only the front pattern is changed.

1. Draw a squared line down from the *front* waist to the width of the ties (Figure 12.35a).
2. Draft the binding tie-strap with enough length to tie into a bow (see Figure 12.35b). To draft the band tie, refer to Figure 12.35c.
3. Draw the grainlines and add a seam allowance.
4. Label the patterns and document the number of patterns to cut for a lined bikini and document the number of patterns to cut.

a)

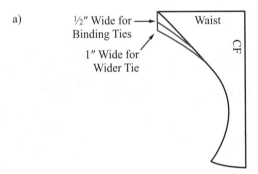

½″ Wide for Binding Ties

1″ Wide for Wider Tie

Waist

CF

Figure 12.35a Draft the front bikini pattern

b)

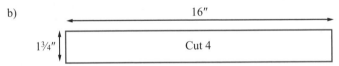

16″

1¾″

Cut 4

Figure 12.35b Draft the binding tie

c)

7″

2″

Cut 4

Figure 12.35c Draft the band tie

Swim Shorts

You draft swim shorts patterns from the boy-cut panty patterns drafted in Chapter 11.

1. To cut the shorts in swim fabric, refer to Figure 4.17 on p. 53.
2. To stitch the swim shorts, refer to the Stitching Order in Table 11.2.

Swim Skirt

The panty and short skirt combined together create the swim skirt. The skirt can sit on the natural waistline or on the hips (mid-rise). (Refer to Figure 4.16 on p. 418.) In this pattern, the skirt is flared to add extra length to the hemline to prevent the skirt from feeling tight around the thighs. The panty does not require a lining; therefore, you should draft the crotch-piece shown in Figure 12.7.

Draft the Pattern

Figures 12.36a and b

You use the skirt pattern for the front and back.

1. Trace the front/back swimsuit slopers to the waist (see Figure 12.36a).
2. Draft an A-line skirt to the required length. Add ½" out from the center front hemline. Draw the new center front squared at the waist and hemline.
3. Slash/spread the pattern, as shown in Figure 12.36b.

a)

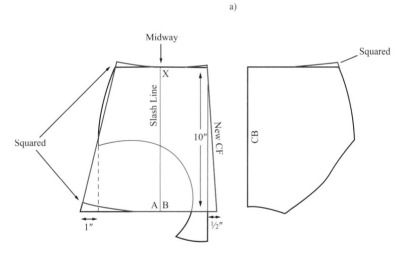

Figure 12.36a Draft a swim skirt

b)

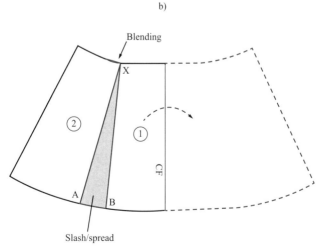

Figure 12.36b Slash/spread the pattern

Cut, Stitch, and Fit

Purchase ¾ yard of 60" wide swimwear fabric. Add ¼" seam allowances to the side and crotch seams to stitch the swim skirt. The swim skirt is shown on the form in Figure 12.25 as a two-piece swimsuit. At this point, only the swim skirt is discussed. Place the skirt on the form, and pin any fitting alterations. Mark these adjustments on the pattern before cutting the final swim skirt.

What to look out for:

✓ Check the fit of the skirt around the hip/thigh area. (If the skirt is tight, it will ride up when it is worn.)

✓ Check that the skirt has enough length.

Finalize the Patterns

Figure 12.37

You can stitch the waist with a turned and topstitched edge using ½" wide elastic (or stitch an elasticized waistband).

1. For a turned and topstitched finish, add a waist allowance the width of the elastic plus ⅛". Draw a directional seamline on the side seam of the waist allowance.
2. Add ¼" seam allowances for stitching seams.
3. Add an allowance for the elasticized leg openings ⅛" wider than the elastic width (including the legline of the crotch-piece).
4. Label the patterns, draw the grainlines, and document the number of pattern pieces to cut.

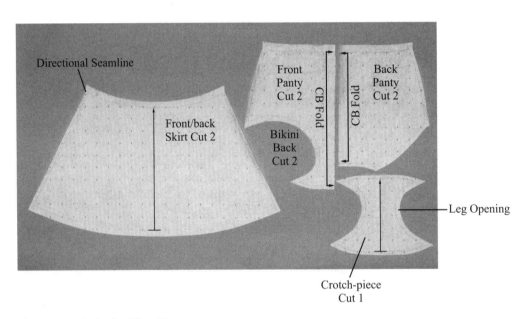

Figure 12.37 Final swim skirt patterns

Stitching Swimsuits

To stitch a one-piece swimsuit and a two-piece bikini, refer to the Stitching Orders in Tables 12.1 through 12.3. One of the most important features of stitching a swimsuit is to elasticize the openings. This section explains how to stitch many facets of a swimsuit, including the elasticized openings.

Lining Swimsuits

Lining improves the fit and helps maintain the shape of a swimsuit. A swimsuit can be fully lined (front and back), partially lined (front only), or not lined at all. (If a swimsuit is not lined, it needs a crotch-piece. A crotch-piece is not necessary, however, when the swimsuit is lined.) Use a lining fabric with equal stretch to the swim fabric, or use another layer of the actual swimsuit fabric as a lining. Cut the lining using the swimsuit pattern pieces.

Front Lining

Figure 12.38

After the crotch seam is stitched, it will be hidden.

1. Place correct sides of the front and back together. Place the back swimsuit facing up.
2. Place the correct side of the front lining over the wrong side of the back.
3. Align the three fabric layers together, and stitch the crotch seam.
4. Turn the lining over the front.
5. Machine or hand baste the edges together, and continue to stitch the swimsuit.

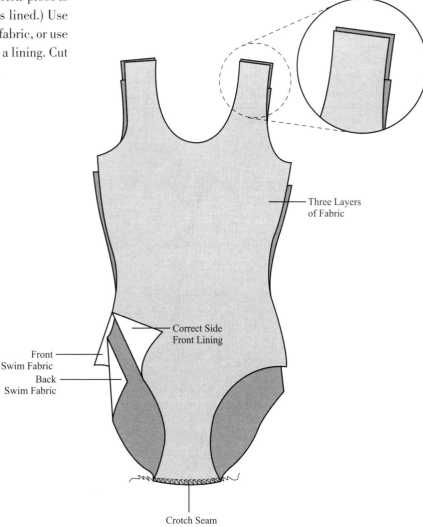

Figure 12.38 Stitching the front lining

Front and Back Lining

Figure 12.39

The swim fabric and lining are layered, and the seams are stitched to produce enclosed hidden seams.

1. Lay the correct sides of the front and back *swimsuit* pieces together.
2. Place the correct sides of the front and back *lining* pieces together.
3. Place the lining pieces over the swimsuit pieces with the wrong sides of the *back* swimsuit and lining placed together.
4. Align the edges and pin the four fabric layers together.
5. Serge the shoulder, side, and crotch seams together.
6. Turn the front lining over to cover the front swimsuit. Then turn the swimsuit to the correct side.
7. Machine or hand baste the edges together. Next, stitch the elasticized openings.

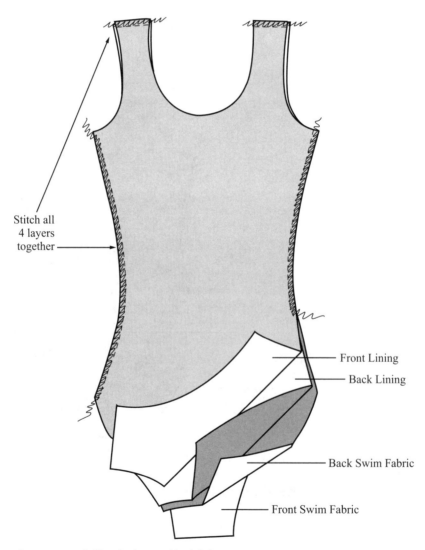

Stitch all 4 layers together

Front Lining

Back Lining

Back Swim Fabric

Front Swim Fabric

Figure 12.39 Stitching the front and back lining

Crotch-Piece

A crotch-piece is required when the swimsuit does not have a lining. To stitch the crotch-piece, refer to the Stitching Order in Table 12.3.

Straps

Different types of straps can be part of a modern swimsuit. If the straps are integral to the fit of the swimsuit or bikini top, they *must* be elasticized. For example, in Figure 12.1b, the *back* strap (with S-hook) is elasticized because it is integral to how the swimsuit fits. The *halter* neck strap is not elasticized. Additionally, the halter tie-straps of the bikinis in Figures 12.2b and c are not elasticized because the straps are not integral to how these bikinis fit. For the swimsuit in Figure 12.1b, you place a seam where the strap is joined. This is necessary when the armhole is elasticized and the strap is not. In this case, you draft a separate shoulder strap pattern. (Refer to Figure 12.15.)

You can use several methods to stitch elasticized straps. First, draft the strap pattern double the elastic width plus a seam allowance. Then cut the strap on the lengthwise grain (see Figure 4.20 on p. 55).

Elasticized

Figures 12.40a and b

Narrow and wise straps can be used for shoulder and back straps of a swimsuit.

1. Use ⅜" wide rubber elastic for *narrow* straps. Cut the fabric 1½" wide to the required length.
2. Use 1" wide braided elastic for *wide* straps. Cut the fabric 2½" wide to the required length.
3. Fold the fabric with correct sides together. Lay the elastic over the wrong side.
4. Align the fabric and elastic edges together. Zigzag stitch or serge a ¼" seam.
5. Turn the strap to the correct side.

Nonelasticized

Figures 12.40c and d

Nonelasticized straps can be used for shoulder straps and tie-straps. The tie sections on the top and bottom bikinis in Figures 12.2b and 12.3b do not need to be elasticized.

1. Cut the strap width double the finished width plus a seam allowance for serging a ¼" seam.
2. Place the correct sides of the fabric together, serge the seam, and turn the strap to the correct side.

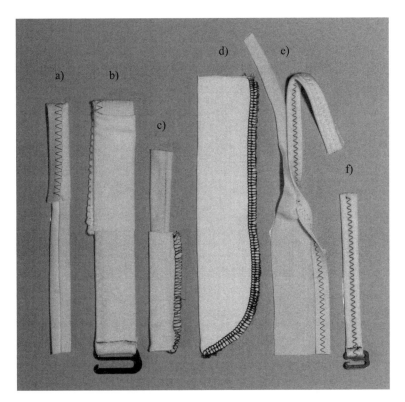

Figure 12.40 **a)** Elasticized narrow straps; **b)** Elasticized wide straps; **c)** Nonelasticized narrow strap; **d)** Nonelasticized tie-strap; **e)** Detachable and elasticized strap; **f)** Detachable strap with S-hook

Detachable and Elasticized

Figures 12.40e and f

Detachable straps are generally part of a strapless swimsuit or a bandeau. You stitch loops to the front/back neckline to provide a slot for fastening the straps. The elasticized straps you stitch in this section can also be used for straps that are stitched permanently to the swimsuit.

1. Add 5" extra to the finished strap length. The extra length is for four loops and the seam allowance for stitching an S-hook to each end of the strap.
2. Use ⅜" wide rubber elastic. Cut the fabric 1½" wide to the required length (see Figure 12.40e).
3. Place the elastic on the wrong side of the fabric; then align the elastic and fabric edges together.
4. Zigzag stitch the elastic to the fabric (do not stretch the elastic as you stitch).
5. Fold the fabric/elastic over *twice*, and zigzag (or twin needle) stitch the center of the strap.

6. Cut away the excess fabric as shown.
7. Place each strap through the S-hook slot and allow a ½" turning. Stitch the turning with a zipper foot and trim to ⅛" (see Figure 12.40f).

STITCHING TIP 12.5: STITCH LOOPS TO NECKLINE

If the swimsuit has detachable straps, you stitch loops to the front/back neckline to provide a slot for the straps to attach/detach. Cut *four* ⅞" pieces from the straps stitched in Figure 12.40f to form the loops.

1. Stitch a loop to the correct side of the swimsuit (see Figure 12.41a).
2. Serge the elastic (and the loop) to the neck edge (see Figure 12.41b).
3. Turn the elasticized neck edge to the wrong side and topstitch (see Figure 12.41b).

b)

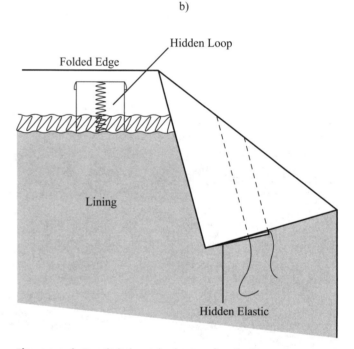

a)

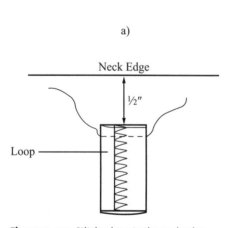

Figure 12.41a Stitch a loop to the neck edge

Figure 12.41b Topstitch the neck edge to secure the loop

Boning

Figure 12.42

A strapless swimsuit or bandeau requires a short piece of boning stitched to the side seam to hold its structure. Use a 3" length of boning (in a casing) for each side seam.

1. Remove the boning from the casing.
2. Position the casing over the seam allowance, and align the casing edge to the seamline.
3. Stitch one side of the casing to the seam, pivot, and stitch across the lower edge.
4. Insert the boning into the casing. When the neck allowance is turned and topstitched, the casing will be secured at the top edge.

Shelf Bra

A shelf bra is a lining stitched inside the swimsuit to provide lift and support to the bustline. Elastic is sewn to the bottom edge to enable the shelf bra to cling under the bust. You can design a shelf bra with or without swim cups. You also can design a shelf bra with removable cups. (Refer to Figure 11.38 on p. 398.) Another type of shelf bra for a swimsuit with inbuilt straps is shown in the Stitching Order in Table 12.1.

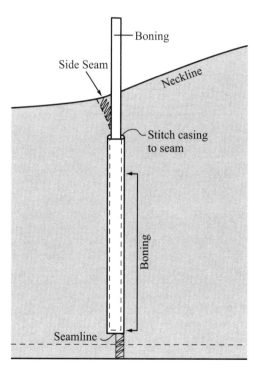

Figure 12.42 Stitching boning to the seam

Elasticized Edges

All openings of swimsuits (neckline, armholes, leg-lines, waistline, and cutouts) *must* be elasticized to ensure the swimsuit stays put on the body during all kinds of motion. You do not apply the elastic in order to pull the swimsuit in to fit the body. The swimsuit (before the elastic is applied) should firmly fit the form or body. You then apply the elastic to keep the swimsuit close-fitting and to enable the edges to stretch so that the swimsuit can be pulled onto the body. It is important that the correct type, width, and length of elastic are used. (Refer to the "Swimwear Supplies" section.)

Before stitching the final swimsuit, stitch a test-fit swimsuit with the elastic stitched to make sure the elastic length is correct. If the leg elastic is too tight, the buttock will not be covered stylishly. If the elastic is too loose, the opening will gape.

Seam Allowance for Elastic

The seam allowance to add to the pattern to stitch elasticized openings is ⅛" wider than the elastic width. For example, add ⅜" seam allowance for ¼" wide elastic, and add ½" seam allowance for ⅜" wide elastic.

Width of Elastic

- *Low back neckline, leg, and armhole edges*—⅜" wide elastic.
- *High round neck*—¼" wide elastic. In this case, also use ¼" wide elastic for armholes.
- *Bandeau and strapless neckline*—½" to ¾" wide elastic.
- *Cutaway section*—¼" wide elastic.
- *Waist of a bikini*—⅜" wide elastic.
- *Waist of swim shorts or swim skirt*—½"-¾" wide elastic.

Length of Elastic

The length of the elastic is crucial to the success of the swimsuit. Determining the length is not guesswork! To calculate the length of elastic required, measure half the pattern seamline and then double the measurement to determine the total seam length.

- *Waistline*—Place side seams together (see Figure 11.22a on p. 378).
- *Leg-line*—Place side seams together (see Figure 11.22b on p. 378).
- *Cutaway section*—Place side seams together (see Figure 12.15a).
- *Neckline and armhole*—Place the front and back shoulder seams together (see Figure 12.18).
- *Strapless neckline and under bust*—Place the front and back side seams together (see Figure 12.21).

- *High-cut neckline*—Reduce ¾".
- *Strapless*—Reduce 2".
- *Armholes*—Reduce ¾".
- *Cutaway sections*—Reduce 1" (the length can vary depending on the size of the cutout.)
- *Waist*—Reduce 1½".
- *Shoulder seams*—Use *clear elastic* to stabilize shoulder seams of a bodysuit or leotard to prevent stretching. You do *not* reduce the elastic length or stretch the elastic when applying it (see Table 3.3 on p. 28).

Reduce the Length

The elastic *must* be cut shorter in length than the edge it is stitched to. If it's not reduced, it will look "wavy" and stretched after it is stitched. After calculating the elastic length, add ½" for joining the elastic.

Elastic length reductions are as follows:

- *Leg elastic*—Reduce 2".
- *Low round neckline with low back*—Reduce 2½".

Join the Elastic

Figures 12.43a and b

If the opening to be elasticized is circular (such as the leg opening), join the seams. Next, overlap the elastic ½" and join so it is circular.

1. Pin or hand stitch rubber elastic together with an overhand stitch.
2. Join natural swimwear elastic with zigzag stitches.

a)

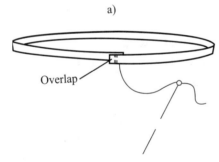

Overlap

Figure 12.43a Joining rubber elastic

b)

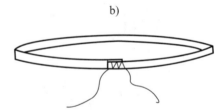

Figure 12.43b Joining natural swimwear elastic

Divide the Garment Edge and Finish into Sections

Figures 12.44a and b, Figure 12.45

1. To evenly distribute the elastic, pin-mark (or chalk-mark) the opening and the elastic into sections (four for the neckline and waist and two for the armholes).

2. Align the elastic and edge markings together and pin (Figure 12.44).

3. For the *leg elastic*, place the elastic join to one side of the crotch seam, and distribute the elastic, as shown in Figure 12.45.

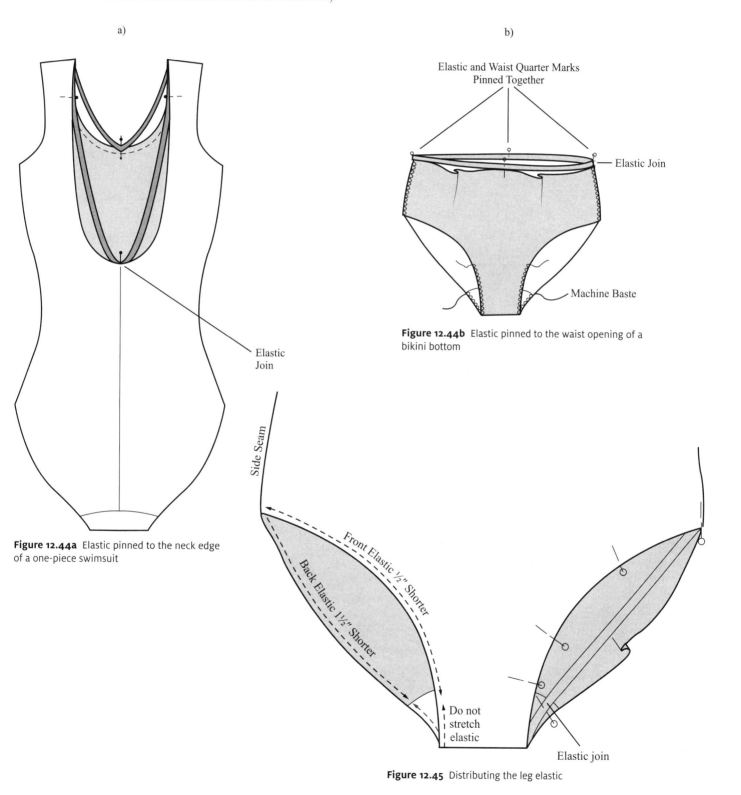

a)

Elastic Join

Figure 12.44a Elastic pinned to the neck edge of a one-piece swimsuit

b)

Elastic and Waist Quarter Marks Pinned Together

Elastic Join

Machine Baste

Figure 12.44b Elastic pinned to the waist opening of a bikini bottom

Side Seam

Front Elastic ½" Shorter

Back Elastic 1½" Shorter

Do not stretch elastic

Elastic join

Figure 12.45 Distributing the leg elastic

Leotard

You draft a leotard pattern from the swimsuit slopers. If
the neckline of a leotard is scooped or wide enough, it can
be pulled onto the body over the hips in the same way a
swimsuit is placed onto the body. If the neckline is high
cut or has a turtleneck neckline, then a zipper or Velcro
(a hook-and-loop fastener), is required on the center back
or across one shoulder. (Refer to the "Unitard with Turtleneck" section in Chapter 10.)

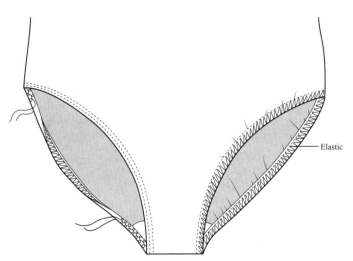

Figure 12.46 Stitch elastic to the opening

Bodysuit

Donna Karan popularized the bodysuit in the 1980s. She knows how versatile a bodysuit is because she wears one for exercise and another paired with skinny pants and a short leather jacket on other occasions.[1] A bodysuit has a crotch closure for practical toiletry reasons. Use snap or hook-and-eye tape to fasten the crotch.

Draft the Crotch Closure

Figure 12.47a

1. Trace the front/back leg-line swimsuit slopers onto pattern paper.
2. Transfer the front crotch section (Y-Z-T-D) to the back. (Refer to Figure 12.7.)
3. To facilitate the crotch opening, add a 1" extension to the back crotch.
4. Add a 1" facing under the *front* (T-D) line and below the extension.
5. Fold the facing (foldline) under the front crotch and back extension.

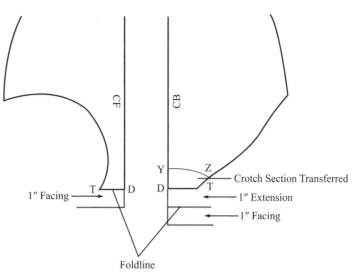

Figure 12.47a Draft the crotch closure

---

1 Anamaria Wilson, "My List, Donna Karan in 24 Hours," *Harper's Bazaar*, September 2012, 237.

Align the Crotch Closure

1. Place both (T-D) lines together, as shown in Figure 12.47b. Trace the front leg-line shape onto the back extension.
2. To finalize the patterns, cut the facing with directional seamlines to reflect the leg-line shape (see Figure 12.48).

> **STITCHING TIP 12.7: STITCHING THE CROTCH CLOSURE**
>
> 1. Apply stable interfacing to the facing.
> 2. Stitch the leg elastic in place.
> 3. Stitch the snap tape to the front crotch and back extension.

b)

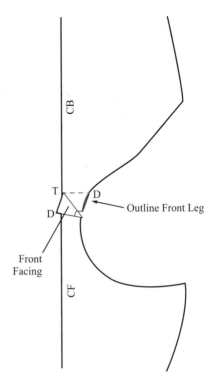

Figure 12.47b Align the crotch closure

c)

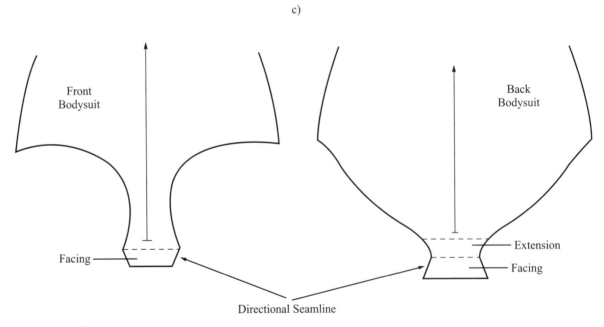

Figure 12.48 Final patterns for the crotch extension

Knit It Together

This checklist summarizes what you have learned about drafting patterns for swimsuits in this chapter.

✓ Swimsuit slopers are drafted from the four-way stretch top foundations and panty slopers.

✓ Swimsuits *must* be constructed from four-way stretch swim fabric with spandex.

✓ Swimsuits must have elasticized openings (neck, armholes, waist, legs, and other openings).

✓ Bodysuit and leotard patterns are drafted from the swimsuit slopers.

✓ Swimsuits can be tightly fitted because swimwear knits have a greater percentage of spandex.

Stop: What Do I Do If . . .

. . . my swimsuit is too big for the form?

To make the pattern smaller, grade the patterns in a *negative direction*. Refer to the "Grading in a Negative Direction" section in Table 3.4. For the total body decrease, you can remove 2" or 3".

. . . my bikini top has gathering under the bust like the bikini in Figure 12.2c? How do I change the bikini top pattern in Figure 12.29 to accommodate the gathering?

1. Slash/spread the pattern through the center of the dart to add fullness for gathering, as shown in Figure 12.49a.
2. After you add the seam allowance, notch the lower seam where the gathering starts (on CF) and finishes (see Figure 12.49b).

a)

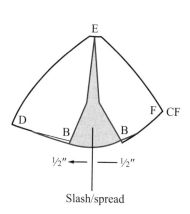

Figure 12.49a Dart intake transferred into gathering

b)

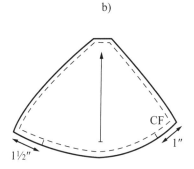

Figure 12.49b Final gathered triangle bikini pattern

Self-Critique

1. What type of knit is required for swimwear? (Refer to the "Swimwear Supplies" section.)
2. Sketch a one-piece swimsuit. Draw an arrow to identify where the swimsuit needs to be elasticized.
3. What elastic would you use? (Refer to the Table 3.3.)
4. What is the purpose of the elastic? (Refer to the "Elasticized Edges" section.)
5. What width seam allowance would you add to the pattern to stitch elasticized edges? (Refer to the "Seam Allowance for Elastic" section.)
6. To topstitch the elasticized openings, what stitches do you use? (Refer to Stitching Tip 12.6.)
7. When must the straps of swimsuits be elasticized? Which swimsuits and swim tops in Figures 12.1 and 12.2 need elasticized straps?
8. What slopers would you use to draft the patterns for a bodysuit?

Key Terms	Leotard
Bandeau	Swim Shorts
Bikini	Swim Skirt
Bodysuit	Swimsuit
Detachable Straps	Tankini
Inbuilt Straps	

ENDNOTES

Chapter 1

1   Hal Rubenstein, "Designer Profile: Donna Karan," *InStyle*, November 2013, 149–150.
2   Justine Picardie, "The Secret Life of Coco Chanel," *Harpers Bazaar*, June 2011, 159. http://www.harpersbazaar.com/fashion /fashion-articles/coco-chanel-secret-life; Sarah Brown, "Jersey Girl Relaxed Chic with a Dash of Liberation, Bottled," *Vogue*, November 2011, 210.
3   Unit III Topic A: Fibers and Fabrics, "Knit Fabrics," accessed November 2, 2014, http://www.uen.org/cte/family/clothing-2 /downloads/textiles/knit.pdf, 87.
4   Claire Shaeffer, *Fabric Sewing Guide* (Iola, WI: Krause Publications, 1994), 77.
5   Unit III Topic A: Fibers and Fabrics, "Knit Fabrics," 87.
6   Rubenstein, "Designer Profile: Donna Karan," 149–150.
7   "Wicking Fabric Demystified," *Healthy Wage Blog*, July 9, 2010, http://healthywage.wordpress.com/2010/07/09/wicking -fabric-demystified/.

Chapter 3

1   Fashionbook, "Terminology Common to Drafting & Draping," accessed September 12, 2014, http://fashionbook.forza6.com/catalogo /term_116.html.

Chapter 4

1   Keith Richardson, *Designing and Patternmaking for Stretch Fabrics* (New York: Fairchild Books, 2008), 19.
2   "The EcoChic Design Award Zero-Waste Design Technique," accessed September 3, 2015, http://www.ecochicdesign award.com/wp-content/blogs.dir/3/files/2013/07 /LEARN_Zero-waste_ENG.pdf.

3   Hal Rubenstein, "Designer Profile: Donna Karan." *InStyle*, November 2013, 149.

Chapter 6

1   Anne Monoky, "Designers Like Lagerfeld Showcase a Cult of Personali-Tee," *Harper's Bazaar*, August 11, 2011, http://www.harpersbazaar.com/fashion/trends/a7267 /designers-showcase-cult-of-personali-tee-081711/.
2   Keith Richardson, *Designing and Patternmaking for Stretch Fabrics* (New York: Fairchild Books, 2008), 71.
3   The Cut, "Ralph Lauren," accessed October 28, 2014, http://nymag .com/fashion/fashionshows/designers/bios/ralphlauren/.

Chapter 7

1   DVF, accessed November 14, 2014, http://www.dvf.com /timeline-70s.html.

Chapter 9

1   Helen Joseph-Armstrong, *Patternmaking for Fashion Design*, 5th ed. (Upple Saddle River, NJ: Pearson Education, Inc., publishing as Prentice Hall, 2010), 291, 292.

Chapter 10

1   Helen Joseph-Armstrong, *Patternmaking for Fashion Design*, 5th ed. (Upper Saddle River, NJ: Pearson Education, Inc., publishing as Prentice Hall, 2010), 570.

Chapter 12

1   Anamaria Wilson, "My List, Donna Karan in 24 Hours," *Harper's Bazaar*, September 2012, 237.

GLOSSARY

A

Activewear Shorts: Tight-fitting shorts designed for sport and fitness.

A-line: The side seams gradually flare out from the hip to hem resembling the letter *A*.

Apex: Center of the breast or bust point on the pattern.

Armscye: The armhole.

Askew Knit: Knit yardage that is distorted and "off grain."

Asymmetrical Garment: A garment that looks different on both sides.

Asymmetrical Patterns: Patterns on which the right and left sides are different.

Awl: A small pointed tool used to pierce a hole in patterns.

Awl-hole: A small hole placed in the pattern to indicate the dart position and other markings.

B

Balloon-hem: A skirt or dress with a rounded, puffed-looking hemline.

Ballpoint Needle: A machine needle with a slightly rounded tip that slides between the knitted loops of the fabric and will not split them apart.

Band: A piece of knit fabric used to finish the neckline, armhole, and wrist or hem edges of a garment.

Bandeau: A swimsuit or top that wraps around a woman's breasts and can tie or clasp at the back or front.

Bandless: The waist of a skirt or pant that does not have a waistband.

Bermuda Shorts: Shorts that extend almost to the knee.

Bikini: A brief two-piece close-fitting swimsuit.

Binding: A strip of fabric used to bind the raw edge of a garment opening.

Blending: The process of drawing a smooth continuous line when two lines emerge together.

Blouson: A garment gathered with a casing (or belt) at the waistline causing it to blouse, that is, to hang in loose folds.

Boatneck: A wide neckline that runs horizontally following the curve of the collar bone.

Bodysuit: A one-piece tight-fitting garment, with or without sleeves and worn with a skirt or pant for casual or for business wear. It hooks or snaps under the crotch.

Boy-cut Panty: A panty with a similar style to men's briefs with short legs extending below the crotch.

Braided Elastic: Soft flexible elastic identified by horizontal narrow ribs. The elastic narrows when stretched.

Bra-top: A separate top piece that gives the garment a defined bust shape.

Button Extension: A section added to the pattern for the buttonholes and button closure.

C

Cami-dress: A camisole of dress length.

Camisole: An underwear/outerwear garment with narrow straps worn on the upper body. A camisole is also referred to as a *cami*.

Capri Pants: Casual pants with a vertical slit on the side seam at the hem.

Cap Sleeve: A small fitted sleeve that conforms to the shape of the upper arm.

Casing: A stitched piece of fabric that forms a tunnel for elastic or a drawstring.

Catchstitch: A cross-shaped hand stitch used to stitch a turned edge to the inside of a garment.

Courses: Loops running across the fabric.

Cowl Neckline: A draped neckline with rounded folds.

Cropkini: A short top that is cut midway between the bust and waist.

Cropped Pant: Pant length that finishes above the ankle.

Crossmark: Two short ¼" intersecting lines drawn to mark and locate various parts of the pattern.

Crotch-piece: A small section of fabric sewn to the crotch of panties to provide strength and comfort.

Cut-in-one Self Lining: The outer garment pattern and lining pattern that are drafted as one pattern piece.

Cut-in-one Waistband: A waistband incorporated into the skirt/pant pattern.

D

Dart Intake: The amount of space between the dart legs.

Dart Legs: Two lines that make up a dart and join at a point.

Dart Manipulation: A pattern drafting technique used to transfer the dart intake from one position to another.

Dart Point: Stitching point of the dart.

Detachable Straps: Straps that are removable.

Differential Feed: The serger mechanism that controls the movement of the front and back feed dogs, which work together to move the fabric through the serger without stretching or puckering the fabric.

Directional Grainline: A grainline that directs how a pattern is to be placed on the fabric and cut.

Directional Seamline: The seam allowance or hem allowance that reflects the identical shape or angle of the pattern section.

Double Knit: A knit fabric knitted with double needles; it is double the thickness of a single knit.

Drawstring: A narrow tie used to tighten the waist or another area of a garment.

Dress/pant form: A three-dimensional model of the torso (or can be a head to toe) and padded with a natural body shape and buttocks.

Dress-piece: A partial pattern drafted from the hipline to knee length.

Drop-match: To place a pattern piece lower than another pattern piece for the purposes of matching the fabric print.

Dropped Shoulder: A style in which the armholes of the garment are positioned on the upper arm rather than placed on the shoulder.

Dropped Waist: Waistline that falls below the natural waistline.

E

Edge Allowance: The width added to the pattern beyond the seamline for turning a folded edge.

Edge Finish: A strip of fabric, lace, or elastic stitched to the neckline, armhole, hem, wrist, or leg opening to finish off the garment edges.

Elastic: A stretchable product used to add elasticity to openings such as the waistline of pants and skirts or a swimsuit.

Empire Waist: Waistline that sits below the bustline and above the natural waistline.

Enclosed Elastic: Elastic that is hidden between two layers of fabric after it is stitched.

Equalize: To draw a new line to eliminate irregularities in line lengths.

F

Facing: A separate fabric piece used to finish exposed edges of the garment such as the neckline or armhole edges.

Final Pattern: Pattern that has been trued, with seam allowance added, notches and grainlines indicated, and patterns labeled.

Finger Press: To use fingers to open a seam so that it is flat.

Fit Flexibility: A system that allows you to choose which sloper to use to draft the patterns for a particular style.

Fitted Slopers: Slopers that are fitted to the body measurements without ease added.

Fitted Waist Finish: Waist that fits close to the natural waistline.

Flared: A pattern that is slashed/spread to add fullness to the garment.

Flat Patternmaking: A method used to draft slopers and patterns. The patterns are drawn directly on pattern paper to a set of measurements.

Flounce: A pattern with inner and outer circles. When the inner circle of the fabric is straightened, the outer circle flutes.

Fold-over Waistband: Waistband that folds over and grips the hips.

Four-way Stretch: A knit that stretches *across* the width of the fabric and *up* and *down* in the length.

Four-way Stretch Interfacing: Interfacing that stretches *across* the width of the fabric and *up* and *down* in the length.

G

Gathering: A series of little puckers that add fullness into a garment.

Godet: A triangular piece of fabric inserted into a garment to make it flared.

Gored Skirt: A shaped skirt created with four, six, or more triangular-shaped panels.

Graded Nest: A set of patterns outlined from largest to smallest.

Grading Grid: Intersecting (vertical and horizontal) lines drawn on pattern paper.

Grading Measurements: Measurements marked on a grading grid in increments.

Gripper Elastic: Elastic with a strip of silicone centered on it. The silicone grips the body and holds the garment in place.

H

Half Pattern: Half of a whole pattern.

Halter: A garment with straps tied around the back neckline that leaves the arms, shoulders, and back bare.

Hi-cut: The legline of panties that are cut high on the leg to allow comfort and freedom of movement and to elongate the length of the leg.

High-rise: Waist that sits on the natural waistline.

Hip Foundation: A partial pattern drafted for the lower part of the body from the waist to the hip.

Horizontal Balance Line: A horizontal line drawn on the sloper that guides and balances the grading.

I

Inbuilt Straps: Straps that are incorporated into the garment.

Inseam Pocket: A pocket inserted into the seam of a garment.

Interfacing: A material that is used to support or reinforce garment parts such as the collar, cuffs, and facings.

Intersecting lines: Vertical and horizontal lines drawn on pattern paper that meet at a 90° (right) angle.

K

Knit Fabric: A stretchable material knitted on huge knitting machines and formed by a series of horizontal interlocking loops.

Knitted Elastic: Elastic that is knitted as per knit fabric.

L

Leggings: Tight-fitting stretch pants covering the legs.

Leg-line Panty: A panty cut around the top of the leg or hi-cut around the legline to elongate the length of the leg.

Leotard: A one-piece tight-fitting garment worn by acrobats, gymnasts, dancers, figure skaters, athletes, and circus performers.

Lining: An inner layer of fabric that covers the inner construction of a garment.

Loose-fit Slopers: Slopers that are graded larger than the minimal stretch slopers. These slopers create patterns for loose-fitting garments in knits.

Loose-fit Waist Finish: A finish with ease added to allow size flexibility and comfort around the waistline.

Low-rise: Waist that sits on the hips.

Lycra®: A synthetic elastic fiber known for its extraordinary ability to stretch many times its original length and then bounce back to its initial size. (In garment labels, *Lycra*, *spandex*, and *elastane* are interchangeable terms.)

M

Master Foundations: The first hip or top foundations to be drafted.

Master Pattern: The first pattern to be drafted.

Master Sloper: The first set of slopers to be drafted.

Matchpoints: Pattern markings indicating two points that must come together when stitching a seam or indicating a pocket placement.

Mechanical Sewing Machine: A home sewing machine.

Mechanical Stretch: A knit fabric that stretches from the loop formation only (it does not have spandex).

Mid-rise: Waist that sits on the high-hip.

Minimal Stretch Foundation: The master foundation drafted to the body measurements and used to draft slopers for minimal stretch knits.

Minimal Stretch Knit: A stretch category of knit with the least amount of stretch.

Minimal Stretch Slopers: Slopers used to draft the patterns for garments constructed from a minimal stretch knit.

Moderate Stretch Foundations: Hip and top foundations drafted for a moderate stretch knit.

Moderate Stretch Knit: A stretch category of knit that stretches 50 percent more than the original length.

Moderate Stretch Slopers: Slopers used to draft the patterns for garments constructed from a moderate stretch knit.

Moisture-Wicking Fabric: Fabric that pulls moisture away from the skin and then releases it for evaporation so you feel comfortable during vigorous activity.

Muslin: (1) A prototype of the actual garment (or section of a garment) used to test the fit of the garment. (2) An inexpensive fabric used to make trial garments for fitting purposes.

N

Nap Layout: A layout in which the top of every pattern piece must be placed on the fabric toward the same end of the fabric in the same direction.

Napped Fabric: A fabric surface that looks different in both directions when touched or viewed.

Narrow Facing: A ½" to 1" wide facing used to finish the raw edges of a neckline, armholes, or cardigan edge.

Negative Direction: The process of grading the patterns to decrease the dimensions.

Negative Ease: Slopers/patterns cut smaller than the body measurements. The stretch factor provides the *ease* and flexibility for movement.

Nonstretch Interfacing: Interfacing that does not stretch.

Notches: Small ⅛" snips on the fabric edge to indicate the fabric pieces that need to be matched together in the stitching process.

O

One-shoulder Dress: An asymmetrical style where the neckline starts from one shoulder and extends diagonally to the opposite underarm.

Oversized Slopers: Slopers that have extra room incorporated for comfort and/or style.

P

Palazzo Pants: Extremely wide-legged floor-length pants.

Patch Pocket: A pocket stitched to the outside of a garment. The lower edge can be square, rounded, or angled.

Pattern Grading: The process of scaling patterns using a mathematical formula to increase or decrease the pattern.

Pattern Manipulation: The process of changing the pattern design by using the slash/spread and slash/separate techniques to add fullness or volume.

Pattern Plotting: The process of planning and drawing the pattern outline or silhouette (neckline, armhole, and hem length) and arranging the placement of seams within the silhouette.

Pegged: A style in which the side seam gradually narrows from the hip to the hemline.

Pick Glass: A tool used to magnify the fabric surface so you can see the loop formation.

Picot Edge Elastic: Lingerie elastic with a delicate edge on one side of it.

Pin-mark: To place pins in the fabric to mark a certain position.

Plush Elastic: Elastic with a satin finish on the correct side and a soft velvety underside that is designed to be comfortable next to the skin.

Pocket Bag: A pouch stitched inside of a garment for the hand to rest in or to use as a compartment for keys, cash, or a cell phone.

Ponte: Double knit fabric.

Positive Direction: The process of grading the patterns to increase the dimensions.

Positive Ease: Slopers/patterns that are cut larger than the body measurements with *ease* incorporated for comfort and movement.

Princess Line: Vertical style lines that contour the body. Can also be called "princess seams."

Puff Sleeve: A short sleeve gathered at the capline to add roundness. The bottom edge of the sleeve can also be gathered.

Pull-on Skirts: Skirts with an elasticized waist finish.

Q

Quarter Pin-mark: Markings that divide an opening (such as the neck, leg opening) into equal sections.

R

Raglan Sleeves: Sleeves joined to the bodice with diagonal seams from the underarm to the neckline.

Rib-line: A column of little "v" stitches that run in lengthwise direction of the fabric.

Ribs: Vertical rows of loops, also called *wales*.

Right Angle: An angle of 90°. It is the corner of a square or at the intersection of two perpendicular straight lines.

Ruffle: A straight fabric piece gathered into fullness.

S

Satin Stitch: A series of zigzag stitches stitched close together to completely cover the edge that is stitched.

Scoop Neckline: A rounded low-cut neckline.

Seam Allowance: The area between the seamline and the cut edge of a pattern (or fabric).

Seamline: A line on the pattern to indicate a seam or the edge of the garment.

Seam Ripper: A tool used to remove unwanted stitches.

Self Fabric: The same fabric as the garment.

Semi-fitted Waist Finish: A finish with *ease* added to allow size flexibility and comfort around the waistline.

Separate Lining: Lining that is attached to the waist or neckline of a garment and is not attached to the hem.

Separate Waistband: A straight strip of fabric prepared and stitched to the waist opening.

Serger: A sewing machine that stitches seams and edge finishes in one stitching process. (A serger is also known as an *overlock machine*.)

Set-in Sleeve: A sleeve that is stitched into the armhole (armscye) of a garment.

Sheath: A dress with straight side seams that contour the body curves.

Shelf bra: A lining that fits under the bust of a top and is edged with plush elastic.

Shift: A short, simple, loose-fitting dress that is often A-line.

Side-front Pocket: A pocket with a slanted opening from the high-hip to the waist.

Single Knit: A jersey knit fabric knitted with a *single* set of needles. A single knit has two distinct sides: vertical ribs show on the correct side, and horizontal loops show on the wrong side.

Single Needle: One needle with one shaft that stitches one row of stitching.

Slash Pocket: A pocket stitched to a vertical, horizontal, or diagonal slit in a garment. A pocket bag is stitched to the slit and placed within the garment.

Slash/separate Technique: The process of cutting a pattern into two sections to add fullness for gathering, tucks, or pleats.

Slash/spread Technique: The process of spreading a pattern to add fullness to create volume and flare.

Sleeve/bodice Combination: A sleeve that combines part or all of the sleeve with the bodice.

Sloper: A basic pattern shaped to the natural neckline, shoulder, armhole, bust, waist, and hip (silhouette) of the form or body.

Sloper System: A method of creating the slopers for drafting patterns in stretch knit fabric.

Spaghetti Straps: Narrow ¼" wide straps.

Spandex: See Lycra®.

Split-hem: A hem that is divided with an opening.

Squared Line: A line drawn perpendicular to another line. There must be an existing line to draw a squared line.

Squared-off Angle: The place where two seamlines meet to form a 90° angle.

Square Neckline: A neckline that forms a square shape.

Stabilizer: A product that is used in clothing construction to add structure to garments.

Stabilizing Tape: A narrow strip of interfacing used to prevent garment edges and seams from stretching.

Stitching Order: The stitching steps used to stitch a garment following a logical order.

Strapless: A garment that does not have straps and exposes the shoulders.

Stretchable Seam: A seam that stretches as much as the knit stretches.

Stretchable Stitches: Stitches that have inbuilt stretch.

Stretch and Recovery: Stretching the fabric and releasing it to see if it bounces back to its original shape.

Stretch Capacity: The extent a knit stretches.

Stretch Categories: Groupings that categorize a particular knit according to the amount of stretch it has.

Stretch Needles: Machine needles with a slightly rounded tip that slides between the knitted loops of the fabric and will not split them apart.

Super Stretchy Foundations: Hip or top foundations drafted for a super stretchy knit.

Super Stretchy Knit: A stretch category of knit that stretches 100 percent or more than the original length.

Super Stretchy Slopers: Slopers used to draft the patterns for garments constructed from a super stretchy knit.

Sweater-jackets: Short cropped jackets with a zipper closure and pockets.

Swim Shorts: Tightly fitted shorts styled similar to men's briefs with short legs extending below the crotch.

Swim Skirt: A panty short and skirt combined.

Symmetrical Garment: A garment that is the same on both sides.

Symmetrical Patterns: Patterns in which both sides are the same.

T

Tank: A sleeveless top or dress with shoulder straps and a low neckline.

Tank Dress: A close-fitting sleeveless dress with shoulder straps and low-cut neckline.

Tankini: A two-piece bathing suit consisting of a tank top and a bikini bottom.

Teddy: An all-in-one garment for sleepwear.

Thread Mark: A needle and thread marking that sews two long tacking stitches together.

Three-quarter Sleeve: Sleeve length between the elbow and the wrist.

Tiered Skirt: A skirt with several flared layers stitched to a base lining.

Top Foundation: A bodice that constitutes the upper part of the body from the waist up to the shoulders.

Trueing: The process to establish correct seam lengths by smoothing, straightening, blending, and establishing correct angles.

Tucks: A folded piece of fabric that is sewn in place.

Turned and Topstitched: An edge turned to the wrong side of the fabric and topstitched.

Twin Needles: Two needles mounted on a single crossbar that simultaneously stitch two parallel rows of stitching.

Two-piece Bra-top: A bra-top that is divided into two sections with horizontal or vertical seamlines.

Two-way Stretch Fabric: A knit fabric that stretches across the width of the fabric.

Two-way Stretch Interfacing: Interfacing that has crosswise stretch and is stable in the length.

U

Understitch: A row of stitches sewn close to the seamline of a facing or collar edge to prevent the seamline rolling to the outside.

Unitards: One-piece tight-fitting garments that cover the body from the neck to the knees or feet.

459

V

Velcro®: A fastener with tiny hooks and "hairier" loops that fasten when pressed together.

Very Stretchy Foundations: Hip or top foundations drafted for a very stretchy knit.

Very Stretchy Knit: A stretch category of knit that stretches 75 percent more than the original length.

Very Stretchy Slopers: Slopers used to draft the patterns for garments constructed from a very stretchy knit.

V-neck: A neckline that comes down to a point in the shape of the letter *V*.

W

Wales: Vertical rows of loops that can also be called *ribs*.

Walk the Pattern: A pattern-drafting technique used to compare the seam lengths. An awl is used to anchor one pattern seamline as it is moved in increments to compare it with another seamline.

Warp Knit: A knit fabric constructed with yarn looped in a lengthwise *warp* direction.

Weft Knit: A knit fabric knitted with one continuous yarn that forms rows of *horizontal* loops across the width of the fabric.

Welt Pocket: A pocket that uses one piece of fabric to form a strip of fabric (the welt) on the correct side and the pocket bag on the inside of the garment.

Working Pattern: A pattern in which the lines are plotted following the sketch of the garment. The pattern pieces are then traced from the working patterns, separated, and finalized.

Woven Elastic: Nonroll elastic constructed by weaving.

Woven Fabric: Nonstretchable material formed when two sets of yarns are woven together.

Z

Zero-waste Pattern Cutting Technique: A technique that eliminates any waste of fabric in drafting a pattern.

Zip-up Pocket: A pocket accessed by a zipper.

INDEX